Basic Grammar in use

P9-ELG-183

WITH ANSWERS

Self-study reference and practice
for students of English

Raymond Murphy
with William R. Smalzer

Second Edition

CAMBRIDGE
UNIVERSITY PRESS

PUBLISHED BY THE PRESS SYNDICATE OF THE UNIVERSITY OF CAMBRIDGE
The Pitt Building, Trumpington Street, Cambridge, United Kingdom

CAMBRIDGE UNIVERSITY PRESS
The Edinburgh Building, Cambridge CB2 2RU, UK
40 West 20th Street, New York, NY 10011–4211, USA
477 Williamstown Road, Port Melbourne, VIC 3207, Australia
Ruiz de Alarcón 13, 28014 Madrid, Spain
Dock House, The Waterfront, Cape Town 8001, South Africa

http://www.cambridge.org

© Cambridge University Press 1989, 2002

This book is in copyright. Subject to statutory exception
and to the provisions of relevant collective licensing agreements,
no reproduction of any part may take place without
the written permission of Cambridge University Press.

First published 1989
Second edition 2002
3rd printing 2003

Printed in Hong Kong, China

Typeface Sabon (Adobe®) 10.5/12pt   *System* QuarkXPress™ 4.1 [KW]

A catalog record for this book is available from the British Library

Library of Congress Cataloging in Publication data available

ISBN 0 521 62600 5 (with answers) paperback with CD (audio)
ISBN 0 521 62599 8 (without answers) paperback with CD (audio)

Illustrations: Randy Jones and Susann Ferris Jones
Book design: Adventure House
Layout: Kate Winter

Contents

**If you are not sure which units you need to study,
use the STUDY GUIDE on page 259.**

> **If you are not sure which units you need to study, use the STUDY GUIDE on page 259.**

If you are not sure which units you need to study,
use the **STUDY GUIDE** on page 259.

If you are not sure which units you need to study, use the STUDY GUIDE on page 259.

To the Student (working without a teacher)

This is a basic grammar book for beginning to low-intermediate students of English. There are 116 units in the book and each unit is about a different point of English grammar. There is a list of units at the beginning of the book *(Contents)*.

Do not study all the units in order from beginning to end. It is better to choose the units that you *need* to do. For example, if you have difficulty with the present perfect *(I have been, he has done, etc.)*, use the *Contents* or the *Index* (at the back of the book) to find the units you need to study (Units 16–21 for the present perfect).

Each unit is two pages. The explanation is on the left-hand page and the exercises are on the right:

explanation 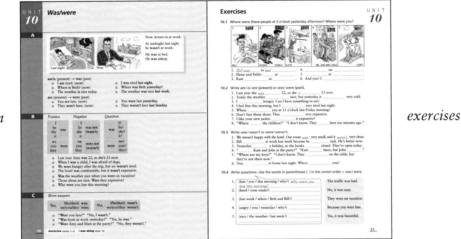 *exercises*

You can use the book in this way:

1. Look in the *Contents* or *Index* to find the units that you need. If you are not sure which units you need to study, use the *Study Guide* on page 259.
2. Study the left-hand page (explanation).
3. Do the exercises on the right-hand page.
4. Use the *Answer Key* to check your answers.
5. Study the left-hand page again if necessary.

Don't forget the seven *Appendixes* at the back of the book (pages 234–242). These will give you information about active and passive forms, irregular verbs, short forms (contractions), spelling, and two-word verbs.

There are also *Additional Exercises* at the back of the book (pages 243–258). There is a list of these exercises on page 243.

There is an audio CD inside the back cover of the book. It contains recordings of the example sentences from selected units. Look for this symbol in the *Contents:* 🎧 .

To the Teacher

The most important features of this book are:

- It is a grammar book. It deals only with grammar and is not a general course book.
- It is for beginning to low-intermediate learners. It does not cover areas of grammar which are not commonly taught at beginning levels.
- It combines reference and practice exercises in one volume.
- It can be used for self-study or as supplementary course material.

The forms used in *Basic Grammar in Use* are those which are most used and generally accepted in standard spoken North American English. Some native speakers may regard some of these usages as "incorrect," but in this book they are treated as standard.

Organization of the Book

There are 116 units in the book, each one focusing on a particular area of grammar. The material is organized in grammatical categories such as tenses, questions, and articles. The book should not be worked through from beginning to end. Units are not ordered according to difficulty, and should therefore be selected and used in the order appropriate for the learners. The units are listed in the *Contents* and there is a comprehensive *Index* at the end of the book.

Each unit has the same format consisting of two facing pages. The grammar point is presented and explained on the left-hand page and the corresponding exercises are on the right. There are seven *Appendixes* (pages 234–242) dealing with active and passive forms, irregular verbs, short forms (contractions), spelling, and two-word (phrasal) verbs. It might be useful to draw students' attention to these.

This new edition of *Basic Grammar in Use* also contains a set of *Additional Exercises* (pages 243–258). These exercises provide mixed practice bringing together grammar points from a number of different units (mainly those concerning verb forms). There are 33 exercises in this section and there is a full list on page 243.

At the back of the book, there is a *Study Guide* (pages 259–270) to help students decide what units to study and an *Answer Key* (pages 271–296) so students can check their work. An edition without the *Study Guide* and *Answer Key* is also available for teachers who would prefer it for their students.

Finally, there is an audio CD inside the back cover of the book, with recordings of the example sentences from selected units. Look for this symbol in the *Contents*: 🎧.

Level

The book is suitable for a range of levels from beginning to low intermediate. However, it is intended mainly for students who are beyond the very earliest stages of a beginners' course, and should *not* be used from the first day of a course for absolute beginners. It could also be used by low-intermediate learners whose grammar is weaker than other aspects of their English or who have problems with particular areas of basic grammar.

The explanations are addressed to the beginning learner and are therefore as simple and as short as possible. The vocabulary used in the examples and exercises has also been restricted so that the book can be used at this level.

Using the Book

The book can be used by students working alone (see *To the Student*) or as supplementary course material. When used as course material, the book can be used for immediate consolidation or for later review or remedial work. It might be used by the whole class or by individual students needing extra help and practice.

In some cases it may be desirable to use the left-hand pages (presentation and explanation) in class, but it should be noted that these have been written for individual study and reference. In most cases, it would probably be better to present the grammar point in whatever way you prefer, with the exercises being done for homework. The left-hand page is then available for later reference by the student.

Some teachers prefer to reserve the book for review and remedial work. In this case, individual students or groups of students can be directed to the appropriate units for self-study and practice.

Basic Grammar in Use, Second Edition

While this is a completely new edition of *Basic Grammar in Use*, the general structure and character of the first edition remain. The main changes are:

- There are eight new units:
  - Unit 9   *I have . . . and I've got . . .*
  - Unit 15   *I used to . . .*
  - Unit 20   *Just, already,* and *yet*
  - Unit 23   *Is being done* and *has been done*
  - Unit 32   *Must*
  - Unit 58   *Do* and *make*
  - Unit 59   *Have*
  - Unit 114 *If I had . . . , if we went . . . ,* etc.

  There is also a new appendix on active and passive forms *(Appendix 1).*

- Some of the material has been reorganized. For example, the content of Units 101–102 *(in/on/at)* in the second edition corresponds to Unit 93 and part of Unit 95 in the first edition.

- Some of the units have been reordered, and after Unit 8, nearly all units have a different number from the first edition. A few units have been moved to different parts of the book. For example, Unit 52 *(work/working,* etc.) was Unit 34 in the first edition.

- Many of the left-hand pages have been rewritten and many of the examples changed. In a few cases there are significant changes to the content, for example, Unit 53 (originally 47), Unit 75 (originally 67), and Unit 84 (originally 76).

- Many of the original exercises have been modified or completely replaced with new exercises (for example, Units 4 and 5).

- There is a new section of *Additional Exercises* at the back of the book (see *Organization of the Book* above).

- The second edition is available both with and without answers at the back of the book.

- In the edition with answers, there is a new *Study Guide* to help students decide which units to study.

- There is an audio CD included with the second edition, inside the back cover of the book. It contains recordings of the example sentences from selected units. Look for this symbol in the *Contents:* 🎧 .

Am/is/are

A

My name is Lisa.

I'm 22.

I'm **not** married.

I'm American.
I'm from Chicago.

My favorite color **is** blue.

I'm a student.

My favorite sports **are**
tennis and swimming.

My father **is** a doctor, and
my mother **is** a journalist.

I'm interested in art.

LISA

B

Positive

I	am	(I'm)
he		(he's)
she	is	(she's)
it		(it's)
we		(we're)
you	are	(you're)
they		(they're)

Negative

I	am not	(I'm not)		
he		(he's **not**	*or*	he **isn't**)
she	is not	(she's **not**	*or*	she **isn't**)
it		(it's **not**	*or*	it **isn't**)
we		(we're **not**	*or*	we **aren't**)
you	are not	(you're **not**	*or*	you **aren't**)
they		(they're **not**	*or*	they **aren't**)

I'm afraid
of dogs.

- I'm cold. Can you close the window, please?
- I'm 32 years old. My sister **is** 29.
- My brother **is** very tall. He's a policeman.
- John **is** afraid of dogs.
- It's ten o'clock. You're late again.
- Mei Lan and I **are** good friends.
- Your keys **are** on the table.

- I'm tired, but I'm **not** hungry.
- Tom **isn't** interested in politics. He's interested in music.
- Jessica **isn't** at home right now. She's at work.
- Those people **aren't** Canadian. They're Australian.
- It's sunny today, but it **isn't** warm.

C

that's = that is   there's = there is   here's = here is

- Thank you. That's very kind of you.
- Look! There's Chris.
- "Here's your key." "Thank you."

Thank you.

Here's
your key.

Am/is/are (Questions) Unit 2   *There is/are* Unit 38

Exercises

1.1 Write the short form (*she's* / *we aren't*, etc.).

1. she is _she's_
2. they are _____
3. it is not _____
4. that is _____
5. I am not _____
6. you are not _____

1.2 Write *am*, *is*, or *are*.

1. The weather _is_ nice today.
2. I _am_ not tired.
3. This bag _____ heavy.
4. These bags _____ heavy.
5. Look! There _____ Carol.
6. My brother and I _____ good tennis players.
7. Amy _____ at home. Her children _____ at school.
8. I _____ a taxi driver. My sister _____ a nurse.

1.3 Write complete sentences. Use *is* / *isn't* / *are* / *aren't*.

1. (your shoes very dirty) _Your shoes are very dirty._
2. (my brother a teacher) My _____ .
3. (this house not very big) _____
4. (the stores not open today) _____
5. (my keys in my bag) _____
6. (Jenny 18 years old) _____

1.4 Look at Lisa's sentences (Section A). Write sentences about yourself.

1. (name?) My _____ .
2. (from?) I _____ .
3. (age?) I _____ .
4. (job?) I _____ .
5. (married?) I _____ .
6. (favorite color or colors?)
   My _____ .
7. (interested in?)
   I _____ .

1.5 Write sentences for the pictures. Use these words:

afraid   angry   cold   hot   hungry   ~~thirsty~~

1. _He's thirsty._
2. They _____ .
3. He _____ .
4. _____
5. _____
6. _____

1.6 Write true sentences, positive or negative. Use *am* / *am not* / *is* / *isn't* / *are* / *aren't*.

1. (I / interested in politics) _I'm interested in politics._ OR _I'm not interested in politics._
2. (I / hungry) I _____ .
3. (it / warm today) It _____ .
4. (I / afraid of dogs) _____
5. (my hands / cold) _____
6. (Canada / a very big country) _____
7. (I / interested in soccer) _____
8. (Tokyo / in China) _____

UNIT 2

Am/is/are (Questions)

A

Positive			Question	
I	am		am	I?
he she it	is		is	he? she? it?
we you they	are		are	we? you? they?

What's your name?
David.
Are you married?
No, I'm single.
How old **are** you?
25.
Are you a student?
Yes, I am.

DAVID

- "**Am** I late?" "No, **you're** on time."
- "**Is your mother** at home?" "No, **she's** out."
- "**Are your parents** at home?" "No, **they're** out."
- "**Is** it cold in your room?" "Yes, a little."
- Your shoes are nice. **Are they** new?

We say:
- **Is she** at home? / **Is your mother** at home? (*not* Is at home your mother?)
- **Are they** new? / **Are your shoes** new? (*not* Are new your shoes?)

B

Where . . . ? / What . . . ? / Who . . . ? / How . . . ? / Why . . . ?

- **Where is** your mother? Is she at home?
- "**Where are** you from?" "Canada."
- "**What color is** your car?" "It's red."
- "**How old is** Joe?" "He's 24."
- "**How are** your parents?" "They're fine."

- "**Why are** you angry?"
  "Because you're late."
- "**How much are** these postcards?"
  "Fifty cents."

where's = where is   what's = what is   who's = who is   how's = how is
- **Where's** Sarah?
- **What's** the temperature?
- **Who's** that man?
- **How's** your father?

C

Short answers

	I	am.		I'm						
Yes,	he she it	is.	No,	he's she's it's	not.	*or*	No,	he she it	isn't.	
	we you they	are.		we're you're they're				we you they	aren't.	

That's my seat.
No, it isn't.

- "**Are you** tired?" "Yes, **I am**."
- "**Are you** hungry?"
  "No, **I'm not**, but I'm thirsty."
- "**Is** your friend Japanese?" "Yes, **he is**."
- "**Are** these **your** keys?" "Yes, **they are**."
- "**That's** my seat." "No, **it isn't**."

4   ***Am/is/are*** Unit 1   **Questions** Unit 45

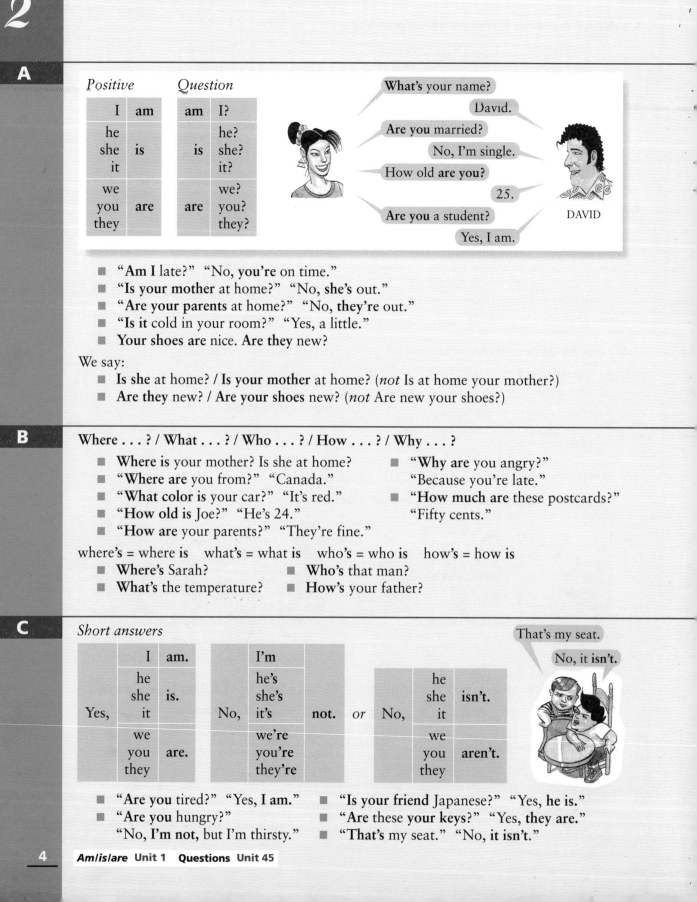

Exercises

2.1 **Find the right answers for the questions.**

1.	Where's the camera?	a) Toronto.	1.	_g_
2.	Is your car blue?	b) No, I'm not.	2.	____
3.	Is Nicole from Boston?	c) Yes, you are.	3.	____
4.	Am I late?	d) My sister.	4.	____
5.	Where's Anne from?	e) Black.	5.	____
6.	What color is your bag?	f) No, it's black.	6.	____
7.	Are you hungry?	g) In your bag.	7.	____
8.	Who's that woman?	h) No, she's Canadian.	8.	____

2.2 **Write questions. Use *is* or *are*.**

1. (at home / your mother?) _Is your mother at home?_ _____
2. (interesting / your job?) _____
3. (the stores / open today?) _____
4. (interested in sports / you?) _____
5. (near here / the post office?) _____
6. (at school / your children?) _____
7. (why / you / late?) _____

2.3 **Write questions. Use *What/Who/Where/How . . . ?*. Read the answers first.**

1.	_How are_ _____ your parents?	They're fine.
2.	_____ the bus stop?	At the end of the block.
3.	_____ your children?	Five, six, and ten.
4.	_____ these oranges?	Seventy-nine cents a pound.
5.	_____ your favorite sport?	Skiing.
6.	_____ the man in this photograph?	That's my father.
7.	_____ your new shoes?	Black.

2.4 **Write questions. Read the answers first.**

1.	(name?) _What's your name?_ _____	Paul.
2.	(married or single?) _____	I'm married.
3.	(Australian?) _____	No, I'm Canadian.
4.	(how old?) _____	I'm 30.
5.	(a lawyer?) _____	No, I'm a teacher.
6.	(wife a teacher?) _____	No, she's a lawyer.
7.	(from?) _____	She's Mexican.
8.	(her name?) _____	Ana.
9.	(how old?) _____	She's 27.

2.5 **Write true short answers (*Yes, I am. / No, he isn't.*, etc.).**

1. Are you married? _No, I'm not._
2. Are you thirsty? _____
3. Is it cold today? _____
4. Are your hands cold? _____
5. Is it dark now? _____
6. Are you a teacher? _____

I am doing (Present Continuous)

She's eating.
She isn't reading.

It's raining.
The sun **isn't shining.**

They're running.
They **aren't walking.**

The *present continuous* is **am/is/are** + **doing/eating/running/writing**, etc.

I	am (not)	
he she it	is (not)	-ing
we you they	are (not)	

- I'm working. I'm not watching TV.
- Chris **is taking** a bath.
- She **isn't eating.** (*or* She's **not eating.**)
- The phone **is ringing.**
- We're **having** dinner.
- You're **not listening** to me. (*or* You **aren't listening** to me.)
- The children **are doing** their homework.

am/is/are + **-ing** = something is happening *now*

I'm working
she's **wearing** a hat
they're **playing** football
I'm **not watching** television

past ———————————————— *now* ———————————————— *future*

- Please be quiet. I'm **working.** (= I'm working now)
- Look at Michiko! She's **wearing** her new hat. (= she is wearing it now)
- The weather is nice. It's **not raining.**
- "Where are the children?" "They're **playing** in the park."
- *(on the phone)* We're **having** dinner now. Can you call back later?
- You can turn off the television. I'm **not watching** it.

Spelling (see Appendix 5)

come → coming	write → writing	dance → dancing
run → running	sit → sitting	swim → swimming
lie → lying		

Am/is/are Unit 1   *Are you doing . . . ?* (Questions) Unit 4   *I am doing* and *I do* Unit 8
What are you doing tomorrow? Unit 26

Exercises

3.1 What are these people doing? Use these verbs to complete the sentences:

~~eat~~ have lie play sit wait

1. _She's eating_____ an apple.
2. He _____ for a bus.
3. They _____ soccer.
4. _____ on the floor.
5. _____ breakfast.
6. _____ on the table.

3.2 Complete the sentences. Use one of these verbs:

build cook leave stand stay swim take ~~work~~

1. Please be quiet. I _'m working_____ .
2. "Where's John?" "He's in the kitchen. He _____ ."
3. "You _____ on my foot." "Oh, I'm sorry."
4. Look! Somebody _____ in the river.
5. We're here on vacation. We _____ at the Far West Motel.
6. "Where's Erin?" "She _____ a shower."
7. They _____ a new hotel downtown.
8. I _____ now. Goodbye.

3.3 Look at the picture. Write sentences about Emily. Use *She's -ing* or *She isn't -ing.*

EMILY

1. (have dinner) _She isn't having dinner.___
2. (watch television) _She's watching television.___
3. (sit on the floor) She _____ .
4. (read a book) _____
5. (play the piano) _____
6. (laugh) _____
7. (wear a hat) _____
8. (write a letter) _____

3.4 What's happening now? Write true sentences.

1. (I / wash / my hair) _I'm not washing my hair.___
2. (it / snow) _It's snowing._ OR _It isn't snowing.___
3. (I / sit / on a chair) _____
4. (I / eat) _____
5. (it / rain) _____
6. (I / study / English) _____
7. (I / listen / to music) _____
8. (the sun / shine) _____
9. (I / wear / shoes) _____
10. (I / read / a newspaper) _____

Are you doing . . . ?
(Present Continuous Questions)

A

Positive

I	am	
he		doing
she	is	working
it		going
we		staying, etc.
you	are	
they		

Question

am	I	
	he	doing?
is	she	working?
	it	going?
	we	staying?, etc.
are	you	
	they	

What **are** you **doing**?

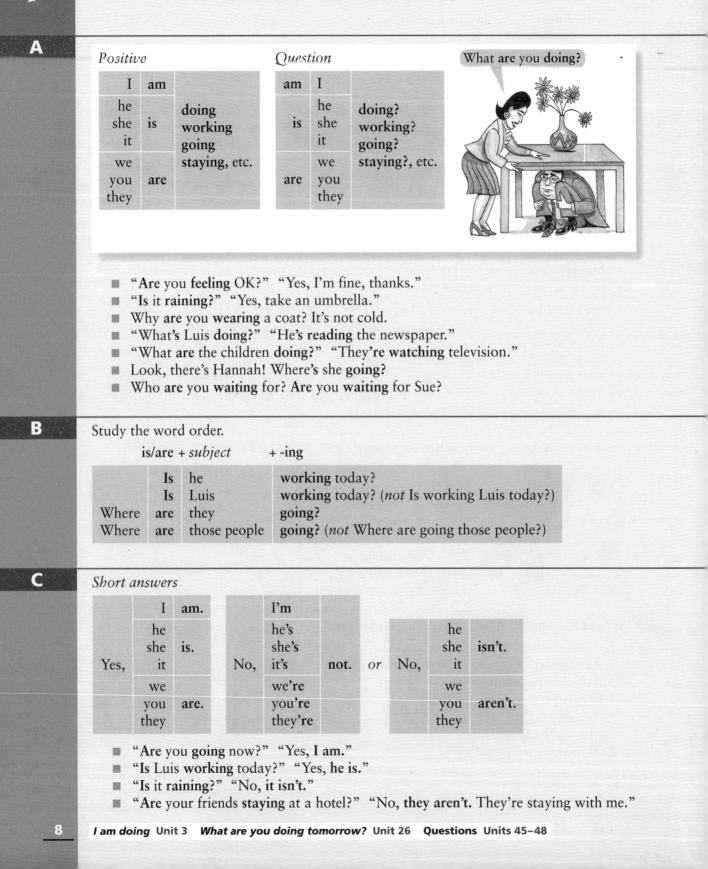

- ■ "Are you **feeling** OK?" "Yes, I'm fine, thanks."
- ■ "Is it **raining**?" "Yes, take an umbrella."
- ■ Why **are** you **wearing** a coat? It's not cold.
- ■ "What's Luis **doing**?" "He's **reading** the newspaper."
- ■ "What **are** the children **doing**?" "They're **watching** television."
- ■ Look, there's Hannah! Where's she **going**?
- ■ Who **are** you **waiting** for? **Are** you **waiting** for Sue?

B

Study the word order.

is/are + *subject*   + -ing

	Is	he	**working** today?
	Is	Luis	**working** today? (*not* Is working Luis today?)
Where	**are**	they	**going**?
Where	**are**	those people	**going**? (*not* Where are going those people?)

C

Short answers

	I	am.
	he	
	she	is.
Yes,	it	
	we	
	you	are.
	they	

No,	I'm	
	he's	
	she's	
	it's	not.
	we're	
	you're	
	they're	

or

No,	he	
	she	isn't.
	it	
	we	
	you	aren't.
	they	

- ■ "Are you **going** now?" "Yes, I am."
- ■ "Is Luis **working** today?" "Yes, he is."
- ■ "Is it **raining**?" "No, it isn't."
- ■ "Are your friends **staying** at a hotel?" "No, they aren't. They're staying with me."

I am doing Unit 3   *What are you doing tomorrow?* Unit 26   **Questions** Units 45–48

Exercises

4.1 Look at the pictures and write the questions.

1 (you / watch / it?)
Are you watching it?
No, you can turn it off.

2 (you / leave / now?)
Yes, see you tomorrow.

3 (it / rain?)
No, not right now.

4 (you/enjoy/the movie?)
Yes, it's very funny.

5 (that clock / work?)
No, it's broken.

6 (you / write / a letter?)
Yes, to my parents.

4.2 Look at the pictures and complete the questions. Use these words:

cry   eat   go   laugh   look at   ~~read~~

1 What *are you reading* ?

2 Where she ?

3 What ?

4 Why ?

5 What ?

6 Why ?

4.3 Write questions with these words. Use *is* or *are* and put the words in order.

1. (working / Luis / today?) *Is Luis working today?*
2. (what / doing / the children?) *What are the children doing?*
3. (you / listening / to me?) _____
4. (where / going / your friends?) _____
5. (your parents / television / watching?) _____
6. (what / cooking / Jessica?) _____
7. (why / you / looking / at me?) _____
8. (coming / the bus?) _____

4.4 Write true short answers (*Yes, I am. / No, he isn't.*, etc.).

1. Are you watching TV? *No, I'm not.*
2. Are you wearing a watch? _____
3. Are you eating something? _____
4. Is it raining? _____
5. Are you sitting on the floor? _____
6. Are you feeling all right? _____

I do, I work, I like, etc. (Simple Present)

We **read** a lot.

They're looking at their books.
They **read** a lot.

I **like** coffee.

He's drinking coffee.
He **likes** coffee.

they **read** / he **likes** / I **work,** etc. = the *simple present*

I/we/you/they	read	like	work	live	watch	do	have
he/she/it	reads	likes	works	lives	watches	does	has

Remember:

he works / she lives / it rains, etc.
- **I work** in an office. **My brother works** in a bank. (*not* My brother work)
- **Anne lives** in Canada. **Her parents live** in the U.S.
- **It rains** a lot in the winter.

he/she/it **has**
- **John has** lunch at home every day. (*not* John haves)

Spelling (see Appendix 5)

-es after -s/-sh/-ch	pass → passes	finish → finishes	watch → watches
-y → -ies	study → studies	try → tries	
and also	do → does	go → goes	

We use the simple present for things that are true in general, or for things that happen sometimes or all the time.
- I **like** big cities.
- The stores **open** at 9 o'clock and **close** at 5:30.
- Mario **works** very hard. He **starts** at 7:30 and **finishes** at 8 o'clock at night.
- The earth **goes** around the sun.
- We **do** a lot of different things in our free time.
- It **costs** a lot of money to stay at luxury hotels.

always/never/often/sometimes/usually + simple present
- Sue **always gets** to work early. (*not* Sue gets always)
- We **often sleep** late on weekends. (*not* We sleep often)
- I **usually drive** to work, but I **sometimes walk.**
- Julia **never eats** breakfast.

I don't . . . Unit 6   *Do you* . . . ? (Questions) Unit 7   *I am doing* and *I do* Unit 8
Always/usually/often, etc. Unit 95

Exercises

5.1 Write these verbs + -s or -es.

1. (read) she _reads_____   3. (fly) it _____   5. (have) she _____
2. (think) he _____   4. (dance) he _____   6. (finish) it _____

5.2 Complete the sentences about the people in the pictures. Use these verbs:

eat   go   live   ~~play~~   play   sleep

1. _He plays_____ the piano.   4. _____ tennis.
2. They _____ in a very big house.   5. _____ to the movies a lot.
3. _____ a lot of fruit.   6. _____ eight hours a night.

5.3 Complete the sentences. Use these verbs:

boil   close   cost   cost   like   like   meet   open   ~~speak~~   teach   wash

1. Megan _speaks_____ four languages.
2. Banks usually _____ at 9:00 in the morning.
3. The Art Museum _____ at 5 o'clock in the afternoon.
4. Isabel is a teacher. She _____ mathematics to young children.
5. My job is very interesting. I _____ a lot of people.
6. Peter _____ his hair every day.
7. Food is expensive. It _____ a lot of money.
8. Shoes are expensive. They _____ a lot of money.
9. Water _____ at 100 degrees Celsius.
10. Julia and I are good friends. I _____ her and she _____ me.

5.4 Write sentences from these words. Put the verb in the right form (*arrive* or *arrives*, etc.).

1. (always / early / Sue / arrive) _Sue always arrives early._____
2. (Julia / parties / enjoy / always) Julia _____ .
3. (work / Megan / hard / usually) _____
4. (Jenny / always / nice clothes / wear) _____
5. (dinner / we / have / always / at 6:30) _____
6. (television / Mario / watch / never) _____
7. (like / chocolate / children / usually) _____
8. (basketball / I / play / often / after work) _____

5.5 Write sentences about yourself. Use *always/never/often/sometimes/usually*.

1. (watch television) _I usually watch television at night._____
2. (read in bed) I _____ .
3. (get up before 7 o'clock) _____
4. (go to work/school by bus) _____
5. (drink coffee) _____

I don't . . . (Simple Present Negative)

The *simple present negative* is **don't/doesn't** + *verb*.

Coffee?

No, thanks. I **don't drink** coffee.

She **doesn't drink** coffee.

I **don't like** my job.

He **doesn't like** his job.

Positive

I we you they	work like do have
he she it	works likes does has

Negative

I we you they	**don't** (do not)	work like do have
he she it	**doesn't** (does not)	

- I **drink** coffee, but I **don't drink** tea.
- Sue **drinks tea,** but she **doesn't drink** coffee.
- You **don't work** very hard.
- We **don't watch** television very often.
- The weather is usually nice. It **doesn't rain** very often.
- Jerry and Nicole **don't know** many people.

Remember:

I/we/you/they **don't . . .** he/she/it **doesn't . . .**

- **I don't** like football.
- **He doesn't** like football.

- **I don't like** Fred, and **Fred doesn't** like me. (*not* Fred don't like)
- **My car doesn't** use much gas. (*not* My car don't use)
- Sometimes he's late, but **it doesn't** happen very often.

We use **don't/doesn't** + *base form* (don't **like** / doesn't **speak** / doesn't **do**, etc.).
- I **don't like** washing the car. I **don't do** it very often.
- Sandra speaks Spanish, but she **doesn't speak** Italian. (*not* doesn't speaks)
- Bill **doesn't do** his job very well. (*not* Bill doesn't his job)
- Paula **doesn't** usually **have** breakfast. (*not* doesn't . . . has)

I do/work/like, etc. **Unit 5**   *Do you . . . ?* (Questions) **Unit 7**

Exercises

6.1 **Write negative sentences.**

1. I play the piano very well. _I don't play the piano very well._
2. Yuki plays the piano very well. Yuki _____ .
3. They know my phone number. _____
4. We work very hard. _____
5. He has a car. _____
6. You do the same thing every day. _____

6.2 **Study the information and write sentences with *like*.**

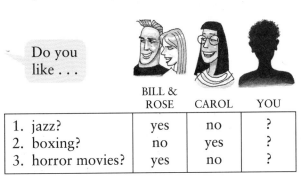

Do you like . . .

	BILL & ROSE	CAROL	YOU
1. jazz?	yes	no	?
2. boxing?	no	yes	?
3. horror movies?	yes	no	?

1. _Bill and Rose like jazz._
   Carol _____ .
   I _____ jazz.
2. Bill and Rose _____ .
   Carol _____ .
   I _____ .
3. _____
   _____
   _____

6.3 **Write about yourself. Use *I never* . . . or *I* . . . *a lot* or *I don't* . . . *very often*.**

1. (watch TV) _I never watch TV._ OR _I watch TV a lot._ OR _I don't . . . very often._
2. (go to the theater) _____
3. (ride a bicycle) _____
4. (eat in restaurants) _____
5. (travel by train) _____

6.4 **Complete the sentences. All of them are negative. Use *don't/doesn't* + one of these verbs:** cost ~~go~~ know ~~read~~ see use wear

1. I buy a newspaper every day, but sometimes I _don't read_ it.
2. Fu Chen has a car, but he _____ it very often.
3. They like films, but they _____ to the movies very often.
4. Amanda is married, but she _____ a ring.
5. I _____ much about science. I'm not interested in it.
6. It's not an expensive hotel. It _____ much to stay there.
7. Brian lives near us, but we _____ him very often.

6.5 **Put the verb in the correct form, positive or negative.**

1. Megan _speaks_ four languages – English, Japanese, Arabic, and Spanish. (speak)
2. I _don't like_ my job. It's very boring. (like)
3. "Where's Mark?" "I'm sorry. I _____ ." (know)
4. Sue is a very quiet person. She _____ very much. (talk)
5. Jim _____ a lot of coffee. It's his favorite drink. (drink)
6. It's not true! I _____ it! (believe)
7. That's a very beautiful picture. I _____ it very much. (like)
8. Mark is a vegetarian. He _____ meat. (eat)

Do you . . . ? (Simple Present Questions)

A

We use **do/does** in *simple present questions.*

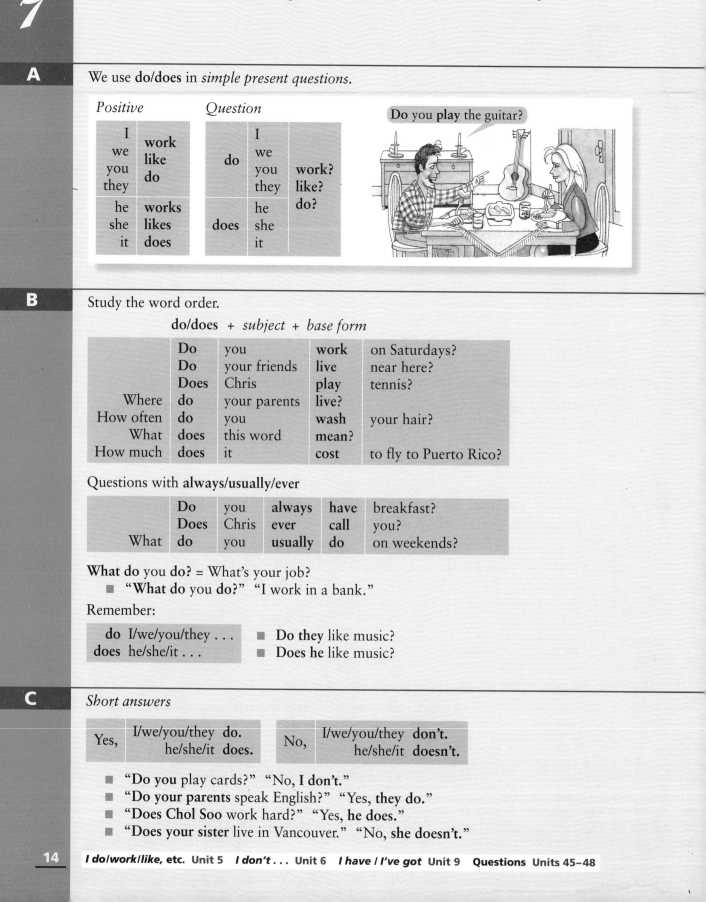

Positive

I we you they	work like do
he she it	works likes does

Question

do	I we you they	**work?** **like?** **do?**
does	he she it	

Do you play the guitar?

B

Study the word order.

do/does + *subject* + *base form*

	Do	you	**work**	on Saturdays?
	Do	your friends	**live**	near here?
	Does	Chris	**play**	tennis?
Where	**do**	your parents	**live?**	
How often	**do**	you	**wash**	your hair?
What	**does**	this word	**mean?**	
How much	**does**	it	**cost**	to fly to Puerto Rico?

Questions with **always/usually/ever**

	Do	you	**always**	**have**	breakfast?
	Does	Chris	**ever**	**call**	you?
What	**do**	you	**usually**	**do**	on weekends?

What do you **do?** = What's your job?
- ■ "**What do** you **do?**" "I work in a bank."

Remember:

do I/we/you/they . . .
does he/she/it . . .

- ■ **Do they** like music?
- ■ **Does he** like music?

C

Short answers

Yes,	I/we/you/they **do.** he/she/it **does.**

No,	I/we/you/they **don't.** he/she/it **doesn't.**

- ■ "**Do you** play cards?" "No, I **don't.**"
- ■ "**Do your parents** speak English?" "Yes, **they do.**"
- ■ "**Does Chol Soo** work hard?" "Yes, **he does.**"
- ■ "**Does your sister** live in Vancouver." "No, **she doesn't.**"

I do/work/like, etc. **Unit 5**   *I don't . . .* **Unit 6**   *I have / I've got* **Unit 9**   **Questions Units 45–48**

Exercises

7.1 **Write questions with *Do . . . ?* and *Does . . . ?***

1. I like chocolate. How about you? *Do you like chocolate?* _____
2. I play tennis. How about you? _____ you _____ ?
3. Paulo plays tennis. How about Lucia? _____ Lucia _____ ?
4. You live near here. How about your friends? _____
5. You speak English. How about your brother? _____
6. I do yoga every morning. How about you? _____
7. Sue often travels on business. How about Paul? _____
8. I want to be famous. How about you? _____
9. You work hard. How about Nicole? _____

7.2 **Write questions. Use the words in parentheses ( ) + *do* / *does*. Put the words in the right order.**

1. (where / live / your parents?) *Where do your parents live?* _____
2. (you / early / always / get up?) *Do you always get up early?* _____
3. (how often / TV / you / watch?) _____
4. (you / want / what / for dinner?) _____
5. (like / you / football?) _____
6. (your brother / like / football?) _____
7. (what / you / do / in your free time?) _____
8. (your sister / work / where?) _____
9. (to the movies / ever / you / go?) _____
10. (what / mean / this word?) _____
11. (ever / snow / it / here?) _____
12. (go / usually / to bed / what time / you?) _____
13. (how much / to call Mexico / it / cost?) _____
14. (you / for breakfast / have / usually / what?) _____

7.3 **Complete the questions. Use these verbs:**

~~do~~   do   enjoy   get   like   start   teach   work

1.	What *do you do* ?	I work in a bookstore.
2.	_____ it?	It's OK.
3.	What time _____ in the morning?	At 9 o'clock.
4.	_____ on Saturdays?	Sometimes.
5.	How _____ to work?	Usually by bus.
6.	And your husband? What _____ ?	He's a teacher.
7.	Where _____ ?	At Lincoln High School.
8.	_____ his job?	Yes, he loves it.

7.4 **Write true short answers (*Yes, he does.* / *No, I don't.*, etc.).**

1. Do you live in a big city? *No, I don't.* OR *Yes, I do.*
2. Does it rain a lot where you live? _____
3. Do your friends watch TV a lot? _____
4. Do you ever ride a bicycle? _____
5. Do you play the piano? _____

I am doing and *I do*
(Present Continuous and Simple Present)

Jim is watching television.
He is not playing the guitar.

But Jim has a guitar.
He plays it often, and he plays very well.

Jim **plays** the guitar, but
he's **not playing** the guitar now.

Is he playing the guitar?	No, he isn't.	*(present continuous)*
Does he play the guitar?	Yes, he does.	*(simple present)*

Present continuous (**I am doing**) = now, at the time of speaking

```
                        I'm doing
_____|_____
past                        now                          future
```

- Please be quiet. **I'm working.** (*not* I work)
- Tom **is taking** a shower right now. (*not* Tom takes)
- Take an umbrella with you. **It's raining.**
- You can turn off the television. **I'm** not **watching** it.
- Why are you under the table? What **are** you **doing?**

Simple present (**I do**) = in general, all the time or sometimes

```
                          I do
<_____|_____>
past                        now                          future
```

- I **work** every day, from 9 o'clock to 5:30.
- Tom **takes** a shower every morning.
- It **rains** a lot in the winter.
- I **don't watch** television very often.
- What **do** you usually **do** on weekends?

We do not use these verbs in the present continuous (**I am -ing**):

like	love	want	know	understand	remember	depend
prefer	hate	need	mean	believe		forget

Use only the simple present (**I want / do you like?**, etc.) with these verbs.
- I'm tired. I **want** to go home. (*not* I'm wanting)
- "**Do** you **know** that girl?" "Yes, but I **don't remember** her name."
- I **don't understand.** What do you **mean?**

Exercises

8.1 Answer the questions about the pictures.

1 I'm a photographer.
2 I'm a bus driver.
3 I'm a window washer.
4 We're teachers.

1. Does he take photographs? _Yes, he does._ Is he taking a photograph? _No, he isn't._
   What's he doing? _He's cooking._
2. Is she driving a bus? _____ Does she drive a bus? _____
   What's she doing? _____
3. Does he wash windows? _____ Is he washing a window? _____
   What's he doing? _____
4. Are they teaching? _____ Do they teach? _____
   What do they do? _____

8.2 Write am/is/are or do/don't/does/doesn't.

1. Excuse me, _do_____ you speak English?
2. "Where's Marta?" "I _____ know."
3. What's so funny? Why _____ you laughing?
4. "What _____ your sister do?" "She's a dentist."
5. It _____ raining. I _____ want to go out in the rain.
6. "Where _____ you come from?" "Canada."
7. How much _____ it cost to send a letter to Canada?
8. Steve is a good tennis player, but he _____ play very often.

8.3 Put the verb in the present continuous (I am doing) or the simple present (I do).

1. Excuse me, _do you speak_____ English? (you / speak)
2. "Where's Tom?" "_He's taking_____ a shower." (he / take)
3. _I don't watch_____ television very often. (I / not / watch)
4. Listen! Somebody _____ . (sing)
5. Sandra is tired. _____ to go home now. (she / want)
6. How often _____ a newspaper? (you / read)
7. "Excuse me, but _____ in my place." "Oh, I'm sorry." (you / sit)
8. I'm sorry, _____ . Can you speak more slowly?
   (I / not / understand)
9. It's late. _____ home now. (I / go)
   _____ with me? (you / come)
10. What time _____ work every day? (your father / finish)
11. You can turn off the radio. _____ to it. (I / not / listen)
12. "Where's Paul?" "In the kitchen. _____ something." (he / cook)
13. Tony _____ to work. (not / usually / drive)
    He _____ . (usually / walk)
14. Achara _____ coffee. (not / like) _____ tea. (she / prefer)

I have . . . and I've got . . .

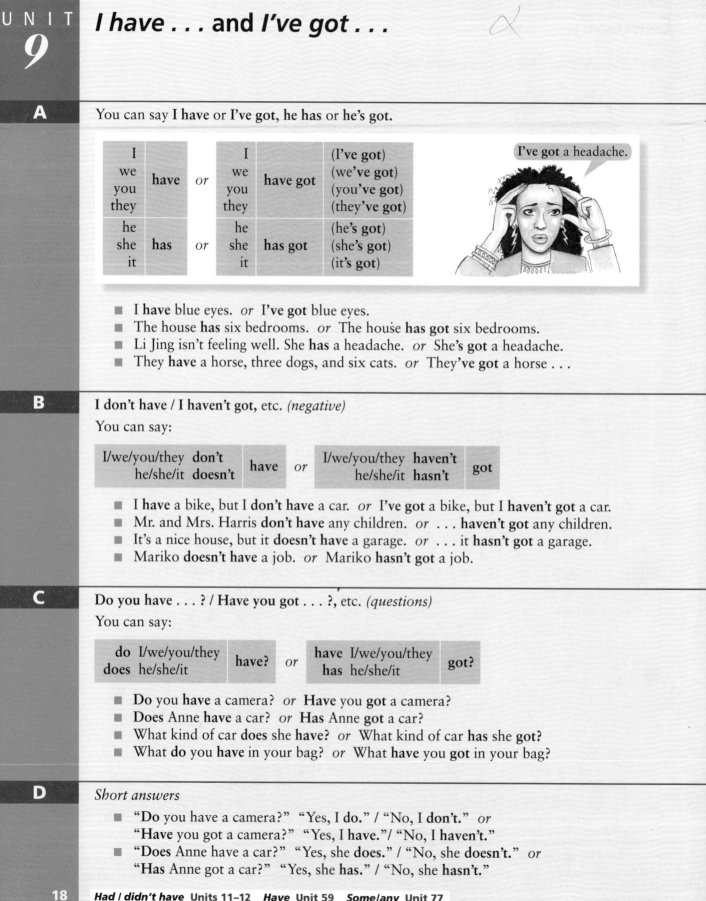

A

You can say **I have** or **I've got**, **he has** or **he's got**.

I we you they	**have**	*or*	I we you they	**have got**	(I've got) (we've got) (you've got) (they've got)
he she it	**has**	*or*	he she it	**has got**	(he's got) (she's got) (it's got)

I've got a headache.

- I **have** blue eyes. *or* I**'ve got** blue eyes.
- The house **has** six bedrooms. *or* The house **has got** six bedrooms.
- Li Jing isn't feeling well. She **has** a headache. *or* She**'s got** a headache.
- They **have** a horse, three dogs, and six cats. *or* They**'ve got** a horse . . .

B

I don't have / I haven't got, etc. *(negative)*

You can say:

I/we/you/they **don't** he/she/it **doesn't**	**have**	*or*	I/we/you/they **haven't** he/she/it **hasn't**	**got**

- I **have** a bike, but I **don't have** a car. *or* I**'ve got** a bike, but I **haven't got** a car.
- Mr. and Mrs. Harris **don't have** any children. *or* . . . **haven't got** any children.
- It's a nice house, but it **doesn't have** a garage. *or* . . . it **hasn't got** a garage.
- Mariko **doesn't have** a job. *or* Mariko **hasn't got** a job.

C

Do you have . . . ? / Have you got . . . ?, etc. *(questions)*

You can say:

do I/we/you/they **does** he/she/it	**have?**	*or*	**have** I/we/you/they **has** he/she/it	**got?**

- **Do** you **have** a camera? *or* **Have** you **got** a camera?
- **Does** Anne **have** a car? *or* **Has** Anne **got** a car?
- What kind of car **does** she **have**? *or* What kind of car **has** she **got**?
- What **do** you **have** in your bag? *or* What **have** you **got** in your bag?

D

Short answers

- "**Do** you have a camera?" "Yes, I **do**." / "No, I **don't**." *or*
  "**Have** you got a camera?" "Yes, I **have**."/ "No, I **haven't**."
- "**Does** Anne have a car?" "Yes, she **does**." / "No, she **doesn't**." *or*
  "**Has** Anne got a car?" "Yes, she **has**." / "No, she **hasn't**."

Had / didn't have Units 11–12   ***Have*** Unit 59   ***Some/any*** Unit 77

Exercises

9.1 Rewrite these sentences with *got* (*have got / hasn't got / have . . . got?*, etc.).

1. They have a car. _They've got a car._
2. Bill has a headache. _____
3. I don't have any free time. _____
4. Do you have a watch? _____
5. We have a lot of work at the office now. _____
6. My brother doesn't have a college degree. _____

Now rewrite these sentences without *got*. Use *have / doesn't have / do . . . have?*, etc.

7. Yoshi hasn't got time to go with us. _Yoshi doesn't have time to go with us._
8. You've got a phone call from Japan. _____
9. Have you got any aspirin? _____
10. Sara hasn't got much money. _____
11. Have your parents got any friends in Hawaii? _____

9.2 Write about Tina and you. Use *has got / hasn't got / have got / haven't got*.

My brothers and sisters.

TINA

1. (a camera) _Tina has got a camera._
   I've got a camera. OR _I haven't got . . ._
2. (a bicycle) Tina _____ .
   I _____ .
3. (long hair) _____
   _____
4. (brothers / sisters) _____
   _____

9.3 Complete the sentences. Use *have/has* or *don't have / doesn't have* + one of these:

~~a big yard~~	a key	a toothache	much time
~~a headache~~	a lot of friends	four wheels	

1. I'm not feeling very well. I _have a headache_ .
2. It's a nice house, but it _doesn't have a big yard_ .
3. Most cars _____ .
4. Everybody likes Tom. He _____ .
5. I'm going to the dentist this morning. I _____ .
6. He can't open the door. He _____ .
7. Hurry! We _____ .

9.4 Complete the sentences with *do, doesn't, don't, got, has,* or *have*.

1. Sarah hasn't _got_ a car. She goes everywhere by bicycle.
2. They like animals. They _have_ three dogs and two cats.
3. Ryan isn't happy. He _____ got a lot of problems.
4. _____ you have change for a dollar?
5. They don't read much. They _____ have many books.
6. "What's wrong?" "I've _____ something in my eye."
7. "Where's my pen?" "I don't know. I don't _____ it."
8. Julia wants to go to the concert, but she _____ have a ticket.
9. _____ you got a minute to help me?

Was/were

A

Last night

Now

Now Arturo **is** at work.

At midnight last night he **wasn't** at work.

He **was** in bed.
He **was** asleep.

am/is (present) → **was** (past)
- I **am** tired. (now)
- Where **is** Beth? (now)
- The weather **is** nice today.

- I **was** tired **last night.**
- Where **was** Beth **yesterday?**
- The weather **was** nice **last week.**

are (present) → **were** (past)
- You **are** late. (now)
- They **aren't** here. (now)

- You **were** late **yesterday.**
- They **weren't** here **last Sunday.**

B

Positive		*Negative*		*Question*	
I he she it	**was**	I he she it	**was not** (**wasn't**)	**was**	I? he? she? it?
we you they	**were**	we you they	**were not** (**weren't**)	**were**	we? you? they?

- Last year Amy **was** 22, so she's 23 now.
- When I **was** a child, I **was** afraid of dogs.
- We **were** hungry after the trip, but we **weren't** tired.
- The hotel **was** comfortable, but it **wasn't** expensive.

- **Was** the weather nice when you **were** on vacation?
- Those shoes are nice. **Were** they expensive?
- Why **were** you late this morning?

C

Short answers

Yes,	I/he/she/it **was.** we/you/they **were.**	No,	I/he/she/it **wasn't.** we/you/they **weren't.**

- "**Were** you late?" "No, I **wasn't.**"
- "**Was** Scott at work yesterday?" "Yes, he **was.**"
- "**Were** Amy and Matt at the party?" "No, they **weren't.**"

Exercises

10.1 Where were these people at 3 o'clock yesterday afternoon? Where were you?

| 1 | 3:00 | 2 | 3:00 | 3 | 3:00 | 4 | 3:00 | 5 | 3:00 |
| BILL | | ELENA | PABLO | KATE | | MR. and MRS. HALL | | | GARY |

1. _Bill was_____ in _bed_____ .
2. Elena and Pablo _____ at _____ .
3. Kate _____ at _____ .
4. _____ on _____ .
5. _____ at _____ .
6. And you? I _____ .

10.2 Write *am / is / are* (present) or *was / were* (past).

1. Last year she _was_____ 22, so she _is_____ 23 now.
2. Today the weather ____is_____ nice, but yesterday it ____was____ very cold.
3. I ____am____ hungry. Can I have something to eat?
4. I feel fine this morning, but I _____ very tired last night.
5. Where _____ you at 11 o'clock last Friday morning?
6. Don't buy those shoes. They _____ very expensive.
7. I like your new jacket. _____ it expensive?
8. "Where _____ the children?" "I don't know. They _____ here ten minutes ago."

10.3 Write *was / wasn't* or *were / weren't*.

1. We weren't happy with the hotel. Our room _was_ very small, and it _wasn't_ very clean.
2. Bill _____ at work last week because he _____ sick. He's better now.
3. Yesterday _____ a holiday, so the banks _____ closed. They're open today.
4. "_____ Kate and John at the party?" "Kate _____ there, but John _____ ."
5. "Where are my keys?" "I don't know. They _____ on the table, but they're not there now."
6. You _____ at home last night. Where _____ you?

10.4 Write questions. Use the words in parentheses ( ) in the correct order + *was / were*.

1. (late / you / this morning / why?) _Why were you late this morning?_   The traffic was bad.

2. (hard / your exam?) _____   No, it was easy.
   _____

3. (last week / where / Beth and Bill?) _____   They were on vacation.

4. (angry / you / yesterday / why?) _____   Because you were late.
   _____

5. (nice / the weather / last week?) _____   Yes, it was beautiful.
   _____

Worked, got, went, etc. (Simple Past)

A

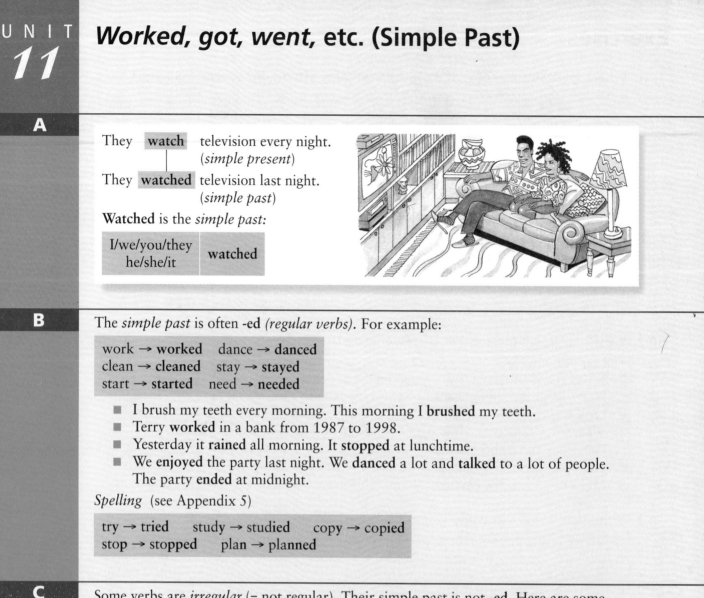

They | watch | television every night.
(*simple present*)

They | watched | television last night.
(*simple past*)

Watched is the *simple past*:

I/we/you/they he/she/it	watched

B

The *simple past* is often -ed *(regular verbs)*. For example:

work → worked	dance → danced
clean → cleaned	stay → stayed
start → started	need → needed

- I brush my teeth every morning. This morning I **brushed** my teeth.
- Terry **worked** in a bank from 1987 to 1998.
- Yesterday it **rained** all morning. It **stopped** at lunchtime.
- We **enjoyed** the party last night. We **danced** a lot and **talked** to a lot of people. The party **ended** at midnight.

Spelling (see Appendix 5)

try → tried	study → studied	copy → copied
stop → stopped	plan → planned	

C

Some verbs are *irregular* (= not regular). Their simple past is not -ed. Here are some important irregular verbs (see also Appendixes 2–3).

begin → began	fall → fell	leave → left	sell → sold
break → broke	find → found	lose → lost	sit → sat
bring → brought	fly → flew	make → made	sleep → slept
build → built	forget → forgot	meet → met	speak → spoke
buy → bought	get → got	pay → paid	stand → stood
catch → caught	give → gave	put → put	take → took
come → came	go → went	read → read*	tell → told
do → did	have → had	ring → rang	think → thought
drink → drank	hear → heard	say → said	win → won
eat → ate	know → knew	see → saw	write → wrote

* *pronounced "red"*

- We **did** a lot of work yesterday.
- I usually get up early, but this morning I **got** up at 9:30.
- Caroline **went** to the movies three times last week.
- Ampol **came** into the room, **took** off his coat, and **sat** down.

Exercises

11.1 Complete the sentences. Use one of these verbs in the simple past:

~~brush~~   die   enjoy   end   happen   rain   start   stay   want

1. I *brushed* my teeth three times yesterday.
2. The concert _____ at 7:30 and _____ at 10 o'clock.
3. When I was a child, I _____ to be a doctor.
4. The accident _____ last Sunday afternoon.
5. It's a nice day today, but yesterday it _____ all day.
6. We _____ our vacation last year. We _____ at a very nice hotel.
7. Amy's grandfather _____ when he was 90 years old.

11.2 Write the simple past of these verbs:

1. get *got*
2. see _____
3. play _____
4. pay _____
5. visit _____
6. buy _____
7. go _____
8. think _____
9. copy _____
10. know _____
11. put _____
12. speak _____

11.3 Read about Anna's trip to Mexico City. Put the verbs in the correct form.

Last Tuesday Anna (1) *flew* from Los Angeles to Mexico   (fly)
City. She (2) _____ up at 6 o'clock in the morning and   (get)
(3) _____ a cup of coffee. At 7:15 she (4) _____   (have) (leave)
home and (5) _____ to the airport. When she   (drive)
(6) _____ , she (7) _____ the car and then   (arrive) (park)
(8) _____ to the ticket counter, where she (9) _____   (go) (check)
in for her flight. Then she (10) _____ breakfast at an airport   (have)
cafe and (11) _____ for her flight. The plane   (wait)
(12) _____ on time and (13) _____ in Mexico City   (depart) (arrive)
four hours later. Finally, she (14) _____ a taxi to her hotel.   (take)

11.4 Write sentences about the past.

1. Jim always goes to work by car. Yesterday he *went to work by car* .
2. Mei Lan often loses her keys. She _____ last week.
3. Kate meets her friends every night. She _____ last night.
4. I usually buy two newspapers every day. Yesterday I _____ ;
5. We usually go to the movies on Sundays. Last Sunday we _____ .
6. I eat an apple every day. Yesterday I _____ .
7. Taro always takes a shower in the morning. This morning he _____ .

11.5 Write sentences about what you did yesterday.

1. *I played volleyball yesterday.*
2. _____
3. _____
4. _____

I didn't ... Did you ...?
(Simple Past Negative and Questions)

A

We use **did** in *simple past negatives* and *questions*.

Base form		Positive		Negative		Question	
play	I	**played**	I		play		I	play?
start	we	**started**	we		start		we	start?
watch	you	**watched**	you		watch		you	watch?
have	they	**had**	they	**did not**	have	**did**	they	have?
see	he	**saw**	he	**(didn't)**	see		he	see?
do	she	**did**	she		do		she	do?
go	it	**went**	it		go		it	go?

B

do/does *(present)* → **did** *(past)*

■ **I don't** watch television very often.   ■ **I didn't** watch television **yesterday.**
■ **Does** she go out often?   ■ **Did** she go out **last night?**

C

We use **did/didn't** + *base form* (**watch/play/go,** etc.)

Positive → *Negative*

I **watched** → I **didn't watch** (*not* I didn't watched)
he **had** → he **didn't have**
they **went** → **did** they **go?** (*not* did they went?)
you **did** → **did** you **do?**

■ I **played** tennis yesterday, but I **didn't win.**
■ "**Did** you **do** your homework?"   "No, I **didn't have** time."
■ We **went** to the movies, but we **didn't enjoy** the film.

D

Study the word order in questions:

	did + *subject*	+ *base form*	
	Did your sister	**call**	you?
What	**did** you	**do**	last night?
How	**did** the accident	**happen?**	
Where	**did** your parents	**go**	for vacation?

E

Short answers

Yes,	I/we/you/they he/she/it	**did.**	No,	I/we/you/they he/she/it	**didn't.**

■ "**Did** you **see** Joe yesterday?"   "No, **I didn't.**"
■ "**Did** it **rain** on Sunday?"   "Yes, **it did.**"
■ "**Did** Helen **come** to the party?"   "No, **she didn't.**"
■ "**Did** your parents **have** a good trip?"   "Yes, **they did.**"

Exercises

12.1 **Complete these sentences. Use *didn't.***

1. I saw Barbara, but I _didn't see_ Mariana.
2. They worked on Monday, but they _____ on Tuesday.
3. We went to the post office, but we _____ to the bank.
4. She had a pen, but she _____ any paper.
5. Brian did some work in the yard, but he _____ any work in the house.

12.2 **Write questions with *Did . . . ?***

1. I watched TV last night. How about you? _Did you watch TV last night?_
2. I enjoyed the party. How about you? _____
3. I had a nice vacation. How about you? _____
4. I finished work early. How about you? _____
5. I slept well last night. How about you? _____

12.3 **What did you do yesterday? Write true sentences, positive or negative.**

1. (watch TV) _I watched TV._ OR _I didn't watch TV._
2. (get up before 7 o'clock) I _____ .
3. (take a shower) _____
4. (buy a magazine) _____
5. (eat meat) _____
6. (go to bed before 10:30) _____

12.4 **Write *B*'s questions. Use:**

cost   get to work   go   go to bed late   happen   have a nice time   ~~stay~~   win

1. A: We went to Vancouver last month.
   B: Where _did you stay_ ?
   A: With some friends.

2. A: I was late this morning.
   B: What time _____ ?
   A: Half past nine.

3. A: I played tennis this afternoon.
   B: _____
   A: No, I lost.

4. A: I had a nice vacation.
   B: Good. Where _____ ?
   A: To the mountains.

5. A: We came home by taxi.
   B: How much _____ ?
   A: Ten dollars.

6. A: I'm tired this morning.
   B: _____
   A: No, but I didn't sleep very well.

7. A: We went to the beach yesterday.
   B: _____
   A: Yes, it was great.

8. A: The window is broken.
   B: How _____ ?
   A: I don't know.

12.5 **Put the verb in the correct form – positive, negative, or question.**

1. We went to the movies, but the film wasn't very good. We _didn't enjoy_ it. (enjoy)
2. Tim _____ some new clothes yesterday – two shirts, a jacket, and a sweater. (buy)
3. "_____ yesterday?" "No, it was a nice day." (rain)
4. We were tired, so we _____ long at the party. (stay)
5. It was very warm in the room, so I _____ a window. (open)
6. "Did you go to the bank this morning?" "No, I _____ time."(have)
7. "I cut my hand this morning." "How _____ that?" (do)

I was doing (Past Continuous)

A

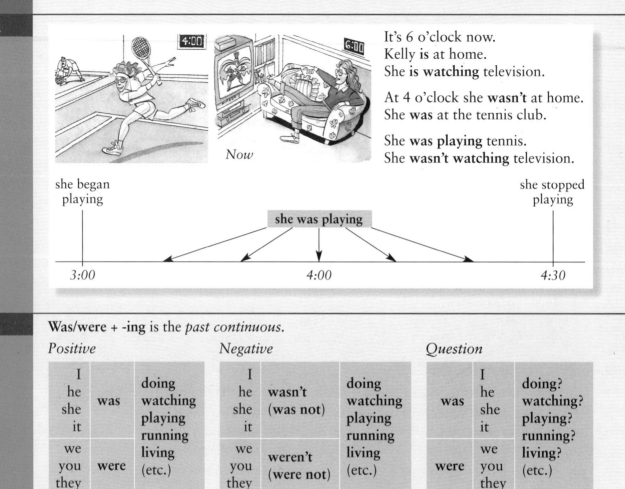

It's 6 o'clock now.
Kelly **is** at home.
She **is watching** television.

At 4 o'clock she **wasn't** at home.
She **was** at the tennis club.

She **was playing** tennis.
She **wasn't watching** television.

Now

she began
playing

she stopped
playing

she was playing

3:00   4:00   4:30

B

Was/were + -ing is the *past continuous*.

Positive

I he she it	was	doing watching playing running
we you they	were	living (etc.)

Negative

I he she it	wasn't (was not)	doing watching playing running
we you they	weren't (were not)	living (etc.)

Question

was	I he she it	doing? watching? playing? running?
were	we you they	living? (etc.)

- What **were** you **doing** at 11:30 yesterday? **Were** you **working**?
- "What did he say?" "I don't know. I **wasn't listening**."
- It **was raining**, so we didn't go out.
- In 1994 we **were living** in Japan.
- Today she's wearing a skirt, but yesterday she **was wearing** pants.
- I woke up early yesterday. It was a beautiful morning. The sun **was shining**, and the birds **were singing**.

Spelling (see Appendix 5)

live → living   run → running   lie → lying

C

am/is/are + -ing *(present)* → was/were + -ing *(past)*

- I'm working (now).
- It isn't raining (now).
- What are you doing (now)?

- I was working at 10:30 last night.
- It wasn't raining when we went out.
- What were you doing at three o'clock?

Was/were **Unit 10** *I was doing* and *I did* **(Past Continuous and Simple Past) Unit 14**

Exercises

13.1 Look at the pictures. Where were these people at 3 o'clock yesterday afternoon?
What were they doing? Write two sentences for each picture.

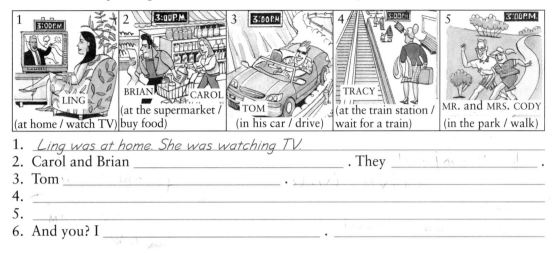

1. *Ling was at home. She was watching TV.*
2. Carol and Brian _____ . They _____ .
3. Tom _____ . _____
4. _____
5. _____
6. And you? I _____ .

13.2 Sarah did a lot of things yesterday morning. Look at the pictures, and complete the
sentences.

| 7:10–7:25 | 7:30–8:10 | 8:30–9:00 | 9:20–10:00 | 10:30–11:00 | 12:00–12:45 |

1. At 8:45 *she was washing her car* .   4. At 12:10 _____ .
2. At 10:45 she _____ .   5. At 7:15 _____ .
3. At 8 o'clock _____ .   6. At 9:30 _____ .

13.3 Complete the questions. Use *was/were -ing*. Use *what/where/why* if necessary.

1. (you / live)   *Where were you living*   in 1990?   In Brazil.
2. (you / do)   _____ at 2 o'clock?   I was asleep.
3. (it / rain)   _____ when you got up?   No, it was sunny.
4. (Ann / drive)   _____ so fast?   Because she was late.
5. (Lee / wear)   _____ a suit yesterday?   No, jeans.

13.4 Look at the picture. You saw Joe yesterday afternoon. What was he doing? Write
positive or negative sentences.

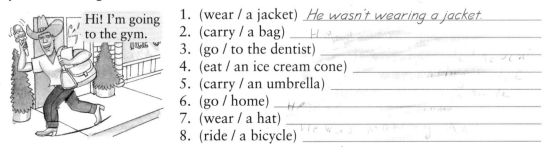

Hi! I'm going to the gym.

1. (wear / a jacket) *He wasn't wearing a jacket.*
2. (carry / a bag) _____
3. (go / to the dentist) _____
4. (eat / an ice cream cone) _____
5. (carry / an umbrella) _____
6. (go / home) _____
7. (wear / a hat) _____
8. (ride / a bicycle) _____

UNIT 14

I was doing and *I did* (Past Continuous and Simple Past)

A

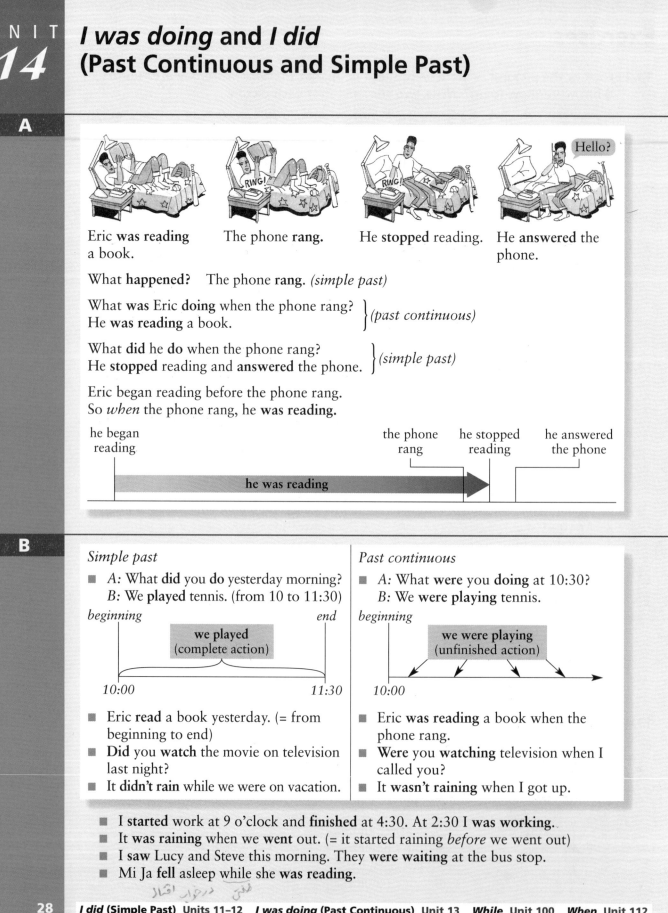

Eric **was reading** a book.

The phone **rang.**

He **stopped** reading.

He **answered** the phone.

What **happened?**   The phone **rang.** *(simple past)*

What **was** Eric **doing** when the phone rang? ⎫
He **was reading** a book. ⎭ *(past continuous)*

What **did** he **do** when the phone rang? ⎫
He **stopped** reading and **answered** the phone. ⎭ *(simple past)*

Eric began reading before the phone rang.
So *when* the phone rang, he **was reading.**

| he began reading | | the phone rang | he stopped reading | he answered the phone |

he was reading

B

Simple past

- A: What **did** you **do** yesterday morning?
  B: We **played** tennis. (from 10 to 11:30)

beginning   *end*

we played
(complete action)

10:00   11:30

- Eric **read** a book yesterday. (= from beginning to end)
- **Did** you **watch** the movie on television last night?
- It **didn't rain** while we were on vacation.

Past continuous

- A: What **were** you **doing** at 10:30?
  B: We **were playing** tennis.

beginning

we were playing
(unfinished action)

10:00

- Eric **was reading** a book when the phone rang.
- **Were** you **watching** television when I called you?
- It **wasn't raining** when I got up.

- I **started** work at 9 o'clock and **finished** at 4:30. At 2:30 I **was working.**
- It **was raining** when we **went** out. (= it started raining *before* we went out)
- I **saw** Lucy and Steve this morning. They **were waiting** at the bus stop.
- Mi Ja **fell** asleep while she **was reading.**

Exercises

14.1 Look at the pictures. Put the verbs in the past continuous or simple past.

1.

Linda _broke_____ (break) her arm last week. It _____ (happen) when she _____ (paint) her room. She _____ (fall) off the ladder.

2.

Hi, Paula!

PAULA

The train _____ (arrive) at the station, and Paula _____ (get) off. Two friends of hers, John and Jenny, _____ (wait) to meet her.

3.

Hello, Jim! | I'm going home.

SUE

Yesterday Sue _____ (walk) down the street when she _____ (meet) Jim. He _____ (go) home, and he _____ (carry) a bag. They _____ (stop) to talk for a few minutes.

14.2 Put the verb in the past continuous or simple past.

1. A: What _were you doing____ (you / do) when the phone _rang_____ (ring)?
   B: I _was watching_____ (watch) television.
2. A: Was Tracy busy when you went to see her?
   B: Yes, she _____ (study).
3. A: What time _____ (the mail / come) this morning?
   B: It _____ (come) while I _____ (have) breakfast.
4. A: Was Megan at work today?
   B: No, she _____ (not / go) to work. She was sick.
5. A: How fast _____ (you / drive) when the police _____ (stop) you?
   B: I don't know exactly, but I _____ (not / drive) very fast.
6. A: _____ (your team / win) the baseball game yesterday?
   B: No, the weather was very bad, so we _____ (not / play).
7. A: How _____ (you / break) the window?
   B: We _____ (play) baseball. I _____ (hit) the ball, and it _____ (break) the window.
8. A: _____ (you / see) Judy last night?
   B: Yes, she _____ (wear) a long dress.
9. A: What _____ (you / do) at 2 o'clock this morning?
   B: I was asleep.
10. A: I _____ (lose) my key last night.
    B: How _____ (you / get) into your apartment?
    A: I _____ (climb) in through a window.

I used to . . .

DAVE *a few years ago*   DAVE *today*

I work in a factory.

I work in a supermarket.
I **used to work** in a factory.

Dave **used to work** in a factory. Now he **works** in a supermarket.

Dave **used to work** in a factory = he worked in a factory in the past, but he doesn't work there now

he used to work	he works
past	*now*

You can say I **used to work** . . . / she **used to have** . . . / they **used to be** . . . , etc.

I/you/we/they he/she/it	used to	be work have play (etc.)

I used to have
very long hair.

- When I was a child, I **used to like** chocolate.
- I **used to read** a lot of books, but I don't read much these days.
- Liz has short hair now, but it **used to be** very long.
- They **used to live** on the same block as us, so we **used to see** them often. But we don't see them very often these days.
- Amy **used to have** a piano, but she sold it when she moved.

The negative is I **didn't use to** . . . .
- When I was a child, I **didn't use to like** tomatoes.

The question is **did you use to** . . . ?
- Where **did** you **use to live** before you came here?

We use **used to** . . . only for the *past*. You cannot say "I use to . . ." *(present)*.
- I **used to play** tennis. These days I **play** golf. (*not* I use to play golf.)
- We **usually get up** early. (*not* We use to get up early.)

Exercises

15.1 Look at the pictures. Complete the sentences with *used to* . . . .

1. *She used to have long hair.*

2. He _____ _____ baseball.

3. _____ _____ a taxi driver.

4. _____ _____ in Dallas.

5. _____ _____

6. This building _____ _____ _____ .

15.2 Karen works very hard and has very little free time. A few years ago, her life was different.

| | KAREN *a few years ago* | KAREN *now* |

Do you play any sports? — Yes, I swim every day and I play volleyball.

Do you go out much? — Yes, three or four nights a week.

Do you play a musical instrument? — Yes, the guitar.

Do you like to read? — Yes, I read a lot.

Do you travel much? — Yes, I take two or three trips a year.

I work very hard at my job. I don't have any free time.

Write sentences about Karen with *used to* . . . .

1. *She used to swim every day.*
2. She _____ .
3. _____
4. _____
5. _____
6. _____

15.3 Complete these sentences. Use *used to* or the simple present (*I play / he lives,* etc.).

1. I *used to play* tennis. I stopped playing a few years ago.
2. "Do you play any sports?" "Yes, I *play* basketball."
3. "Do you have a car?" "No, I _____ one, but I sold it."
4. Fu Chen _____ a waiter. Now he's the manager of a restaurant.
5. "Do you go to work by car?" "Sometimes, but usually I _____ by train."
6. When I was a child, I never _____ vegetables, but I eat them now.
7. Suree loves to watch TV. She _____ TV every night.
8. We _____ near the airport, but we moved to the city a few years ago.
9. Normally I start work at 7 o'clock, so I _____ up very early.
10. What games _____ you _____ when you were a child?

Have you ever . . . ? (Present Perfect)

كامل - درجة بك

A

Have you been to Mexico City?

Yes, I have. Many times.

Have you ever driven a car there?

No, I've never driven in Mexico City.

Have been / have driven / have played, etc., is the *present perfect* (**have** + *past participle*).

I we you they	have ('ve) have not (haven't)	played lived visited	have	I we you they	played? lived? visited?	} *Regular verbs*
he she it	has ('s) has not (hasn't)	read lost been flown	has	he she it	read? lost? been? flown?	} *Irregular verbs*

Regular verbs: The past participle is **-ed** (the same as the simple past).

play → we **have played**   live → I **have lived**   visit → she **has visited**

Irregular verbs: The past participle is sometimes the same as the simple past.

buy → I **bought** / I **have bought**   have → he **had** / he **has had**

Sometimes it is different (see Appendixes 2–3).

break → I **broke** / I **have broken**   see → you **saw** / you **have seen**

B

We use the present perfect when we talk about a time from the past until now, for example, a person's life.

Have you ever been to Japan?

past   *now*

- "**Have** you **been** to France?" (in your life) "No, I **haven't**."
- We've **been** to Canada, but we **haven't been** to Alaska.
- Mary **has had** many different jobs and **has lived** in many places.
- I've **seen** that woman before, but I can't remember where.
- How many times **has** Brazil **won** the World Cup?
- "**Have** you **read** this book?" "Yes, I've **read** it twice." (twice = two times)

C

Present perfect + **ever** (in *questions*) and **never**
- "**Has** Amy **ever been** to Australia?" "Yes, once." (once = one time)
- "**Have** you **ever played** golf?" "Yes, I play golf a lot."
- My mother **has never traveled** by plane.
- I've **never ridden** a horse.
- "Who is that man?" "I don't know. I've **never seen** him before."

Exercises

16.1 You are asking Angela questions. Write the questions. Begin with *Have you ever . . . ?*

YOU   ANGELA

1. (Montreal?)
2. (play / golf?)
3. (Australia?)
4. (lose / your passport?)
5. (fly / in a helicopter?)
6. (eat / Chinese food?)
7. (London?)
8. (drive / a bus?)

Have you ever been to Montreal?
Have you ever played golf?
Have _____ ?
_____
_____
_____
_____
_____

No, never.
Yes, many times.
No, never.
Yes, once.
No, never.
Yes, a few times.
Yes, twice.
No, never.

16.2 Look at Angela's answers in Exercise 16.1. Write sentences about Angela.

1. (London) *Angela has been to London twice.* _____
2. (Australia) She _____ .
3. (Chinese food) _____
4. (drive / a bus) _____

Now write about yourself. How many times have you done these things?

5. (London) I _____ .
6. (play / tennis) _____
7. (fly / in a helicopter) _____

16.3 Mary is 85 years old. She has had an interesting life. What has she done?

MARY

be	meet
do	travel
~~have~~	write

all over the world	~~many different jobs~~
a lot of interesting people	married three times
a lot of interesting things	ten books

1. *She has had many different jobs.* _____
2. She _____ .
3. _____
4. _____
5. _____
6. _____

16.4 Put the verbs in the present perfect.

1. *I've seen* _____ (I / see) that woman before, but I can't remember where.
2. " *Have you ever played* (you / ever / play) golf?" "Yes, I play golf a lot."
3. " _____ (you / ever / write) a poem?" "Yes, in high school."
4. "Does Emma know Sam?" "No, _____ (she / never / meet) him."
5. Ann and Eli have lots of books, and _____ (they / read) all of them.
6. _____ (I / never / be) to Australia, but _____ (my brother / be) there twice.
7. Joy's favorite film is *Howard and Belinda.* _____ (she / see) it five times, but _____ (I / never / see) it.
8. _____ (I / travel) by plane, bus, and train. Someday, I want to take a trip by boat.

UNIT 17 — How long have you . . . ?

A

Susan is on vacation in New York.
She is there now.

She arrived in New York on Monday.
Today is Thursday.

How long **has she been** in New York?

She **has been** in New York { since Monday.
for three days.

How long have you been in New York?

Since Monday.

Compare **is** and **has been**:

She **has been** in New York { since Monday.
for three days.

She is in
New York now.

is = *present*

has been = *present perfect*

Monday

now
Thursday

B

Compare:

Simple present	*Present perfect*
■ Dan and Kate **are** married.	■ They **have been** married **for** five years. (*not* They are married for five years.)
■ **Are** you married?	■ **How long have** you **been** married? (*not* How long are you married?)
■ **Do** you **know** Lynn?	■ **How long have** you **known** her? (*not* How long do you know her?)
■ I **know** Lynn.	■ I've **known** her **for** a long time. (*not* I know her for a long time.)
■ Vera **lives** in Brasilia.	■ **How long has** she **lived** in Brasilia? She **has lived** there **all her life.**
■ I **have** a car.	■ **How long have** you **had** your car? I've **had** it **since** April.

Present continuous	*Present perfect continuous*
■ **I'm studying** German.	■ **How long have** you **been studying** German? (*not* How long are you studying German?) I've **been studying** German **for** two years.
■ Bruce **is watching** TV.	■ **How long has** he **been watching** TV? He's **been watching** TV **since** 5 o'clock. (he's been = he has been)
■ It's **raining**.	■ It's **been raining** all day. (it's been = it has been)

For and **since** Units 18, 99

Exercises

17.1 **Complete these sentences.**

1. Susan is in New York. She _has been_ there since Monday.
2. I know Isabel. I _have known_ her for a long time.
3. Nancy and Seth are married. They _____ married since 1997.
4. Bill is sick. He _____ sick for the last few days.
5. We live on Main Street. We _____ there for ten years.
6. Chris works in a bank. She _____ in a bank for five years.
7. Andy has a headache. He _____ a headache since he got up this morning.
8. I'm studying English. I _____ English for six months.

17.2 **Write questions with *How long . . . ?***

1.	Susan is on vacation.
2.	Seth and Nancy are in Canada.
3.	I know Amy.
4.	Diana is studying Italian.
5.	My brother lives in Seattle.
6.	I'm a teacher.
7.	It is raining.

How long has she been on vacation?
How long _____ ?
How long _____ you _____ ?
_____
_____
_____
_____

17.3

1 We're married.
2 I live in Korea.
3 We're on vacation.
4 The sun is shining.
5 I'm waiting.
6 I have a beard.

Look at the pictures and complete the sentences with:

all day   all her life   for ten minutes   ~~for ten years~~   since he was 20   since Sunday

1. _They have been married for ten years._
2. She _____ .
3. They _____ .
4. The sun _____ .
5. She _____ .
6. He _____ .

17.4 **Which is right?**

1. Vinai ~~lives~~ / has lived in Canada since 1999. (*has lived* is right)
2. Ruth is a good friend of mine. I know / have known her very well.
3. Ruth is a good friend of mine. I know / have known her for a long time.
4. "Sorry I'm late. How long are you / have you been waiting?" "Only five minutes."
5. Ted works / has worked in a hotel now. He likes his job a lot.
6. Amy is reading the newspaper. She is / has been reading it for two hours.
7. "How long do you live / have you lived in this house?" "About ten years."
8. "Is that a new coat?" "No, I have / I've had this coat for a long time."
9. Ed is / has been in Seattle right now. He is / has been there for the last three days.

For, since, and ago

for and **since**

We use **for** and **since** to say *how long*.

- Rachel is in Brazil. She **has been** there { **for three days.** **since Monday.**

We use **for** + a period of time (**three days / two years**, etc.).

| for three days | | |
| Monday | Tuesday | Wednesday |

past   *now*

for	
three days	ten minutes
an hour	two hours
a week	four weeks
a month	six months
five years	a long time

- Richard has been in Canada **for six months.** (*not* since six months)
- We've been waiting **for two hours.** (*not* since two hours)
- I've lived in Chicago **for a long time.**

We use **since** + the start of the period (**Monday / 9 o'clock**, etc.).

| Monday | **since Monday** |

past   *now*

since	
Monday	Wednesday
9 o'clock	12:30
July 4th	my birthday
January	I was ten years old
1995	we arrived

- Richard has been in Canada **since January.** (= from January to now)
- We've been waiting **since 9 o'clock.** (= from 9 o'clock to now)
- I've lived in Chicago **since I was ten years old.**

ago

ago = before now

- Ji Yoo started her new job **three weeks ago.** (= three weeks before now)
- "When did Tom go out?" "**Ten minutes ago.**" (= ten minutes before now)
- I had dinner **an hour ago.**
- Life was very different **a hundred years ago.**

We use **ago** with the *past* (**started/did/had/was**, etc.).

Compare **ago** and **for**:

- **When did** Rachel **arrive** in Brazil?
  She **arrived** in Brazil **three days ago.**
- **How long has** she **been** in Brazil?
  She **has been** in Brazil **for three days.**

Present Perfect + for/since Unit 17   **From/until/since/for** Unit 99   **For and during** Unit 100

Exercises

18.1 Write *for* or *since*.

1. Rachel has been in Brazil *since* Monday.
2. Rachel has been in Brazil *for* three days.
3. My aunt has lived in Australia _____ 15 years.
4. Jennifer is in her office. She has been there _____ 7 o'clock.
5. Mexico has been an independent country _____ 1821.
6. The bus is late. We've been waiting _____ 20 minutes.
7. Nobody lives in those houses. They have been empty _____ many years.
8. Luis has been sick _____ a long time. He has been in the hospital _____ October.

18.2 Answer these questions. Use *ago*.

1. When was your last meal? *Three hours ago.*
2. When was the last time you were sick? _____
3. When was the last time you went to the movies? _____
4. When was the last time you were in a car? _____
5. When was the last time you took a vacation? _____

18.3 Complete the sentences. Use the words in parentheses ( ) + *for* or *ago*.

1. Rachel arrived in Brazil *three days ago* . (three days)
2. Rachel has been in Brazil *for three days* . (three days)
3. Linda and Frank have been married _____ . (20 years)
4. Linda and Frank got married _____ . (20 years)
5. We arrived _____ . (ten minutes)
6. It started to rain _____ . (an hour)
7. Silvia has been studying English _____ . (six months)
8. I bought these shoes _____ . (a few days)

18.4 Complete the sentences with *for* or *since*.

1. Pam is in Cuba now. She arrived three days ago. *She has been there for three days.*
2. Carlos is here. He arrived here on Tuesday. He has _____ .
3. It's raining. It started an hour ago. It's been _____ .
4. I know Sue. I met her two years ago. I've _____ .
5. I have a camera. I bought it in 1999. I've _____ .
6. Liz is studying medicine at the university. She started three years ago. She has
   _____ .
7. Toshi plays the piano. He started when he was seven years old. Toshi has
   _____ .

18.5 Write sentences about yourself with *for* and *since*. Begin with the words in parentheses ( ).

1. (I've lived) _____
2. (I've been) _____
3. (I've been studying) _____
4. (I've known) _____
5. (I've had) _____

I have done and *I did*
(Present Perfect and Simple Past 1)

A

His car is dirty.

He is washing his car.

He **has washed** his car.
(= his car is clean *now*)

They are at home.

They are going out.

They **have gone** out.
(= they are not at home *now*)

B

We use the *present perfect* (he **has washed** / they **have gone**, etc.) for an action in the past with a result *now*.

■ I've **lost** my passport. (= I can't find my passport *now*)
■ "Where's Tiffany?" "She's **gone** to bed." (= she is in bed *now*)
■ We've **bought** a new car. (= we have a new car *now*)
■ Rachel has a headache because she **hasn't taken** her medicine.
■ "Bob is on vacation." "Oh, where **has he gone?**"
■ **Have** you **met** my brother, or should I introduce you?
■ I was a very slow typist in college, but I've **gotten** faster.

Usually you can also use the *simple past* (he **washed** / I **lost**, etc.) in these situations. So you can say:

■ "Where's your key?" "I've **lost** it." *or* "I **lost** it."
■ "Is Peter here?" "No, he's **gone** home." *or* "He **went** home."
■ We've **bought** a new car. *or* We **bought** a new car.

C

We use only the simple past (not the present perfect) with a *finished* time (**yesterday, last week,** etc.).

■ I **lost** my key **yesterday.** (*not* I have lost)
■ We **bought** a new car **last week.** (*not* we have bought)

Present Perfect Units 16–18   Present Perfect and Simple Past Units 20–21

Exercises

19.1 Look at the pictures. What has happened? Use the present perfect. Choose from:

close the door   fall down   go to bed   stop raining   take a shower   ~~wash her car~~

1. *before* → *now*

   She has washed her car.

2. *before* → *now*

   He _____.

3. *before* → *now*

   They _____.

4. *before* → *now*

   It *ha* _____.

5. *before* → *now*

   He _____.

6. *before* → *now*

   The _____.

19.2 Rewrite the sentences that have <u>underlined</u> verbs. Use the present perfect.

1. Lee Ming isn't here. He <u>went</u> home. *He has gone home.* _____
2. I don't need to call them. I <u>wrote</u> them a letter. _____
3. Karen's not coming to the party. She <u>broke</u> her arm. _____
4. My brother and his wife don't live here anymore. They <u>moved</u> to Seattle.

   _____
5. I <u>made</u> a big mistake. _____
6. I <u>lost</u> my wallet. _____
   <u>Did</u> you <u>see</u> it anywhere? _____
7. <u>Did</u> you <u>hear</u>? _____
   Mark <u>got</u> married! _____

Now rewrite these present perfect sentences in the simple past.

8. I've <u>done</u> the shopping. *I did the shopping.* _____
9. Brian <u>has taken</u> my bike again without asking. _____
10. <u>Have</u> you <u>told</u> your friends the good news? _____
11. We <u>haven't paid</u> the electric bill. _____

Just, already, and *yet* (Present Perfect and Simple Past 2)

A

just (= a short time ago)

We use **just** with the *present perfect* or the *simple past*.

- A: Are Diane and Paul here?
  B: Yes, they**'ve just arrived.** *or* Yes, they **just arrived.**
- A: Are you hungry?
  B: No, I**'ve just had** dinner. *or* I **just had** dinner.
- A: Is Jiro here?
  B: Sorry, he**'s just left.** *or* Sorry, he **just left.**

Hi! Come in.

They **have just arrived.**

B

already (= before you expected / before I expected)

We use **already** with the present perfect or the simple past.

- A: What time are Diane and Paul coming?
  B: They**'ve already arrived.** *or* They **already arrived.**
- It's only nine o'clock, and Anne **has already gone** to bed.
  or . . . Anne **already went** to bed.
- A: John, this is Mary.
  B: Yes, I know. We**'ve already met.** *or* We **already met.**

John, this is Mary.

Yes, I know. We've already met.

C

yet (= until now)

We use **yet** with the present perfect or simple past. We use **yet** in negative sentences (I **haven't** . . . **yet**) and questions (**Have** you . . . **yet?**). **Yet** is usually at the end.

yet in *negative sentences*

- A: Are Diane and Paul here?
  B: No, they **haven't arrived yet.** *or* . . . they **didn't arrive yet.**
    (but B expects Diane and Paul to arrive soon)
- A: Does John know that you're going away?
  B: No, I **haven't told** him yet. *or* . . . I **didn't tell** him yet.
    (but B is going to tell him soon)
- Joy bought a new dress, but she **hasn't worn** it yet. *or* . . . she **didn't wear** it yet.

yet in *questions*

- A: **Have** Diane and Paul **arrived yet?** *or*
     Did Diane and Paul **arrive yet?**
  B: No, not yet. We're still waiting for them.
- A: **Has** Nicole **started** her new job yet? *or*
     Did Nicole **start** her new job yet?
  B: No, she's starting next week.
- A: This is my new dress.
  B: Oh, it's nice. **Have** you **worn** it yet? *or*
     Did you **wear** it yet?

This is my new dress.

Oh, it's nice. **Have** you **worn** it yet?

Exercises

20.1 Write a sentence for each picture. Use *just* and the present perfect.

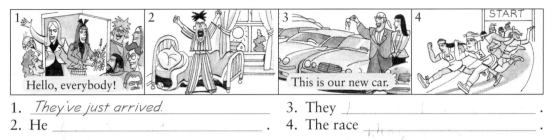

1. *They've just arrived.*   3. They _____ .
2. He _____ .   4. The race _____ .

20.2 Complete the sentences. Use *already* and the present perfect.

1. What time is Yong Jin arriving?   *He's already arrived.*
2. Do Sue and Bill want to see the movie?   No, they _____ it.
3. Don't forget to call Eric.   I _____ .
4. When is Mark going to work?   He _____ .
5. Do you want to read the newspaper?   I _____ .
6. When does Nicole start her new job?   She _____ .

20.3 Rewrite these sentences. Use the present perfect.

1. <u>Did Nicole start</u> her new job yet?   *Has Nicole started her new job yet?*
2. <u>Did you tell</u> your father about the accident yet? _____
3. <u>I just ate</u> a big dinner, so I'm not hungry. _____
4. Jenny can watch TV because <u>she already did</u> her homework. _____
5. You can't go to bed – <u>you didn't brush</u> your teeth yet. _____
6. You can't talk to Pete because <u>he just went</u> home. _____
7. <u>Sarah just got out</u> of the hospital, so she can't go to work. _____

Now rewrite these sentences in the simple past.

8. <u>Have you given</u> the mailman our new address yet?
 Did you give the mailman our new address yet?
9. <u>The mailman hasn't come</u> yet. _____
10. <u>I've just spoken</u> to your sister. _____
11. <u>Has Mario bought</u> a new computer yet? _____
12. <u>Ted and Alice haven't told</u> anyone they're getting married yet.
 _____
13. <u>We've already done</u> our packing for our trip. _____
14. <u>I've just been to</u> the gym. I feel great! _____

20.4 Write questions with the present perfect and *yet.*

1. Your friend has gotten a new job. Perhaps she has started it. You ask her,
 Have you started your new job yet ?
2. Your friend has some new neighbors. Maybe he has met them. You ask him,
 _____ you _____ ?
3. Your friend has to write a letter. Perhaps she has written it now. You ask her,
 _____ ?
4. Jiro was trying to sell his car. Maybe he has sold it now. You ask a friend about Jiro.
 _____ ?

I've lost my key. I lost my key last week.
(Present Perfect and Simple Past 3)

Sometimes you can use the *present perfect* (I **have lost** / he **has gone**, etc.) *or the simple past* (I **lost** / he **went**, etc.).

■ "Is Peter here?" "No, he's **gone** home." *or* "No, he **went** home."

But with a finished time (**yesterday** / **last week**, etc.), we use only the simple past (not the present perfect).

Simple past + finished time

We **arrived**	yesterday. last week. at 3 o'clock. in 1991. six months ago.		yesterday last week six months ago (finished time)	
		past		*now*

Do not use the present perfect with a finished time.

■ I **saw** Ratana **yesterday**. (*not* I have seen)
■ Where **were** you **on Sunday afternoon**? (*not* Where have you been)
■ We **didn't take** a vacation **last year**. (*not* We haven't taken)
■ "What **did** you **do last night**?" "I **stayed** at home."
■ William Shakespeare **lived from 1564 to 1616**. He **was** a writer. He **wrote** many plays and poems.

Use the simple past to ask **When . . . ?** or **What time . . . ?**.

■ **When did** they **arrive**? (*not* When have they arrived?)

Compare:

Present perfect or simple past

■ I **have lost** my key. *or* I **lost** my key. (= I can't find it *now*)
■ Bill **has gone** home. *or* Bill **went** home. (= he isn't here *now*)
■ **Have** you **had** lunch? *or* **Did** you **have** lunch?
■ The letter **hasn't arrived** yet. *or* The letter **didn't arrive** yet.

Present perfect only

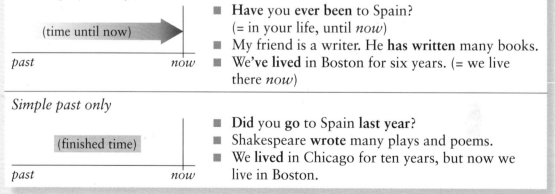

■ **Have** you **ever been** to Spain?
  (= in your life, until *now*)
■ My friend is a writer. He **has written** many books.
■ We've **lived** in Boston for six years. (= we live there *now*)

Simple past only

■ **Did** you **go** to Spain **last year**?
■ Shakespeare **wrote** many plays and poems.
■ We **lived** in Chicago for ten years, but now we live in Boston.

Exercises

21.1 Use the words in parentheses ( ) to answer the questions.

1. (an hour ago)
2. (last week)
3. (on Friday)
4. (at 5 o'clock)
5. (yesterday)

Have you had lunch? | _Yes, I had it an hour ago._
Have you started your new job? | Yes, I _____ last week.
Have your friends arrived? | Yes, they _____ .
Has Sarah gone out? | Yes, _____ .
Have you worn your new suit? | Yes, _____ .

21.2 Right or wrong? Correct the underlined parts that are wrong.

1. I've lost my key. I can't find it. _RIGHT_
2. Have you seen Anne yesterday? _WRONG   Did you see_
3. I've finished my work at two o'clock. _____
4. I'm ready now. I've finished my work. _____
5. What time have you finished your work? _____
6. Gloria isn't here. She's gone out. _____
7. Jim's grandmother has died last night. _____
8. Where have you been in 1998? _____

21.3 Put the verb in the present perfect or simple past.

1. My friend is a writer. He _has written_ many books. (write)
2. We _didn't take_ a vacation last year. (not / take)
3. I _____ tennis yesterday afternoon. (play)
4. What time _____ to bed last night? (you / go)
5. Kathy travels a lot. She _____ many countries. (visit)
6. I live in New York now, but I _____ in Mexico for many years. (live)
7. The weather _____ very good yesterday. (not / be)
8. Sonia is an actress now. She _____ in several plays. (be)
9. I _____ my hair before breakfast this morning. (wash)

21.4 Put the verb in the present perfect or simple past.

1. A: _Have you ever been_ (you / ever / be) to Florida? B: Yes, we _went_ (go) there on vacation two years ago. A: _____ (you / have) a good time? B: Yes, it _____ (be) great.	2. A: What does your friend do? B: She's a painter. She _____ (win) many prizes for her paintings. A: _____ (you / see) any of her paintings? B: Yes, _____ (I / see) some of her work last week.
3. Rose works in a factory now, but she _____ (have) a lot of different jobs. Five years ago, she _____ (be) a waitress in a restaurant. After that, she _____ (work) on a ranch, but she _____ (not / enjoy) it very much.	4. A: Do you know Mark's sister? B: I _____ (see) her a few times but I _____ (never / speak) to her. _____ (you / ever / speak) to her? A: Yes, I _____ (meet) her at a party last week. She's very nice.

Is done and *was done* (Passive 1)

A

The office **is cleaned** every day.

The office **was cleaned** yesterday.

Compare *active* and *passive*:

Somebody **cleans** the office every day. *(active)*

The office **is cleaned** every day. *(passive)*

Somebody **cleaned** the office yesterday. *(active)*

The office **was cleaned** yesterday. *(passive)*

B

The passive is:

			Past participle	
Simple present	am/is/are	(not)	cleaned	done
Simple past	was/were		invented	built
			injured	taken, etc.

The *past participle* of regular verbs is -ed (**cleaned/damaged**, etc.).
For a list of irregular past participles (**done/built/taken**, etc.), see Appendixes 2–3.

- Butter **is made** from cream.
- Oranges **are imported** into Canada.
- How often **are** these rooms **cleaned**?
- I **am** never **invited** to parties.

- This house **was built** 100 years ago.
- These houses **were built** 100 years ago.
- When **was** the telephone **invented**?
- We **weren't invited** to the party last week.
- "**Was** anybody **injured** in the accident?" "Yes, two people **were taken** to the hospital."

C

was/were born
- I **was born** in Los Angeles in 1981. (*not* I am born)
- Where **were** you **born**?

D

Passive + by . . .
- We **were woken up by a loud noise.** (= The noise woke us up.)
- The telephone was invented **by Alexander Graham Bell** in 1876.
- My brother was bitten **by a dog** last week.

Is being done / has been done Unit 23   Irregular Verbs Unit 25, Appendixes 2–3
By Unit 106   Active and Passive Appendix 1

Exercises

22.1 Write sentences with the words in parentheses ( ). Sentences 1–7 are present.

1. (the office / clean / every day) _The office is cleaned every day._
2. (these rooms / clean / every day?) _Are these rooms cleaned every day?_
3. (glass / make / from sand) Glass _____ .
4. (stamps / sell / in a post office) _____
5. (this word / not / use / very often) _____
6. (we / allow / to park here?) _____
7. (how / this word / pronounce?) _____

Sentences 8–14 are past.

8. (the office / clean / yesterday) _The office was cleaned yesterday._
9. (the house / paint / last month) The house _____ .
10. (three people / injure / in the accident) _____
11. (my bicycle / steal / a few days ago) _____
12. (when / this bridge / build?) _____
13. (you / invite / to the party last week?) _____
14. (I / not / wake up / by the noise) _____

22.2 Correct these sentences.

1. This house built 100 years ago. _This house was built 100 years ago._
2. Soccer plays in most countries of the world. _____
3. Why did the letter send to the wrong address? _____
4. A garage is a place where cars repair. _____
5. Where are you born? _____
6. How many languages are speaking in Canada? _____
7. Somebody broke into our house, but nothing stolen. _____
8. When was invented the bicycle? _____

22.3 Complete the sentences. Use the passive (present or past) of these verbs:

~~clean~~   damage   find   give   invite   make   make   show   steal   ~~take~~

1. The room _is cleaned_____ every day.
2. I saw an accident yesterday. Two people _were taken_____ to the hospital.
3. Paper _____ from wood.
4. There was a fire at the hotel last week. Two of the rooms _____ .
5. "Where did you get this picture?" "It _____ to me by a friend of mine."
6. Many British programs _____ on American television.
7. "Did Jim and Sue go to the wedding?" "No. They _____ , but they didn't go."
8. "How old is this movie?" "It _____ in 1965."
9. My car _____ last week, but the next day it _____ by the police.

22.4 Where were they born?

1. (Makoto / Kyoto) _Makoto was born in Kyoto._
2. (Isabel / São Paulo) Isabel _____ .
3. (her parents / Rio de Janeiro) Her _____ .
4. (you / ???) I _____ .
5. (your mother / ???) _____

Is being done and *has been done* (Passive 2)

A

is/are being . . . *(present continuous passive)*

Somebody **is painting** the door . *(active)*

The door **is being painted.** *(passive)*

- I took the bus this morning. My car **is being repaired.** (= somebody is repairing it)
- Some new houses **are being built** across from the park. (= somebody is building them)

Compare the *present continuous* and *simple present:*
- The office **is being cleaned** right now. *(present continuous)*
  The office **is cleaned** every day. *(simple present)*
- In the U.S., football games **are** usually **shown** on TV on Mondays, but no games **are being shown** next Monday.

B

has/have been . . . *(present perfect passive)*

before   *now*

Somebody **has painted** the door . *(active)*

The door **has been painted.** *(passive)*

- My key **has been stolen.** (= somebody has stolen it)
- My keys **have been stolen.** (= somebody has stolen them)
- I'm not going to the party. I **haven't been invited.** (= nobody has invited me)
- **Has** this window **been washed?** (= Has somebody washed it?)

Compare the *present perfect* and *simple past:*
- The room is clean now. It **has been cleaned.** *(present perfect)*
  The room **was cleaned** yesterday. *(simple past)*
- I can't find my keys. I think they**'ve been stolen.** *(present perfect)*
  My keys **were stolen** last week. *(simple past)*

Present Continuous and Simple Present Units 8, 26   **Present Perfect and Simple Past** Unit 21
Is done / was done Unit 18   **Active and Passive** Appendix 1

Exercises

23.1 What's happening?

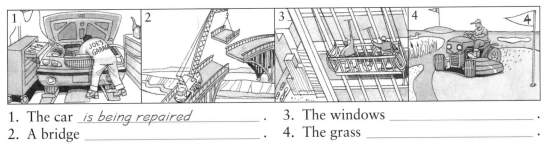

1. The car *is being repaired* .
2. A bridge _____ .
3. The windows _____ .
4. The grass _____ .

23.2 Look at the pictures. What is happening or what has happened? Use the present continuous *(is/are being . . .)* or the present perfect *(has/have been . . .)*.

1. (the office / clean) *The office is being cleaned.*
2. (the shirts / iron) *The shirts have been ironed.*
3. (the window / break) The window _____ .
4. (the roof / repair) The roof _____ .
5. (the car / damage) _____
6. (the buildings / knock / down) _____
7. (the trees / cut / down) _____
8. (they / invite / to a party) _____

23.3 Use the words in parentheses ( ) to complete the sentences. (Study Unit 22 first.)

1. I can't use my office right now. It *is being painted* . (paint)
2. We didn't go to the party. We *weren't invited* . (not / invite)
3. The washing machine was broken, but it's OK now.
   It _____ . (repair)
4. The washing machine _____ yesterday afternoon. (repair)
5. A factory is a place where things _____ . (make)
6. How old are these houses? When _____ ? (they / build)
7. *A:* _____ right now? (the computer / use)
   B: Yes, Jim is using it.
8. I've never seen these flowers before. What _____ ? (they / call)
9. My sunglasses _____ at the beach yesterday. (steal)
10. The bridge is closed. It _____ last week and it
    _____ yet. (damage) (not / repair)

Be, have, and do in Present and Past Tenses

A

be (am/is/are/was/were) + -ing (cleaning/working, etc.)

am/is/are + -ing *(present continuous)* See Units 3–4 and 26.	■ Please be quiet. **I'm working**. ■ It **isn't raining** right now. ■ What **are** you **doing** tonight?
was/were + -ing *(past continuous)* See Unit 13.	■ I **was working** when she arrived. ■ It **wasn't raining**, so we went out. ■ What **were** you **doing** at three o'clock?

B

be + *past participle* (cleaned/made/eaten, etc.)

am/is/are + *past participle* *(simple present passive)* See Unit 22.	■ The room **is cleaned** every day. ■ I'm never **invited** to parties. ■ Oranges **are imported** into Canada.
was/were + *past participle* *(simple past passive)* See Unit 22.	■ The room **was cleaned** yesterday. ■ These houses **were built** 100 years ago. ■ How **was** the window **broken**? ■ Where **were** you **born**?

C

have/has + *past participle* (cleaned/lost/eaten/been, etc.)

have/has + *past participle* *(present perfect)* See Units 16–17, 19–21.	■ **I've lived** in this house for ten years. ■ Tom **has never ridden** a horse. ■ Barbara **hasn't been** to South America. ■ Where **have** Paul and Nicole **gone**?

D

do/does/did + *base form* (clean/like/eat/go, etc.)

do/does + *base form* *(simple present negative* *and questions)* See Units 6–7.	■ I like coffee, but I **don't like** tea. ■ Chris **doesn't go** out very often. ■ What **do** you usually **do** on weekends? ■ **Does** Barbara **live** alone?
did + *base form* *(simple past negative* *and questions)* See Unit 12.	■ I **didn't watch** TV yesterday. ■ It **didn't rain** last week. ■ What time **did** Paul and Nicole **go** out?

Exercises

24.1 Write *is/are/do/does*.

1. _Do_____ you work on weekends?
2. Where _are_____ they going?
3. Why _____ you looking at me?
4. _____ Bill live near you?
5. _____ you like to cook?
6. _____ the sun shining?
7. What time _____ the stores close?
8. _____ Ratana working today?
9. What _____ this word mean?
10. _____ you feeling all right?

24.2 Write *am not / isn't / aren't / don't / doesn't*. All these sentences are negative.

1. Tom _doesn't_____ work on weekends.
2. I'm very tired. I _____ want to go out tonight.
3. I'm very tired. I _____ going out tonight.
4. Eric _____ working this week. He's on vacation.
5. My parents are usually at home. They _____ go out very often.
6. Barbara has traveled a lot, but she _____ speak any foreign languages.
7. You can turn off the television. I _____ watching it.
8. There's a party next week, but we _____ going.

24.3 Write *was/were/did/have/has*.

1. Where _were_____ your shoes made?
2. _____ you go out last night?
3. What _____ you doing at 10:30?
4. Where _____ your mother born?
5. _____ Barbara gone home?
6. What time _____ she go?
7. When _____ these houses built?
8. _____ Sanun arrived yet?
9. Why _____ you go home early?
10. How long _____ they been married?

24.4 Write *is/are/was/were/have/has*.

1. Joe _has_____ never ridden a horse.
2. This bridge _____ built ten years ago.
3. _____ you finished your work yet?
4. This town is always clean. The streets _____ cleaned every day.
5. Where _____ you born?
6. I _____ just made some coffee. Would you like some?
7. Glass _____ made from sand.
8. This is a very old photograph. It _____ taken a long time ago.
9. Joe _____ bought a new car.

24.5 Complete the sentences. Choose verbs from the list. Use the correct forms.

damage	enjoy	go away	open	rain	use
eat	go	listen	pronounce	understand	

1. I'm going to take an umbrella with me. It's _raining_____ .
2. Why are you so tired? Did you _go_____ to bed late last night?
3. Where are the chocolates? Have you _____ them all?
4. How is your new job? Are you _____ it?
5. My car was badly _____ in the accident, but I was OK.
6. Chris has a car but she doesn't _____ it very often.
7. Mary isn't at home. She has _____ for a few days.
8. I don't _____ the problem. Can you explain it again?
9. Mark is in his room. He's _____ to music.
10. I don't know how to say this word. How is it _____ ?
11. How do you _____ this window? Can you show me?

49

Regular and Irregular Verbs

A

Regular verbs

The *simple past* and *past participle* of regular verbs is **-ed.**

clean → cleaned   live → lived   paint → painted   study → studied

Simple past (see Unit 11)

- I **cleaned** my room yesterday.
- Charlie **studied** engineering in college.

Past participle

Present perfect = **have/has** + *past participle* (see Units 16–17, 19–21)
- I **have cleaned** my room.
- Tracy **has lived** in Miami for ten years.

Passive = **be** (**is / are / were / has been,** etc.) + *past participle* (see Units 22–23)
- These rooms **are cleaned** every day.
- My car **has been repaired.**

B

Irregular verbs

The simple past and past participle of irregular verbs are not **-ed.** For example:

Base form	make	break	cut
Simple past	made	broke	cut
Past participle	made	broken	cut

Sometimes the simple past and past participle are the same. For example:

Base form	make	find	buy	cut
Simple past / Past participle	made	found	bought	cut

- I **made** a cake yesterday. (simple past)
- I've just **made** some coffee. (past participle in the present perfect)
- Butter **is made** from cream. (past participle in the passive)

Sometimes the simple past and past participle are different. For example:

Base form	break	know	begin	go
Simple past	broke	knew	begin	went
Past participle	broken	known	began	gone

- Somebody **broke** this window last night. (simple past)
- Somebody **has broken** this window. (past participle in the present perfect)
- This window **was broken** last night. (past participle in the passive)

Exercises

25.1 Write the simple past / past participle of these verbs. (The simple past and past participle are the same for all the verbs in this exercise.)

1. make *made*
2. cut *cut*
3. say _____
4. bring _____
5. pay _____

6. enjoy _____
7. buy _____
8. sit _____
9. leave _____
10. happen _____

11. hear _____
12. put _____
13. catch _____
14. watch _____
15. understand _____

25.2 Write the simple past and past participle of these verbs.

1. break *broke   broken*
2. begin _____ _____
3. eat _____ _____
4. drink _____ _____
5. drive _____ _____

6. run _____ _____
7. speak _____ _____
8. write _____ _____
9. come _____ _____
10. know _____ _____

11. take _____ _____
12. go _____ _____
13. give _____ _____
14. throw _____ _____
15. get _____ _____

25.3 Put the verb in the right form.

1. I *washed* my hands because they were dirty. (wash)
2. Somebody has *broken* this window. (break)
3. I feel good. I _____ very well last night. (sleep)
4. We _____ a really good movie yesterday. (see)
5. It _____ a lot while we were on vacation. (rain)
6. I've _____ my bag. (lose) Have you _____ it? (see)
7. Rosa's bicycle was _____ last week. (steal)
8. I _____ to bed early because I was tired. (go)
9. Have you _____ your work yet? (finish)
10. The shopping mall was _____ about 20 years ago. (build)
11. Annie _____ to drive when she was 16. (learn)
12. I've never _____ a horse. (ride)
13. Julia is a good friend of mine. I've _____ her for a long time. (know)
14. Yesterday I _____ and _____ my leg. (fall / hurt)

25.4 Complete these sentences. Choose from the list and put the verb in the correct form.

cost   drive   fly   ~~make~~   meet   sell   speak   swim   tell   think   wake up

1. I've just *made* some coffee. Would you like some?
2. Have you _____ John about your new job?
3. I know Aldo, but I've never _____ his wife.
4. We were _____ by loud music in the middle of the night.
5. Stephanie jumped into the river and _____ to the other side.
6. "Did you like the movie?" "Yes, I _____ it was very good."
7. Many different languages are _____ in Guatemala.
8. Our vacation _____ a lot of money because we stayed at an expensive hotel.
9. Have you ever _____ a very fast car?
10. All the tickets for the concert were _____ very quickly.
11. A bird _____ in through the open window while we were eating dinner.

UNIT 26

What are you doing tomorrow?

A

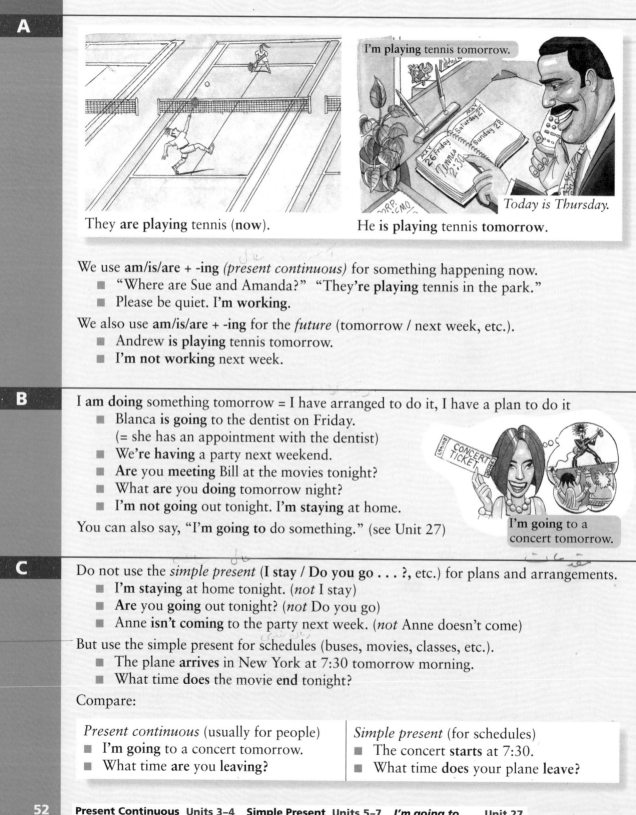

They **are playing** tennis (**now**).

I'm playing tennis tomorrow.

Today is Thursday.

He **is playing** tennis **tomorrow**.

We use **am/is/are + -ing** (*present continuous*) for something happening now.
- "Where are Sue and Amanda?" "They're **playing** tennis in the park."
- Please be quiet. I'm **working**.

We also use **am/is/are + -ing** for the *future* (tomorrow / next week, etc.).
- Andrew **is playing** tennis tomorrow.
- I'm **not working** next week.

B

I **am doing** something tomorrow = I have arranged to do it, I have a plan to do it
- Blanca **is going** to the dentist on Friday.
  (= she has an appointment with the dentist)
- We're **having** a party next weekend.
- **Are** you **meeting** Bill at the movies tonight?
- What **are** you **doing** tomorrow night?
- I'm **not going** out tonight. I'm **staying** at home.

You can also say, "I'm **going to** do something." (see Unit 27)

I'm going to a concert tomorrow.

C

Do not use the *simple present* (I stay / Do you go . . . ?, etc.) for plans and arrangements.
- I'm **staying** at home tonight. (*not* I stay)
- **Are** you **going** out tonight? (*not* Do you go)
- Anne **isn't coming** to the party next week. (*not* Anne doesn't come)

But use the simple present for schedules (buses, movies, classes, etc.).
- The plane **arrives** in New York at 7:30 tomorrow morning.
- What time **does** the movie **end** tonight?

Compare:

Present continuous (usually for people)	*Simple present* (for schedules)
▪ I'm **going** to a concert tomorrow.	▪ The concert **starts** at 7:30.
▪ What time **are** you **leaving**?	▪ What time **does** your plane **leave**?

Present Continuous Units 3–4   **Simple Present** Units 5–7   *I'm going to . . .* Unit 27

Exercises

26.1 Look at the pictures. What are these people doing next Friday?

ANDREW   RICHARD   BARBARA   DENISE   SUE AND TOM

1. *Andrew is playing tennis on Friday.*   4. _____ lunch with Ken.
2. Richard _____ to the movies.   5. _____
3. Barbara _____ .

26.2 Write questions. All the sentences are future.

1. (you / go / out / tonight?) *Are you going out tonight?* _____
2. (you / work / next week?) _____
3. (what / you / do / tomorrow night?) _____
4. (what time / your friends / come?) _____
5. (when / Liz / go / on vacation?) _____

26.3 Write sentences about yourself. What are you doing in the next few days?

1. *I'm staying at home tonight.* _____
2. *I'm going to the theater on Monday.* _____
3. _____
4. _____
5. _____
6. _____

26.4 Put the verb in the present continuous (*he is leaving,* etc.) or simple present (*the train leaves,* etc.).

1. " *Are you going* _____ out tonight?" (you / go) "No, I'm too tired."
2. *We're going* _____ to a concert tonight. (we / go) *It starts* _____ at 7:30. (it / start)
3. Listen to this! _____ married next month! (Karen / get)
4. *A:* My parents _____ on vacation soon. (go)
   B: Oh, that's nice. Where _____ ? (they / go)
5. Silvia is taking an English course this semester. The course _____
   on Friday. (end)
6. There's a football game tomorrow, but _____ . (I / not / go)
7. _____ out with some friends tonight. (I / go) Why don't you
   come too? _____ at John's house at 8 o'clock. (we / meet)
8. *A:* How _____ home after the party tomorrow? (you / get) By taxi?
   B: No, I can take the bus. The last bus _____ at midnight. (leave)
9. *A:* Do you want to go to the movies tonight?
   B: Yes, what time _____ ? (the movie / begin)
10. *A:* What _____ next Monday afternoon? (you / do)
    B: _____ (I / work)

I'm going to . . .

A

I'm going to do something.

Morning

I'm going to watch TV tonight.

Tonight

She **is going to watch** TV tonight.

We use **am/is/are** + **going to** . . . for the *future*.

I **am**		do	**am** I			buy . . . ?
he/she/it **is**	**(not) going to**	drink	**is** he/she/it	**going to**		eat . . . ?
we/you/they **are**		watch	**are** we/you/they			wear . . . ?

B

I am going to do something = I have decided to do it, my intention is to do it

I decided to do it   **I'm going to do it**

past   *now*   *future*

- ■ **I'm going to buy** some books tomorrow.
- ■ Sarah **is going to sell** her car.
- ■ **I'm not going to have** breakfast this morning. I'm not hungry.
- ■ What **are you going to wear** to the party tonight?
- ■ "Your hands are dirty." "Yes, I know. **I'm going to wash** them."
- ■ **Are** you **going to invite** Min Fang to your party?

We also use the *present continuous* (**I am doing**) for the future, usually for arrangements (see Unit 26).

- ■ **I am playing** tennis with Julia tomorrow.

C

Something **is going to happen** = it is clear now that it is sure to happen

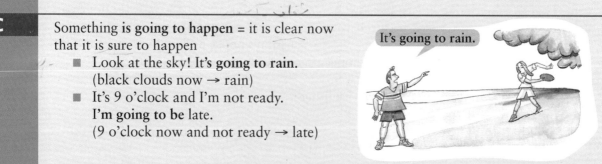

It's going to rain.

- ■ Look at the sky! It's **going to rain**.
  (black clouds now → rain)
- ■ It's 9 o'clock and I'm not ready.
  I'm going to be late.
  (9 o'clock now and not ready → late)

Present for the Future Unit 26   *Will* Units 28–29

Exercises

27.1 What are these people saying?

1. I 'm going to watch TV .
2. I _____ .
3. We at _____ .
4. I _____ .

27.2 Complete the sentences. Use *am/is/are* + *going to* + one of these verbs:

do eat give lie down visit walk ~~wash~~ watch ~~wear~~

1. My hands are dirty. I *'m going to wash* _____ them.
2. What *are you going to wear* _____ to the party tonight?
3. It's a nice day. I don't want to take the bus. I _____ .
4. John is going to Seattle next week. He _____ some friends.
5. I'm hungry. I _____ a sandwich.
6. It's Sharon's birthday next week. We _____ her a present.
7. Maria says she's feeling very tired. She _____ for an hour.
8. There's a good program on Channel 13 at 9:00 tonight. _____
   you _____ it?
9. What _____ Rachel _____ when she finishes school?

27.3 Look at the pictures. What is going to happen?

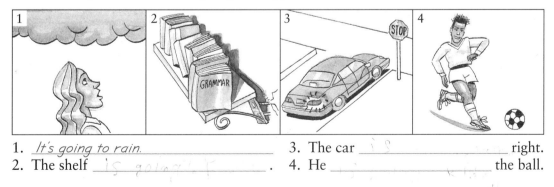

1. *It's going to rain.* _____
2. The shelf *is going t* _____ .
3. The car *is* _____ right.
4. He _____ the ball.

27.4 What are you going to do today or tomorrow? Write three sentences.

1. I'm _____ .
2. _____
3. _____

Will (1)

A

SOO MI

Soo Mi goes to work every day. She is always there from 8:30 until 4:30.

It is 11 o'clock now. Soo Mi **is** at work.

At 11 o'clock yesterday, she **was** at work.

At 11 o'clock tomorrow, she **will be** at work.

will + *base form* (**will be** / **will win** / **will come**, etc.)

I/we/you/they he/she/it	will ('ll) will not (won't)	be win eat come, etc.

will	I/we/you/they he/she/it	be? win? eat? come?, etc.

'll = will: I**'ll** (I will) / you**'ll** / she**'ll**, etc.
won't = will not: I **won't** (I will not) / you **won't** / she **won't**, etc.

B

We use **will** for the *future* (tomorrow / next week, etc.).
- Sue travels a lot. Today she is in Los Angeles. Tomorrow she**'ll be** in Mexico City. Next week she**'ll be** in New York.
- You can call me tonight. I**'ll be** home.
- Put this bread in the back yard. The birds **will eat** it.
- We**'ll** probably **go** out tonight.
- **Will** you **be** home tonight?

- I **won't be** here tomorrow. (= I will not be here)
- Don't drink coffee before you go to bed. You **won't sleep**.

We often say **I think . . . will . . . .**
- **I think** Diana **will pass** her driver's test.
- **Do you think** the test **will be** difficult?
- **I don't think** it **will rain** this afternoon.

We say **I don't think . . . will . . .** (*not* I think . . . won't . . .).
- **I don't think** the test **will be** difficult. (*not* I think the test won't be . . .)

C

We do not use **will** for things we have already *arranged* or *decided* to do (see Units 26–27).
- We**'re going** to the movies on Saturday. (*not* We will go)
- I**'m** not **working** tomorrow. (*not* I won't work)
- Are you **going to cook** dinner tonight? (*not* Will you cook)

What are you doing tomorrow? Unit 26   *I'm going to . . .* Unit 27   *Will* (2) Unit 29

Exercises

28.1 Tracy is traveling in South America. Complete the sentences with *she was, she's,* or *she'll be.*

CARACAS (next week)
BOGOTA (tomorrow)
LIMA (now)
RIO DE JANEIRO (yesterday)
SANTIAGO (Last week)
BUENOS AIRES (three days ago)
TRACY

1. Yesterday _she was_ in Rio de Janeiro.
2. Tomorrow _____ in Bogota.
3. Last week _____ in Santiago.
4. Next week _____ in Caracas.
5. Right now _____ in Lima.
6. Three days ago _____ in Buenos Aires.
7. At the end of her trip _____ very tired.

28.2 Where will you be? Write answers about yourself. Use one of these:

I'll be . . .   I'll probably be . . .   I don't know where I'll be.

1. At 10 o'clock tomorrow? _I'll be at work._ OR _I'll probably be at the beach._
2. One hour from now? _____
3. At midnight tonight? _____
4. At 3 o'clock tomorrow afternoon? _____
5. Two years from now? _____

28.3 Write *will ('ll)* or *won't.*

1. Don't drink coffee before you go to bed. You _won't_ sleep.
2. "Are you ready yet?" "Not yet. I _____ be ready in five minutes."
3. I'm going away for a few days. I'm leaving tonight, so I _____ be at home tomorrow.
4. It _won't_ rain, so you don't need to take an umbrella.
5. *A:* I don't feel very well tonight.
   B: Well, go to bed early and you _____ feel better in the morning.
6. It's Bill's birthday next Monday. He _____ be 25.
7. I'm sorry I was late this morning. It _____ happen again.

28.4 Rewrite these sentences. Use *I think . . .* or *I don't think . . . .*

1. (Diana will pass the driver's test.) _I think Diana will pass the driver's test._
2. (Diana won't pass the driver's test.) _I don't think Diana will pass the driver's test._
3. (We'll win the game.) I _____ .
4. (I won't be here tomorrow.) _____
5. (Rika will like her present.) _____
6. (They won't get married.) _____
7. (You won't like the movie.) _____

28.5 Which is right? (Study Unit 26 before you do this exercise.)

1. ~~We'll go~~ / We're going to the theater tonight. We've got tickets. (*We're going* is right.)
2. "What will you do / are you doing tomorrow night?" "Nothing. I'm free."
3. They'll leave / They're leaving tomorrow morning. Their train is at 8:40.
4. I'm sure she'll lend / she's lending us some money. She's very rich.
5. "Why are you putting on your coat?" "I'll go / I'm going out."
6. Do you think Claire will call / is calling us tonight?
7. Steve can't meet us on Saturday. He'll work / He's working.

Will (2)

I'll **carry** it for you, Dad.

Bye! I'll **call** you tomorrow, OK?

X CORP

You can use **I'll . . . (I will)** when you offer or decide to do something.
- ■ "My suitcase is very heavy." "**I'll carry** it for you."
- ■ "**I'll call** you tomorrow, OK?" "OK. Goodbye."

We often say **I think I'll . . . / I don't think I'll . . .** when we decide to do something.
- ■ I'm tired. **I think I'll go** to bed early tonight.
- ■ It's a nice day. **I think I'll sit** outside.
- ■ It's raining. **I don't think I'll go** out.

Do not use the simple present (**I go / I call,** etc.) in sentences like these:
- ■ **I'll call** you tomorrow, OK? (*not* I call you)
- ■ I think **I'll go** to bed early. (*not* I go to bed)

Do not use **I'll . . .** for something you decided before (see Units 26–27).
- ■ **I'm working** tomorrow. (*not* I'll work)
- ■ There's a good program on TV tonight. **I'm going to watch** it. (*not* I'll watch)
- ■ What **are** you **doing** this weekend? (*not* What will you do)

Shall I/we . . . ?

Shall I answer the phone?

RING!

No, that's OK. I'll **answer** it.

Shall I/we . . . ? = Do you think this is a good thing to do? Do you think this is a good idea?
- ■ "**Shall I call** you tonight?" "OK."
- ■ It's a nice day. **Shall we go** for a walk?

We use **should** in the same way.
- ■ "**Should I call** you tonight?" "OK."
- ■ It's a nice day. **Should we go** for a walk?

Exercises

29.1 Complete the sentences. Use *I'll* (*I will*) + one of these verbs:

~~carry~~ do eat send show sit stay

1. My suitcase is very heavy.	*I'll carry* _____ it for you.
2. Enjoy your vacation.	Thank you. _____ you a postcard.
3. I don't want this banana.	Well, I'm hungry. _____ it.
4. Do you want a chair?	No, that's OK. _____ on the floor.
5. Did you call Jenny?	Oh no, I forgot. _____ it now.
6. Are you coming with me?	No, I don't think so. _____ here.
7. How do you use this camera?	Give it to me and _____ you.

29.2 Complete the sentences. Use *I think I'll . . .* or *I don't think I'll . . .* + one of these verbs:

buy ~~go~~ have play

1. It's cold today. *I don't think I'll go* _____ out.
2. I'm hungry. I _____ something to eat.
3. I feel tired. _____ tennis.
4. This camera is too expensive. _____ it.

29.3 Which is right?

1. ~~I call~~ / I'll call you tomorrow, OK? (*I'll call* is right.)
2. I haven't done the shopping yet. <u>I do</u> / <u>I'll do</u> it later.
3. I like sports. <u>I watch</u> / <u>I'll watch</u> a lot of sports on TV.
4. I need some exercise. I think <u>I go</u> / <u>I'll go</u> for a walk.
5. Jim <u>is going to buy</u> / <u>will buy</u> a new car. He told me last week.
6. "This letter is for Alicia." "OK. <u>I give</u> / <u>I'll give</u> / <u>I'm going to give</u> it to her."
7. *A:* <u>Are you doing</u> / <u>Will you do</u> anything this evening?
   B: Yes, <u>I'm going</u> / <u>I'll go</u> out with some friends.
8. "Can you tell Ted I'll be late tonight?" "Sure, <u>I tell</u> / <u>I'm going to tell</u> / <u>I'll tell</u> him."
9. "Why are you going out?" "<u>I do</u> / <u>I'll do</u> / <u>I'm going to do</u> the shopping."
10. I can't go out with you tomorrow night. <u>I work</u> / <u>I'm working</u> / <u>I'll work</u>.
11. I like this hat. I think <u>I buy</u> / <u>I'll buy</u> it.

29.4 What does B say to A? Find the right answers.

	A		B
1.	It's very warm in this room.	*d*	a) If you want. Where should we go?
2.	This TV program is boring.		b) Yes, who shall we invite?
3.	Should we have a party?		c) No, shall I go and get some?
4.	It's dark in this room.		d) Shall I open the window?
5.	Should I go to the store?		e) Should I turn on the light?
6.	Shall we go out?		f) OK, how many shall we buy?
7.	Shall I wait here?		g) Should I turn it off?
8.	Have we got any bread?		h) No, come with me.
9.	Should we get some lottery tickets?		i) No, it's OK. I'll go.

Might

A

Where are you going for vacation?

I'm not sure. I **might go** to New York.

It **might rain**.

He **might go** to New York.
(= it is possible that he will go to New York)

It **might rain**.
(= it is possible that it will rain)

might + *base form* (**might go** / **might be** / **might rain,** etc.)

I/we/you/they he/she/it	**might** (not)	be go play come, etc.

B

I might = it is possible that I will

- I **might go** to the movies tonight. (= it is possible that I will go)
- *A:* When is Kanya going to call you?
  B: I don't know. She **might call** this afternoon.
- Take an umbrella with you. It **might rain**.
- Buy a lottery ticket. You **might be** lucky. (= perhaps you will be lucky)
- "Are you going out tonight?" "I **might**." (= I might go out)

Study the difference:

- I'm **playing** tennis tomorrow. *(sure)*
  I **might play** tennis tomorrow. *(possible)*
- Kanya **is going to call** later. *(sure)*
  Kanya **might call** later. *(possible)*

C

The negative is **might not**.

- I **might not** go to work tomorrow. (= it is possible that I will not go)
- Sonia **might not come** to the party. (= it is possible that she will not come)

D

may

You can use **may** in the same way. **I may** = **I might**.

- I **may go** to the movies tonight. (= I might go)
- Sonia **may not come** to the party. (= Sonia might not come)

May I . . . ? = Is it OK to . . . ? / Can I . . . ?

- **May I** ask a question? (= Can I ask?)
- "**May I** sit here?" "Sure."

Exercises

30.1 Write sentences with *might*.

1. (it's possible that I'll go to the movies) *I might go to the movies.*
2. (it's possible that I'll see you tomorrow) I _____ .
3. (it's possible that Sarah will forget to call) _____
4. (it's possible that it will snow today) _____
5. (it's possible that I'll be late tonight) _____

Write sentences with *might not*.

6. (it's possible that Mark won't be here) _____
7. (it's possible that I won't have time to go out tonight) _____

30.2 Somebody is asking you about your plans. You have some ideas, but you are not sure. Choose from the list and write sentences with *I might*.

~~Europe~~   fish   Monday   new car   take a trip   take a taxi

1. Where are you going for vacation? | I'm not sure. *I might go to Europe.*
2. What are you doing this weekend? | I don't know. I _____ .
3. When will you see Amy again? | I'm not sure. _____
4. What are you going to have for dinner? | I don't know. _____
5. How are you going to get home tonight? | I'm not sure. _____
6. I hear you won some money. What are you going to buy? | I haven't decided yet. _____

30.3 You ask Adam about his plans. Sometimes he is sure, but usually he is not sure.

1. Are you playing tennis tomorrow? | Yes, in the afternoon.
2. Are you going out tonight? | Possibly.
3. Are you going to get up early? | Maybe. might
4. Are you working tomorrow? | No, I'm not.
5. Will you be home tomorrow night? | Maybe.
6. Are you going to watch television? | I might.
7. Are you going out this afternoon? | Yes, I am. might
8. Are you going shopping? | Maybe, I'm not sure.

YOU   ADAM

Now write about Adam. Use *might* where necessary.

1. *He's playing tennis tomorrow afternoon.*
2. *He might go out tonight.*
3. He _____ .
4. _____
5. _____
6. _____
7. _____
8. _____

30.4 Write three things that you might do tomorrow.

1. _____
2. _____
3. _____

Can and could ℓ

I can play the piano.

He **can play** the piano.

Could you **open** the door, please?

can + *base form* (**can do** / **can play** / **can come**, etc.)

I/we/you/they he/she/it	can can't/cannot	do play see come, etc.

can	I/we/you/they he/she/it	do? play? see? come?, etc.

I can do something = I *know how* to do it or *it is possible* for me to do it

- I **can play** the piano. My brother **can play** the piano too.
- Sarah **can speak** Italian, but she **can't speak** Spanish.
- "**Can** you **swim**?" "Yes, but I'm not a very good swimmer."
- "**Can** you **change** a ten-dollar bill?" "I'm sorry, **I can't.**"
- I'm having a party next week, but Scott and Angela **can't come.**

For the *past* (**yesterday** / **last week**, etc.), we use **could/couldn't.**

- When I was young, I **could run** very fast.
- Before Shu Ling came to Canada, she **couldn't understand** much English. Now she **can understand** everything.
- I was tired last night, but I **couldn't sleep.**
- I had a party last week, but Scott and Angela **couldn't come.**

Can you . . . ? Could you . . . ? Can I . . . ? Could I . . . ?

We use **Can you . . . ?** or **Could you . . . ?** when we ask people to do things.

- **Can you** open the door, please? *or* **Could you** open the door, please?
- **Can you** tell me the time, please? *or* **Could you** tell . . . ?

We use **Can I have . . . ?** or **Could I have . . . ?** to ask for something.

- *(in a store)* **Can I have** change for a dollar, please? *or* **Could I have** . . . ?

Can I . . . ? or **Could I . . . ?** = is it OK to do something?

- Tom, **can I** borrow your pen? *or* Tom, **could I** borrow your pen?
- *(on the phone)* Hello, **can I** speak to Jerry, please? *or* . . . **could I** speak . . . ?

May I . . . ? Unit 30

Exercises

31.1 Ask Steve if he can do these things:

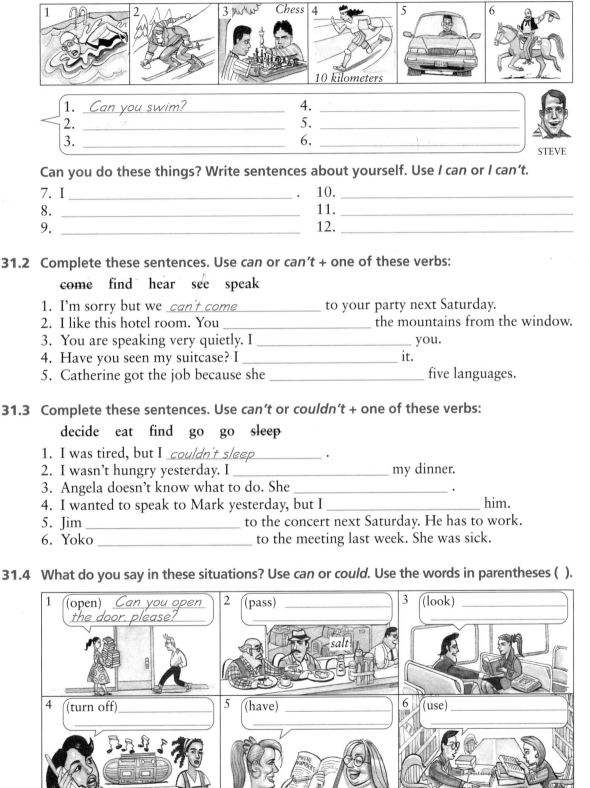

1. _Can you swim?_
2. _____
3. _____
4. _____
5. _____
6. _____

STEVE

Can you do these things? Write sentences about yourself. Use *I can* or *I can't.*

7. I _____ .
8. _____
9. _____
10. _____
11. _____
12. _____

31.2 Complete these sentences. Use *can* or *can't* + one of these verbs:

~~come~~   find   hear   see   speak

1. I'm sorry but we _can't come_ to your party next Saturday.
2. I like this hotel room. You _____ the mountains from the window.
3. You are speaking very quietly. I _____ you.
4. Have you seen my suitcase? I _____ it.
5. Catherine got the job because she _____ five languages.

31.3 Complete these sentences. Use *can't* or *couldn't* + one of these verbs:

decide   eat   find   go   go   ~~sleep~~

1. I was tired, but I _couldn't sleep_ .
2. I wasn't hungry yesterday. I _____ my dinner.
3. Angela doesn't know what to do. She _____ .
4. I wanted to speak to Mark yesterday, but I _____ him.
5. Jim _____ to the concert next Saturday. He has to work.
6. Yoko _____ to the meeting last week. She was sick.

31.4 What do you say in these situations? Use *can* or *could*. Use the words in parentheses ( ).

1 (open) _Can you open the door, please?_
2 (pass) _____   salt
3 (look) _____
4 (turn off) _____
5 (have) _____
6 (use) _____

Must

A

Tracy's not at work today. | She **must be** sick.

She **must be** sick = I am sure she is sick, it is clear that she is sick

Must + *base form*
(**must be** / **must know**, etc.)

I/we/you/they he/she/it	must (not)	be know have live, etc.

We use **must** when we believe that something is true.

- You worked ten hours today. You **must be** tired.
- My brother has worked at your company for years. You **must know** him.
- My friends have the same zip code as you. They **must live** close to you.
- (*on the telephone*) This isn't the Smiths'? I'm sorry. I **must have** the wrong number.

We use **must not** when we believe that something is *not* true.

- The phone rang eight times and Karen didn't answer. She **must not be** at home.
- Carlos takes the bus everywhere. He **must not have** a car.
- The Silvas are always home on Friday. They **must not work** then.

B

Must also has another meaning. You **must do** something = it is necessary to do it

- You **must be** careful with this knife. It's very sharp.
- Workers **must wear** safety glasses at this machine.
- In the U.S., you **must be** 18 to vote.

For the *past* (**yesterday, last week**, etc.), we use **had to ...** (*not* **must**).

- They were in a dangerous situation. They **had to be** careful. (*not* They must be careful.)
- We **had to wear** safety glasses when we visited the factory last week. (*not* we must wear)

You **must not do** something = it is necessary *not* to do it, it is the wrong thing to do

- Bicyclists **must not ride** on the sidewalk. (= they must ride in the street)
- You **must not be** late for school again!

Should Unit 33   *I have to ...* Unit 34

Exercises

32.1 Complete the sentences. Use *must be* + one of these:

for you   good   hungry   in the kitchen   ~~tired~~   very happy

1. Silvia worked ten hours today. She *must be tired* _____ .
2. It's evening and you haven't eaten anything all day. You _____ .
3. It's the most popular restaurant in town, so the food _____ .
4. "I got the job!" "You did? That's great. You _____ ."
5. The phone's ringing. I know it's not for me. It _____ .
6. My keys aren't in the living room, so they _____ .

32.2 Complete the sentences. Use *must* + one of these:

drink   have   ~~know~~   like   work

1. My brother has worked at your company for years. You *must know* _____ him.
2. Marilyn wears something blue every day. She _____ the color blue.
3. The Hills have six children and three dogs. They _____ a big house.
4. Mrs. Lee bought three gallons of milk at the store. Her children _____ a lot of milk.
5. I know Mrs. Romo has a job, but she's always home during the day. She _____ nights.

32.3 Write *must* or *must not.*

1. (*on the telephone*) This isn't the Smiths'? I'm sorry. I *must* have the wrong number.
2. Carlos takes the bus everywhere. He *must not* have a car.
3. Brandon is very thin. He _____ eat very much.
4. I never see my neighbor in the morning. He _____ leave for work very early.
5. I always have to repeat things when I talk to Kelly. She _____ hear very well.
6. Jim wears the same clothes every day. He _____ have many clothes.
7. You have a cold and a fever? Poor thing! You _____ feel awful.

32.4 Complete the sentences. Use *must* + one of these:

~~be~~   be   get   know   take   wear

1. In most of the U.S., you *must be* _____ at least 16 to get a driver's license.
2. For this job, you _____ both English and Spanish.
3. People in the front seat of a car _____ a seat belt.
4. High school students who want to go to college _____ good grades.
5. This highway is closed. Drivers _____ another road.
6. A tennis player _____ very good to play professionally.

32.5 Write *must, mustn't,* or *had to.*

1. We *mustn't* forget to send Sam a birthday card.
2. We *had to* wear safety glasses when we visited the factory.
3. I _____ hurry or I'll be late.
4. "Why were you so late?" "I _____ wait half an hour for the bus."
5. Keep these papers in a safe place. You _____ lose them.
6. Bicyclists _____ follow the same traffic rules as drivers.
7. We _____ forget to turn off the lights when we leave.
8. I don't usually work on Saturdays, but last Saturday I _____ work.

Should

A

You **shouldn't watch** TV so much.

Should + *base form*
(should do / should watch, etc.)

		do
I/we/you/they	should	stop
he/she/it	shouldn't	go
		watch, etc.

B

You **should do** something = it is a good thing to do, it is the right thing to do

- Tom **should go** to bed earlier. He goes to bed very late, and he's always tired.
- It's a good movie. You **should go** and see it.
- When you play tennis, you **should** always **watch** the ball.

Should I do something? = is it a good thing to do?

- **Should** I **invite** Karen to dinner?
- **Should** we **buy** something special for dinner?

C

You **shouldn't do** something = it is not a good thing to do (**shouldn't = should not**)

- Tom **shouldn't go** to bed so late.
- You watch TV all the time. You **shouldn't watch** TV so much.

D

We often use **think** with **should**.

I think . . . should . . .

- I think Gary **should buy** some new clothes. (= I think it is a good idea.)
- It's late. **I think** I **should go** home now.

I don't think . . . should . . .

- I **don't think** you **should work** so hard.
  (= I don't think it is a good idea.)
- I **don't think** we **should go** yet. It's too early.

Do you think . . . should . . . ?

Do you think I should buy this coat?

- **Do you think** I **should buy** this coat?
- What time **do you think** we **should go** home?

E

Should is different from **have to.**

- I **should** study tonight, but I think I'll go to the movies.
- I **have to** study tonight. I can't go to the movies.

F

Another way to say **should** is **ought to.**

- I **ought to study** tonight, but I think I'll go to the movies. (= I should study)
- I think Gary **ought to buy** some new clothes. (= Gary should buy)

Shall/should Unit 29   *Can* Unit 31   *Must* Unit 32   *Have to* Unit 34

Exercises

33.1 Complete the sentences. Use *you should* + one of these verbs:

brush   g̶o̶   read   visit   w̶a̶t̶c̶h̶   wear

1. When you play tennis, *you should watch* _____ the ball.
2. It's late and you're very tired. _____ to bed.
3. _____ your teeth twice a day.
4. If you have time, _____ the Science Museum. It's very interesting.
5. When you're driving, _____ a seat belt.
6. It's a very good book. _____ it.

33.2 Write about the people in the pictures. Use *He/She shouldn't . . . so . . . .*

1. *She shouldn't watch TV so much.*   3. _____ hard.
2. He _____ .   4. _____

33.3 You ask a friend for advice. Write questions with *Do you think I should . . . ?*

1. You are in a store. You are trying on a jacket. You ask your friend:
   (buy) *Do you think I should buy this jacket?* _____
2. You can't drive. You ask your friend:
   (learn) Do you think _____ ?
3. You don't like your job. You ask your friend:
   (get another job) _____
4. You are going to have a party. You ask your friend:
   (invite Scott) _____

33.4 Write sentences with *I think . . . should* or *I don't think . . . should.*

1. We have to get up early tomorrow. *I think we should go home now.* (go home now)
2. That coat is too big for you. *I don't think you should buy it.* (buy it)
3. You don't need your car. _____ (sell it)
4. Diane needs a change. _____ (take a trip)
5. Karen and Don are too young. _____ (get married)
6. You're still sick. _____ (go to work)
7. James isn't feeling well today. _____ (go to the doctor)
8. This hotel is too expensive for us. _____ (stay here)

33.5 What do you think? Write sentences with *should.*

1. I think *everybody should learn another language* _____ .
2. I think everybody _____ .
3. I think _____ .
4. I don't think _____ .
5. I think I should _____ .

I have to . . .

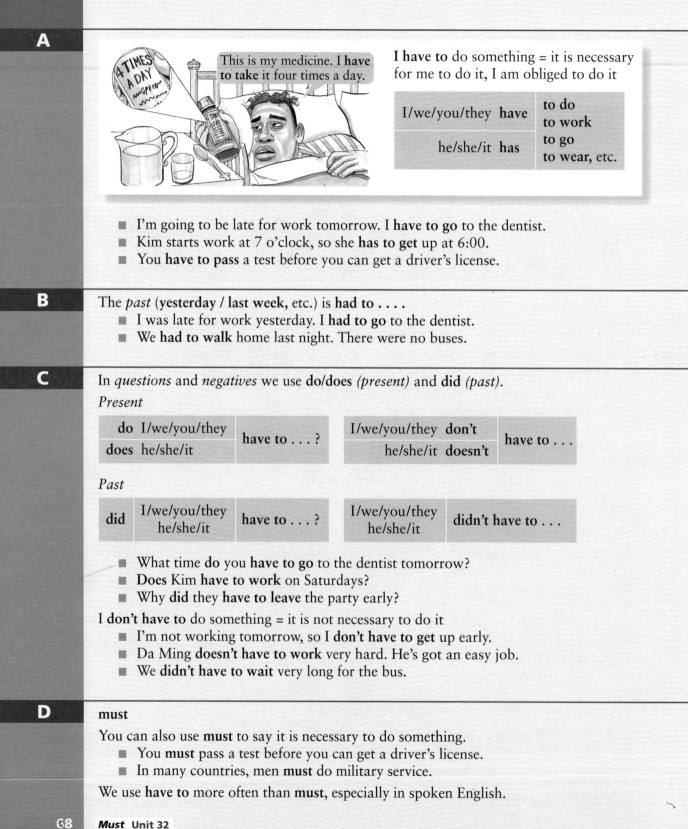

This is my medicine. I **have to take** it four times a day.

I **have to** do something = it is necessary for me to do it, I am obliged to do it

I/we/you/they **have**	to do to work
he/she/it **has**	to go to wear, etc.

- I'm going to be late for work tomorrow. I **have to go** to the dentist.
- Kim starts work at 7 o'clock, so she **has to get** up at 6:00.
- You **have to pass** a test before you can get a driver's license.

The *past* (**yesterday / last week**, etc.) is **had to . . . .**
- I was late for work yesterday. I **had to go** to the dentist.
- We **had to walk** home last night. There were no buses.

In *questions* and *negatives* we use **do/does** *(present)* and **did** *(past)*.

Present

do I/we/you/they **does** he/she/it	**have to . . . ?**

I/we/you/they **don't** he/she/it **doesn't**	**have to . . .**

Past

did	I/we/you/they he/she/it	**have to . . . ?**

I/we/you/they he/she/it	**didn't have to . . .**

- What time **do** you **have to go** to the dentist tomorrow?
- **Does** Kim **have to work** on Saturdays?
- Why **did** they **have to leave** the party early?

I **don't have to** do something = it is not necessary to do it
- I'm not working tomorrow, so I **don't have to get** up early.
- Da Ming **doesn't have to work** very hard. He's got an easy job.
- We **didn't have to wait** very long for the bus.

must

You can also use **must** to say it is necessary to do something.
- You **must** pass a test before you can get a driver's license.
- In many countries, men **must** do military service.

We use **have to** more often than **must**, especially in spoken English.

Must Unit 32

Exercises

34.1 Complete the sentences. Use *have to* or *has to* + one of these verbs:

   hit   read   speak   take   travel   ~~wear~~

1. My eyes are not very good. I *have to wear* glasses.
2. At the end of the course, all the students _____ a test.
3. Marta is studying literature. She _____ a lot of books.
4. Alberto doesn't understand much English. You _____ to him very slowly.
5. Kate is not at home much. She _____ a lot for her job.
6. In tennis you _____ the ball over the net.

34.2 Complete the sentences. Use *have to* or *had to* + one of these verbs:

   answer   buy   change   go   take   wake   ~~walk~~

1. We *had to walk* home last night. There were no buses.
2. It's late. I _____ now. I'll see you tomorrow.
3. I went to the store after work yesterday. I _____ some food.
4. This bus doesn't go all the way downtown. You _____ at First Avenue.
5. We took an exam yesterday. We _____ six questions out of ten.
6. I'm going to bed early. I _____ up early tomorrow.
7. Amy and her cousin can't go out with us tonight. They _____ care of Amy's little brother.

34.3 Complete the questions. Some are present and some are past.

1.	I have to get up early tomorrow.	What time *do you have to get up* ?
2.	Eric had to wait a long time.	How long _____ ?
3.	Liz has to go somewhere.	Where _____ ?
4.	We had to pay a lot of money.	How much _____ ?
5.	I have to do some work.	What exactly _____ ?
6.	They had to leave early.	Why _____ ?

34.4 Write sentences with *don't/doesn't/didn't have to* . . . .

1. Why do you want to pay the bill now? You *don't have to pay* it now.
2. Why is Hannah waiting? She _____ .
3. Why did you get up early? You _____ .
4. Why is Joel working so hard? He _____ .
5. Why do you want to leave now? We _____ .

34.5 Write some things that you (or your friends or family) *have to do* or *had to do*.

1. (every day) *I have to drive fifty miles to work every day.*
2. (every day) _____
3. (tomorrow) _____
4. (yesterday) _____
5. (last week) _____
6. (when I was younger) _____

Would you like . . . ?   I'd like . . .

A

Would you like . . . ? = Do you want . . . ?

We use **Would you like . . . ?** to offer things.

- *A:* **Would you like** some coffee?
  B: No, thank you.
- *A:* **Would you like** a piece of candy?
  B: Yes, thanks.
- *A:* What **would you like,** tea or coffee?
  B: Tea, please.

We use **Would you like to . . . ?** to invite somebody.

- **Would you like to go** for a walk?
- *A:* **Would you like to have** dinner with us on Sunday?
  B: Yes, **I'd love to.** (= I would love to have dinner with you.)
- What **would you like to do** tonight?

Would you like a piece of candy?

Yes, thanks.

B

I'd like . . . is a polite way to say "I want." (**I'd like = I would** like)

- I'm thirsty. **I'd like** a drink.
- *(in a tourist office)* **I'd like** a road map, please.
- **I'd like to watch** the news on television tonight.

C

Would you like . . . ? and **Do you like . . . ?**

Would you like . . . ? / I'd like . . .	**Do you like . . . ? / I like . . .**
Would you like some coffee?	**Do you like** coffee?
Yes, thanks.	Yes, I do.
	Would you like some now?
	No, thank you. Not now.
Would you like some coffee? = Do you want some coffee?	**Do you like** coffee? = Do you think coffee is good?
■ *A:* **Would you like** to go to the movies tonight? (= Do you want to go tonight?) *B:* Yes, I'd love to.	■ *A:* **Do you like** to go to the movies? *(in general)* *B:* Yes, I go to the movies a lot.
■ **I'd like** an orange, please. (= Can I have an orange?)	■ **I like** oranges. *(in general)*
■ What **would you like** to do next weekend?	■ What **do you like** to do on weekends?

Exercises

35.1 What are the people in the pictures saying? Use _Would you like . . . ?_

1. *Would you like a piece of candy?*
2.
3.
4.
5.
6.

35.2 What do you say to Sue in these situations? Use _Would you like to . . . ?_ and the words in parentheses ( ).

1. You want to go to the movies tonight. You hope Sue will go too.
   You say: (go) _Would you like to go to the movies tonight?_
2. You want to play tennis tomorrow. You hope Sue will play with you.
   You say: (play) _____
3. You've got some vacation pictures. Sue hasn't seen them yet.
   You say: (see) _____
4. You have an extra ticket for a concert next week. You hope Sue will go with you.
   You say: (go) _____
5. It's raining and Sue is going out. She doesn't have an umbrella, but you have one.
   You say: (borrow) _____

35.3 Which is right?

1. "~~Do you like~~ / Would you like a piece of candy?" "Yes, thanks." (_Would you like_ is right.)
2. "Do you like / Would you like bananas?" "Yes, I love them."
3. "Do you like / Would you like some ice cream?" "No, thank you."
4. "What do you like / would you like to drink?" "A glass of water, please."
5. "Do you like / Would you like to go out for a walk?" "Not now. Maybe later."
6. I like / I'd like tomatoes, but I don't eat them very often.
7. What time do you like / would you like to have dinner tonight?
8. "Do you like / Would you like something to eat?" "No, thanks. I'm not hungry."
9. "Do you like / Would you like your new job?" "Yes, I'm enjoying it."
10. I'm tired. I like / I'd like to go to sleep now.

I'd rather . . .

ناد ترجیح داردم(ترجیح)

> Would you like to sit here?   No, thanks. **I'd rather** sit on the floor.

Angela likes to sit on the floor. She doesn't
want to sit on a chair. So she says:
I'd rather sit on the floor.
(= I would prefer to sit on the floor.)
I'd rather . . . = I **would** rather . . .

I **would rather** do something = I would prefer to do something

Positive		*Negative*		*Question*	
I'd rather (I **would rather**)	do stay have be	**I'd rather not** (I **would rather not**)	do stay have be	**Would** you **rather**	do? stay? have? be?

- ■ I don't really want to go out. **I'd rather stay** home. (= I'd prefer to stay home.)
- ■ "Should we go now?" "No, **I'd rather wait** until later."
- ■ I want to go now, but Tom **would rather wait** until later.
- ■ I don't like to be late. **I'd rather be** early.

- ■ I'm feeling tired. **I'd rather not go out** tonight. (= I'd prefer not to go out.)
- ■ Beth is feeling tired. She**'d rather not go out** tonight.
- ■ We're not hungry. We**'d rather not eat** yet.
- ■ "Do you want to go out tonight?" "**I'd rather not**." (= I'd rather not go out.)

- ■ "**Would** you **rather have** milk or juice?" "Juice, please."
- ■ Which **would** you **rather do** – go to the movies or watch a video at home?

We say "**I'd rather do** something." (*not* to do something)
- ■ I'd rather **sit** on the floor. (*not* I'd rather to sit)
- ■ Beth would rather not **go** out. (*not* would rather not to go)

But we say "**I'd prefer to do** something."
- ■ I'd prefer **to sit** on the floor.
- ■ Beth would prefer not **to go** out.

You can say "**I'd rather** . . . **than** . . . ."
- ■ **I'd rather** go out **than** stay home.
- ■ **I'd rather** have a dog **than** a cat.
- ■ We**'d rather** go to the movies **than** watch a video at home.
- ■ **I'd rather** be at home right now **than** here.

Prefer Unit 53

Exercises

36.1 Look at the pictures and complete B's sentences. Use *I'd rather* . . . .

1. Would you like to sit here?

No, thanks. *I'd rather sit* on the floor.

2. Do you want to watch TV?

No, I _____ my book.

3. Would you like some tea?

Well, _____ coffee if you have some.

4. Should we go out now?

_____ until it stops raining.

36.2 Complete these questions. Use *would you rather* . . . .

1. Do you want to go out, or *would you rather stay* home?
2. Should we have dinner now, or _____ later?
3. Would you like a glass of iced tea, or _____ water?
4. Do you want to go to the movies, or _____ TV?

36.3 Complete the sentences with a verb. Sometimes you need *to*.

1. I'd rather *stay* home tonight. I'd prefer not *to go* out.
2. Should we walk home, or would you rather _____ a taxi?
3. Do you want me to go with you, or would you prefer _____ alone?
4. Vera doesn't want to go to college. She'd rather _____ a job.
5. "Can I help you with your suitcase?" "No, thanks. I'd rather _____ it myself."
6. I'd rather not _____ him. I'd prefer _____ him a letter.

36.4 Write sentences about yourself with *I'd rather . . . than*.

1. Which would you prefer to be – a bus driver or an airline pilot?
   I'd rather be an airplane pilot than a bus driver.
2. Which would you prefer to be – a journalist or a teacher?
   I'd rather _____ .
3. Where would you prefer to live – in a big city or a small town?
   _____
4. Which would you prefer to have – a cat or a dog?
   _____
5. What would you prefer to study – electronics or philosophy?
   _____

Do this! Don't do that! Let's do this!

A

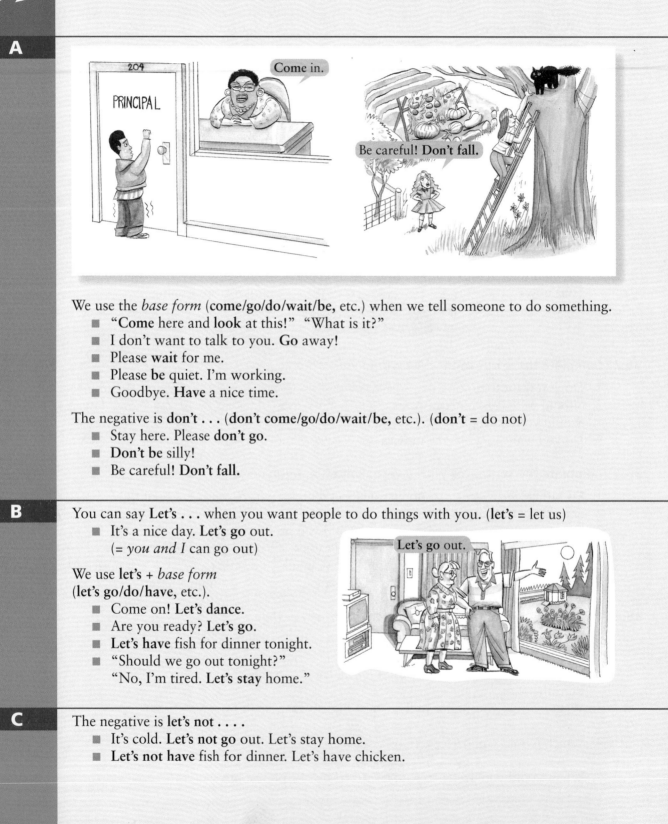

We use the *base form* (**come/go/do/wait/be**, etc.) when we tell someone to do something.

- ■ "**Come** here and **look** at this!" "What is it?"
- ■ I don't want to talk to you. **Go** away!
- ■ Please **wait** for me.
- ■ Please **be** quiet. I'm working.
- ■ Goodbye. **Have** a nice time.

The negative is **don't . . .** (**don't come/go/do/wait/be**, etc.). (**don't** = do not)

- ■ Stay here. Please **don't go**.
- ■ **Don't be** silly!
- ■ Be careful! **Don't fall**.

B

You can say **Let's . . .** when you want people to do things with you. (**let's** = let us)

- ■ It's a nice day. **Let's go** out.
  (= *you and I* can go out)

We use **let's** + *base form*
(**let's go/do/have**, etc.).

- ■ Come on! **Let's dance**.
- ■ Are you ready? **Let's go**.
- ■ **Let's have** fish for dinner tonight.
- ■ "Should we go out tonight?"
  "No, I'm tired. **Let's stay** home."

C

The negative is **let's not . . . .**

- ■ It's cold. **Let's not go** out. Let's stay home.
- ■ **Let's not have** fish for dinner. Let's have chicken.

Exercises

37.1 Look at the pictures. What are the people saying? Sometimes the sentence is positive (*go/eat*, etc.) and sometimes it is negative (*don't go / don't eat*, etc.). Use these verbs:

buy ~~come~~ drink sit sleep smile talk turn

1 <u>Come</u> in.

2 It's too expensive. _____ it.

3 OK, _____ !

4 _____ the water!

5 _____ left!

6 _____ on the cat!

7 Please _____

8 I'm going to bed. _____ well.

37.2 Complete the sentences. Use *No, let's . . .* + one of these:

~~go for a swim~~   go to a restaurant   take the bus   wait   watch TV

1. Would you like to play tennis? *No, let's go for a swim.*
2. Do you want to drive downtown? No, _____ .
3. Shall we go to the movies?
4. Should we have dinner at home?
5. Would you like to begin now?

37.3 Answer with *No, don't . . .* or *No, let's not . . . .*

1. Shall I wait for you? *No, don't wait for me.*
2. Should we go home now? *No, let's not go home now.*
3. Shall we go out?
4. Should I close the door?
5. Should I call you tonight?
6. Should we wait for Dave?
7. Shall I turn on the light?
8. Should we take a taxi?

There is/are

A

There's a man on the roof.   There's a train at 10:30.   **There are** seven days in a week.

Singular

there is . . .   (there's)
is there . . . ?
there is not . . . (there isn't
or there's not)

- There's a big tree in the yard.
- There's a good movie on TV tonight.
- A: Do you have any money?
  B: Yes, **there's** some in my wallet.
- A: Excuse me, **is there** a hotel near here?
  B: Yes, **there is**. / No, **there isn't**.
- We can't go skiing. **There isn't** any snow.

Plural

there are . . .
are there . . . ?
there are not . . . (there aren't)

- There are some big trees in the yard.
- There are a lot of accidents on this road.
- A: **Are there** any mistakes in my letter?
  B: Yes, **there are**. / No, **there aren't**.
- This restaurant is very quiet. **There aren't** many people here.
- How many players **are there** on a soccer team?
- There are 11 players on a soccer team.

B   there is and it is

there is

There's a book on the table.
(*not* It's a book on the table.)

it is

I like this book . **It's** funny. (it = this book)

Compare:
- "What's **that noise**?" "**It's** a train." (it = that noise)
  There's a train at 10:30. **It's** a fast train. (it = the 10:30 train)
- There's a lot of salt in this soup.
  I don't like **this soup**. **It's** too salty. (it = this soup)

There was / were / has been, etc. Unit 39   *It and there* Unit 40   *Some and any* Unit 77

Exercises

38.1 Springfield is a small town. Write sentences about Springfield with *There is/are* or *There isn't/aren't*. Use the information in the box.

1. A golf course?	No
2. Any restaurants?	Yes (a lot)
3. A hospital?	Yes
4. A swimming pool?	No
5. Any movie theaters?	Yes (two)
6. A university?	No
7. Any big hotels?	No

1. *There isn't a golf course.*
2. *There are a lot of restaurants.*
3. _____
4. _____
5. _____
6. _____
7. _____

38.2 Write about your town (or a town that you know). Use *There is/are/isn't/aren't.*

1. *There are a few restaurants.*
2. *There's a big park.*
3. _____
4. _____
5. _____
6. _____

38.3 Write *there is / there isn't / is there / there are / there aren't / are there.*

1. Springfield isn't an old town. *There aren't* _____ any old buildings.
2. Look! _____ a picture of your brother in the newspaper!
3. "Excuse me, _____ a bank near here?" "Yes, at the end of the block."
4. _____ five people in my family: my parents, my two sisters, and me.
5. "How many students _____ in the class?" "Twenty."
6. "Can we take a picture?" "No, _____ any film in the camera."
7. "_____ a bus downtown from the airport?" "Yes. Every 20 minutes."
8. "_____ any problems?" "No, everything is OK."
9. _____ nowhere to sit down. _____ any chairs.

38.4 Write sentences with *There are . . . .* Choose from the boxes.

~~seven~~	twenty-six	~~days~~	planets	a hockey team	the English alphabet
nine	thirty	days	players	~~a week~~	the solar system
eleven	fifty	letters	states	September	the USA

1. *There are seven days in a week.*
2. _____
3. _____
4. _____
5. _____
6. _____

38.5 Write *there's / is there / it's / is it.*

1. "*There's* a flight at 10:30." "*Is it* a non-stop flight?"
2. I'm not going to buy this shirt. _____ too expensive.
3. "What's wrong?" "_____ something in my eye."
4. _____ a red car outside the house. _____ yours?
5. "_____ anything good on TV tonight?" "Yes, _____ a movie at 8:00."
6. "What's that building?" "_____ a school."
7. "_____ a restaurant in this hotel?" "No, I'm sorry."

There was/were   there has been / have been
there will be

A   there was/were *(past)*

> There **is** a train every hour.
> It's 11:15 now.
> There **was** a train at 11 o'clock.

Compare:

there is/are *(present)*	**there was/were** *(past)*
■ **There is** a good movie on TV tonight.	■ **There was** a good movie on TV last night.
■ We are staying at a big hotel. **There are** 1,250 rooms.	■ We stayed at a very big hotel. **There were** 1,250 rooms.
■ **Are there** any phone messages for me today?	■ **Were there** any phone messages for me yesterday?
■ I'm hungry, but **there isn't** anything to eat.	■ When I got home, I was hungry, but **there wasn't** anything to eat.

B   there has been / have been *(present perfect)*

There's been an accident.

■ Look! **There's been** an accident.
   (**there's been** = there has been)
■ This road is very dangerous. **There have been** a lot of accidents here.

Compare **there was** *(past)*:
■ **There was** an accident **last night.**
   (*not* There has been an accident last night.)

For present perfect and simple past, see Unit 19.

C   there will be

There will be rain tomorrow afternoon.

■ Do you think **there will be** a lot of people at the party on Saturday?
■ The manager of the company is leaving, so **there will be** a new manager soon.
■ I'm going away tomorrow. I'm packing my things today because **there won't be** time tomorrow. (**there won't be** = there will not be)

Was/were Unit 10   **Has/have been** Units 16, 19–21   **Will** Unit 28   **There is/are** Unit 38
There and **it** Units 38, 40   **Some/any** Unit 77

Exercises

39.1 Look at the two pictures. The room is empty now. What was in the room last
week? Write sentences with *There was . . .* or *There were . . .* + one of these:

a clock	an armchair	a sofa	some flowers
a coffee table	a rug	some books	three pictures

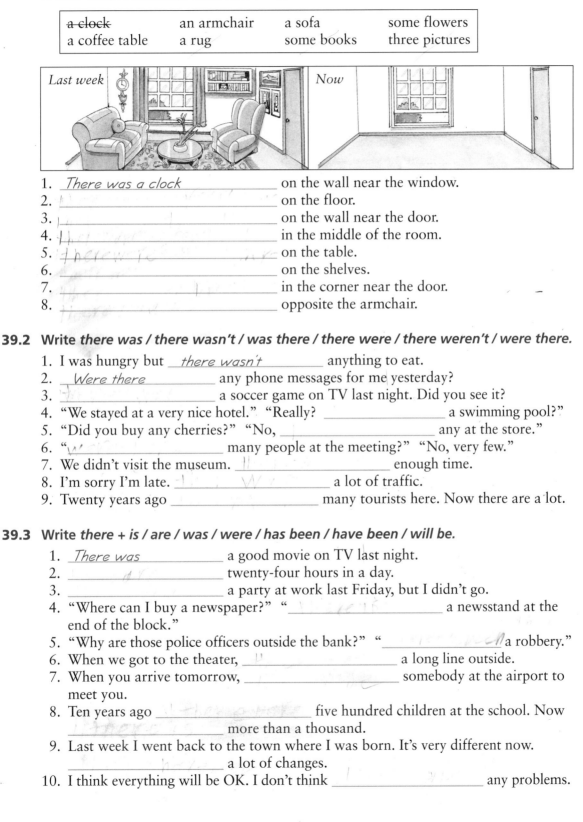

1. *There was a clock* _____ on the wall near the window.
2. _____ on the floor.
3. _____ on the wall near the door.
4. _____ in the middle of the room.
5. _____ on the table.
6. _____ on the shelves.
7. _____ in the corner near the door.
8. _____ opposite the armchair.

39.2 Write *there was / there wasn't / was there / there were / there weren't / were there.*

1. I was hungry but ___*there wasn't*___ anything to eat.
2. ___*Were there*___ any phone messages for me yesterday?
3. _____ a soccer game on TV last night. Did you see it?
4. "We stayed at a very nice hotel." "Really? _____ a swimming pool?"
5. "Did you buy any cherries?" "No, _____ any at the store."
6. "_____ many people at the meeting?" "No, very few."
7. We didn't visit the museum. _____ enough time.
8. I'm sorry I'm late. _____ a lot of traffic.
9. Twenty years ago _____ many tourists here. Now there are a lot.

39.3 Write *there + is / are / was / were / has been / have been / will be.*

1. *There was* _____ a good movie on TV last night.
2. _____ twenty-four hours in a day.
3. _____ a party at work last Friday, but I didn't go.
4. "Where can I buy a newspaper?" "_____ a newsstand at the
   end of the block."
5. "Why are those police officers outside the bank?" "_____ a robbery."
6. When we got to the theater, _____ a long line outside.
7. When you arrive tomorrow, _____ somebody at the airport to
   meet you.
8. Ten years ago _____ five hundred children at the school. Now
   _____ more than a thousand.
9. Last week I went back to the town where I was born. It's very different now.
   _____ a lot of changes.
10. I think everything will be OK. I don't think _____ any problems.

It . . .

A

We use **it** for time/day/distance/weather.

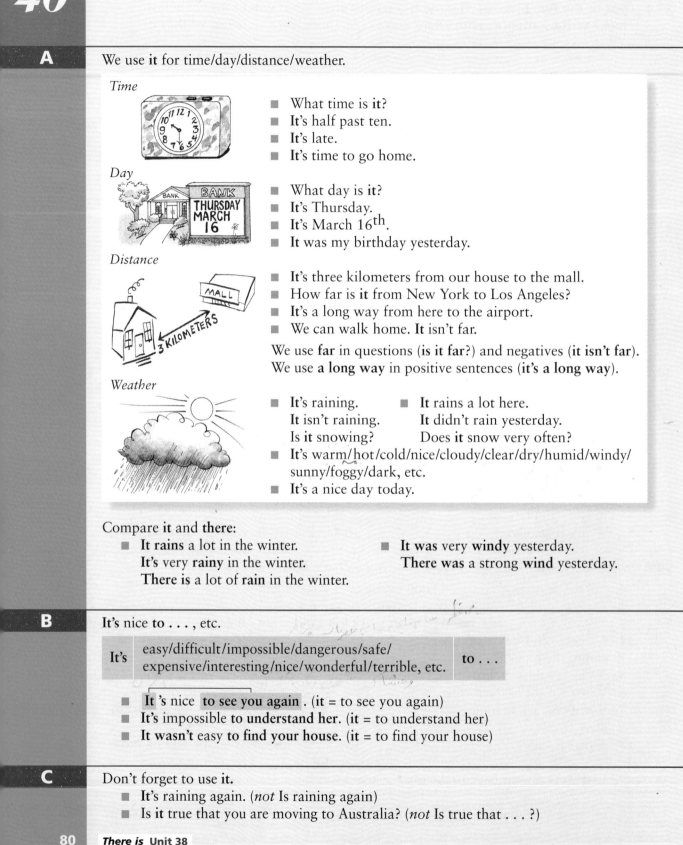

Time

- What time is **it**?
- **It's** half past ten.
- **It's** late.
- **It's** time to go home.

Day

- What day is **it**?
- **It's** Thursday.
- **It's** March 16th.
- **It** was my birthday yesterday.

Distance

- **It's** three kilometers from our house to the mall.
- How far is **it** from New York to Los Angeles?
- **It's** a long way from here to the airport.
- We can walk home. **It** isn't far.

We use **far** in questions (**is it far?**) and negatives (**it isn't far**).
We use **a long way** in positive sentences (**it's a long way**).

Weather

- **It's** raining.   ■ **It** rains a lot here.
  It isn't raining.   **It** didn't rain yesterday.
  Is **it** snowing?   Does **it** snow very often?
- **It's** warm/hot/cold/nice/cloudy/clear/dry/humid/windy/
  sunny/foggy/dark, etc.
- **It's** a nice day today.

Compare **it** and **there**:

- **It rains** a lot in the winter.
  It's very **rainy** in the winter.
  There is a lot of **rain** in the winter.

- **It was** very **windy** yesterday.
  There was a strong **wind** yesterday.

B

It's nice to . . . , etc.

It's	easy/difficult/impossible/dangerous/safe/ expensive/interesting/nice/wonderful/terrible, etc.	to . . .

- **It** 's nice **to see you again** . (it = to see you again)
- **It's** impossible **to understand her.** (it = to understand her)
- **It wasn't** easy **to find your house.** (it = to find your house)

C

Don't forget to use **it**.

- **It's** raining again. (*not* Is raining again)
- Is **it** true that you are moving to Australia? (*not* Is true that . . . ?)

***There is** Unit 38*

Exercises

40.1 Write about the weather in the pictures. Use *It's* . . . .

1. *It's raining.*
2. _____
3. _____
4. _____
5. _____
6. _____

40.2 Write *it's* (it is) or *is it*.

1. What time *is it* ?
2. We must go now. _____ very late.
3. _____ true that Bill can fly a helicopter?
4. "What day _____ today? Tuesday?"
   "No, _____ Wednesday."
5. _____ OK to call you at the office?
6. _____ twelve kilometers from downtown to the airport.
7. "Do you want to walk to the restaurant?"
   "I don't know. How far _____ ?"
8. _____ Linda's birthday today. She's 27.
9. I don't believe it! _____ impossible.

40.3 Write questions with *How far* . . . ?

1. (here / the station) *How far is it from here to the station?*
2. (the hotel / the beach) How _____ ?
3. (New York / Washington) _____
4. (your house / the airport) _____

40.4 Write *it* or *there*.

1. *It* rains a lot in the winter.
2. *There* was a strong wind yesterday.
3. _____ was a nice day yesterday.
4. We can't go skiing. _____ isn't any snow.
5. _____'s hot in this room. Open a window.
6. I was afraid because _____ was very dark.
7. _____ was a storm last night. Did you hear it?
8. _____'s a long way from here to the nearest gas station.

40.5 Complete the sentences. Choose from the boxes.

it's	easy	dangerous	to	work in this office	~~get up early~~
	~~difficult~~	~~nice~~		visit different places	go out alone
	impossible	interesting		~~see you again~~	~~make friends~~

1. If you go to bed late, *it's difficult to get up early* _____ in the morning.
2. Hello, Jill. _____ How are you?
3. _____ There is too much noise.
4. Everybody is very nice at work. _____
5. I like traveling. _____
6. Some cities are not safe. _____ at night.

I am, I don't, etc.

I'm not tired.

I am.

Do you like tea?

No, I don't.

Yes, I do.

She isn't tired, but **he is.**
(= he is tired)

He likes tea, but **she doesn't.**
(= she doesn't like tea)

In these examples, it is not necessary to repeat some words (he is *tired*, she doesn't *like tea*).

You can use these verbs in the same way.

am/is/are was/were have/has do/does/did can will might should

- I haven't seen the movie, but my sister **has.** (= She has seen the movie.)
- *A:* Please help me.
  B: I'm sorry. I **can't.** (= I can't help you.)
- *A:* Are you tired?
  B: I **was,** but **I'm not** now. (= I was tired, but I'm not tired now.)
- *A:* Do you think Marta will call tonight?
  B: She **might.** (= she might call)
- *A:* Are you going to study tonight?
  B: I **should,** but I probably **won't.**
  (= I should study, but I probably won't study.)

You *cannot* use 'm/'s/'ve, etc. *(short forms)* in this way. You must use **am/is/have,** etc.

- She isn't tired, but he **is.** (*not* . . . but he's)

But you *can* use **isn't/haven't/won't,** etc. (negative short forms).

- My sister has seen the movie, but I **haven't.**
- "Are you and Jim working tomorrow?" "I am, but Jim **isn't.**"

You can use **I am / I'm not,** etc., after **Yes** and **No.**

- "Are you tired?" "Yes, I **am.** / No, I'm **not.**"
- "Will Alan be here tomorrow?" "Yes, he **will.** / No, he **won't.**"
- "Is there a bus to the airport?" "Yes, there **is.** / No, there **isn't.**"

We use **do/does** for the *simple present* (see Units 6–7).

- I don't like hot weather, but Megan **does.** (= Megan likes hot weather.)
- Megan works hard, but I **don't.** (= I don't work hard.)
- "Do you enjoy your work?" "Yes, I **do.**"

We use **did** for the *simple past* (see Unit 12).

- *A:* Did you and John like the movie?
  B: I **did,** but John **didn't.** (= I liked it, but John didn't like it.)
- "I had a good time." "I **did** too." (= I had a good time too.)
- "Did it rain yesterday?" "No, it **didn't.**"

You have? / I have you?, etc. **Unit 42** *So am I / neither do I,* etc. **Unit 43**

Exercises

41.1 **Complete these sentences. Use only one verb (*is/have/can*, etc.) each time.**

1. Kate wasn't hungry, but we _were_ .
2. I'm not married, but my sister _is_ .
3. Bill can't help you, but I _can_ .
4. I haven't read the book, but Ed _has_
5. Ken won't be here, but Sue _will_ .
6. You weren't late, but I _was_ .

41.2 **Complete these sentences with a negative verb (*isn't/haven't/can't*, etc.).**

1. Sam can play the piano, but I _can't_ .
2. Marta is working today, but I _____ .
3. I was working, but my friends _____ .
4. Bob has been to China, but I _haven't_
5. I'm ready to go, but Tom _isn't_ .
6. I've seen the movie, but Kim _hasn't_

41.3 **Complete these sentences with *do/does/did* or *don't/doesn't/didn't*.**

1. I don't like hot weather, but Megan _does_ .
2. Megan likes hot weather, but I _don't_ .
3. My mother wears glasses, but my father _____ .
4. You don't know Paul very well, but I _____ .
5. I didn't enjoy the party, but my friends _____ .
6. I don't watch TV much, but Peter _____ .
7. Kate lives in Canada, but her parents _____ .
8. You had breakfast this morning, but I _____ .

41.4 **Complete the sentences. Write about yourself and other people.**

1. I didn't _go out last night, but my friends did_ .
2. I like _____ , but _____ .
3. I don't _____ , but _____ .
4. I'm _____ .
5. I haven't _____ .

41.5 **Write a verb – positive or negative.**

1. "Are you tired?" "I _was_ earlier, but I'm not now."
2. Fu Chen is happy today, but he _____ yesterday.
3. The stores aren't open yet, but the post office _____ .
4. I don't have a video camera, but I know somebody who _____ .
5. I would like to help you, but I'm sorry, I _____ .
6. I don't usually go to work by car, but I _____ yesterday.
7. *A:* Have you ever been to Alaska?
   B: No, but Sandra _had_ . She went there on vacation last year.
8. "Do you and Luke watch TV a lot?" "I _____ , but Luke doesn't."
9. "Do you think Diane will pass her driving test?" "Yes, I'm sure she _____ ."
10. "Are you going out tonight?" "I _____ . I don't know for sure."

41.6 **Answer these questions about yourself. Use *Yes, I have. / No, I'm not.*, etc.**

1. Are you Canadian? _No, I'm not._
2. Do you have a car? _____
3. Is it snowing? _____
4. Do you feel OK? _____
5. Are you hungry? _____
6. Do you like classical music? _____
7. Will you be in Rome tomorrow? _____
8. Have you ever been to Oslo? _____
9. Did you go out last night? _____
10. Were you asleep at 1:00 A.M.? _____

You have? / have you?
you are? / are you?, etc.

A

You can say **you have?** / **you are?** / **you don't?**, etc., to show that you are interested or surprised.

- "**You're** late." "**I am?** I'm sorry."
- "**I was** sick last week." "**You were?** I didn't know that."
- "**It's** raining again." "**It is?** It was sunny ten minutes ago."
- "**There's** a letter for you." "**There is?** Where is it?"
- "**Bill can't** drive." "**He can't?** I didn't know that."
- "**I'm not** hungry." "**You aren't?** I am."
- "**Sue isn't** at work today." "**She isn't?** Is she sick?"

Use **do/does** for the *simple present* and **did** for the *simple past*.

- "**I speak** four languages." "**You do?** Which ones?"
- "**Tom doesn't** eat meat." "**He doesn't?** Does he eat fish?"
- "**Nicole got** married last week." "**She did?** Really?"

B

Tag questions

You can use **have you?** / **is it?** / **can't she?**, etc., at the end of a sentence.

These "mini-questions" are called *tag questions*.

A *positive* sentence → a *negative* tag question

It's a nice day,	**isn't it?**	Yes, it's perfect.
Karen lives in Seattle,	**doesn't she?**	Yes, that's right.
You closed the window,	**didn't you?**	Yes, I did.
Those shoes are nice,	**aren't they?**	Yes, very nice.
Tom will be here soon,	**won't he?**	Yes, probably.

A *negative* sentence → a *positive* tag question

That isn't your car,	**is it?**	No, my car is white.
You haven't met my mother,	**have you?**	No, I haven't.
Lucia doesn't have a car,	**does she?**	No, she doesn't.
You won't be late,	**will you?**	No, I'm never late.

I am, I don't, etc. Unit 41

Exercises

42.1 Answer with *You do? / She doesn't? / They did?*, etc.

1. I speak four languages.
2. I work in a bank.
3. I didn't go to work yesterday.
4. Paula doesn't like me.
5. You look tired.
6. Julia called me last night.

You do?	Which ones?
_____	I work in a bank too.
_____	Were you sick?
_____	Why not?
_____	I feel fine.
_____	What did she say?

42.2 Answer with *You have? / You haven't? / She did? / She didn't?*, etc.

1. I've decided to buy a new car.
2. Tim doesn't eat meat.
3. I've already had dinner.
4. Sue can't drive.
5. I was born in Italy.
6. I didn't sleep well last night.
7. There's a good movie on TV.
8. I'm not happy.
9. I saw Amy last week.
10. Anne works in a factory.
11. I won't be here next week.
12. The clock isn't working.

You have?	What kind?
He doesn't?	Does he eat fish?
_____	When did you have it last?
_____	She should learn.
_____	I didn't know that.
_____	Was the bed uncomfortable?
_____	Are you going to watch it?
_____	Why not?
_____	How is she?
_____	What kind of factory?
_____	Where will you be?
_____	It was working yesterday.

42.3 Complete these sentences with a tag question (*isn't it? / haven't you?*, etc.).

1. It's a nice day, *isn't it* _____ ? Yes, it's beautiful.
2. These flowers are nice, _____ ? Yes, what kind are they?
3. Anne was at the party, _____ ? Yes, but I didn't speak to her.
4. You've been to Chile, _____ ? Yes, many times.
5. You speak Thai, _____ ? Yes, but not very well.
6. Bill looks tired, _____ ? Yes, he works very hard.
7. You'll help me, _____ ? Yes, of course I will.

42.4 Complete these sentences. Use a positive tag question (*is it? / do you?* etc.) or a negative tag question (*isn't it? / don't you?*, etc.).

1. You haven't eaten yet, *have you* _____ ? No, I'm not hungry.
2. You aren't tired, _____ ? No, I feel fine.
3. Mary is a very nice person, _____ ? Yes, everybody likes her.
4. You can play the piano, _____ ? Yes, but I'm not very good.
5. You don't know Mike's sister, _____ ? No, I've never met her.
6. John went to college, _____ ? Yes, she studied economics.
7. The movie wasn't very good, _____ ? No, it was terrible.
8. Anne lives near you, _____ ? Yes, just a few blocks away.
9. You won't tell her what I said, _____ ? No, of course not.

Too/either and so am I / neither do I, etc.

A

too and either

I'm happy.
I'm happy too.

I'm not happy.
I'm not happy either.

We use **too** and **either** at the end of a sentence.

We use **too** after a *positive* verb.	We use **either** after a *negative* verb.

■ A: I'm happy.
   B: **I'm** happy **too**. (*or* I am too.)
■ A: I liked the movie.
   B: I **liked** it **too**. (*or* I did too.)
■ Mei Lan is a doctor. Her husband **is** a doctor **too**. (*or* Her husband is too.)
	■ A: I'm not happy.
	   B: **I'm not** happy **either**.
	     (*or* I'm not either.)
	■ A: I can't cook.
	   B: I **can't either**.
	■ Bill doesn't watch TV. He **doesn't** read newspapers **either**.

B

so am I / neither do I, etc.

I'm happy.

So am I.

	am/is/are . . .
	was/were . . .
	do/does . . .
so	did . . .
neither	have/has . . .
	can . . .
	will . . .
	would . . .

I'm not happy.

Neither am I.

so am I = I am too so do I = I do too (etc.)	neither am I = I'm not either neither can I = I can't either (etc.)

■ A: **I'm** working.
   B: **So am I**. (= I'm working too.)
■ A: **I was** late for work today.
   B: **So was John**. (= John was late too.)
■ A: **I have** a key.
   B: **So do I**.
■ A: **We went** to the movies last night.
   B: You did? **So did we**.
■ A: **I'd** like to go to Australia.
   B: **So would I**.
	■ A: **I haven't** been to China.
	   B: **Neither have I**. (= I haven't either.)
	■ A: **Anne can't** cook.
	   B: **Neither can Tom**.
	     (= Tom can't either.)
	■ A: **I won't** (= will not) be here tomorrow.
	   B: **Neither will I**.
	■ A: **I never go** to the movies.
	   B: **Neither do I**.

Remember: so **am** I (*not* so I am), neither **have** I (*not* neither I have)

I am, I don't, etc. Unit 41

Exercises

43.1 Write *too* or *either*.

1. I'm happy.
2. I'm not hungry.
3. I'm going out.
4. It rained on Saturday.
5. Gloria can't ride a bicycle.
6. I don't like to go shopping.
7. Tracy's mother is a teacher.

I'm happy _too_ .
I'm not hungry _either_ .
I'm going out _too_ .
It rained on Sunday _either · too_ .
She can't drive a car _____ .
I don't like to go shopping _____ .
Her father is a teacher _____ .

43.2 Answer with *So . . . I* (*So am I / So do I / So can I*, etc.).

1. I went to bed late last night.
2. I'm thirsty.
3. I've already read this book.
4. I need a vacation.
5. I'll be late tomorrow.
6. I was very tired this morning.

So did I.

Answer with *Neither . . . I.*

7. I can't go to the party.
8. I didn't call Alex last night.
9. I haven't eaten lunch yet.
10. I'm not going out tonight.
11. I don't have much time.

43.3 You are talking to Maria. Write true sentences about yourself. Where possible, use *So . . . I* or *Neither . . . I.* Look at these examples carefully:

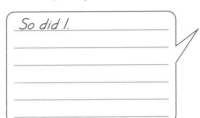

I'm tired today.

You can say: So am I. or I'm not.

I don't work very hard.

You can say: Neither do I. or I do.

MARIA
YOU

1. I'm studying English.
2. I can ride a bicycle.
3. I'm not American.
4. I like to cook.
5. I don't like cold weather.
6. I slept well last night.
7. I've never been to India.
8. I don't write letters very often.
9. I'm going out tomorrow night.
10. I wasn't sick last week.
11. I didn't watch TV last night.
12. I go to the movies a lot.

Isn't . . . , haven't . . . , don't . . . , etc. (Negatives)

A

We use **not** (**n't**) in negative sentences.

Positive → Negative

am	**am not** (**'m not**)
is	**is not** (**isn't** *or* **'s not**)
are	**are not** (**aren't** *or* **'re not**)
was	**was not** (**wasn't**)
were	**were not** (**weren't**)
have	**have not** (**haven't**)
has	**has not** (**hasn't**)
will	**will not** (**won't**)
can	**cannot** (**can't**)
could	**could not** (**couldn't**)
should	**should not** (**shouldn't**)
would	**would not** (**wouldn't**)
must	**must not**

- I'm **not** tired.
- It **isn't** (*or* It's **not**) raining.
- They **aren't** (*or* They're **not**) here.
- Brian **wasn't** hungry.
- The stores **weren't** open.
- I **haven't** finished my work.
- Sue **hasn't** been to Mexico.
- We **won't** be here tomorrow.
- Eric **can't** drive.
- I **couldn't** sleep last night.
- You **shouldn't** work so hard.
- I **wouldn't** like to be an actor.
- They **must not** have a car.

B

don't/doesn't/didn't

Simple present negative	I/we/you/they **do not** (**don't**)	**work/live/have**, etc.
	he/she/it **does not** (**doesn't**)	
Simple past negative	I/they/he/she, etc. **did not** (**didn't**)	

Positive → Negative

I **want** to go out. → I **don't want** to go out.
They **work** hard. → They **don't work** hard.
Liz **has** a car. → Liz **doesn't have** a car.
My father **likes** his job. → My father **doesn't like** his job.

I **got** up early this morning. → I **didn't get** up early this morning.
They **worked** hard yesterday. → They **didn't work** hard yesterday.
We **played** tennis. → We **didn't play** tennis.
Diane **had** dinner with us. → Diane **didn't have** dinner with us.

don't . . .

Look! → **Don't look!**
Wait for me. → **Don't wait** for me.

Sometimes **do** is the main verb.

Do something! → **Don't do** anything!
Sue **does** a lot on weekends. → Sue **doesn't do** much on weekends.
I **did** what you said. → I **didn't do** what you said.

Simple Present Negative Unit 6   **Simple Past Negative** Unit 12
Don't! Unit 37   **Why isn't/don't . . . ?** Unit 45

Exercises

44.1 Make these sentences negative.

1. He's gone out. *He hasn't gone out.*
2. They're married. _____
3. I've had dinner. _____
4. It's cold today. _____
5. We'll be late. _____
6. You should go. _____

44.2 Make these sentences negative. Use *don't/doesn't/didn't*.

1. She saw me. *She didn't see me.*
2. I like cheese. _____
3. They understood. _____
4. He lives here. _____
5. Go away! _____
6. I did the dishes. _____

44.3 Make these sentences negative.

1. She can swim. *She can't swim.*
2. They've arrived. _____
3. I went to the bank. _____
4. He speaks Japanese. _____
5. We were angry. _____
6. He'll be pleased. _____
7. Call me tonight. _____
8. It rained yesterday. _____
9. I could hear them. _____
10. I have a camera. _____

44.4 Complete these sentences with a negative verb (*isn't/haven't/don't*, etc.).

1. They aren't rich. They *don't* _____ have much money.
2. "Would you like something to eat?" "No, thank you. I _____ hungry."
3. I _____ find my glasses. Have you seen them?
4. Eric _____ write letters very often. He prefers to use the phone.
5. We can walk to the station from here. It _____ very far.
6. "Where's Kim?" "I _____ know. I _____ seen her today."
7. Be careful! _____ fall!
8. I _____ have a ticket, so I couldn't go to the concert.
9. I've been to Japan many times, but I _____ been to Korea.
10. Julia _____ be here tomorrow. She's going away.
11. "Who broke that window?" "Not me. I _____ do it."
12. We didn't see what happened. We _____ looking at the time.

44.5

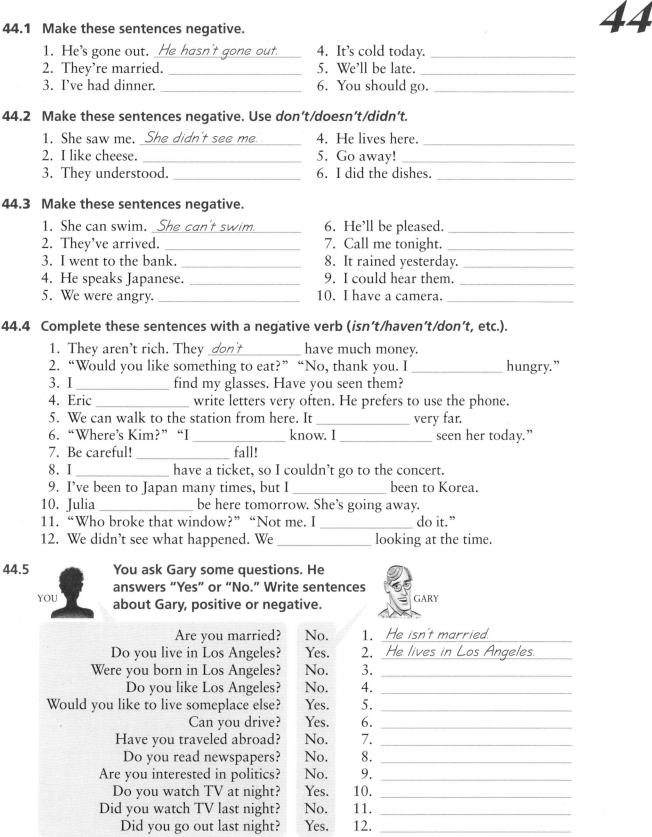

YOU

GARY

You ask Gary some questions. He answers "Yes" or "No." Write sentences about Gary, positive or negative.

Are you married?	No.	1. *He isn't married.*
Do you live in Los Angeles?	Yes.	2. *He lives in Los Angeles.*
Were you born in Los Angeles?	No.	3. _____
Do you like Los Angeles?	No.	4. _____
Would you like to live someplace else?	Yes.	5. _____
Can you drive?	Yes.	6. _____
Have you traveled abroad?	No.	7. _____
Do you read newspapers?	No.	8. _____
Are you interested in politics?	No.	9. _____
Do you watch TV at night?	Yes.	10. _____
Did you watch TV last night?	No.	11. _____
Did you go out last night?	Yes.	12. _____

Is it . . . ?, Have you . . . ?, Do they . . . ?, etc.

A

Positive | you | are | You are eating.

Question | are | you | Are you eating? What are you eating?

Positive subject + verb		Question verb + subject	
I	am late.	→	Am	I late?
That seat	is free.	→	Is	that seat free?
She	was angry.	→	Why was	she angry?
David	has gone out.	→	Where has	David gone?
You	have been to Japan.	→	Have	you been to Japan?
They	will be here soon.	→	When will	they be here?
Paula	can swim.	→	Can	Paula swim?

Be careful with word order – the *subject* is after the first *verb*.

- Where **has David** gone? (*not* Where has gone David?)
- **Are those people** waiting for something? (*not* Are waiting . . . ?)
- When **was the telephone** invented? (*not* When was invented . . . ?)

B

do . . . ? / does . . . ? / did . . . ?

Simple present questions	**do** I/we/you/they **does** he/she/it	**work/live/have** (etc.) . . . ?
Simple past questions	**did** you/she/they (etc.)	

Positive			Question	
They	**work** hard.	→	**Do** they	**work** hard?
You	**watch** television.	→	How often **do** you	**watch** television?
Chris	**has** a car.	→	**Does** Chris	**have** a car?
She	**gets up** early.	→	What time **does** she	**get** up?
They	**worked** hard.	→	**Did** they	**work** hard?
You	**had** dinner.	→	What **did** you	**have** for dinner?
She	**got** up early.	→	What time **did** she	**get** up?

Sometimes **do** is the *main verb* (do you **do** / did he **do**, etc.).

- What do you usually **do** on weekends?
- "What does your brother **do**?" "He works in a bank."
- "I broke my finger last week." "How did you **do** that?"

C

Why isn't . . . ? / Why don't . . . ?, etc. (Why + *negative*)

- Where's Pedro? **Why isn't he** here? (*not* Why he isn't here?)
- **Why can't Ratana** come to the meeting tomorrow? (*not* Why Ratana can't . . . ?)
- **Why didn't you** call me last night?

Simple Present Questions Unit 7 **Simple Past Questions** Unit 12
Questions Units 46–47 **What/which/how** . . . ? Units 48–49

Exercises

45.1 Write questions.

1. I can swim. (and you?) *Can you swim?*
2. I work hard. (and Jim?) *Does Jim work hard?*
3. I was late this morning. (and you?) _____
4. I've had lunch. (and Anne?) _____
5. I'll be here tomorrow. (and you?) _____
6. I'm going out tonight. (and Paul?) _____
7. I like my job. (and you?) _____
8. I live near here. (and Nicole?) _____
9. I enjoyed the movie. (and you?) _____
10. I had a nice vacation. (and you?) _____

45.2 You are talking to a friend about driving. Write the questions.

YOU

1. (have / a car?) *Do you have a car?* _____ Yes, I do.
2. (use / a lot?) _____ it _____ ? Yes, almost every day.
3. (use / yesterday?) _____ Yes, to go to work.
4. (enjoy driving?) _____ Not very much.
5. (a good driver?) _____ I think I am.
6. (ever / have / an accident?) _____ No, never.

45.3 Put the words in the right order. All the sentences are questions.

1. (has / gone / where / David?) *Where has David gone?*
2. (working / Rachel / is / today?) *Is Rachel working today?*
3. (the children / what / are / doing?) What _____ ?
4. (made / is / how / cheese?) _____
5. (to the party / coming / is / your sister?) _____
6. (you / the truth / tell / don't / why?) _____
7. (your guests / have / yet / arrived?) _____
8. (leave / what time / your plane / does?) _____
9. (your car / in the accident / was / damaged?) _____
10. (to work / Anne / why / go / didn't?) _____

45.4 Complete the questions.

1.	I want to go out.	Where *do you want to go*	?
2.	Al and Joe aren't going to the party.	Why *aren't they going*	?
3.	I'm reading.	What _____	?
4.	Sue went to bed early.	What time _____	?
5.	My parents are going on vacation.	When _____	?
6.	I saw Tom a few days ago.	Where _____	?
7.	I can't come to the party.	Why _____	?
8.	I need some money.	How much _____	?
9.	Angela doesn't like me.	Why _____	?
10.	It sometimes rains.	How often _____	?
11.	I did the shopping.	When _____	?

Who saw you?   Who did you see?

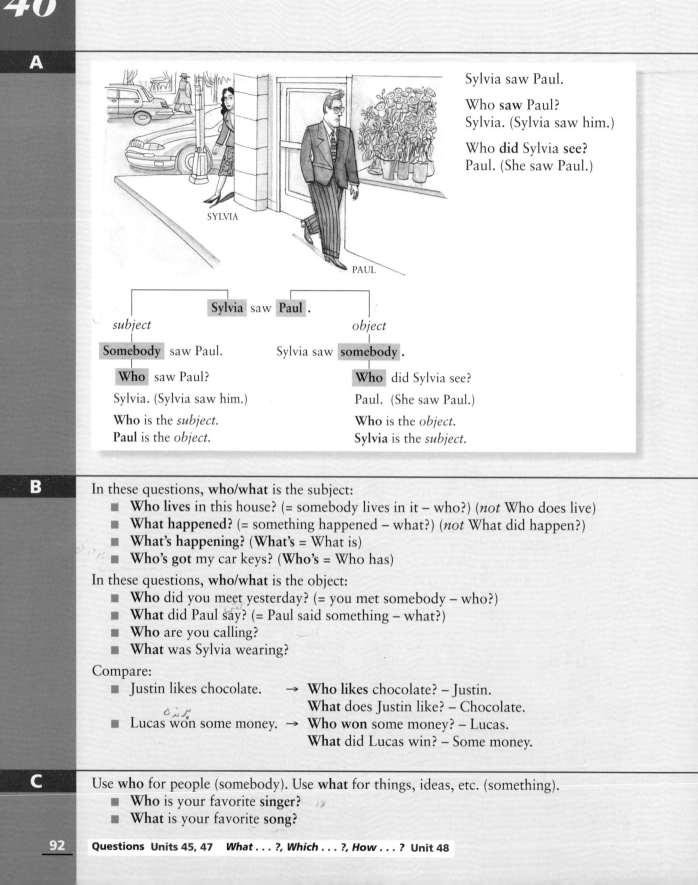

Sylvia saw Paul.

Who **saw** Paul?
Sylvia. (Sylvia saw him.)

Who **did** Sylvia **see?**
Paul. (She saw Paul.)

SYLVIA

PAUL

Sylvia saw **Paul** .

subject   *object*

Somebody saw Paul.   Sylvia saw **somebody** .

Who saw Paul?   **Who** did Sylvia see?

Sylvia. (Sylvia saw him.)   Paul. (She saw Paul.)

Who is the *subject*.   **Who** is the *object*.
Paul is the *object*.   **Sylvia** is the *subject*.

In these questions, **who/what** is the subject:
- **Who lives** in this house? (= somebody lives in it – who?) (*not* Who does live)
- **What happened?** (= something happened – what?) (*not* What did happen?)
- **What's happening?** (**What's** = What is)
- **Who's got** my car keys? (**Who's** = Who has)

In these questions, **who/what** is the object:
- **Who** did you meet yesterday? (= you met somebody – who?)
- **What** did Paul say? (= Paul said something – what?)
- **Who** are you calling?
- **What** was Sylvia wearing?

Compare:
- Justin likes chocolate.   → **Who likes** chocolate? – Justin.
                                What does Justin like? – Chocolate.
- Lucas won some money.   → **Who won** some money? – Lucas.
                                What did Lucas win? – Some money.

Use **who** for people (somebody). Use **what** for things, ideas, etc. (something).
- **Who** is your favorite **singer?**
- **What** is your favorite **song?**

Exercises

46.1 Write questions with *who* or *what*. In these questions, *who/what* is the subject.

1. Somebody broke the window.
2. Something fell off the shelf.
3. Somebody wants to see you.
4. Somebody took my umbrella.
5. Something made me sick.
6. Somebody is coming.

Who broke the window?
What _____ ?
_____ me?
_____
_____
_____

46.2 Write questions with *who* or *what* (subject or object).

1. I bought something.
2. Somebody lives in this house.
3. I called somebody.
4. Something happened last night.
5. Somebody knows the answer.
6. Somebody did the dishes.
7. Jane did something.
8. Something woke me up.
9. Somebody saw the accident.
10. I saw somebody.
11. Somebody has my pen.
12. This word means something.

What did you buy?
Who lives in this house?
_____
_____
_____
_____
_____
_____
_____
_____
_____
_____

46.3 You want the missing information (XXXXX). Write questions with *who* or *what*.

1. I lost XXXXX yesterday, but fortunately XXXXX found it and gave it back to me.

2. XXXXX called me last night. She wanted XXXXX.

3. I needed some advice, so I asked XXXXX. He said XXXXX.

4. I hear that XXXXX got married last week. XXXXX told me.

5. I met XXXXX on my way home tonight. She told me XXXXX.

6. Steve and I played tennis yesterday. XXXXX won. After the game, we XXXXX.

7. It was my birthday last week, and I got some presents. XXXXX gave me a book, and Catherine gave me XXXXX.

What did you lose?
Who found it?
_____
_____
_____
_____
_____
_____
_____
_____
_____
_____
_____
_____

Who is she talking to?   What is it like?

A

JULIA

Julia is talking to somebody.

Who is she talking to ?
|
preposition

In questions beginning **Who** . . . ? / **What** . . . ? /
Where . . . ? / **Which** . . . ?, *prepositions*
(**to/from/with**, etc.) usually go at the end.

- "**Where** are you **from?**" "I'm from Thailand."
- "John was afraid." "**What** was he afraid **of?**"
- "**Who** do these books belong **to?**" "They're mine."
- "Tom's father is in the hospital." "**Which hospital** is he **in?**"
- "Kate is going on vacation." "**Who** is she going **with?**"
- "Can we talk?" "Sure. **What** do you want to talk **about?**"

B

What's it like? / What are they like?, etc.

What's your new house like?

It's big.

What's it like? = What **is** it like?

What's it like? = tell me
something about it (is it good
or bad?, big or small?, old or
new?, etc.)

When we say, "What is it like?," **like** is a *preposition*.
It is not the *verb* **like**. (Do you **like** your new house?)

- A: There's a new restaurant near my
  house.
  B: **What's** it **like?** Is it good?
  A: I don't know. I haven't eaten there yet.

- A: **What's** your new teacher **like?**
  B: She's really good. We learn a lot.

- A: I met Nicole's parents yesterday.
  B: You did? **What** are they **like?**
  A: They're very nice.

- A: Did you have a good vacation?
  What was the weather **like?**
  B: It was great. It was sunny every day.

Exercises

47.1 You want the missing information (XXXXX). Write questions with *Who* or *What*.

1. The letter is from XXXXX.
2. I'm looking for a XXXXX.
3. I went to the movies with XXXXX.
4. The movie was about XXXXX.
5. I gave the money to XXXXX.
6. The book was written by XXXXX.

Who is the letter from?
What _are_ you _____ ?
_____
_____
_____
_____

47.2 Complete the questions about the pictures. Use one of these verbs + a preposition:

listen   look   ~~talk~~   talk   wait   write

4 It was very good.

Yes, very interesting.

5

6 BUS 10 32

1. Who *is she talking to* ?
2. What _____ ?
3. Who _____ ?
4. What _____ ?
5. What _____ ?
6. Which bus _____ ?

47.3 Write questions with *Which*.

1. Tom's father is in the hospital.
2. We stayed at a hotel.
3. Jack belongs to a tennis club.
4. I went to high school in this town.

Which hospital is he in?
_____ you _____ ?
_____
_____

47.4 You want some information about another country. You ask somebody who has been there. Ask questions with *What is/are . . . like?*

1. (the roads) *What are the roads like?*
2. (the food) _____
3. (the people) _____
4. (the weather) _____

47.5 Ask questions with *What was/were . . . like?*

1. Your friend has just come back from a trip. Ask about the weather.
   What was the weather like?
2. Your friend has just come back from the movies. Ask about the movie.
   _____
3. Your friend has just finished a computer course. Ask about the classes.
   _____
4. Your friend has just come back from a business trip. Ask about the hotel.
   _____

UNIT 48

What . . . ?, Which . . . ?, and How . . . ? α

A

what + *noun* (**What color** . . . ? / **What kind** . . . ?, etc.)

- **What color** is your car?
- **What size** is this shirt?
- **What day** is it today?
- **What kind** of job do you want? (*or* **What type** of job . . . ?)

- **What color** are your eyes?
- **What nationality** is she?
- **What time** is it?

what without a noun

- **What's** your favorite color?
- **What** do you want to do tonight?

B

which + noun (things or people)

- **Which train** did you catch – the 9:50 or the 10:30?
- **Which doctor** did you see – Doctor Vega, Doctor Gray, or Doctor Hill?

We use **which** without a noun for things, not people.

- **Which** is bigger – Canada or Australia?

We use **who** for people (without a noun).

- **Who** is taller – Bill or Sam? (*not* Which is taller?)

C

What or which?

We use **which** when we are thinking about a small number of possibilities (perhaps two, three, or four).

- We can go this way or that way. **Which way** should we go?
- There are four umbrellas here. **Which** is yours?

What is more general.

- **What** is the capital of Argentina? (of all the cities in Argentina)
- **What kind** of music do you like? (of all kinds of music)

Compare:

- **What color** are his eyes? (*not* Which color . . . ?)
  Which color do you prefer, **pink** or **yellow**?
- **What** is the longest river in the world?
  Which is the longest river – **the Mississippi, the Amazon,** or **the Nile**?

? or **?** or **?** or **?**
Which?

D

How . . . ?

- "**How** was the party last night?" "It was great."
- "**How** do you usually get to work?" "By bus."

You can use **how** + *adjective/adverb* (**how tall** / **how old** / **how often,** etc.).

	tall are you?" "I'm five feet 10."(five feet 10 inches *or* one meter 70)
	big is the house?" "Not very big."
	old is your mother?" "She's 45."
"**How**	**far** is it from here to the airport?" "Ten miles." (about 17 kilometers)
	often do you use your car?" "Every day."
	long have they been married?" "Ten years."
	much was the taxi?" "Ten dollars."

Questions Units 45–47   *How long does it take . . . ?* Unit 49   *Which one(s)?* Unit 76

Exercises

48.1 Write questions with *What . . . ?*

1. This shirt is nice.   (size) _What size is it?_
2. I want a job.   (kind) _What kind of job do you want?_
3. I've got a new sweater.   (color) What _____ ?
4. I got up early this morning.   (time) _____ get up?
5. I like music.   (type) _____
6. I want to buy a car.   (kind) _____

48.2 Complete the questions. Use *Which . . . ?*

1. _Which way_ should we go?
2. _____ is yours?
3. _____ do you want to see?
4. _____ goes to the museum?

48.3 Write *What, Which,* or *Who.*

1. _What_ is that man's name?
2. _Which_ way is it? Left or right?
3. Tea or coffee? _____ do you prefer?
4. "_____ day is it today?" "Friday."
5. This is a nice office.
   _____ desk is yours?
6. _____ is your favorite sport?
7. _____ is cheaper, meat or fish?
8. _____ is older, Anne or Justin?
9. _____ kind of camera do you have?
10. *A:* Mary has three cameras.
    B: _____ camera does she use most?

48.4 Complete the questions with *How* + adjective or adverb (*How high, How long,* etc.).

1. _How high_ is Mount Everest?   Almost 9,000 meters.
2. _____ is it to the station?   About two miles.
3. _____ is Sarah?   She's 26.
4. _____ do the buses run?   Every ten minutes.
5. _____ is the water in the pool?   Two meters.
6. _____ have you lived here?   Almost three years.

48.5 Write questions with *How . . . ?*

1. Are you five feet nine? Five feet ten? Five feet eleven? _How tall are you?_
2. Is this box one kilogram? Two? Three? _____
3. Are you 20 years old? 21? 22? _____
4. Did you spend $10? $15? $20? _____
5. Do you watch TV every day? Once a week? Never?

   _____
6. Is it 2,000 miles from New York to Los Angeles? 2,500? 3,000?

   _____

How long does it take . . . ?

A

How long **does it take to get from . . . to . . . ?**

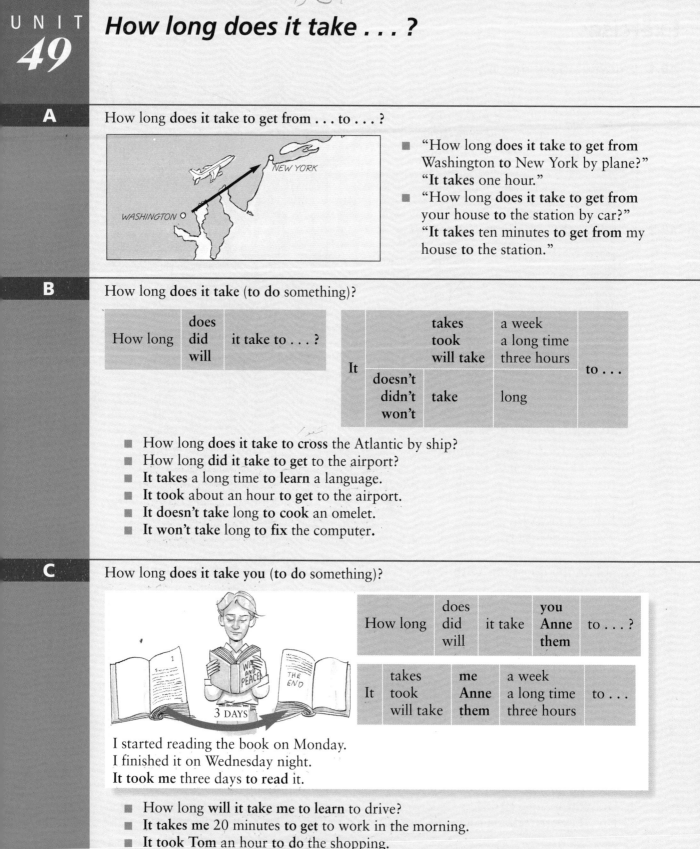

- "How long **does it take to get from** Washington **to** New York by plane?"
  "**It takes** one hour."
- "How long **does it take to get from** your house **to** the station by car?"
  "**It takes** ten minutes **to get from** my house **to** the station."

B

How long **does it take (to do** something)?

How long	does did will	it take to . . . ?

It	takes took will take	a week a long time three hours	to . . .
	doesn't didn't won't	take	long	

- How long **does it take to cross** the Atlantic by ship?
- How long **did it take to get** to the airport?
- **It takes** a long time **to learn** a language.
- **It took** about an hour **to get** to the airport.
- **It doesn't take** long **to cook** an omelet.
- **It won't take** long **to fix** the computer.

C

How long **does it take you (to do** something)?

How long	does did will	it take	**you** **Anne** **them**	to . . . ?

It	takes took will take	**me** **Anne** **them**	a week a long time three hours	to . . .

I started reading the book on Monday.
I finished it on Wednesday night.
It took me three days **to read** it.

- How long **will it take me to learn** to drive?
- **It takes me** 20 minutes **to get** to work in the morning.
- **It took Tom** an hour **to do** the shopping.
- **Did it take you** a long time **to find** a job?
- **It will take us** an hour **to cook** dinner.

Exercises

49.1 Look at the pictures and write questions with *How long . . . ?*

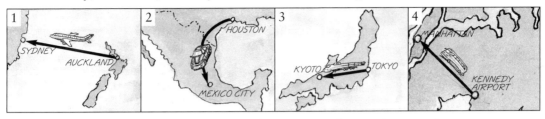

1. _How long does it take to get from Auckland to Sydney by plane?_
2. _____
3. _____
4. _____

49.2 How long does it take to do these things? Write full sentences.

1. fly from your city/country to New York
   It takes a day to fly from Tokyo to New York.
2. fly from your city/country to Australia
   _____
3. become a doctor in your country
   _____
4. walk from your house to the nearest school
   _____
5. get from your house to the nearest airport
   _____

49.3 Write questions with *How long did it take . . . ?*

1. She found a place to live. _How long did it take her to find a place to live?_
2. I walked to the station. _____ you _____ ?
3. He washed the windows. _____
4. I learned to ski. _____
5. They repaired the car. _____

49.4 Read the situations and write sentences with *It took . . . .*

1. I read a book last week. I started reading it on Monday. I finished it three days later.
   It took me three days to read the book.
2. We walked home last night. We left at 10 o'clock, and we got home at 10:20.
   _____
3. I learned to fly last year. I had my first flying lesson in January. I got my pilot's license nine months later.
   _____
4. Mark drove to Houston yesterday. He left home at eight o'clock and got to Houston at 10:00.
   _____
5. Nicole began looking for a job a long time ago. She found a job last week.
   _____
6. (Now write a true sentence about yourself.)
   _____

Do you know where . . . ?,
I don't know what . . . , etc.

A

Do you know where Paula is?

We say: Where **is** Paula?

but: **Do you know** where Paula **is** ?
(*not* Do you know where is Paula?)

In the same way we say:
I know where **Paula is.**
I don't know where **Paula is.**
Can you tell me where **Paula is?**

Compare:

Who **are those people?**		
How old **is Nicole?**		
What time **is it?**		
Where **can I go?**		
How much **is this camera?**		
When **are you** leaving town?		
Where **have they** gone?		
What **was Dawn** wearing?		

but

Do you know	who **those people are**	?
Can you tell me	how old **Nicole is**	
	what time **it is**	
	where **I can** go	
I know	how much **this camera is**	
I don't know	when **you're** leaving town	.
I don't remember	where **they've** gone	
	what **Dawn was** wearing	

B

Questions with **do/does/did** (*simple present* and *simple past*)

Where **does he live** ?

Do you know where **he lives** ? (*not* Do you know where does he live?)

Compare:

How **do airplanes** fly?		
What **does Jessica** want?		
Why **did she** go home?		
Where **did I** put the key?		

but

Do you know	how **airplanes fly**	?
I don't know	what **Jessica wants**	
I don't remember	why **she went** home	.
I know	where **I put** the key	

C

Questions beginning **Is . . . ?** / **Do . . . ?** / **Can . . . ?**, etc. (*yes/no questions*)

Compare:

Is Jack at home?		
Have they left yet?		
Can Brian swim?		
Do they live near here?		
Did anybody see you?		

but

Do you know	**if**	**Jack is** at home	?
	or	**they've** left yet	
I don't know	**whether**	**Brian can** swim	.
		they live near here	
		anybody saw you	

You can use **if** or **whether** in these sentences:

■ Do you know **if** they've got a car? *or* Do you know **whether** they've got a car?
■ I don't know **if** he's married. *or* I don't know **whether** he's married.

Exercises

50.1 Answer these questions with *I don't know where/when/why . . .*, etc.

1. Have your friends gone home?   (where) *I don't know where they've gone.*
2. Is Kate in her office?   (where) I don't know _____.
3. Is the building very old?   (how old) _____
4. Will Paul be here soon?   (when) _____
5. Was he angry because I was late?   (why) _____
6. Has Mary lived here a long time?   (how long) _____

50.2 Complete the sentences.

1. (How do airplanes fly?) Do you know *how airplanes fly* ?
2. (Where does Susan work?) I don't know _____.
3. (What did Peter say?) Do you remember _____?
4. (Why did he go home early?) I don't know _____.
5. (What time does the meeting begin?) Do you know _____?
6. (How did the accident happen?) I don't remember _____.

50.3 Which is right?

1. Do you know what time is it / it is? (*it is* is right)
2. Why are you / you are leaving?
3. I don't know where are they / they are going.
4. Can you tell me where is the museum / the museum is?
5. Where do you want / you want to go for vacation?
6. Do you know what do elephants eat / elephants eat?

50.4 Write questions with *Do you know if . . . ?*

1. (Have they got a car?) *Do you know if they've got a car?*
2. (Are they married?) Do you know _____?
3. (Does Sue know Bill?) _____
4. (Will Justin be here tomorrow?) _____
5. (Did he pass his exam?) _____

50.5 Write questions beginning with *Do you know . . . ?*

1. (What does Tomiko want?) *Do you know what Tomiko wants?*
2. (Where is Lynn?) Do _____?
3. (Is she working today?) _____
4. (What time does she start work?) _____
5. (Are the banks open tomorrow?) _____
6. (Where do Sarah and Tim live?) _____
7. (Did they go to Ji Yoo's party?) _____

50.6 Use your own ideas to complete these sentences.

1. Do you know why *the train was late* ?
2. Do you know what time _____?
3. Excuse me, can you tell me where _____?
4. I don't know what _____?
5. Do you know if _____?

She said that . . .   He told me that . . .

Last week you went to a party. A lot of your friends were there. Here are some things they said to you.

Today you meet Paul. You tell him about the party. You tell Paul what your friends said.

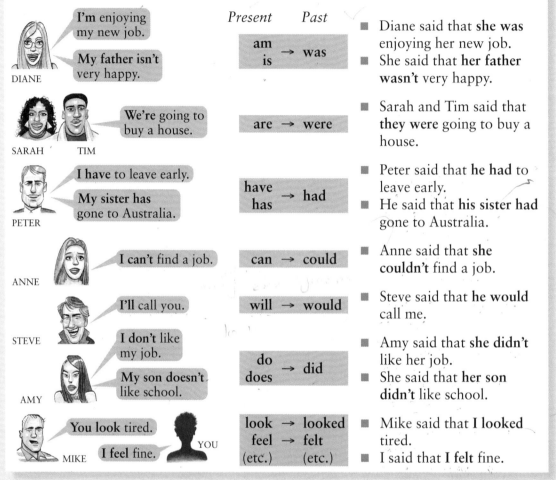

Present		Past
am is	→	was
are	→	were
have has	→	had
can	→	could
will	→	would
do does	→	did
look feel (etc.)	→	looked felt (etc.)

DIANE — I'm enjoying my new job. / My father isn't very happy.

SARAH TIM — We're going to buy a house.

PETER — I have to leave early. / My sister has gone to Australia.

ANNE — I can't find a job.

STEVE — I'll call you.

AMY — I don't like my job. / My son doesn't like school.

MIKE — You look tired. YOU — I feel fine.

- Diane said that **she was** enjoying her new job.
- She said that **her father wasn't** very happy.

- Sarah and Tim said that **they were** going to buy a house.

- Peter said that **he had** to leave early.
- He said that **his sister had** gone to Australia.

- Anne said that **she couldn't** find a job.

- Steve said that **he would** call me.

- Amy said that **she didn't** like her job.
- She said that **her son didn't** like school.

- Mike said that **I looked** tired.
- I said that **I felt** fine.

say and **tell**

say (→ **said**)
- He **said** that he was tired.
  (*not* He said me)
- What did she **say to** you? (*not* say you)

Do not say: "he said me," "I said Anne," etc.

tell (→ **told**)
- He **told me** that he was tired.
  (*not* He told that . . .)
- What did she **tell you**? (*not* tell to you)

Do not say: "he told to me," "I told to Anne," etc.

You can say:
- He said **that** he was tired. *or* He said he was tired. (*without* that)
- Amy told me **that** she didn't like her job. *or* Amy told me she didn't like her job.

Exercises

51.1 Read what these people say and write sentences with *He/She/They said (that)* . . . .

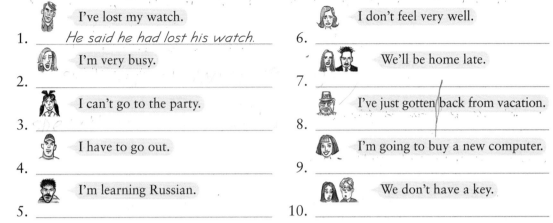

1. ___He said he had lost his watch.___ *(I've lost my watch.)*
2. _____ *(I'm very busy.)*
3. _____ *(I can't go to the party.)*
4. _____ *(I have to go out.)*
5. _____ *(I'm learning Russian.)*

6. _____ *(I don't feel very well.)*
7. _____ *(We'll be home late.)*
8. _____ *(I've just gotten back from vacation.)*
9. _____ *(I'm going to buy a new computer.)*
10. _____ *(We don't have a key.)*

51.2 Use the pictures to complete the sentences.

1. I saw Diane last week. She said ___she was enjoying her new job___ .
2. Emily didn't want anything to eat. She said _____ .
3. I wanted to borrow Don's ladder but he said _____ .
4. Hannah was invited to the party but she said _____ .
5. Sharon told me she didn't want the picture. She said _____ .
6. Mark just left on vacation. He said _____ .
7. I was looking for Robert. Nicole said _____ .
8. "Why did Jiro stay home?" "He said _____ ."
9. "Has Mary gone out?" "I think so. She said _____ ."

51.3 Write *say/said* or *tell/told*.

1. He _say__ he was tired.
2. What did she _tell__ you?
3. Anne _____ she didn't like Peter.
4. Jack _____ me that you were sick.
5. Please don't _____ Jim what happened.
6. Did Pat _____ she would be late?
7. The woman _____ she was a reporter.
8. The woman _____ us she was a reporter.
9. They asked me a lot of questions, but I didn't _____ them anything.
10. They asked me a lot of questions, but I didn't _____ anything.

Work/working, go/going, do/doing

work/go/be, etc. *(base form)*

We use the base form with will/can/must, etc.

will	■ Amy **will be** here soon.	} (see Units 28–29)
shall	■ **Shall** I **open** the window?	
might	■ I **might call** you later.	} (see Unit 30)
may	■ **May** I **sit** here?	
can	■ I **can't meet** you tomorrow.	} (see Unit 31)
could	■ **Could** you **pass** the salt, please?	
must	■ It's late. You **must be** tired.	(see Unit 32)
should	■ You **shouldn't work** so hard.	(see Unit 33)
would	■ **Would** you **like** some coffee?	(see Unit 35)

We use the base form with do/does and did.

do/does *(simple present)*	■ **Do** you **work?**	(see Units 6–7)
	■ They **don't work** very hard.	
	■ Elena **doesn't know** many people.	
	■ How much **does** it **cost?**	
did *(simple past)*	■ What time **did** the train **leave?**	(see Unit 12)
	■ We **didn't sleep** well.	

To work / to go / to be, etc. *(infinitive)*

(I'm) going to . . .	■ I'm **going to play** tennis tomorrow.	(see Unit 27)
	■ What **are** you **going to do?**	
(I) have to . . .	■ I **have to go** now.	(see Unit 34)
	■ Everybody **has to eat.**	
(I) want to . . .	■ Do you **want to go** out?	(see Unit 51)
	■ They don't **want to come** with us.	
(I) would like to . . .	■ I'd **like to talk** to you.	(see Unit 35)
	■ **Would** you **like to go** out?	
(I) used to . . .	■ Dave **used to work** in a factory.	(see Unit 25)

Working/going/playing, etc.

am/is/are + -ing *(present continuous)*	■ Please be quiet. I'm **working.**	(see Units 3–4, 8, 26)
	■ Tom **isn't working** today.	
	■ What time **are** you **going** out?	
was/were + -ing *(past continuous)*	■ It **was raining**, so we didn't go out.	(see Units 13–14)
	■ What **were** you **doing** when the phone rang?	

Verbs + *to* . . . and *-ing (I want to do / I enjoy doing)* Unit 53   *Go + -ing* Unit 56

Exercises

52.1 Complete the sentences. Write: *call Paul* or *to call Paul.*

1. I'll _call Paul_ .
2. I'm going _to call Paul_ .
3. You can _____ .
4. Shall I _____ ?
5. I'd like _____ .
6. Do you have _____ ?
7. You should _____ .
8. I want _____ .
9. I might _____ .
10. Could you _____ ?

52.2 Complete the sentences with a verb from the list. Sometimes you need the base form (*work, go,* etc.) and sometimes you need *-ing* (*working, going,* etc.).

do / doing	get / getting	~~sleep / sleeping~~	watch / watching
eat / eating	go / going	stay / staying	wear / wearing
fly / flying	listen / listening	wait / waiting	~~work / working~~

1. Please be quiet. I'm _working_ .
2. I feel tired today. I didn't _sleep_ very well last night.
3. What time do you usually _____ up in the morning?
4. "Where are you _____ ?" "To the bank."
5. Did you _____ television last night?
6. Look at that plane! It's _____ very low.
7. You can turn off the radio. I'm not _____ to it.
8. They didn't _____ anything because they weren't hungry.
9. My friends were _____ for me when I arrived.
10. "Does Sharon always _____ glasses?" "No, only for reading."
11. "What are you _____ tonight?" "I'm _____ home."

52.3 Put the verb in the correct form. Choose the base form (*work/go,* etc.), the infinitive (*to work / to go,* etc.), or *-ing* (*working/going,* etc.).

1. Shall I _open_ the window? (open)
2. It's late. I have _to go_ now. (go)
3. Amy isn't _working_ this week. She's on vacation. (work)
4. I'm tired. I don't want _____ out. (go)
5. It might _____ . Take an umbrella with you. (rain)
6. What time do you have _____ tomorrow morning? (leave)
7. I'm sorry I can't _____ you. (help)
8. My brother is a student. He's _____ physics. (study)
9. Would you like _____ on a trip around the world? (go)
10. When you saw Chol Su, what was he _____ ? (wear)
11. When you go to London, where are you going _____ ? (stay)
12. It's cold, but Carlos isn't wearing a jacket. He must _____ cold. (be)
13. "Where's Eric?" "He's _____ a bath." (take)
14. I used _____ a car, but I sold it last year. (have)
15. He spoke very quietly. I couldn't _____ him. (hear)
16. You don't look well. I don't think you should _____ to work today. (go)
17. I don't know what he said. I wasn't _____ to him. (listen)
18. I'm sorry I'm late. I had _____ a phone call. (make)
19. Medical students must _____ courses in biology and chemistry. (take)
20. May I please _____ your phone? (use)

To . . . (I want to do) and -ing (I enjoy doing)

A   *Verbs* + **to** . . . (I want to do)

want	plan	decide	try	
hope	expect	offer	forget	+ **to** . . . (to do / to work / to be, etc.)
need	promise	refuse	learn	

- What do you **want to do** tonight?
- It's not very late. We don't **need to go** home yet.
- Tina has **decided to sell** her house.
- You **forgot to turn** off the light when you went out.
- My brother is **learning to drive**.
- I **tried to read** my book, but I was too tired.

B   *Verbs* + **-ing** (I enjoy doing)

enjoy	stop	suggest	
mind	finish		+ **-ing** (doing / working / being, etc.)

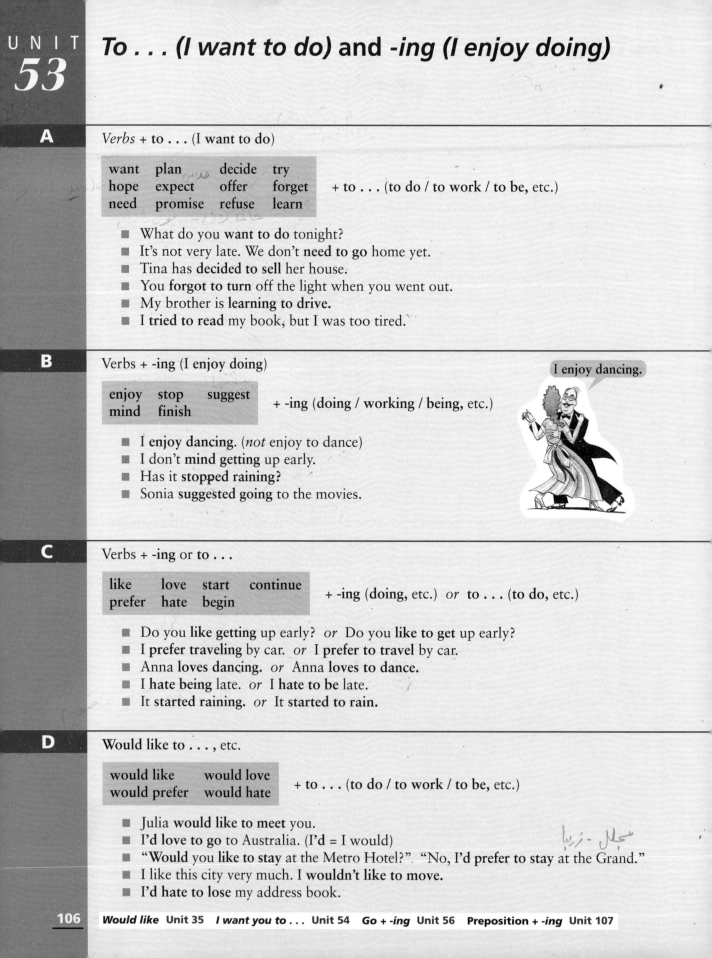

I enjoy dancing.

- I **enjoy dancing**. (*not* enjoy to dance)
- I don't **mind getting** up early.
- Has it **stopped raining**?
- Sonia **suggested going** to the movies.

C   *Verbs* + **-ing** or **to** . . .

like	love	start	continue	
prefer	hate	begin		+ **-ing** (doing, etc.) *or* **to** . . . (to do, etc.)

- Do you **like getting** up early? *or* Do you **like to get** up early?
- I **prefer traveling** by car. *or* I **prefer to travel** by car.
- Anna **loves dancing**. *or* Anna **loves to dance**.
- I **hate being** late. *or* I **hate to be** late.
- It **started raining**. *or* It **started to rain**.

D   Would like to . . . , etc.

would like	would love	
would prefer	would hate	+ **to** . . . (to do / to work / to be, etc.)

- Julia **would like to meet** you.
- I'd **love to go** to Australia. (I'd = I would)
- "**Would** you **like to stay** at the Metro Hotel?" "No, I'd **prefer to stay** at the Grand."
- I like this city very much. I **wouldn't like to move**.
- I'd **hate to lose** my address book.

Would like **Unit 35**   ***I want you to*** **. . . Unit 54**   ***Go*** **+ -ing Unit 56**   **Preposition + -ing Unit 107**

Exercises

53.1 Put the verb in the right form – *to* . . . or *-ing.*

1. I enjoy *dancing* . (dance)
2. What do you want *to do* tonight? (do)
3. Goodbye! I hope _____ you again soon. (see)
4. I learned *to* _____ when I was five years old. (swim)
5. Have you finished _____ the kitchen? (clean)
6. I'm tired. I want _____ to bed. (go)
7. Do you enjoy _____ other countries? (visit)
8. The weather was nice, so I suggested _____ for a walk by the river. (go)
9. Where's Bill? He promised _____ here on time. (be)
10. I'm not in a hurry. I don't mind _____. (wait)
11. What have you decided *to do* ? (do)
12. Eric was very angry and refused _____ to me. (speak)
13. Where's Anna? I need _____ her something. (ask)
14. They were very upset and started _____. (cry)
15. I'm trying _____. (work) Please stop _____. (talk)

53.2 Complete the sentences with *to* . . . or *-ing.* Use one of these verbs:

cook   go   help   lose   ~~meet~~   rain   read   see   send   wait   walk   watch

1. Julia would like *to meet* you.
2. Nicole has a lot of books. She enjoys _____.
3. I'm surprised that you're here. I didn't expect _____ you.
4. Don't forget _____ us a postcard when you're on vacation.
5. "Should we take a taxi to the restaurant?" "If you want, but it isn't far. I don't mind _____."
6. This ring was my grandmother's. I'd hate _____ it.
7. Rita had a lot to do, so I offered _____ her.
8. What should we do this afternoon? Would you like _____ to the beach?
9. When I'm tired in the evening, I like _____ television.
10. "Do you want to go now?" "No, I'd prefer _____ a few minutes."
11. I'm not going out until it stops _____.
12. Dinner is going to be late. I just started _____.

53.3 Read the questions and complete the answers.

1. Do you usually get up early ?
2. Do you ever go to museums?
3. Do you write letters often?
4. Have you ever been to Rome?
5. Do you ever travel by train?
6. Do you want to eat at home or go to a restaurant?

Yes, I like *getting up early* OR *to get up early* .
Yes, I love _____.
No, I don't like _____.
No, but I'd love _____ sometime.
Yes, I enjoy _____.
I don't mind _____ a restaurant, but I'd prefer _____ home.

53.4 Complete these sentences. Write about yourself. Use *to* . . . or *-ing.*

1. I enjoy _____.
2. I don't like _____.
3. If it's a nice day tomorrow, I'd like _____.
4. When I'm on vacation, I like _____.
5. I don't mind _____, but _____.
6. I wouldn't like _____.

I want you to . . . and *I told you to . . .*

A

I want you to . . .

The woman **wants to leave.**

The man **doesn't want** the woman **to leave.**
He **wants** her **to stay.**

We say:

I want	you somebody Anne	to do something

- **I want you to be** happy. (*not* I want that you are happy)
- They didn't **want anybody to know** their secret.
- Do you **want me to lend** you some money?

We use **would like** in the same way.
- **Would** you **like me to lend** you some money?

B

We also use this structure (*verb* + somebody + **to** . . .) with:

	verb	+	somebody + **to** . . .		

ask		Sue	**asked**	a friend	**to lend**	her some money.
tell		I	**told**	you	**to be**	careful. تَ دِقَت
advise		What do you	**advise**	me	**to do?**	
expect		I didn't	**expect**	them	**to be**	here. اينما
persuade		We	**persuaded**	Eric	**to come**	with us.
teach		I	**am teaching**	my brother	**to swim.**	

C

I told you **to . . . / I told** you **not to . . .**

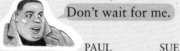

ANNE   ME

Anne **told** me **to wait** for her.

PAUL   SUE

Paul **told** Sue **not to wait** for him.

D

make and **let**

After **make** and **let,** we do not use **to.**
- He's very funny. He **makes** me **laugh.** (*not* makes me to laugh)
- At school our teachers **made** us **work** very hard.
- Ada **let** me **use** her computer because mine wasn't working. (*not* let me to use)

You can say **Let's . . .** (= **Let us**) when you want people to do things with you.
- Come on! **Let's dance.**
- "Do you want to go out tonight?" "No, I'm tired. **Let's stay** home."

He told me that . . . **Unit 51**

Exercises

54.1 Write sentences beginning *I want you … / I don't want you … / Do you want me …?*

1. (you have to come with me) *I want you to come with me.*
2. (listen carefully) I want _____.
3. (please don't be angry) I don't _____.
4. (shall I wait for you?) Do you _____.
5. (don't call me tonight) _____ call me _____
6. (you should meet Sarah) _____

54.2 Look at the pictures and complete the sentences.

1. Brian was sick. I advised *him to see a doctor* _____.
2. I wanted to get to the station. A woman told _____.
3. Linda had a lot of luggage. She asked _____.
4. Sue is going to call later. I told _____.
5. I wanted to make a phone call. Yoshi let _____.
6. Lee's mother taught _____.

54.3 Complete these sentences with the verbs in the list. Sometimes *to* is necessary
(*to go / to wait*, etc.); sometimes *to* is not necessary (*go/wait*, etc.).

arrive   borrow   get   go   ~~leave~~   make   repeat   tell   think   wait

1. Please stay! I don't want you *to leave* _____ yet.
2. I didn't hear what she said, so I asked her _____ it.
3. "Should we begin?" "No, let's _____ a few minutes."
4. Are they already here? I expected them _____ much later.
5. Kevin's parents didn't want him _____ married.
6. I want to stay here. You can't make me _____ with you.
7. "Is that your bicycle?" "No, it's John's. He let me _____ it."
8. Mika can't come to the party. She told me _____ you.
9. Do you want something to drink? Would you like me _____ some coffee?
10. "Achara doesn't like me." "What makes you _____ that?"

I went to the store to . . .

A

Kelly wanted a newspaper, so she went to the store.

Why did she go to the store? **To buy** a newspaper.

She went to the store **to buy** a newspaper.

To . . . (**to buy** / **to see**, etc.) tells us *why* a person does something.

- "Why are you going out?" "**To get** some bread."
- Amy went to the airport **to meet** her friend.
- Fu Chen turned on the television **to watch** the news.
- I'd like to go to Mexico **to learn** Spanish.

money/time to (do something)

- We need some **money to buy** food.
- I don't have **time to watch** television.

B

to . . . and **for . . .**

to + *verb* (**to buy** / **to see**, etc.)	**for +** *noun* (**for a newspaper** / **for food**, etc.)
■ I went to the store **to buy** a newspaper. (*not* for buy)	■ I went to the store **for a newspaper**.
■ They're going to Brazil **to see** their friends.	■ They're going to Brazil **for a holiday**.
■ We need some money **to buy** food.	■ We need some money **for food**.

C

wait for . . .

- Please **wait for me**.
- Are you **waiting for the bus**?

wait to (do something)

- I'm **waiting to talk** to the manager.
- Are you **waiting to see** the doctor?

wait for (somebody/something) **to . . .**

- I can't leave yet. I'm **waiting for John to call**.
- Are you **waiting for the mail to come**?

I can't leave yet. I'm waiting for John to call.

Go to . . . , go for . . . Unit 56   *Something to eat / nothing to do*, etc. Unit 80
Enough to/for . . . Unit 92   *Too . . . to/for . . .* Unit 93

Exercises

55.1 Write sentences beginning *I went to . . . .* Choose from the boxes.

~~the station~~	the post office
a coffee shop	the supermarket

buy some food	get some stamps
~~catch a train~~	meet a friend

1. *I went to the station to catch a train.*
2. I went _____ .
3. _____
4. _____

55.2 Finish the sentences. Choose from the box.

to open this door	to wake him up	to see who it was
~~to watch the news~~	to read the newspaper	to get some fresh air

1. I turned on the television *to watch the news* _____ .
2. Alice sat down in an armchair _____ .
3. Do I need a key _____ ?
4. I went for a walk by the river _____ .
5. Dave was sleeping. I knocked on his door _____ .
6. The doorbell rang, so I looked out the window _____ .

55.3 Use your own ideas to finish these sentences. Use *to . . . .*

1. I went to the store *to buy a newspaper* _____ .
2. I'm very busy. I haven't got time _____ .
3. I called Amy _____ .
4. I'm going out _____ .
5. I borrowed some money _____ .

55.4 Write *to* or *for.*

1. Ampol went to the store *to* buy some bread.
2. We went to a restaurant _____ have dinner.
3. Robert wants to go to college _____ study economics.
4. I'm going to Toronto _____ an interview next week.
5. I'm going to Vancouver _____ visit some friends of mine.
6. Do you have time _____ a cup of coffee?
7. I was late this morning. I didn't have time _____ comb my hair.
8. Everybody needs money _____ live.
9. My office is very small. There's only enough room _____ a desk and a chair.
10. *A:* Excuse me, are you waiting _____ use the phone?
    B: No, I'm waiting _____ somebody.

55.5 Finish these sentences. Choose from the list:

~~John / call~~   it / to arrive   you / tell me   the film / begin

1. I can't leave yet. I'm waiting *for John to call* _____ .
2. I sat down in the movie theater and waited _____ .
3. We called an ambulance and waited _____ .
4. "Do you know what to do?" "No, I'm waiting _____ ."

Go to . . .   go on . . .   go for . . .   go -ing

A

go to . . . (go to work / go to San Francisco / go to a concert, etc.)

- ■ What time do you usually **go to work**?
- ■ I'm **going to China** next week.
- ■ Tom didn't want to **go to the concert**.
- ■ What time did you **go to bed** last night?
- ■ I **went to the dentist** last week.

go to →

go home (without to)

- ■ I'm **going home** now. (*not* going to home)

B

go on . . .

go on	a trip
	a tour
	an excursion
	a cruise
	vacation
	strike

- ■ Children often **go on school trips**.
- ■ When we were in Egypt, we **went on a tour** of the Pyramids.
- ■ We're **going on vacation** next week.
- ■ Last year I **went** to Costa Rica **on vacation**.
- ■ The workers have **gone on strike**. (= they are refusing to work)

C

go for . . .

go (somewhere) for	a walk
	a run
	a swim
	lunch, dinner, etc.

- ■ "Where's John?" "He **went for a walk**."
- ■ Did you **go for a run** this morning?
- ■ The water looks nice. Let's **go for a swim**.
- ■ Should we **go out for dinner**? I know a good restaurant.

D

go + -ing

We use **go + -ing** for many sports (**swimming/skiing**, etc.) and also for **shopping**:

	shopping
I **go**	swimming
he is **going**	fishing
we **went**	sailing
they have **gone**	skiing
she wants to **go**	jogging
	running, etc.

I'm going skiing.

- ■ Are you **going shopping** this afternoon?
- ■ It's a nice day. Let's **go swimming**. (*or* Let's **go for a swim**.)
- ■ Richard has a small boat, and he often **goes sailing**.
- ■ I **went jogging** before breakfast this morning.

Exercises

56.1 Write *to/on/for* where necessary.

1. I'm going _to_ China next week.
2. Richard often goes ___—___ sailing.
3. Sue went _____ Mexico last year.
4. Would you like to go _____ the movies tonight?
5. Brian goes _____ jogging every morning.
6. I'm going out _____ a walk. Do you want to come?
7. I'm tired because I went _____ bed very late.
8. Mark is going _____ a trip _____ Turkey next week.
9. The weather was warm and the lake was clean, so we went _____ a swim.
10. The taxi drivers went _____ strike when I was in New York.
11. I need some stamps, so I'm going _____ the post office.
12. It's late. I have to go _____ home now.
13. Would you like to go _____ a tour of the city?
14. Do you want to go out _____ lunch today?
15. My parents are going _____ a cruise this summer.

56.2 Use the pictures to complete the sentences. Use *go/goes/going/went + -ing*.

1 *often*   2 *last Saturday*   3 *every day*   4 *next month*   5 *later*   6 *yesterday*

RICHARD   DIANE   JOHN   NICOLE   PETER   SALLY

1. Richard has a boat. He often _goes sailing_____ .
2. Last Saturday Diane went _____ .
3. John _____ every day.
4. Nicole is going to Colorado next month. She's _____ .
5. Peter is going out later. He has to _____ .
6. Sally _____ after work yesterday.

56.3 Complete these sentences. Use the words in the box. Use *to/on/for* if necessary.

~~a swim~~	bed	home	shopping	the bank
a walk	Hawaii	riding	skiing	vacation

1. The water looks great! Let's go _for a swim_____ .
2. "Is John at home?" "No, he went _____ to get some money."
3. I'm going _____ now. I have to buy some presents.
4. I was very tired last night. I went _____ early.
5. I wasn't enjoying the party, so I went _____ early.
6. We live near the mountains. In winter we go _____ almost every weekend.
7. Richard has a horse. He goes _____ a lot.
8. It's a beautiful day! Would you like to go _____ in the park?
9. *A:* Are you going _____ soon?
   B: Yes, next month. We're going _____ .

Get

A

get a letter / get a job, etc. (**get** + *noun*) = receive/buy/find

| you **don't have** something | you **get** it ➤ | you **have** it |

- "Did you **get** my post card?" "Yes, I **got** it yesterday." (= receive)
- I like your sweater. Where did you **get** it? (= buy)
- *(on the phone)* "Hello, can I speak to Amy, please?"
  "Sure. I'll **get** her." (= find and bring back)
- Is it difficult to **get** a job in your country? (= find)

B

get hungry / get cold / get tired, etc. (**get** + *adjective*) = become

| you're **not hungry** | you **get hungry** ➤ | you are **hungry** |

- If you don't eat, you **get hungry.**
- Drink your coffee. It's **getting cold.**
- I'm sorry your mother is sick. I hope she **gets better** soon.
- We **got wet** because we didn't take an umbrella.

Also: **get married**
    get dressed = put your clothes on
    get lost = lose your way

- Nicole and Frank **are getting married** soon.
- I got up and **got dressed** quickly.
- We didn't have a map, so we **got lost.**

C

get to a place = arrive
- I usually **get to work** before 8:30. (= arrive at work)
- We left Boston at 10:15 and **got to Ottawa** at 11:30.

get here/there (without **to**)
- How did you **get here?** By bus?

get home (without **to**)
- What time did you **get home** last night?

get to

D

get in / get out / get on / get off

get in (a car)   get out (of a car)   get on   get off
(a bus / a train / a plane)

- Kate **got in the car** and drove away. (You can also say: Kate got **into** the car . . .)
- A car stopped and a man **got out.** (*but* a man got out **of the car**)
- We **got on the bus** outside the hotel and **got off** at Church Street.

Get to Unit 103   **In/out/on/off** Units 105,109   **Get up** Unit 109

Exercises

57.1 Complete these sentences. Use *get/gets* and choose from the box.

~~my letter~~	a lot of snow	a room	the manager
your jacket	a new computer	a ticket	the job

1. I wrote to you last week. Did you *get my letter* ?
2. Where did you _____ ? It's really nice.
3. We couldn't _____ . All the hotels were full.
4. I had an interview with the manager, but I didn't _____ .
5. Chicago has terrible weather. They _____ in winter.
6. "Are you going to the concert?" "Yes, if I can _____ ."
7. I'm going to _____ . The one I have is too slow.
8. I have a problem. Could you _____ , please?

57.2 Complete these sentences. Use *getting* + one of these words:

~~cold~~   dark   late   married   ready

1. Drink your coffee. It's *getting cold* .
2. Turn on the light. It's _____ .
3. "I'm _____ next week." "Oh, really? Congratulations!"
4. "Where's Karen?" "She's _____ to go out."
5. It's _____ . It's time to go home.

57.3 Complete the sentences. Use *get/got* + one of these words:

angry   better   ~~hungry~~   lost   married   nervous   old   wet

1. If you don't eat, you'll *get hungry* .
2. Don't go out in the rain. You'll _____ .
3. My brother _____ last year. His wife's name is Julia.
4. My boss _____ and shouted at us yesterday.
5. We tried to find the hotel, but we _____ .
6. Everybody wants to stay young, but we all _____ .
7. The beginning of the film wasn't very good, but it _____ .
8. Most people _____ before exams.

57.4 Write sentences with *I left . . .* and *got to . . . .*

1. (home / 7:30 → work / 8:15) *I left home at 7:30 and got to work at 8:15.*
2. (Toronto / 10:15 → New York / 11:45)
   I left Toronto at 10:15 and _____ .
3. (the party / 11:15 → home / midnight)

   _____

   Write a true sentence about yourself.

4. I left _____ .

57.5 Write *got in / got out of / got on / got off.*

1. Mei Lan *got in* the car and drove away.
2. I _____ the bus and walked to my house from the bus stop.
3. Isabel _____ the car, locked the doors, and went into a store.
4. I made a stupid mistake. I _____ the wrong train.

UNIT 58

Do and *make*

A

Do is a general word for actions.

- What are you **doing** tonight? (*not* What are you making)
- "Shall I open the window?" "No, it's OK. I'll **do** it."
- Julia's job is very boring. She **does** the same thing every day.
- I **did** a lot of things yesterday.

What do you do? = What's your job?

- "What do you **do**?" "I work in a bank."

B

Make = produce/create. For example:

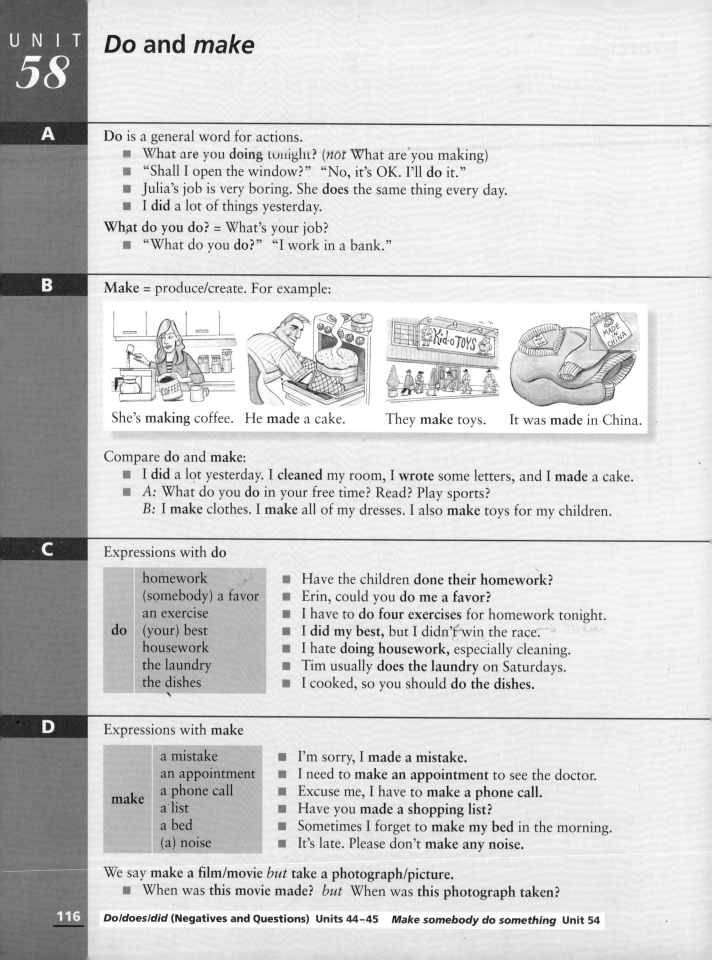

She's **making** coffee.　He **made** a cake.　They **make** toys.　It was **made** in China.

Compare **do** and **make**:

- I **did** a lot yesterday. I **cleaned** my room, I **wrote** some letters, and I **made** a cake.
- A: What do you **do** in your free time? Read? Play sports?
  B: I **make** clothes. I **make** all of my dresses. I also **make** toys for my children.

C

Expressions with **do**

do	homework (somebody) a favor an exercise (your) best housework the laundry the dishes

- Have the children **done their homework?**
- Erin, could you **do me a favor?**
- I have to **do four exercises** for homework tonight.
- I **did my best,** but I didn't win the race.
- I hate **doing housework,** especially cleaning.
- Tim usually **does the laundry** on Saturdays.
- I cooked, so you should **do the dishes.**

D

Expressions with **make**

make	a mistake an appointment a phone call a list a bed (a) noise

- I'm sorry, I **made a mistake.**
- I need to **make an appointment** to see the doctor.
- Excuse me, I have to **make a phone call.**
- Have you **made a shopping list?**
- Sometimes I forget to **make my bed** in the morning.
- It's late. Please don't **make any noise.**

We say **make a film/movie** *but* **take a photograph/picture.**

- When was **this movie made?** *but* When was **this photograph taken?**

Exercises

58.1 Write *make/making/made* or *do/doing/did/done*.

1. "Shall I open the window?" "No, it's OK. I'll _do_ it."
2. What did you _____ last weekend? Did you leave town?
3. Do you know how to _____ bread?
4. Paper is _____ from wood.
5. Fernando didn't help me. He sat in an armchair and _____ nothing.
6. "What do you _____?" "I'm a doctor."
7. I asked you to clean the bathroom. Have you _____ it?
8. "What do they _____ in that factory?" "Shoes."
9. I'm _____ some coffee. Would you like some?
10. Why are you mad at me? I didn't _____ anything wrong.
11. "What are you _____ tomorrow afternoon?" "I'm working."

58.2 What are these people doing?

1. _He's making a cake._
2. They _____ .
3. She _____ .
4. _____
5. _____
6. _____
7. _____
8. _____
9. _____
10. _____

58.3 Write *make* or *do* in the correct form.

1. I hate _doing_ housework, especially cleaning.
2. Why do you always _____ the same mistake?
3. "Can you _____ me a favor?" "It depends on what it is."
4. "Have you _____ your homework?" "Not yet."
5. I need to see the dentist, but I haven't _____ an appointment yet.
6. Chayan _____ his best, but he didn't pass his driver's test.
7. I painted the door, but I didn't _____ it very well.
8. When you've finished Exercise 1, you can _____ Exercise 2.
9. There's something wrong with the car. The engine is _____ a strange noise.
10. It was a bad mistake. It was the worst mistake I've ever _____ .
11. Let's _____ a list of all the things we have to _____ today.

Have

have and **have got** (see Unit 9)

I **have** (something) or I**'ve got** (something) = it is mine

- I **have** a new car. *or* I**'ve got** a new car.
- She **has** long hair. *or* She**'s got** long hair. (= She has got)
- **Do** Amy and Ed **have** any children? *or* **Have** Amy and Ed **got** any children?
- Tim **doesn't have** a job. *or* Tim **hasn't got** a job.
- How much time **do you have**? *or* How much time **have you got**?

Also:

I **have**	a headache / a toothache / a stomachache / a pain (in my leg, etc.)
I**'ve got**	a cold / a cough / a sore throat / a fever / the flu, etc.

- I **have** a headache. *or* I**'ve got** a headache.
- **Do** you **have** a cold? *or* **Have** you **got** a cold?

The past is **I had** (without **got**) / **I didn't have** / **Did you have?**, etc.

- When I first met Li Jing, she **had** short hair.
- He **didn't have** any money because he **didn't have** a job.
- **Did** you **have** a cold last week?

have breakfast / **have a good time**, etc.

In these expressions **have** = **eat** or **drink**. You can't use "have got."

have	a sandwich / a pizza / a snack, etc. a cup of coffee / a glass of milk, etc. something to eat/drink

- "Where's Amy?" "She's **having** lunch."
- "**Have** a cookie!" "Oh, thank you."
- I **had** three cups of coffee this morning.
- Can I **have** something to eat?

We also use **have** (*not* have got) in these expressions:

have	a vacation / a party a dream an accident a baby an argument

- We're **having** a party next Friday. Can you come?
- Fu Chen **had** an accident on the way to work.
- Sandra just **had** a baby. It's a boy.
- Jack and I never agree. We **have** an argument every time we meet.

We also say:

have	fun / a (good) time a (nice) day / a (nice) weekend / a (great) vacation a (good) flight / a (great) trip, etc.

- "My vacation starts tomorrow." "**Have** a great time!"
- "How was your trip?" "We **had** a terrible flight, but after that I **had** fun."
- "Did you **have** a nice weekend?" "Yes, thanks. Very nice!"
- I'm **having** a bad day. Everything is going wrong.

I have / I've got Unit 9   *I've (done)* **(Present Perfect)** Units 16, 19–20   *I have to . . .* Unit 34

Exercises

59.1 Write the correct form of *have* or *have got.*

1. *I didn't have* _____ time to do the shopping yesterday. (I / not / have)
2. "*Has Lisa got* OR *Does Lisa have* a car?" "No, she can't drive." (Lisa / have?)
3. He can't open the door. _____ a key. (he / not / have)
4. _____ a cold last week. He's better now. (Eric / have)
5. What's wrong? _____ a headache? (you / have?)
6. We wanted to go by taxi, but we _____ enough money. (we / not / have)
7. Liz is very busy. _____ much free time. (she / not / have)
8. _____ any problems when you were on vacation? (you / have?)

59.2 What are these people doing? Choose from the list.

an argument   breakfast   a cup of tea   a terrible flight   fun   ~~a party~~

1. *They're having a party.* _____
2. She _____ .
3. He _____ .
4. They _____ .
5. _____
6. _____

59.3 What do you say in these situations? Use *have.*

1. Mariko is going on vacation. What do you say to her before she goes?
   Have a nice vacation!
2. You meet Claire at the airport. She has just arrived. Ask her about her flight.
   Did you have a good flight?
3. Jiro is going on a long trip. What do you say to him before he leaves?
   _____
4. It's Monday morning. You are at work. Ask Paula about her weekend.
   _____
5. Paul has just come back from vacation. Ask him about his vacation.
   _____
6. Rachel is going out tonight. What do you say to her before she leaves?
   _____

59.4 Complete the sentences. Use *have/had* and choose from the list.

an accident   ~~a glass of water~~   a baby   ~~a party~~   a bad dream   something to eat

1. We *had a party* _____ a few weeks ago. We invited fifty people.
2. "Should we _____ ?" "No, I'm not hungry."
3. I was thirsty, so I _____ .
4. I _____ last night. It woke me up.
5. Soo Mi is a very good driver. She has never _____ .
6. Rachel is going to _____ . It will be her first child.

I/me, he/him, they/them, etc.

A

People

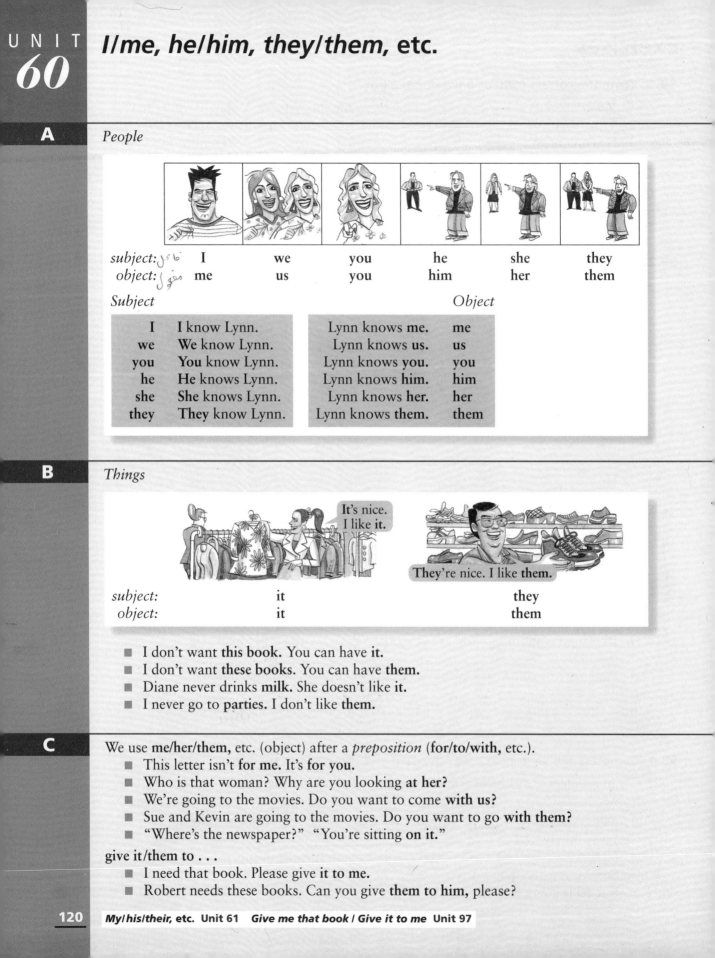

subject:	I	we	you	he	she	they
object:	me	us	you	him	her	them

Subject   **Object**

I	I know Lynn.		Lynn knows **me**.	me
we	We know Lynn.		Lynn knows **us**.	us
you	You know Lynn.		Lynn knows **you**.	you
he	He knows Lynn.		Lynn knows **him**.	him
she	She knows Lynn.		Lynn knows **her**.	her
they	They know Lynn.		Lynn knows **them**.	them

B

Things

It's nice. I like **it**.

They're nice. I like **them**.

subject:	it	they
object:	it	them

- I don't want **this book**. You can have **it**.
- I don't want **these books**. You can have **them**.
- Diane never drinks **milk**. She doesn't like **it**.
- I never go to **parties**. I don't like **them**.

C

We use **me/her/them**, etc. (object) after a *preposition* (**for/to/with**, etc.).

- This letter isn't **for me**. It's **for you**.
- Who is that woman? Why are you looking **at her**?
- We're going to the movies. Do you want to come **with us**?
- Sue and Kevin are going to the movies. Do you want to go **with them**?
- "Where's the newspaper?" "You're sitting **on it**."

give it/them to . . .

- I need that book. Please give **it to me**.
- Robert needs these books. Can you give **them to him**, please?

Exercises

60.1 Complete the sentences with *him/her/them.*

1. I don't know those girls. Do you know _them_ ?
2. I don't know that man. Do you know _____ ?
3. I don't know those people. Do you know _____ ?
4. I don't know Dave's wife. Do you know _____ ?
5. I don't know Mr. Kwang. Do you know _____ ?
6. I don't know Sarah's parents. Do you know _____ ?
7. I don't know the woman in the black coat. Do you know _____ ?

60.2 Complete the sentences. Use *I/me/you/she/her,* etc.

1. I want to see her, but _she_ doesn't want to see _me_ .
2. They want to see me, but _____ don't want to see _____ .
3. She wants to see him, but _____ doesn't want to see _____ .
4. We want to see them, but _____ don't want to see _____ .
5. He wants to see us, but _____ don't want to see _____ .
6. They want to see her, but _____ doesn't want to see _____ .
7. I want to see them, but _____ don't want to see _____ .
8. You want to see her, but _____ doesn't want to see _____ .

60.3 Write sentences with *I like . . . , I don't like . . . ,* or *Do you like . . . ?*

1. I don't eat tomatoes. _I don't like them._
2. Eric is a very nice man. I like _____ .
3. This jacket isn't very nice. I don't _____ .
4. This is my new car. Do _____ ?
5. Mrs. Clark is not very friendly. I _____ .
6. These are my new shoes. _____ ?

60.4 Complete the sentences. Use *I/me/he/him,* etc.

1. Who is that woman? Why are you looking at _her_ ?
2. "Do you know that man?" "Yes, I work with _____ ."
3. Where are the tickets? I can't find _____ .
4. I can't find my keys. Where are _____ ?
5. We're going out. You can come with _____ .
6. Mary likes music. _____ plays the piano.
7. I don't like dogs. I'm afraid of _____ .
8. I'm talking to you. Please listen to _____ .
9. Where is Anne? I want to talk to _____ .
10. My brother has a new job. _____ doesn't like _____ very much.

60.5 Complete the sentences.

1. I need that book. Can you _give it to me_ ?
2. He wants the key. Can you give _____ ?
3. She wants the keys. Can you _____ ?
4. I need that letter. Can you _____ ?
5. They want the money. Can you _____ ?
6. We need the photographs. Can you _____ ?

My / his / their, etc.

A

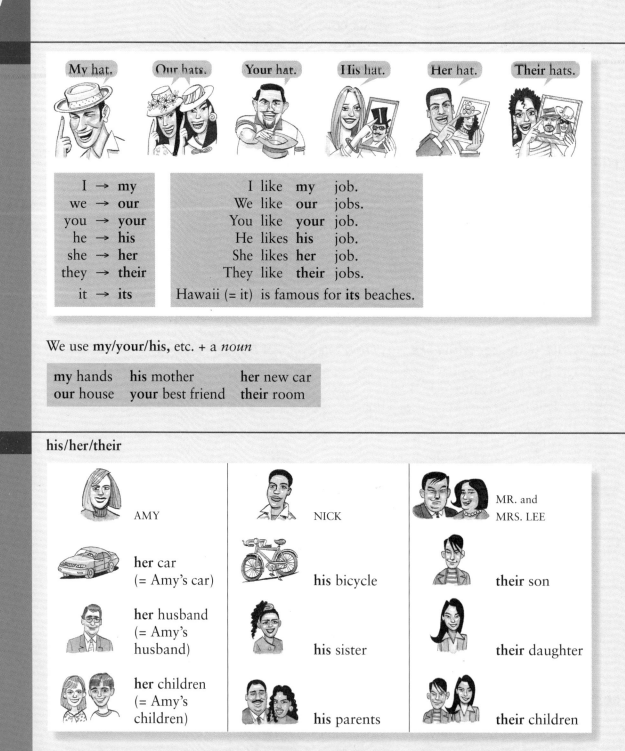

I → my	I like **my** job.
we → our	We like **our** jobs.
you → your	You like **your** job.
he → his	He likes **his** job.
she → her	She likes **her** job.
they → their	They like **their** jobs.
it → its	Hawaii (= it) is famous for **its** beaches.

We use **my/your/his,** etc. + a *noun*

my hands	**his** mother	**her** new car
our house	**your** best friend	**their** room

B

his/her/their

AMY

her car
(= Amy's car)

her husband
(= Amy's husband)

her children
(= Amy's children)

NICK

his bicycle

his sister

his parents

MR. and MRS. LEE

their son

their daughter

their children

C

its and it's

its   Hawaii is famous for **its** beaches.
it's (= it is)   I like Hawaii. **It's** a beautiful place. (= **It is** a beautiful place.)

Exercises

61.1 Complete these sentences.

1. I'm going to wash _my hands_ .
2. She's going to wash _____ .
3. We're going to wash _____ .
4. He's going to wash _____ .
5. They're going to wash _____ .
6. Are you going to wash _____ ?

61.2 Complete these sentences.

1. He _lives with his parents_ .
2. They live with _____ parents.
3. We _____ parents.
4. Mary lives _____ .
5. I _____ parents.
6. John _____ .
7. Do you live _____ ?
8. Most children _____ .

61.3 Look at the family tree, and complete the sentences with *his/her/their*.

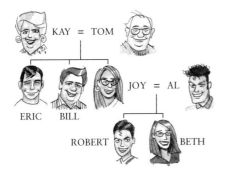

KAY = TOM

JOY = AL

ERIC   BILL

ROBERT   BETH

1. I saw Kay with _her_ husband, Tom.
2. I saw Joy and Al with _____ children.
3. I saw Al with _____ wife, Joy.
4. I saw Eric with _____ brother, Bill.
5. I saw Joy with _____ brother Bill.
6. I saw Kay and Tom with _____ son Bill.
7. I saw Joy with _____ parents.
8. I saw Beth and Robert with _____ parents.

61.4 Write *my/our/your/his/her/their/its*.

1. Do you like _your_ job?
2. I know Mr. Chu, but I don't know _____ wife.
3. Mr. and Mrs. Romo live in San Francisco. _____ son lives in Canada.
4. We're going to have a party. We're going to invite all _____ friends.
5. Amy is going out with _____ friends tonight.
6. I like tennis. It's _____ favorite sport.
7. "Is that _____ car?" "No, I don't have a car."
8. I want to call Amy. Do you know _____ phone number?
9. Do you think most people are happy with _____ jobs?
10. I'm going to wash _____ hair before I go out.
11. That's a beautiful tree. _____ leaves are a beautiful color.
12. John has a brother and a sister. _____ brother is 25, and _his_ sister is 21.

61.5 Complete the sentences. Use *my/his/their*, etc., with one of these words:

coat   homework   house   husband   ~~job~~   key   name

1. Jim doesn't enjoy _his job_ . It's not very interesting.
2. I can't open the door. I don't have _____ .
3. Amy is married. _____ works in a bank.
4. It's very cold today. Put on _____ when you go out.
5. "What are the children doing?" "They're doing _____ ."
6. "Do you know that man?" "Yes, but I don't know _____ ."
7. We live on Main Street. _____ is on the corner of Main and First.

Whose is this? It's mine/yours/hers, etc.

A

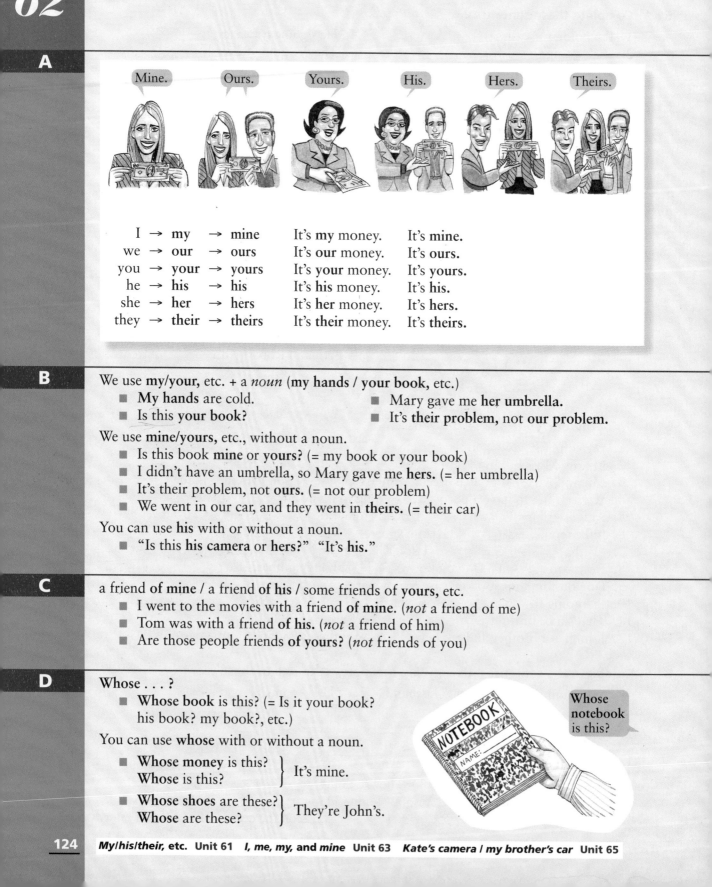

Mine. Ours. Yours. His. Hers. Theirs.

I	→	my	→	mine	It's **my** money.	It's **mine**.
we	→	our	→	ours	It's **our** money.	It's **ours**.
you	→	your	→	yours	It's **your** money.	It's **yours**.
he	→	his	→	his	It's **his** money.	It's **his**.
she	→	her	→	hers	It's **her** money.	It's **hers**.
they	→	their	→	theirs	It's **their** money.	It's **theirs**.

B

We use **my/your**, etc. + a *noun* (**my hands** / **your book**, etc.)

- **My hands** are cold.
- Is this **your book**?
- Mary gave me **her umbrella**.
- It's **their problem**, not **our problem**.

We use **mine/yours**, etc., without a noun.

- Is this book **mine** or **yours**? (= my book or your book)
- I didn't have an umbrella, so Mary gave me **hers**. (= her umbrella)
- It's their problem, not **ours**. (= not our problem)
- We went in our car, and they went in **theirs**. (= their car)

You can use **his** with or without a noun.

- "Is this **his camera** or hers?" "It's **his**."

C

a friend **of mine** / a friend **of his** / some friends of **yours**, etc.

- I went to the movies with a friend **of mine**. (*not* a friend of me)
- Tom was with a friend **of his**. (*not* a friend of him)
- Are those people friends **of yours**? (*not* friends of you)

D

Whose . . . ?

- **Whose book** is this? (= Is it your book? his book? my book?, etc.)

You can use **whose** with or without a noun.

- **Whose money** is this?
  Whose is this? } It's mine.

- **Whose shoes** are these?
  Whose are these? } They're John's.

Whose notebook is this?

NOTEBOOK
NAME:

My/his/their, etc. Unit 61   *I, me, my, and mine* Unit 63   *Kate's camera / my brother's car* Unit 65

Exercises

62.1 Complete the sentences with *mine/yours*, etc.

1. It's your money. It's _yours_____ .
2. It's my bag. It's _____ .
3. It's our car. It's _____ .
4. They're her shoes. They're _____ .
5. It's their house. It's _____ .
6. They're your books. They're _____ .
7. They're my glasses. They're _____ .
8. It's his coat. It's _____ .

62.2 Choose the right word.

1. It's their/~~theirs~~ problem, not ~~our~~/ours. (*their* and *ours* are right)
2. This is a nice camera. Is it your/yours?
3. That's not my/mine umbrella. My/Mine is black.
4. Whose books are these? Your/Yours or my/mine?
5. Catherine is going out with her/hers friends tonight.
6. My/Mine room is bigger than her/hers.
7. They've got two children but I don't know their/theirs names.
8. Can we use your telephone? Our/Ours isn't working.

62.3 Complete these sentences. Use *friend(s) of mine/yours*, etc.

1. I went to the movies with a _friend of mine_____ .
2. They went on vacation with some _friends of theirs_____ .
3. She's going out with a _____ .
4. We had dinner with some _____ .
5. I played tennis with a _____ .
6. Tom is going to meet a _____ .
7. Do you know those people? Are they _____ ?

62.4 Look at the pictures. What are the people saying?

125

I, me, my, and *mine*

I can see him, but he can't see **me**.

You give **me** your address, and I'll give you **mine**.

I, etc. (Unit 60)	me, etc. (Unit 60)	my, etc. (Unit 61)	mine, etc. (Unit 62)
I know Tom.	Tom knows **me**.	It's **my** car.	It's **mine**.
We know Tom.	Tom knows **us**.	It's **our** car.	It's **ours**.
You know Tom.	Tom knows **you**.	It's **your** car.	It's **yours**.
He knows Tom.	Tom knows **him**.	It's **his** car.	It's **his**.
She knows Tom.	Tom knows **her**.	It's **her** car.	It's **hers**.
They know Tom.	Tom knows **them**.	It's **their** car.	It's **theirs**.

■ "Do **you** know that man?" "Yes, I know **him**, but I can't remember **his name**."
■ **She** was very happy because **we** invited **her** to stay with **us** at **our house**.
■ *A:* Where are the children? Have **you** seen **them**?
  B: Yes, **they**'re playing with **their friends** in the park.
■ That's **my pen**. Can you give it to **me**, please?
■ "Is this **your umbrella**?" "No, it's **yours**."
■ **He** didn't have an umbrella, so **she** gave **him hers**. (= she gave her umbrella to him)
■ I'm going out with a friend of **mine** tonight. (*not* a friend of me)

Myself/yourself, etc. Unit 64   *Give me that book / Give it to me* Unit 97

Exercises

63.1 **Answer the questions in the same way.**

1. Yes, I _know him, but I can't remember_
   his name _____ .

2. Yes, I know _____ ,
   but I can't remember _____ .

3. Yes, I _____ , but I
   _____ names.

4. Yes, I _____ , but
   _____ .

63.2 **Complete the sentences in the same way.**

1. We invited her _to stay with us at our house_ _____ .
2. He invited us to stay with _____ house.
3. They invited me to stay with _____ house.
4. I invited them _____ .
5. She invited us _____ .
6. Did you invite him _____ ?

63.3 **Complete the sentences in the same way.**

1. I gave him _my address, and he gave me his_ _____ .
2. I gave her _____ address, and she gave me _____ .
3. He gave me _____ address, and I gave _____ .
4. We gave them _____ address, and they gave _____ .
5. She gave him _____ address, and _____ .
6. You gave us _____ address, and _____ .
7. They gave you _____ address, and _____ .

63.4 **Write *him/her/yours*, etc.**

1. Where's Amy? Have you seen _her_ _____ ?
2. Where are my keys? Where did I put _____ ?
3. This letter is for Bill. Can you give it to _____ ?
4. We wrote to John but he didn't answer _____ letter.
5. "I can't find my pen. Can I use _____ ?" "Sure."
6. We're going to the movies. Why don't you come with _____ ?
7. Did your sister pass _____ driver's test?
8. Some people talk about _____ jobs all the time.
9. Last night I went out for dinner with a friend of _____ .

Myself/yourself/themselves, etc.

A

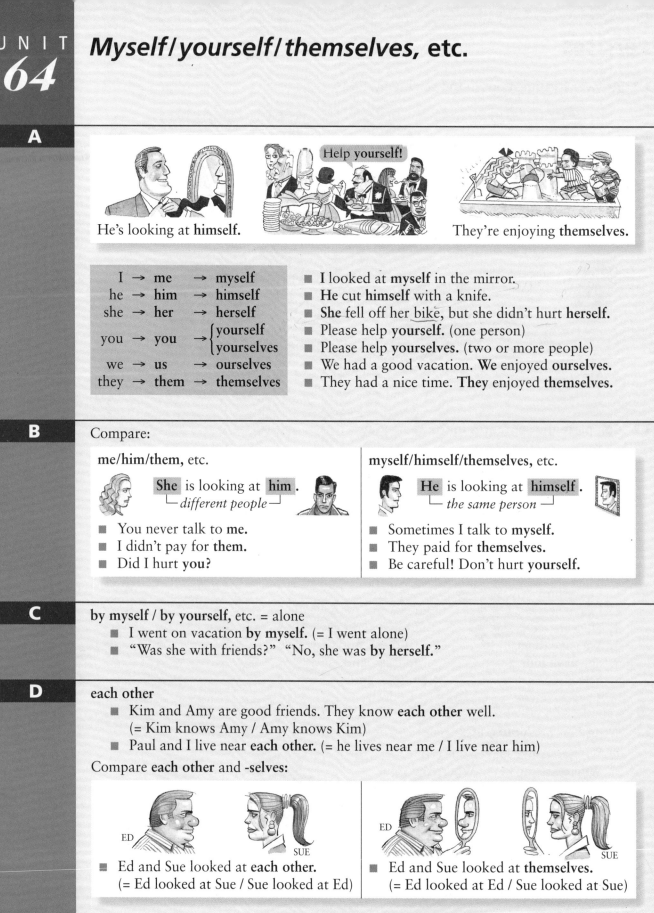

He's looking at **himself**.　　Help **yourself**!　　They're enjoying **themselves**.

I →	me →	myself
he →	him →	himself
she →	her →	herself
you →	you →	{ yourself / yourselves }
we →	us →	ourselves
they →	them →	themselves

- I looked at **myself** in the mirror.
- He cut **himself** with a knife.
- **She** fell off her bike, but she didn't hurt **herself**.
- Please help **yourself**. (one person)
- Please help **yourselves**. (two or more people)
- We had a good vacation. **We** enjoyed **ourselves**.
- They had a nice time. **They** enjoyed **themselves**.

B

Compare:

me/him/them, etc.

She is looking at him.
└─ *different people* ─┘

- You never talk to **me**.
- I didn't pay for **them**.
- Did I hurt **you**?

myself/himself/themselves, etc.

He is looking at himself.
└─ *the same person* ─┘

- Sometimes I talk to **myself**.
- They paid for **themselves**.
- Be careful! Don't hurt **yourself**.

C

by myself / by yourself, etc. = alone
- I went on vacation **by myself**. (= I went alone)
- "Was she with friends?" "No, she was **by herself**."

D

each other
- Kim and Amy are good friends. They know **each other** well.
  (= Kim knows Amy / Amy knows Kim)
- Paul and I live near **each other**. (= he lives near me / I live near him)

Compare **each other** and **-selves**:

- Ed and Sue looked at **each other**.
  (= Ed looked at Sue / Sue looked at Ed)

- Ed and Sue looked at **themselves**.
  (= Ed looked at Ed / Sue looked at Sue)

Exercises

64.1 Complete the sentences with *myself/yourself*, etc.

1. He looked at _himself_____ in the mirror.
2. I'm not angry with you. I'm angry with _____ .
3. Jennifer had a good time in Mexico. She enjoyed _____ .
4. My friends had a good time in Mexico. They enjoyed _____ .
5. He never thinks about other people. He only thinks about _____ .
6. I want to know more about you. Tell me about _____ . *(one person)*
7. Goodbye! Have a good trip and take care of _____ ! *(two people)*

64.2 Write sentences with *by myself / by yourself*, etc.

1. I went to South America alone.   _I went to South America by myself._____
2. When I saw him, he was alone.   When I saw him, he _____ .
3. Don't go out alone.   Don't _____ .
4. I went to the movies alone.   I _____ .
5. My sister lives alone.   My sister _____ .
6. Many people live alone.   Many people _____ .

64.3 Write sentences with *each other*.

1. _They like each other._____
2. They can't _____ .
3. They _____ .

4. _____
5. _____
6. _____

64.4 Complete the sentences. Use:

> each other   ourselves/yourselves/themselves   us/you/them

1. Paul and I live near _each other_____ .
2. Who are those people? Do you know _them_____ ?
3. You can help Taro, and Taro can help you. So you and Taro can help _____ .
4. There's food in the kitchen. If you and Bob are hungry, you can help _____ .
5. We didn't go to Megan's party. She didn't invite _____ .
6. When we go on vacation, we always enjoy _____ .
7. Diane and I are very good friends. We've known _____ for a long time.
8. "Did you see Sam and Sue at the party?" "Yes, but I didn't speak to _____ ."
9. Many people talk to _____ when they're alone.

-'s (Kate's camera / my brother's car, etc.)

A

My camera.

My car.

MANAGER

KATE

MY
BROTHER

Kate's camera
(**her** camera)

my **brother's** car
(**his** car)

the **manager's** office
(**his** or **her** office)

We normally use -'s for *people*.

- I stayed at **my sister's** house. (*not* the house of my sister)
- Have you met **Mr. Suzuki's** wife? (*not* the wife of Mr. Suzuki)
- Are you going to **James's** party?
- Paul is **a man's** name. Paula is **a woman's** name.

You can use -'s without a noun after it.

- Mi Ja's hair is longer than **Megan's.** (= Megan's hair)
- "Whose umbrella is this?" "It's **my mother's.**" (= my mother's umbrella)
- "Where were you last night?" "I was at **Paul's.**" (= Paul's house)

B

friend's and **friends'**

MY FRIEND My house.

my **friend's** house = *one friend*
(= **his** house *or* **her** house)

We write -'s after **friend/student/mother**,
etc. *(singular):*

  my **mother's** car *(one mother)*
  my **father's** car *(one father)*

Our house.

MY FRIENDS

my **friends'** house = *two or more friends*
(= **their** house)

We write -' after **friends/students/parents**,
etc. *(plural):*

  my **parents'** car *(two parents)*

C

We use **of . . .** for *things, places*, etc.

- Look at the roof **of that building.** (*not* that building's roof)
- We didn't see the beginning **of the film.** (*not* the film's beginning)
- What's the name **of this town?**
- Do you know the cause **of the problem?**
- We had to sit in the back **of the theater.**
- Madrid is the capital **of Spain.**

Exercises

65.1 Look at the family tree. Write sentences about the people in the family.

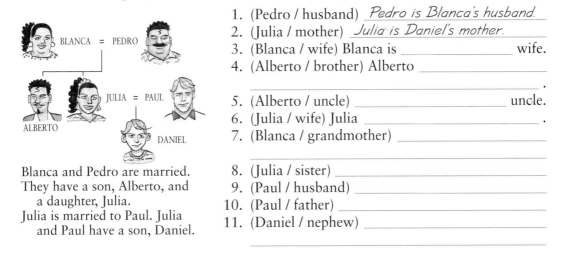

BLANCA = PEDRO

JULIA = PAUL

ALBERTO

DANIEL

Blanca and Pedro are married.
They have a son, Alberto, and
   a daughter, Julia.
Julia is married to Paul. Julia
   and Paul have a son, Daniel.

1. (Pedro / husband) *Pedro is Blanca's husband.*
2. (Julia / mother) *Julia is Daniel's mother.*
3. (Blanca / wife) Blanca is _____ wife.
4. (Alberto / brother) Alberto _____
   _____ .
5. (Alberto / uncle) _____ uncle.
6. (Julia / wife) Julia _____ .
7. (Blanca / grandmother) _____
   _____
8. (Julia / sister) _____
9. (Paul / husband) _____
10. (Paul / father) _____
11. (Daniel / nephew) _____
    _____

65.2 Look at the pictures and answer the questions. Use only one word.

JANE   ANDY   ALICE   DIANE   DAVE

1. Whose is this?
   Alice's.
2. Whose is this?
   _____
3. And this?
   _____
4. And these?
   _____
5. And this?
   _____
6. And these?
   _____

65.3 Are these sentences right? Correct the sentences that are wrong.

1. I stayed at <u>the house of my sister</u>.   *my sister's house*
2. What is <u>the name of this town</u>?   *OK*
3. Do you like <u>the color of this coat</u>? _____
4. Do you know <u>the phone number of Bill</u>? _____
5. <u>The job of my brother</u> is very interesting. _____
6. Write your name at <u>the top of the page</u>. _____
7. For me, morning is <u>the best part of the day</u>. _____
8. <u>The favorite color of Paula</u> is blue. _____
9. When is <u>the birthday of your mother</u>? _____
10. <u>The house of my parents</u> isn't very big. _____
11. <u>The walls of this house</u> are very thin. _____
12. The car stopped at <u>the end of the street</u>. _____
13. Are you going to <u>the party of Silvia</u> next week? _____
14. <u>The manager of the hotel</u> is in a meeting right now. _____

A/an . . .

A

He has **a camera**.   She's waiting for **a taxi**.   It's **a beautiful day**.

a . . . = one thing or person
- Alice works in **a bank**. (*not* in bank)
- Can I ask **a question**? (*not* ask question)
- I don't have **a car**.
- There's **a woman** at the bus stop.

B

an (*not* a) **before a/e/i/o/u**
- Do you want **an apple** or **a banana**?
- I'm going to buy **a hat** and **an umbrella**.
- There was **an interesting** program on TV last night.

Also: **an hour** ("h" is not pronounced: an h̷our)
But: **a university** (pronounced *yuniversity*)
      a European country (pronounced *yuropean*)

Another (= an + other) is one word.
- Can I have **another** cup of coffee?

C

We use **a/an** . . . when we say what a thing or a person is. For example:
- The sun is **a star**.
- Football is **a game**.
- Dallas is **a city** in Texas.
- A mouse is **an animal**. It's **a small animal**.
- Joe is **a very nice person**.

We use **a/an** . . . for jobs.
- *A:* What do you do?
  B: I'm **a dentist**. (*not* I'm dentist.)
- "What does Mark do?" "He's **an engineer**."
- Would you like to be **a teacher**?
- Beethoven was **a composer**.
- Picasso was **a famous painter**.
- Are you **a student**?

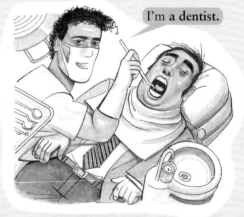

I'm a dentist.

Exercises

66.1 Write *a* or *an*.

1. _an_ old book
2. _____ window
3. _____ horse
4. _____ airport
5. _____ new airport
6. _____ organization
7. _____ university
8. _____ hour
9. _____ economic problem

66.2 What are these things? Choose from the list.

airplane	flower	insect	planet	sport
~~bird~~	fruit	mountain	river	vegetable

1. A duck is _a bird_ .
2. A carrot is _____ .
3. Tennis is _____ .
4. A 747 is _____ .
5. Everest is _____ .
6. Saturn is _____ .
7. A banana is _____ .
8. The Amazon is _____ .
9. A rose is _____ .
10. A fly is _____ .

66.3 What are their jobs? Choose from the list and complete the sentences.

architect   auto mechanic   ~~dentist~~   electrician   photographer   sales clerk   taxi driver

1. _She's a dentist._
2. He's _____ .
3. He _____ .
4. _____
5. _____
6. _____
7. _____
8. And you? I'm _____ .

66.4 Write sentences. Choose from each box. Use *a/an*.

~~I want to ask you~~	I can't ride
Lucia works in	Jim lives in
Tom never wears	My brother is
Amy wants to learn	Tonight I'm going to

+

old house	office
artist	foreign language
party	hat
~~question~~	bicycle

1. _I want to ask you a question._
2. _____
3. _____
4. _____
5. _____
6. _____
7. _____
8. _____

Flower(s) and *bus(es)* (Singular and Plural)

A

The plural of a noun is usually **-s.**

singular = one → *plural* = two or more

a flower	→ some **flowers**
a week	→ two **weeks**
a nice place	→ many nice **places**
this hat	→ these **hats**

a flower   some **flowers**

Spelling (see Appendixes 5.1–5.2)

-s / -sh / -ch / -x → -es	bus → buses dish → dishes church → churches	
	box → boxes	
also	potato → potatoes tomato → tomatoes	
-y → -ies	baby → babies dictionary → dictionaries party → parties	
but -ay / -ey / -oy → -ys	day → days monkey → monkeys boy → boys	
-f / -fe → -ves	shelf → shelves leaf → leaves wife → wives	

B

These things are plural in English:

scissors   glasses   pants   jeans   shorts   pajamas

- Do you wear **glasses?**
- Where **are** the **scissors?** I need **them.**

You can also say **a pair of scissors / a pair of pants / a pair of pajamas,** etc.

- I need a new **pair of jeans.** *or* I need **some** new **jeans.** (*not* a new jeans)

C

Some plurals do *not* end in **-s.**

this **man** → these **men**	one **foot** → two **feet**	that **sheep** → those **sheep**
a **woman** → some **women**	a **tooth** → all my **teeth**	a **fish** → a lot of **fish**
a **child** → many **children**	a **mouse** → some **mice**	

Also: a **person** → two **people / some people / a lot of people,** etc.

- She's a nice **person.**
- They are nice **people.** (*not* nice persons)

D

People is plural (= they), so we say **people are / people have,** etc.

- A lot of **people speak** English. (*not* speaks)
- I like the **people** here. **They are** very friendly.

Police is plural.

- "The **police are** here." "Why? What **do they** want?"

Exercises

67.1 Write the plural.

1. flower *flowers*
2. boat _____
3. woman _____
4. city _____

5. umbrella _____
6. address _____
7. knife _____
8. sandwich _____

9. family _____
10. foot _____
11. holiday _____
12. potato _____

67.2 Look at the pictures and complete the sentences.

1. There are a lot of *sheep* in the field.
2. Eric is brushing his _____ .
3. There are three _____ at the bus stop.

4. Kim has two _____ .
5. There are a lot of _____ in the river.
6. The _____ are falling from the tree.

67.3 Are these sentences right? Correct the sentences that are wrong.

1. I'm going to buy some flowers. *OK* _____
2. I need a new jeans. *a new pair of jeans* OR *some new jeans* _____
3. It's a lovely park with a lot of beautiful tree. _____
4. There was a woman in the car with two mens. _____
5. Sheep eat grass. _____
6. Fernando is married and has three childs. _____
7. Most of my friend are student. _____
8. He put on his pajama and went to bed. _____
9. We went fishing, but we didn't catch many fish. _____
10. Do you know many persons in this town? _____
11. I like your pant. Where did you get it? _____
12. Montreal is usually full of tourist. _____
13. I don't like mice. I'm afraid of them. _____
14. This scissor isn't very sharp. _____

67.4 Which is right? Complete the sentences.

1. It's a nice place. Many people *go* there on vacation. (go *or* goes?)
2. Some people _____ always late. (is *or* are?)
3. Their president is not popular. The people _____ like him. (don't *or* doesn't?)
4. A lot of people _____ television every day. (watch *or* watches?)
5. Three people _____ injured in the accident. (was *or* were?)
6. How many people _____ in that house? (live *or* lives?)
7. _____ the police carry guns in your country? (Do *or* Does?)
8. The police _____ looking for the stolen car. (is *or* are?)
9. I need my glasses, but I can't find _____ . (it *or* them?)
10. I'm going to buy _____ new jeans today. (a *or* some?)

A car, some money
(Countable and Uncountable 1)

A noun can be *countable* or *uncountable*.

A

Countable nouns

For example: (a) **car** (a) **man** (a) **key** (a) **house** (a) **flower** (an) **idea** (an) **accident**

You can use **one/two/three** (etc.) + *countable nouns* (you can count them)

one **car**   two **cars**   three **men**   four **houses**

Countable nouns can be *singular* (= one) or *plural* (= two or more).

singular	**a car, the car, my car,** etc.
plural	**cars, the cars, his cars, two cars, some cars, many cars,** etc.

- ■ I've got **a car.**
- ■ New **cars** are very expensive.
- ■ There aren't **many cars** in the parking lot.

You can't use the singular (**car/house/key,** etc.) alone. You need **a/an** (Unit 66).
- ■ We can't get in without **a key.** (*not* without key)

B

Uncountable nouns

For example: **water   air   rice   salt   plastic   money   music   tennis**

water   salt   money   music

You can't say **one/two/three** (etc.) + *uncountable nouns* (you can't count them)
~~one water~~   ~~two musics~~

Uncountable nouns have only *one* form.
money   the **money**   my **money**   some **money**   much **money,** etc.

- ■ I've got **some money.**
- ■ **Money** isn't everything.
- ■ There isn't **much money** in the box.

You can't use **a/an** + uncountable nouns: ~~a money~~   ~~a music~~

But you can use **a piece of . . . / a glass of . . . ,** etc. + uncountable nouns.

a glass of water	**a carton of** milk	**a bowl of** rice	**a piece of** candy
a cup of coffee	**a bottle of** perfume	**a can of** fruit	**a game of** tennis

---

Exercises

68.1 What are these things? Some are countable and some are uncountable. Write *a/an* if necessary. The names of these things are:

bucket	envelope	~~salt~~	~~spoon~~	teapot	toothpaste
egg	money	sand	tea	toothbrush	wallet

1. It's _salt_ .
2. It's _a spoon_ .
3. It's _____ .
4. It's _____ .

5. It's _____ .
6. It's _____ .
7. It's _____ .
8. It's _____ .

9. It's _____ .
10. It's _____ .
11. It's _____ .
12. It's _____ .

68.2 Some of these sentences are right, but some need *a/an*. Write *a/an* if necessary.

1. I haven't got watch. _a watch_
2. Do you like cheese? _OK_
3. Beth never wears hat. _____
4. Are you looking for job? _____
5. Eve doesn't eat meat. _____
6. Eve eats apple every day. _____
7. I'm going to concert tonight. _____
8. It was beautiful day. _____
9. Jamaica is island. _____
10. I don't need key. _____
11. Everybody needs food. _____
12. I've got good idea. _____
13. Can you drive car? _____
14. Do you want cup of tea? _____
15. I don't like tea without milk. _____
16. Don't go out without coat. _____

68.3 What are these things? Write *a . . . of . . .* for each picture. Choose from each box.

bottle	~~carton~~	jar	beans	juice	soup
bowl	cup	piece	coffee	~~milk~~	water
can	glass	piece	honey	paper	wood

+

1. _a carton of milk_
2. _____
3. _____
4. _____
5. _____
6. _____
7. _____
8. _____
9. _____

UNIT 69

A car, some money
(Countable and Uncountable 2)

A

a/an and some

> A/an + *singular countable nouns* (car/apple/shoe, etc.):
> - I need **a** new **car**.
> - Would you like **an apple**?
>
> an apple
>
> Some + *plural countable nouns* (cars/apples/shoes, etc.):
> - I need **some** new **shoes**.
> - Would you like **some apples**?
>
> some apples
>
> Some + *uncountable nouns* (water/money/music, etc.):
> - I need **some money**.
> - Would you like **some cheese**? *or*
> - Would you like **a piece of** cheese?
>
> some cheese *or*
> **a piece of** cheese

Compare **a** and **some**:
- Nicole bought **a hat**, **some shoes**, and **some perfume**.
- I read **a newspaper**, wrote **some letters**, and listened to **some music**.

B

Many nouns are sometimes countable and sometimes uncountable. For example:

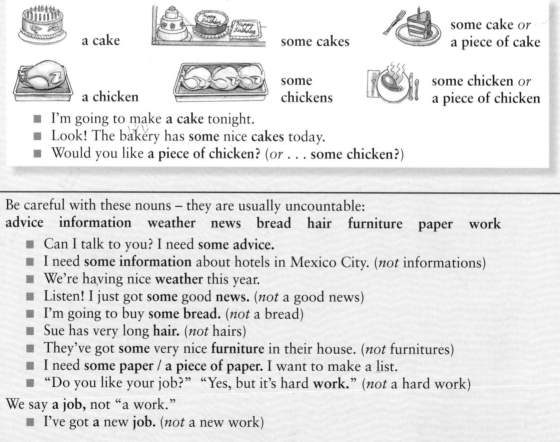

a cake | some cakes | some cake *or* a piece of cake

a chicken | some chickens | some chicken *or* a piece of chicken

- I'm going to make **a cake** tonight.
- Look! The bakery has **some** nice **cakes** today.
- Would you like **a piece of chicken**? (*or* . . . **some chicken**?)

C

Be careful with these nouns – they are usually uncountable:
advice   information   weather   news   bread   hair   furniture   paper   work

- Can I talk to you? I need **some advice**.
- I need **some information** about hotels in Mexico City. (*not* informations)
- We're having nice **weather** this year.
- Listen! I just got **some** good **news**. (*not* a good news)
- I'm going to buy **some bread**. (*not* a bread)
- Sue has very long **hair**. (*not* hairs)
- They've got **some** very nice **furniture** in their house. (*not* furnitures)
- I need **some paper** / **a piece of paper**. I want to make a list.
- "Do you like your job?" "Yes, but it's hard **work**." (*not* a hard work)

We say **a job**, not "a work."
- I've got **a** new **job**. (*not* a new work)

Exercises

69.1 **What did you buy? Use the pictures and write sentences (*I bought . . .*).**

1. *I bought a hat, some shoes, and some perfume.*
2. I bought _____ .
3. _____
4. _____

69.2 **Write sentences with *Would you like a . . . ?* or *Would you like some . . . ?*.**

1. *Would you like some cheese?*   4. _____
2. Would you like _____ ?   5. _____
3. Would _____ ?   6. _____

69.3 **Write *a/an* or *some*.**

1. I read *a* book and listened to *some* music.
2. I need _____ money. I want to buy _____ food.
3. We met _____ interesting people at the party.
4. I'm going to open _____ window to get _____ fresh air.
5. Ratana didn't eat much for lunch – only _____ apple and _____ bread.
6. We live in _____ big house. There's _____ nice yard with _____ beautiful trees.
7. I'm going to make a table. First I need _____ wood.
8. Listen to me. I'm going to give you _____ advice.
9. I want to write a letter. I need _____ paper and _____ pen.

69.4 **Which is right?**

1. I'm going to buy some new ~~shoe~~/shoes. (*shoes* is right)
2. Mark has brown eye/eyes.
3. Shu Ling has short black hair/hairs.
4. The guidebook had some information/informations about the city.
5. We're going to buy some new chair/chairs.
6. We're going to buy some new furniture/furnitures.
7. It's hard to find a work/job right now.
8. We had wonderful weather / a wonderful weather when we were on vacation.

A/an and the

a/an

Can you open **a window**?

There are *three* windows here.
a window = window 1 or 2 or 3

- I have **a car**. (There are many cars and I have one.)
- Can I ask **a question?** (There are many questions – can I ask one?)
- Is there **a hotel** near here? (There are many hotels – is there one near here?)
- Paris is **an interesting city**. (There are many interesting cities and Paris is one.)
- Lisa is **a student**. (There are many students and Lisa is one.)

the

Can you open **the window**?

There is only *one* window here –
the window.

- I'm going to wash **the car** tomorrow. (= my car)
- Can you repeat **the question,** please? (= the question that you asked)
- We enjoyed our vacation. **The hotel** was very nice. (= our hotel)
- Paris is **the capital of France**. (There is only one capital of France.)
- Lisa is **the youngest student** in her class. (There is only one youngest student.)

Compare **a** and **the:**

I bought **a jacket** and **a shirt** . **The jacket** was cheap, but **the shirt** was expensive.

(= **the** jacket and **the** shirt that I bought)

We say **the . . .** when it is clear which thing or person we mean. For example:

the door / the ceiling / the floor / the light, etc. *(of a room)*
the roof / the backyard / the kitchen / the bathroom, etc. *(of a house)*
the airport / the police station / the train station / the mayor's office, etc. *(of a city)*

- "Where's Tom?" "In **the kitchen**."
  (= the kitchen of this house or apartment)
- Turn off **the light** and close **the door**.
  (= the light and the door of the room)
- Do you live far from **the airport?**
  (= the airport of your town)
- I'd like to speak to **the manager,** please.
  (= the manager of this store, etc.)

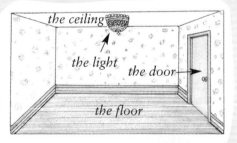

the ceiling
the light
the door
the floor

Exercises

70.1 Write *a/an* or *the*.

1. We enjoyed our trip. *The* hotel was very nice.
2. "Can I ask _*a*___ question?" "Sure. What do you want to know?"
3. You look very tired. You need _____ vacation.
4. "Where's Tom?" "He's in _____ kitchen."
5. Tracy is _____ interesting person. You should meet her.
6. Excuse me, can you tell me how to get to _____ post office?
7. *A:* Let's go and see _____ movie tonight.
   B: OK, that's _____ good idea. What do you want to see?
8. It's _____ nice morning. Let's go for _____ walk.
9. Amanda is _____ student. When she finishes school, she wants to be _____ journalist. She lives in _____ apartment near _____ college where she is studying. _____ apartment is small, but she likes it.
10. Peter and Mary have two children, _____ boy and _____ girl. _____ boy is seven years old, and _____ girl is three. Peter works in _____ factory. Mary doesn't have _____ job right now.

70.2 Complete the sentences. Use *a* or *the* + one of these words:

airport   cup   ~~door~~   floor   picture   radio

1. Can you open _*the door*_, please?
2. How far is it to _____?
3. Can I have _____ of coffee, please?
4. That's _____ nice _____ – I like it.
5. Can you turn off _____, please?
6. Why are you sitting on _____?

70.3 Write *a/an* or *the* where necessary.

1. Don't forget to turn off light when you go out.   *turn off the light*
2. Enjoy your trip, and don't forget to send me postcard. _____
3. What is name of this town? _____
4. Canada is very big country. _____
5. What is largest city in Canada? _____
6. I like this room, but I don't like color of ceiling. _____
7. "Are you OK?" "No, I've got headache." _____
8. We live in old house near station. _____
9. What is name of director of movie we saw last night? _____

The . . .

We use **the** when it is clear which thing or person we mean.

- What is **the name** of this street? (This street has only one name.)
- Who is **the best player** on your team?
- Can you tell me **the time,** please? (= the time *now*)
- My office is on **the first floor.** (= the first floor of the building)

Don't forget to use **the.**

- Do you live near **the airport?** (*not* near airport)
- Excuse me, where is **the nearest bank?** (*not* where is nearest . . .)

the same . . .

- We live on **the same street.** (*not* on same street)
- "Are these two books different?" "No, they're **the same.**" (*not* they're same)

We say:

the sun / the moon / the world / the sky / the ocean / the country

- **The sky** is blue and **the sun** is shining.
- Do you live in a city or in **the country?**

the police

- After the robbery, **the police** asked us a lot of questions.

the top / the end / the middle / the left, etc.

- Write your name at **the top** of the page.
- My house is at **the end** of this block.
- The table is in **the middle** of the room.
- Do you drive on **the right** or on **the left** in your country?

the top
the left | *the middle* | *the right*
the bottom

play the piano / the guitar / the trumpet, etc. (musical instruments)

- Paula is learning to play **the piano.**

the radio

- I listen to **the radio** a lot.

We do *not* use **the** with:

television/TV

- I watch **television/TV** a lot.
- What's on **television** tonight?

but ■ Can you turn off **the TV?** (= the TV set)

breakfast/lunch/dinner

- What did you have for **breakfast?** (*not* the breakfast)
- **Dinner** is ready!

next/last + week/month/year/summer/Monday, etc.

- I'm not working **next week.** (*not* the next week)
- Did you take a vacation **last summer?** (*not* the last summer)

Exercises

71.1 Write *the* where necessary. Write *OK* if the sentence is correct.

1. What is name of this street?   *the name*
2. What's on television tonight?   *OK*
3. Our apartment is on second floor.   _____
4. Would you like to go to moon?   _____
5. What's best hotel in this town?   _____
6. What time is lunch?   _____
7. How far is it to football stadium?   _____
8. We're taking a trip at end of May.   _____
9. What are you doing next weekend?   _____
10. I didn't like her first time I met her.   _____
11. I'm going out after dinner.   _____
12. What's biggest city in world?   _____
13. My sister got married last month.   _____
14. My dictionary is on top shelf on right.   _____
15. We live in country about five miles from nearest town.   _____

71.2 Complete the sentences. Use *the same* + one of these words:

age   color   problem   ~~street~~   time

1. I live on Water Street and you live on Water Street. We live on *the same street* .
2. I arrived at 8:30 and you arrived at 8:30. We arrived at _____ .
3. Jim is 25 and Sue is 25. Jim and Sue are _____ .
4. My shirt is dark blue and so is my jacket. My shirt and jacket are _____ .
5. I have no money and you have no money. We have _____ .

71.3 Look at the pictures and complete the sentences. Use *the* if necessary.

1. *The sun* _____ is shining.   4. He's listening to _____ .
2. She's playing _____ .   5. They're watching _____ .
3. They're having _____ .   6. They're swimming in _____ .

71.4 Complete these sentences. Choose from the list. Use *the* if necessary.

capital   ~~dinner~~   police   lunch   middle   name   sky   television

1. We had *dinner* _____ at a restaurant last night.
2. We stayed at a very nice hotel, but I don't remember _____ .
3. _____ is very clear tonight. You can see all the stars.
4. I watched three movies on _____ last night.
5. _____ stopped me because I was driving too fast.
6. Tokyo is _____ of Japan.
7. "What did you have for _____?" "A salad."
8. I woke up in _____ of the night.

Go to work   go home   go to the movies

A

She's **at work.**

They're going **to school.**

He's **in bed.**

We say:

(go) **to work,** (be) **at work,** start **work,** finish **work**
- Goodbye! I'm **going to work** now. (*not* to the work)
- I **finish work** at 5 o'clock every day.

(go) **to school,** (be) **at school,** start **school,** finish **school,** etc.
- What did you learn **at school** today? (*not* at the school)
- Some children don't like **school.**

(go) **to college,** (be) **in college**
- Helen wants to **go to college** when she finishes high school.
- What did you study **in college?**

(go) **to prison/jail,** (be) **in prison/jail**
- Why is he **in prison?** What did he do?

(go) **to church,** (be) **in/at church**
- Dave usually **goes to church** on Sundays.

(go) **to bed,** (be) **in bed**
- I'm tired. I'm **going to bed** (*not* to the bed)
- "Where's Kim?" "She's **in bed.**"

(go) **home,** (be) **(at) home,** etc.
- I'm tired. I'm **going home.** (*not* to home)
- Are you going out tonight, or are you **staying home?** (*or* staying **at** home)

B

We say:

(go to) **the bank / the post office / the hospital / the station / the airport**
- "Are you going to **the bank?**" "No, **the post office.**"
- Brian was in an accident. He had to go to **the hospital.**
- Does this bus go to **the airport?**

(go to) **the theater / the movies**
- I never go to **the theater,** but I go to **the movies** a lot.

(go to) **the doctor, the dentist**
- You're sick. Why don't you go to **the doctor?**
- I'm going to **the dentist** tomorrow.

Exercises

72.1 Where are these people? Complete the sentences. Sometimes you need *the*.

1. He's in *bed* .
2. They're at _____ .
3. She's in _____ .
4. She's at _____ .
5. They're at _____ .
6. He's in _____ .

72.2 Complete the sentences. Choose from the list. Use *the* if necessary.

~~bank~~   bed   ~~church~~   home   post office   school   station

1. I need some money. I have to go to *the bank* .
2. Dave usually goes to *church* on Sundays.
3. In the U.S., children start _____ at the age of five.
4. There were a lot of people at _____ waiting for the train.
5. I called you last night, but you weren't at _____ .
6. I'm going to _____ now. Good night!
7. I'm going to _____ to get some stamps.

72.3 Complete the sentences. Use *go*. Sometimes you need *the*.

1. If you want to catch a plane, you *go to the airport* .
2. If you want to see a movie, you go to _____ .
3. If you are tired and you want to sleep, you _____ .
4. If you rob a bank and the police catch you, you _____ .
5. If you have a problem with your teeth, you _____ .
6. If you want to study after you finish high school, you _____ .
7. If you are injured in an accident, you _____ .

72.4 Write *the* where necessary. Write *OK* if the sentence is correct.

1. We went to movies last night.   *to the movies*
2. I finish work at 5 o'clock every day.   *OK*
3. Yuki wasn't feeling well yesterday, so she went to doctor.   _____
4. I wasn't feeling well this morning, so I stayed in bed.   _____
5. Why is Angela always late for work?   _____
6. "Where are your children?" "They're at school."   _____
7. We have no money in bank.   _____
8. When I was younger, I went to church every Sunday.   _____
9. What time do you usually get home from work?   _____
10. "Where shall we meet?" "At station."   _____
11. Jim is sick. He's in hospital.   _____
12. Makoto takes his children to school every day.   _____
13. Would you like to go to college?   _____
14. Would you like to go to theater tonight?   _____

I like music. I hate exams.

I like music. | I hate exams. | I don't like cold weather.

Do not use **the** for general ideas.

- I like **music**, especially **classical music**.
  (*not* the music . . . the classical music)
- We don't eat **meat** very often. (*not* the meat)
- **Life** is not possible without **water**.
  (*not* The life . . . the water)
- I hate **exams**. (*not* the exams)
- Do you know where they sell **foreign newspapers**?
- I'm not very good at writing **letters**.

Do not use **the** for games and sports.

- My favorite sports are **tennis** and **skiing**. (*not* the tennis . . . the skiing)

Do not use **the** for languages or academic subjects (**history/geography/physics/biology**, etc.).

- Do you think **English** is difficult? (*not* the English)
- Tom's brother is studying **physics** and **chemistry**.

Flowers or **the flowers**?

Compare:

- **Flowers** are beautiful.
  (= flowers in general)

- I don't like **cold weather**.
  (= cold weather in general)

- We don't eat **fish** very often. (= fish in general)

- Are you interested in **history**? (= history in general)

- I love your garden!
  The flowers are beautiful.
  (= the flowers in this garden)

- **The weather** isn't very good today. (= the weather today)

- We had a great meal last night. **The fish** was excellent. (= the fish we ate last night)

- Are you interested in **the history** of your country?

The flowers are beautiful.

Exercises

73.1 What do you think about these things?

dogs	big cities	fishing	TV quiz shows	exams	parties
museums	tea	basketball	computer games	loud music	hard work

Choose seven things from the box. Write sentences beginning:

I like   I don't like   I love   I hate   I don't mind (= it's OK)

1. _I hate exams._
2. _____
3. _____
4. _____
5. _____
6. _____
7. _____
8. _____

73.2 Are you interested in these things? Write sentences with:

I'm (very) interested in . . .	I know a lot about . . .	I don't know much about . . .
I'm not interested in . . .	I know a little about . . .	I don't know anything about . . .

1. (history) _I'm very interested in history._
2. (politics) I _____ .
3. (sports) _____
4. (art) _____
5. (astronomy) _____
6. (economics) _____

73.3 Which is right?

1. My favorite sport is tennis / ~~the tennis~~. (*tennis* is right)
2. I like this hotel. ~~Rooms~~ / The rooms are very nice. (*The rooms* is right)
3. Everybody needs friends / ~~the friends~~.
4. Tracy doesn't go to parties / the parties very often.
5. I went shopping this morning. Stores / The stores were very crowded.
6. "Where's milk / the milk?" "It's in the fridge."
7. I don't like milk / the milk. I never drink it.
8. "Do you play any sports?" "Yes, I play football / the football."
9. These days a lot of people use computers / the computers.
10. We went for a swim. Water / The water was very cold.
11. I don't like swimming in cold water / the cold water.
12. Excuse me, can you pass salt / the salt, please?
13. I like this town. I like people / the people here.
14. Vegetables / The vegetables are good for you.
15. I can't sing this song. I don't know words / the words.
16. I enjoy taking pictures / the pictures. It's my hobby.
17. Look at pictures / the pictures that I took when I was on vacation.
18. English / The English is used a lot in international business / the international business.
19. Money / The money doesn't always bring happiness / the happiness.

UNIT 74

The . . . (Names of Places)

A

Places (continents, countries, states, islands, cities, etc.)

In general we do not use **the** + names of places.

■ **Bangkok** is the capital of **Thailand**.

■ **Easter Island** is in the Pacific.

■ **Peru** is in **South America**.

■ **Quebec** is a province of **Canada**.

(the) *[crossed out]*

But we use **the** in names with **republic/states/kingdom**.

the Dominican **Republic**	the United **States** of America (**the** USA)
the Czech **Republic**	the United **Kingdom** (**the** UK)

(the)

B

the -s (plural names)

We use **the** + plural names of countries/islands/mountains.

the Netherlands	the Canary Islands
the Philippines	the Andes

(the)

C

Oceans, rivers, etc.

We use **the** + names of oceans/seas/rivers/canals.

the Pacific (Ocean)	the Amazon (River)
the Mediterranean (Sea)	the Panama Canal

(the)

D

Places in towns (streets, buildings, etc.)

In general we do not use **the** + names of streets, squares, etc.

■ Kevin lives on **Central Avenue**.   ■ **Times Square** is in New York.

■ Where is **Main Street**, please?

(the) *[crossed out]*

We do not use **the** + names + airports/stations/universities/parks, etc.

Kennedy Airport	**McGill University**
Pennsylvania Station	**Yosemite** (National **Park**)

But we use **the** + names of universities with **of** (see Section E).

(the) *[crossed out]*

We generally use **the** with names of hotels, restaurants, theaters, museums, monuments.

the Milton (Hotel)	the New Broadway (Theater)
the Millhouse (Restaurant)	the Metropolitan (Museum)
the Springfield Cineplex (movie theater)	the Lincoln Memorial

(the)

E

the . . . of . . .

We use **the** + names with **of** . . . .

the University of California	the Great Wall of China
the Bank of Nova Scotia	the Tower of London

(the)

F

the north / the south / the east / the west

■ "Which part of Canada did you go to?" "To **the** west/north."

(the)

---

148   *The* Units 70–73

Exercises

74.1 Answer these geography questions. Choose from the box. Use *The* if necessary.

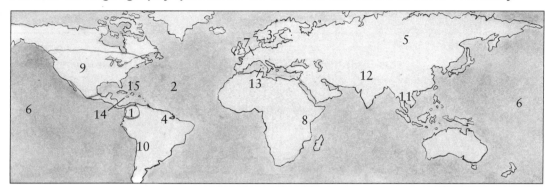

1. _Bogota_	is the capital of Colombia.	Amazon
2. _The Atlantic_	is between Africa and the Americas.	Andes
3. _Sweden_	is a country in northern Europe.	Asia
4. _Am_	is a river in South America.	~~Atlantic~~
5. _____	is the largest continent in the world.	Bahamas
6. _____	is the largest ocean.	Bangkok
7. _____	is a river in Europe.	~~Bogota~~
8. _____	is a country in East Africa.	Himalayas
9. _____	is between Canada and Mexico.	Jamaica
10. _____	are mountains in South America.	Kenya
11. _____	is the capital of Thailand.	Mediterranean
12. _____	are mountains in Asia.	Pacific
13. _____	is between Europe and Africa.	Rhine
14. _____	is an island in the Caribbean.	Sweden
15. _____	are a group of islands near Florida.	United States

74.2 Write *the* where necessary. If the sentence is correct, write *OK*.

1. Kevin lives on Central Avenue. _OK_
2. We went to see a play at National Theater. _at the National Theater_
3. Have you ever been to China? _____
4. Have you ever been to Philippines? _____
5. Can you tell me where Westside Cineplex is? _____
6. Can you tell me where Fifth Street is? _____
7. Can you tell me where Museum of Modern Art is? _____
8. I'll meet you in front of Washington Monument. _____
9. The sun rises in east and sets in west. _____
10. Europe is bigger than Australia. _____
11. Which river is longer – Mississippi or Nile? _____
12. We stayed at Park Hotel near Central Park. _____
13. How far is it from Times Square to Penn Station? _____
14. Rocky Mountains are in North America. _____
15. Texas is famous for oil and cowboys. _____
16. Panama Canal joins Atlantic Ocean and Pacific Ocean. _____
17. I hope to go to United States next year. _____
18. Alan went to University of Michigan. _____

This/these and *that/those*

A

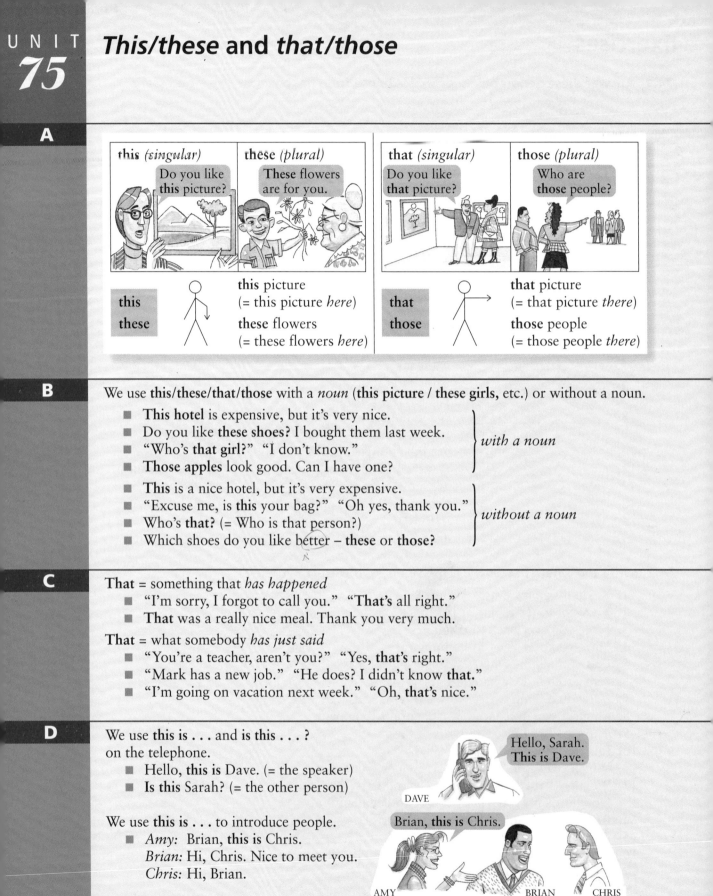

this *(singular)*
Do you like **this picture?**

these *(plural)*
These flowers are for you.

that *(singular)*
Do you like **that picture?**

those *(plural)*
Who are **those people?**

this these		**this** picture (= this picture *here*)
		these flowers (= these flowers *here*)

that those		**that** picture (= that picture *there*)
		those people (= those people *there*)

B

We use **this/these/that/those** with a *noun* (**this picture / these girls,** etc.) or without a noun.

- **This hotel** is expensive, but it's very nice.
- Do you like **these shoes?** I bought them last week.
- "Who's **that girl?**" "I don't know."
- **Those apples** look good. Can I have one?

} with a noun

- **This** is a nice hotel, but it's very expensive.
- "Excuse me, is **this** your bag?" "Oh yes, thank you."
- Who's **that?** (= Who is that person?)
- Which shoes do you like better – **these** or **those?**

} without a noun

C

That = something that *has happened*

- "I'm sorry, I forgot to call you." "**That's** all right."
- **That** was a really nice meal. Thank you very much.

That = what somebody *has just said*

- "You're a teacher, aren't you?" "Yes, **that's** right."
- "Mark has a new job." "He does? I didn't know **that.**"
- "I'm going on vacation next week." "Oh, **that's** nice."

D

We use **this is . . .** and **is this . . . ?**
on the telephone.

- Hello, **this is** Dave. (= the speaker)
- **Is this** Sarah? (= the other person)

Hello, Sarah. **This is Dave.**

DAVE

We use **this is . . .** to introduce people.

- *Amy:* Brian, **this is** Chris.
  Brian: Hi, Chris. Nice to meet you.
  Chris: Hi, Brian.

Brian, **this is Chris.**

AMY   BRIAN   CHRIS

This one / that one Unit 76

Exercises

75.1 Complete the sentences. Use *this/these/that/those* + one of these words:

birds   dishes   house   postcards   chair   ~~shoes~~

1 Do you like _these shoes_ ?
2 Who lives in _____ ?
3 How much are _____ ?
4 Look at _____ !
5 Excuse me, is _____ free?
6 _____ are dirty.

75.2 Write questions: *Is this/that your . . . ?* or *Are these/those your . . . ?*

1 _Is this your bag?_
2
3
4
5
6
7
8
9
10

75.3 Complete the sentences with *this is* or *that's* or *that*.

1. *A:* I'm sorry I'm late.
   B: _That's_ all right.
2. *A:* I can't come to the party tomorrow.
   B: Oh, _____ too bad. Why not?
3. *(on the telephone)*
   Sue: Hello, Kim. _____ Sue.
   Kim: Oh, hi, Sue. How are you?
4. *A:* You're lazy!
   B: _____ not true!

5. *A:* Beth plays the piano very well.
   B: Really? I didn't know _____ .
6. *(Mark meets Paul's sister Amy.)*
   Paul: Mark, _____ my sister Amy.
   Mark: Hi, Amy.
7. *A:* I'm sorry I was angry yesterday.
   B: _____ OK. Forget it!
8. *A:* You're a friend of John's, aren't you?
   B: Yes, _____ right.

One/ones

one (= a . . .)

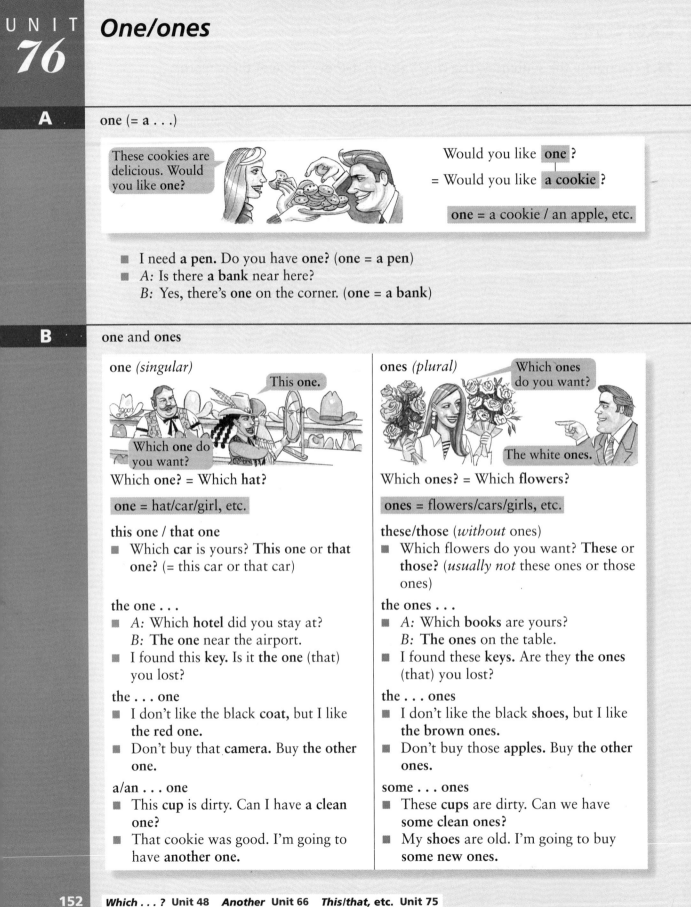

These cookies are delicious. Would you like **one**?

Would you like **one**?
= Would you like **a cookie**?

one = a cookie / an apple, etc.

- I need **a pen**. Do you have **one**? (one = a pen)
- *A:* Is there **a bank** near here?
  B: Yes, there's **one** on the corner. (one = a bank)

one and ones

one *(singular)*

This **one**.

Which **one** do you want?

Which **one**? = Which **hat**?

one = hat/car/girl, etc.

this one / that one
- Which **car** is yours? **This one** or **that one**? (= this car or that car)

the one . . .
- *A:* Which **hotel** did you stay at?
  B: **The one** near the airport.
- I found this **key**. Is it **the one** (that) you lost?

the . . . one
- I don't like the black **coat**, but I like **the red one**.
- Don't buy that **camera**. Buy **the other one**.

a/an . . . one
- This **cup** is dirty. Can I have **a clean one**?
- That cookie was good. I'm going to have **another one**.

ones *(plural)*

Which **ones** do you want?

The white **ones**.

Which **ones**? = Which **flowers**?

ones = flowers/cars/girls, etc.

these/those *(without* ones*)*
- Which flowers do you want? **These** or **those**? (*usually not* these ones or those ones)

the ones . . .
- *A:* Which **books** are yours?
  B: **The ones** on the table.
- I found these **keys**. Are they **the ones** (that) you lost?

the . . . ones
- I don't like the black **shoes**, but I like **the brown ones**.
- Don't buy those **apples**. Buy **the other ones**.

some . . . ones
- These **cups** are dirty. Can we have **some clean ones**?
- My **shoes** are old. I'm going to buy **some new ones**.

Exercises

76.1 A asks B some questions. Use the information in the box to write B's answers. Use
one (not *a/an . . .*) in the answers.

B doesn't need a car.	✗ B just had a cup of coffee.
There's a drugstore on First Avenue.	✗ B is going to buy a bicycle.
~~B doesn't have a pen.~~	✗ B doesn't have an umbrella.

1. *A:* Can you lend me a pen?   *B:* I'm sorry, *I don't have one* .
2. *A:* Would you like to have a car?   *B:* No, I don't _____ .
3. *A:* Do you have a bicycle?   *B:* No, but _____ .
4. *A:* Can you lend me an umbrella?   *B:* I'm sorry, but _____ .
5. *A:* Would you like a cup of coffee?   *B:* No, thank you. _____ .
6. *A:* Is there a drugstore near here?   *B:* Yes, _____ .

76.2 Complete the sentences. Use *a/an . . . one*. Use the words in the list.

    better big ~~clean~~ different new old

1. This cup is dirty. Can I have *a clean one* ?
2. I'm going to sell my old car and buy _____ .
3. That's not a very good photograph. This is _____ .
4. I want today's newspaper. This is _____ .
5. This box is too small. I need _____ .
6. Why do we always go to the same restaurant? Let's go to _____ .

76.3 Use the information in the box to complete these conversations. Use *one/ones*.

The coat is black.	I took the photos at the beach last week.
The girl is tall with long hair.	The shoes are brown.
~~The hotel is near the airport.~~	The picture is on the wall.
The house has a red door.	The books are on the top shelf.
The flowers are yellow.	The man has a mustache and glasses.

1. *A:* We stayed at a hotel.
   B: *Which one* ?
   A: *The one near the airport.*

2. *A:* Those shoes are nice.
   B: Which _____ ?
   A: The _____ ones.

3. *A:* That's a nice house.
   B: _____ ?
   A: _____ with _____ .

4. *A:* I like that coat.
   B: _____ ?
   A: _____

5. *A:* I like that picture.
   B: _____ ?
   A: _____

6. *A:* Are those your books?
   B: _____ ?
   A: _____

7. *A:* Do you know that girl?
   B: _____ ?
   A: _____

8. *A:* Those flowers are beautiful.
   B: _____ ?
   A: _____

9. *A:* Who's that man?
   B: _____ ?
   A: _____

10. *A:* Have you seen my photos yet?
   B: _____ ?
   A: _____

Some and *any*

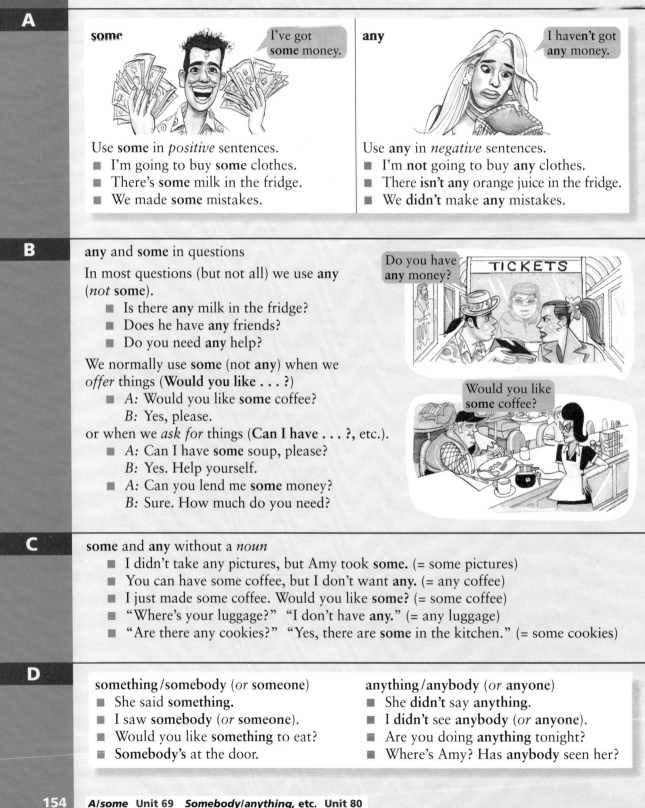

A

some

I've got **some** money.

Use **some** in *positive* sentences.
- I'm going to buy **some** clothes.
- There's **some** milk in the fridge.
- We made **some** mistakes.

any

I haven't got **any** money.

Use **any** in *negative* sentences.
- I'm **not** going to buy **any** clothes.
- There **isn't any** orange juice in the fridge.
- We **didn't** make **any** mistakes.

B

any and **some** in questions

In most questions (but not all) we use **any** (*not* **some**).
- Is there **any** milk in the fridge?
- Does he have **any** friends?
- Do you need **any** help?

Do you have **any** money?

TICKETS

We normally use **some** (not **any**) when we *offer* things (**Would you like . . . ?**)
- *A:* Would you like **some** coffee?
  B: Yes, please.

or when we *ask for* things (**Can I have . . . ?**, etc.).
- *A:* Can I have **some** soup, please?
  B: Yes. Help yourself.
- *A:* Can you lend me **some** money?
  B: Sure. How much do you need?

Would you like **some** coffee?

C

some and **any** without a *noun*
- I didn't take any pictures, but Amy took **some.** (= some pictures)
- You can have some coffee, but I don't want **any.** (= any coffee)
- I just made some coffee. Would you like **some?** (= some coffee)
- "Where's your luggage?" "I don't have **any.**" (= any luggage)
- "Are there any cookies?" "Yes, there are **some** in the kitchen." (= some cookies)

D

something / **somebody** (*or* **someone**)
- She said **something.**
- I saw **somebody** (*or* **someone**).
- Would you like **something** to eat?
- **Somebody's** at the door.

anything / **anybody** (*or* **anyone**)
- She **didn't** say **anything.**
- I **didn't** see **anybody** (*or* **anyone**).
- Are you doing **anything** tonight?
- Where's Amy? Has **anybody** seen her?

Exercises

77.1 Write *some* or *any*.

1. I bought *some* cheese, but I didn't buy *any* bread.
2. I'm going to the post office. I need _____ stamps.
3. There aren't _____ gas stations in this part of town.
4. Eric and Alice don't have _____ children.
5. Have you got _____ brothers or sisters?
6. There are _____ beautiful flowers in the park.
7. Do you know _____ good hotels in Miami?
8. "Would you like _____ coffee?" "Yes, please."
9. When we were on vacation, we visited _____ very interesting places.
10. Don't buy _____ rice. We don't need _____ .
11. I went out to buy _____ oranges, but they didn't have _____ at the store.
12. I'm thirsty. Can I have _____ water, please?

77.2 Complete the sentences. Use *some* or *any* + one of these words:

air	friends	help	letters	pictures
batteries	fruit	languages	milk	~~shampoo~~

1. I want to wash my hair. Is there *any shampoo* _____ ?
2. This evening I'm going to write _____ .
3. I don't have my camera, so I can't take _____ .
4. Do you speak _____ foreign _____ ?
5. Last night I went to a restaurant with _____ of mine.
6. Can I have _____ in my coffee, please?
7. That clock isn't working. There aren't _____ in it.
8. It's hot in this office. I'm going out for _____ fresh _____ .
9. "Would you like _____ ?" "No, thank you. I'm not hungry right now."
10. I can do this job alone. I don't need _____ .

77.3 Complete the sentences. Use *some* or *any*.

1. Min Fang didn't take any pictures, but *I took some* . (I / take)
2. "Where's your luggage?" "*I don't have any* ." (I / not / have)
3. "Do you need any money?" "No, thank you. _____ ." (I / have)
4. "Can I borrow some money?" "Sorry, _____ ." (I / not / have)
5. The tomatoes weren't very good, so _____ . (I / not / buy)
6. There were some nice oranges at the store, so _____ . (I / buy)

77.4 Write *something/somebody/anything/anybody*.

1. Luis said *something* to me, but I didn't understand it.
2. "What's wrong?" "There's _____ in my eye."
3. Do you know _____ about politics?
4. I went to the store, but I didn't buy _____ .
5. _____ broke the window. I don't know who.
6. There isn't _____ in the bag. It's empty.
7. I'm looking for my keys. Has _____ seen them?
8. Would you like _____ to drink?
9. I didn't eat _____ because I wasn't hungry.
10. This is a secret. Please don't tell _____ .

Not + any, no, and none

The parking lot is empty.

There **aren't any** cars
There are **no** cars } in the parking lot.

How many cars are there in the parking lot?
None.

not (-n't) + any

- There **aren't any** cars in the parking lot.
- Karen and Steve **don't** have **any** children.
- You can have some coffee, but I **don't** want **any**.

no + *noun* (no cars / no garage, etc.)

no . . . = not + any *or* not + a

- There are **no** cars in the parking lot. (= there **aren't any** cars)
- We have **no coffee**. (= we **don't have any** coffee)
- It's a nice house, but there's **no garage**. (= there **isn't a** garage)

We use **no . . .** especially after **have/has** and **there is/are**.

***negative verb* + any = *positive verb* + no**

- They **don't** have **any** children. *or* They **have no** children.
  (*not* They don't have no children)
- There **isn't any** sugar in your coffee. *or* **There's no** sugar in your coffee.

Compare **no** and **none**:

Use **no + *noun* (no money / no children**, etc.).
- We have **no money**.
- Everything was OK. There were **no problems**.

Use **none** alone (*without* a noun).
- "How much money do you have?" "**None.**" (= no money)
- "Were there any problems?" "No, **none.**" (= no problems)

none and **no one**

none = 0 (zero)
no one = nobody

None is an answer for **How much? / How many?** (things or people).
- "**How much** money do you have?" "**None.**" (= no money)
- "**How many** people did you meet?" "**None.**" (= no people)

No one is an answer for **Who?**.
- "**Who** did you meet?" "**No one.**" *or* "**Nobody.**"

Exercises

78.1 **Write these sentences again with *no*.**

1. We don't have any money.   We have no money.
2. There aren't any stores near here.   There are _____.
3. Carol doesn't have any free time.   _____
4. There isn't a light in this room.   _____

Write these sentences again with *any*.

5. We have no money.   We don't have any money.
6. There's no gas in the car.   _____
7. There are no buses today.   _____
8. Marcos has no brothers or sisters.   _____

78.2 **Write *no* or *any*.**

1. There's _no_____ sugar in your coffee.
2. My brother is married, but he doesn't have _____ children.
3. Sue doesn't speak _____ foreign languages.
4. I'm afraid there's _____ coffee. Would you like some tea?
5. "Look at those birds!" "Birds? Where? I can't see _____ birds."
6. "Do you know where Jessica is?" "No, I have _____ idea."

Write *no*, *any*, or *none*.

7. There aren't _____ pictures on the wall.
8. The weather was cold, but there was _____ wind.
9. I wanted to buy some oranges, but they didn't have _____ at the store.
10. Everything was correct. There were _____ mistakes.
11. "How much luggage have you got?" "_____."
12. "How much luggage have you got?" "I haven't got _____."

78.3 **Complete the sentences. Use *any* or *no* + one of these words:**

| air conditioning | difference | friends | money | ~~problems~~ |
| answer | film | furniture | photographs | questions |

1. Everything was OK. There were _no problems_____ .
2. They want to take a vacation, but they have _____ .
3. I'm not going to answer _____ .
4. He's always alone. He has _____ .
5. There is _____ between these two machines. They're exactly the same.
6. There wasn't _____ in the room. It was completely empty.
7. I tried to call you yesterday, but there was _____ .
8. The house is hot because there isn't _____ .
9. I can't take _____ . There's _____ in the camera.

78.4 **Write short answers (one or two words) to these questions. Use *None* where necessary.**

1. How many letters did you write yesterday? _Two._ OR _A lot._ OR _None._
2. How many sisters do you have? _____
3. How much coffee did you drink yesterday? _____
4. How many pictures have you taken today? _____
5. How many legs does a snake have? _____

Not + anybody/anyone/anything and nobody/no one/nothing

A

not + anybody / anyone
nobody / no one
(for *people*)

not + anything
nothing
(for *things*)

There **isn't** $\begin{Bmatrix} \textbf{anybody} \\ \textbf{anyone} \end{Bmatrix}$ in the room.

There **isn't anything** in the bag.

There **is** $\begin{Bmatrix} \textbf{nobody} \\ \textbf{no one} \end{Bmatrix}$ in the room.

There **is nothing** in the bag.

A: **Who** is in the room?
B: **Nobody. / No one.**

A: **What's** in the bag?
B: **Nothing.**

-body and **-one** are the same:
anybody = **anyone**   **nobody** = **no one**

B

not + anybody/anyone
■ I **don't** know **anybody** (*or* **anyone**) here.

not + anything
■ I **can't** remember **anything**.

nobody = not + anybody
no one = not + anyone
■ I'm lonely. I have **nobody** to talk to.
   (= I **don't** have **anybody**.)
■ The house is empty. There is **no one** in it.
   (= There **isn't anyone** in it.)

nothing = not + anything
■ She said **nothing**.
   (= She **didn't** say **anything**.)
■ There's **nothing** to eat.
   (= There **isn't anything** to eat.)

C

You can use **nobody / no one / nothing** at the beginning of a sentence or alone (to answer a question).

■ The house is empty. **Nobody** lives there.
   (*not* Anybody lives there)
■ "Who did you speak to?" "**No one.**"

■ **Nothing** happened.
   (*not* Anything happened)
■ "What did you say?" "**Nothing.**"

D

Remember: *negative verb* + anybody/anyone/anything
           positive verb + nobody/no one/nothing

   ■ He **doesn't** know **anything.** (*not* he doesn't know nothing)
   ■ **Don't** tell **anybody.** (*not* don't tell nobody)
   ■ There is **nothing** to do in this town. (*not* there isn't nothing)

Exercises

79.1 Write these sentences again with *nobody / no one* or *nothing*.

1. There isn't anything in the bag.   *There's nothing in the bag.*
2. There isn't anybody in the office.   There's _____ .
3. I don't have anything to do.   I _____ .
4. There isn't anything on TV.   _____
5. There wasn't anyone at home.   _____
6. We didn't find anything.   _____

79.2 Write these sentences again with *anybody/anyone* or *anything*.

1. There's nothing in the bag.   *There isn't anything in the bag.*
2. There was nobody on the bus.   There wasn't _____ .
3. I have nothing to read.   _____
4. I have no one to help me.   _____
5. Sarai heard nothing.   _____
6. We have nothing for dinner.   _____

79.3 Answer these questions with *nobody / no one* or *nothing*.

1a. What did you say? *Nothing.*   5a. Who knows the answer? _____
2a. Who saw you? *Nobody.*   6a. What did you buy? _____
3a. What do you want? _____   7a. What happened? _____
4a. Who did you meet? _____   8a. Who was late? _____

**Now answer the same questions with full sentences. Use *nobody / no one / nothing*
or *anybody / anyone / anything*.**

1b. *I didn't say anything.*   5b. _____ the answer.
2b. *Nobody saw me.*   6b. _____
3b. I don't _____ .   7b. _____
4b. I _____ .   8b. _____

**79.4 Complete the sentences. Use *nobody / no one / nothing / anybody / anyone /
anything*.**

1. That house is empty. *Nobody* lives there.
2. Brian has a bad memory. He can't remember *anything* .
3. Be quiet! Don't say _____ .
4. I didn't know about the meeting. _____ told me.
5. "What did you have to eat?" "_____ . I wasn't hungry."
6. I didn't eat _____ . I wasn't hungry.
7. Jenny was sitting alone. She wasn't with _____ .
8. I'm sorry I can't help you. There's _____ I can do.
9. I don't know _____ about car engines.
10. The museum is free. It doesn't cost _____ to go in.
11. I heard a knock on the door, but when I opened it, there was _____ there.
12. Antonio spoke very fast. I didn't understand _____ .
13. "What are you doing tonight?" "_____ . Why?"
14. Helen is out of town. _____ knows where she is. She didn't tell
_____ where she was going.

Somebody, anything, nowhere, etc.

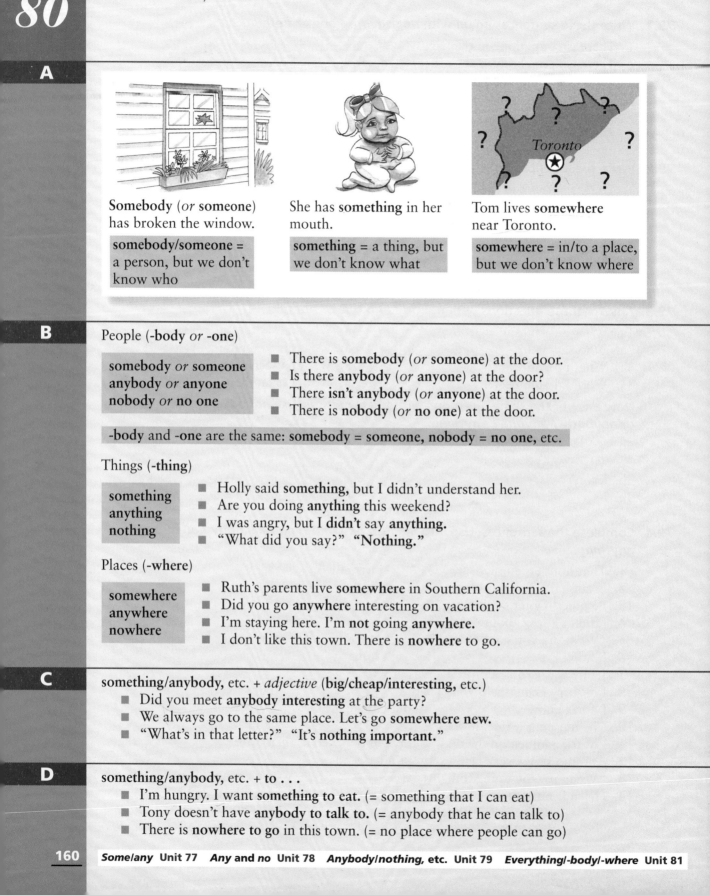

Somebody (*or* **someone**) has broken the window.

> **somebody/someone** = a person, but we don't know who

She has **something** in her mouth.

> **something** = a thing, but we don't know what

Tom lives **somewhere** near Toronto.

> **somewhere** = in/to a place, but we don't know where

People (**-body** *or* **-one**)

> somebody *or* someone
> anybody *or* anyone
> nobody *or* no one

- There is **somebody** (*or* **someone**) at the door.
- Is there **anybody** (*or* **anyone**) at the door?
- There **isn't anybody** (*or* **anyone**) at the door.
- There is **nobody** (*or* **no one**) at the door.

> **-body** and **-one** are the same: **somebody** = **someone**, **nobody** = **no one**, etc.

Things (**-thing**)

> something
> anything
> nothing

- Holly said **something**, but I didn't understand her.
- Are you doing **anything** this weekend?
- I was angry, but I **didn't** say **anything**.
- "What did you say?" "**Nothing**."

Places (**-where**)

> somewhere
> anywhere
> nowhere

- Ruth's parents live **somewhere** in Southern California.
- Did you go **anywhere** interesting on vacation?
- I'm staying here. I'm **not** going **anywhere**.
- I don't like this town. There is **nowhere** to go.

something/anybody, etc. + *adjective* (**big/cheap/interesting**, etc.)
- Did you meet **anybody interesting** at the party?
- We always go to the same place. Let's go **somewhere new**.
- "What's in that letter?" "It's **nothing important**."

something/anybody, etc. + **to** . . .
- I'm hungry. I want **something to eat**. (= something that I can eat)
- Tony doesn't have **anybody to talk to**. (= anybody that he can talk to)
- There is **nowhere to go** in this town. (= no place where people can go)

Exercises

80.1 Write *somebody* (or *someone*) / *something* / *somewhere*.

1. Holly said _something_ .   What did she say?
2. I lost _____ this morning.   What did you lose?
3. Sue and Tom have gone _____ .   Where have they gone?
4. I'm going to call _____ .   Who are you going to call?

80.2 Write *nobody* (or *no one*) / *nothing* / *nowhere*.

1a. What did you say?   _Nothing._
2a. Where are you going?   _____
3a. What do you want?   _____
4a. Who are you looking for?   _____

Answer the same questions with full sentences. Use *not + anybody/anything/anywhere*.

1b. _I didn't say anything._   3b. _____
2b. I'm not _____ .   4b. _____

80.3 Write *somebody/anything/nowhere*, etc.

1. It's dark. I can't see _anything_ .
2. Jay lives _somewhere_ near Toronto.
3. Do you know _____ about computers?
4. "Listen!" "What? I can't hear _____ ."
5. "What are you doing here?" "I'm waiting for _____ ."
6. We need to talk. There's _____ I want to tell you.
7. "Did _____ see the accident?" "No, _____ ."
8. We weren't hungry, so we didn't eat _____ .
9. "What's going to happen?" "I don't know. _____ knows."
10. "Do you know _____ in Tokyo?" "Yes, a few people."
11. "What's in that suitcase?" "_____ . It's empty."
12. I'm looking for my glasses. I can't find them _____ .
13. I don't like cold weather. I want to live _____ warm.
14. Is there _____ interesting on TV tonight?
15. Have you ever met _____ famous?

80.4 Complete the sentences. Choose from the boxes.

You can use these words more than once: **Use these words once:**

something	anything	nothing
somewhere	anywhere	nowhere

do	eat	play	sit
drink	~~go~~	read	stay

1. We don't go out very much because there's _nowhere to go_ .
2. There isn't any food in the house. We don't have _____ .
3. I'm bored. I have _____ .
4. "Why are you standing?" "Because there isn't _____ ."
5. "Would you like _____ ?" "Yes, please – a glass of water."
6. All the hotels were full. There was _____ .
7. I want _____ . I'm going to buy a magazine.
8. We're going to buy a house with a yard. Our boys need _____ .

Every and *all*

every

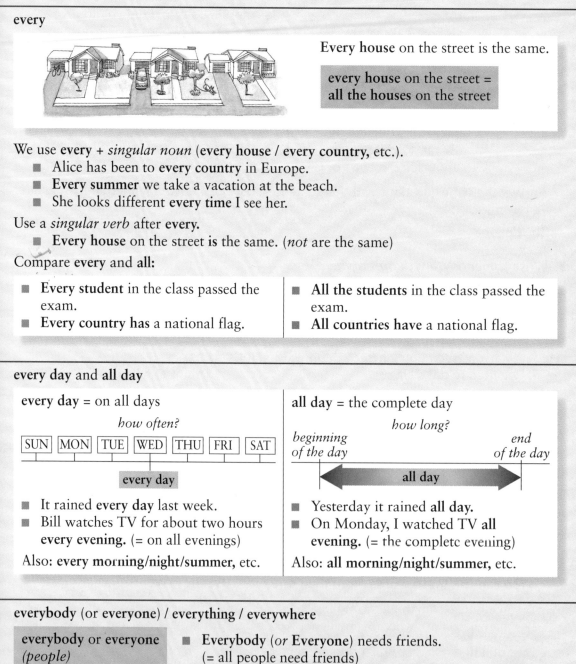

Every house on the street is the same.

> every house on the street =
> all the houses on the street

We use **every** + *singular noun* (**every house** / **every country**, etc.).

- Alice has been to **every country** in Europe.
- **Every summer** we take a vacation at the beach.
- She looks different **every time** I see her.

Use a *singular verb* after **every**.

- **Every house** on the street **is** the same. (*not* are the same)

Compare **every** and **all**:

■ **Every student** in the class passed the exam.	■ **All the students** in the class passed the exam.
■ **Every country has** a national flag.	■ **All countries have** a national flag.

every day and **all day**

every day = on all days	**all day** = the complete day
how often?	*how long?*
SUN MON TUE WED THU FRI SAT	*beginning of the day* ←——— all day ———→ *end of the day*
every day	

■ It rained **every day** last week.	■ Yesterday it rained **all day**.
■ Bill watches TV for about two hours **every evening**. (= on all evenings)	■ On Monday, I watched TV **all evening**. (= the complete evening)
Also: **every morning/night/summer**, etc.	Also: **all morning/night/summer**, etc.

everybody (or **everyone**) / **everything** / **everywhere**

everybody or **everyone** *(people)*	■ **Everybody** (*or* **Everyone**) needs friends. (= all people need friends)
everything *(things)*	■ Have you got **everything** you need? (= all the things you need)
everywhere *(places)*	■ I lost my watch. I've looked **everywhere** for it. (= I've looked in all places)

Use a *singular verb* after **everybody/everyone/everything**.

- **Everybody has** problems. (*not* everybody have)

Exercises

81.1 **Complete the sentences. Use *every* + one of these words:**

day   room   ~~student~~   time   word

1. _Every student_____ in the class passed the exam.
2. My job is very boring. _____ is the same.
3. Kate is a very good tennis player. When we play, she wins _____ .
4. _____ in the hotel has a color TV.
5. "Did you understand what she said?" "Most of it but not _____ ."

81.2 **Complete the sentences with *every day* or *all day*.**

1. Yesterday it rained _all day_____ .
2. I buy a newspaper _____ , but sometimes I don't read it.
3. I'm not going out tomorrow. I'll be at home _____ .
4. I drink about four cups of coffee _____ .
5. Paula was sick yesterday, so she stayed in bed _____ .
6. Last year we went to the beach for a week, and it rained _____ .
7. I'm tired because I've been working hard _____ .

81.3 **Write *every* or *all*.**

1. Bill watches TV for about two hours _every_____ evening.
2. Barbara gets up at 6:30 _____ morning.
3. The weather was nice yesterday, so we sat outside _____ afternoon.
4. I'm leaving town on Monday. I'll be away _____ week.
5. "How often do you go skiing?" "_____ year. Usually in March."
6. *A:* Were you at home at 10 A.M. yesterday?
   B: Yes, I was home _____ morning. I went out after lunch.
7. My sister likes new cars. She buys one _____ year.
8. I saw Brian at the party, but he didn't speak to me _____ evening.
9. We take a vacation for two or three weeks _____ summer.

81.4 **Write *everybody/everything/everywhere*.**

1. _Everybody_____ needs friends.
2. Chris knows _____ about computers.
3. I like the people here. _____ is very friendly.
4. This is a nice hotel. It's comfortable and _____ is very clean.
5. Kevin never uses his car. He goes _____ on his motorcycle.
6. Let's have dinner. _____ is hungry.
7. Sue's house is full of books. There are books _____ .
8. You're right. _____ you say is true.

81.5 **Write a verb (one word).**

1. Everybody _has_____ problems.
2. Are you ready yet? Everybody _____ waiting for you.
3. Eric is very popular. Everyone _____ him.
4. This town is completely different. Everything _____ changed.
5. I got home very late. I came in quietly because everyone _____ asleep.
6. Everybody _____ mistakes!

All, most, some, any, and no/none

Compare:

children/money/books, etc. (in general)	the children / the money / these books, etc.
■ **Children** like to play. (= children in general) ■ **Money** isn't everything. (= money in general) ■ I enjoy reading **books**. ■ Everybody needs **friends**.	■ Where are **the children**? (= our children) ■ I want to buy a car, but I haven't got **the money**. (= the money for a car) ■ Have you read **these books**? ■ I often go out with **my friends**.

most / most of / some / some of, etc.

all   most   some   any   no / none / not + any

most/some, etc. + noun

all most some any no	~~of~~	cities children books money

■ **Most children** like to play.
  (= children in general)
■ I don't want **any money**.
■ **Some books** are better than others.
■ He has **no friends**.
■ **All cities** have the same problems.
  (= cities in general)

Do not use **of** in these sentences:
■ **Most people** drive too fast.
  (*not* most of people)
■ **Some birds** can't fly. (*not* some of birds)

most of / some of, etc. + **the/this/my**, etc.

all	(of)	the this/that these/those my/your, etc.
most some any none	of	

■ **Most of the children in this school** are
  under 11 years old.
■ I don't want **any of this money**.
■ **Some of these books** are very old.
■ **None of my friends** can ski.

But we say **all the . . . / all my . . .**, etc.
(with or without **of**).
■ **All the students in our class** passed the
  exam. (*or* All of the students . . .)
■ Silvia has lived in Miami **all her life**.
  (*or* . . . **all of her life**.)

all of it / most of them / none of us, etc.

all most some any none	of	it them us you

■ We can have **some of this cake** but not **all of it**.
■ *A:* Do you know those people?
  B: **Most of them**, but not **all of them**.
■ **Some of us** are going out tonight. Why don't you come with us?
■ I have a lot of history books, but I haven't read **any of them**.
■ "How many of these books have you read?" "**None of them**."

The (children / the children, etc.) Unit 73 *Some/any* Unit 77 *No/none/any* Unit 78 *Every and all* Unit 81

Exercises

82.1 Complete the sentences. Use the word in parentheses (*some*/*most*, etc.). Sometimes you need *of* (*some of* / *most of*, etc.).

1. _Most_____ children like to play. (most)
2. _Some of_____ this money is yours. (some)
3. _____ people never stop talking. (some)
4. _____ the stores downtown close at 6:00. (most)
5. You can change your money in _____ banks. (some)
6. I don't like _____ the pictures in the living room. (any)
7. He's lost _____ his money. (all)
8. _____ my friends are married. (none)
9. Do you know _____ the people in this photograph? (any)
10. _____ birds can fly. (most)
11. I enjoyed _____ the film, but I didn't like the ending. (most)
12. _____ sports are very dangerous. (some)
13. We can't find anywhere to stay. _____ the hotels are full. (all)
14. Try _So me of_____ this cheese. It's delicious. (some)
15. The weather was bad when we were on vacation. It rained _most of_ the time. (most)

82.2 Look at the pictures and answer the questions. Use *all*/*most*/*some*/*none* + *of them* / *of it*.

1. How many of the people are women?   _Most of them._____
2. How many of the boxes are on the table?   _____
3. How many of the men are wearing hats?   _____
4. How many of the windows are open?   _____
5. How many of the people are standing?   _____
6. How much of the money is Ben's?   _____

82.3 Right or wrong? Correct the sentences that are wrong. Write *OK* if the sentence is correct.

1. Most of children like to play.   _Most children_____
2. All the students failed the exam.   _OK_____
3. Some of people work too hard.   _____
4. Some of questions on the exam were very easy.   _____
5. I haven't seen any of those people before.   _____
6. All of insects have six legs.   _____
7. Have you read all these books?   _____
8. Most of students in our class are very nice.   _____
9. Most of my friends are going to the party.   _____
10. I'm very tired this morning – I was awake most of night. _____

Both, either, and neither

A

We use **both/either/neither** to talk about two things or people.

both	either	neither (not + either)

- Rosemary has two children. **Both** are married. (**both** = the two children)
- Would you like tea or coffee? You can have **either**. (**either** = tea or coffee)
- A: Do you want to go to the movies or the theater?
  B: **Neither.** I want to stay home. (**neither** = not the movies *or* the theater)

Compare **either** and **neither**:

- "Would you like **tea or coffee?**"
  - "**Either.** It doesn't matter." (= tea or coffee)
  - "**I don't** want **either.**" (*not* I don't want neither)
  - "**Neither.**" (= not tea *or* coffee)

B

Both/either/neither + *noun*

both + *plural*	**both**	**windows/books/children,** etc.
either neither } + *singular*	**either neither**	**window/book/child,** etc.

- Last year I went to Miami and Seattle. I liked **both cities** very much.
- First I worked in an office, and then in a store. **Neither job** was very interesting.
- There are two ways to get to the airport. You can go **either way.**

C

both of . . . / either of . . . / neither of . . .

both either neither	of	the these/those my/your/Amy's, etc.

I like both of those pictures.

- **Neither of my parents** is Canadian.
- I haven't read **either of these books.**

You can say **both (of) the . . . / both (of) those . . . / both (of) my . . . ,** etc. (with or without of).

- I like **both of those pictures.** *or* I like **both those pictures.**
- **Both of Amy's sisters** are married. *or* **Both Amy's sisters** are married.

D

both of them / neither of us, etc.

both		them
either	of	us
neither		you

- Tiffany has two sisters. **Both of them** are married.
- Tom and I didn't eat anything. **Neither of us** was hungry.
- Who are those two people? I don't know **either of them.**

I can't either / neither can I **Unit 43**

Exercises

83.1 Write *both/either/neither.* Use *of* where necessary.

1. Last year I went to Miami and Seattle. I liked *both* _____ cities very much.
2. There were two pictures on the wall. I didn't like *either of* _____ them.
3. It was a good football game. _____ teams played well.
4. It wasn't a good football game. _____ team played well.
5. "Is your friend Canadian or American?" "_____ . She's Australian."
6. We went away for two days, but the weather was bad. It rained _____ days.
7. *A:* I bought two newspapers. Which one do you want?
   B: _____ . It doesn't matter which one.
8. I invited Diana and Mike to the party, but _____ them came.
9. "Do you go to work by car or by bus?" "_____ . I always walk."
10. "Which hat do you like, this one or that one?" "I don't like _____ them."
11. "Do you work, or are you a student?" "_____ . I work and I'm a student, too."
12. Paula and I didn't know the time because _____ us had a watch.
13. Lee has two sisters and a brother. _____ sisters are married.
14. Lee has two sisters and a brother. I know her brother, but I haven't met
    _____ her sisters.

83.2 Complete the sentences for the pictures. Use *Both . . .* or *Neither . . . .*

1. *Both cups are* _____ empty.   4. _____ cameras.
2. _____ are open.   5. _____ to the airport.
3. _____ wearing a hat.   6. _____ right.

83.3 A man and a woman answered some questions. Their answers were the same. Write sentences with *Both of them / Neither of them . . . .*

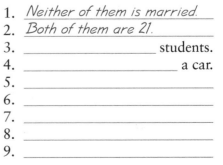

Are you married?	No	No
How old are you?	21	21
Are you a student?	Yes	Yes
Do you have a car?	No	No
Where do you live?	Boston	Boston
Do you like to cook?	Yes	Yes
Can you play the piano?	No	No
Do you read the newspaper?	Yes	Yes
Are you interested in sports?	No	No

1. *Neither of them is married.*
2. *Both of them are 21.*
3. _____ students.
4. _____ a car.
5. _____
6. _____
7. _____
8. _____
9. _____

A lot, much, and many

A

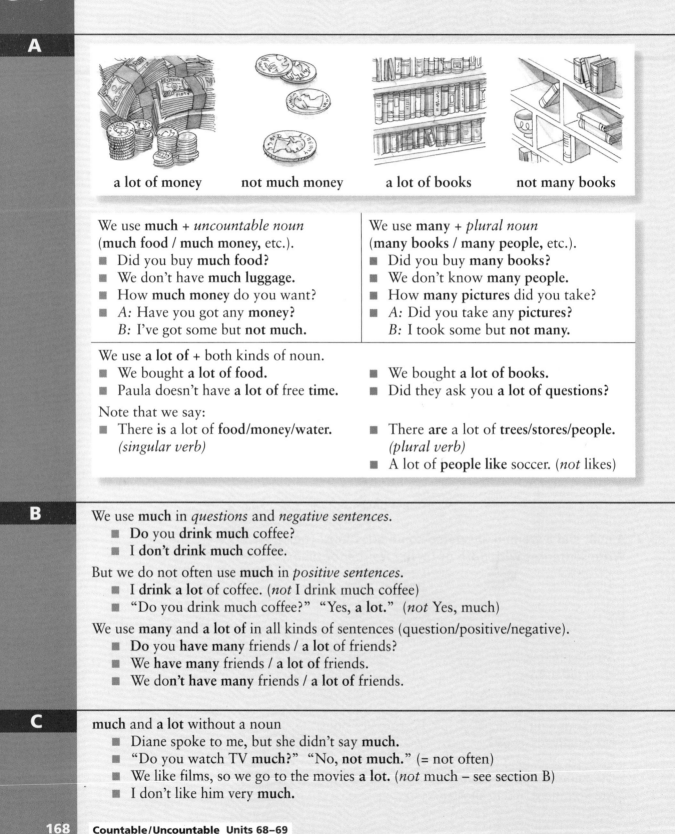

a lot of money   not much money   a lot of books   not many books

We use **much** + *uncountable noun*
(**much food / much money**, etc.).
- Did you buy **much food?**
- We don't have **much luggage.**
- How **much money** do you want?
- *A:* Have you got any **money?**
  B: I've got some but **not much.**

We use **many** + *plural noun*
(**many books / many people**, etc.).
- Did you buy **many books?**
- We don't know **many people.**
- How **many pictures** did you take?
- *A:* Did you take any **pictures?**
  B: I took some but **not many.**

We use **a lot of** + both kinds of noun.
- We bought **a lot of food.**
- Paula doesn't have **a lot of** free **time.**

- We bought **a lot of books.**
- Did they ask you **a lot of questions?**

Note that we say:
- There **is** a lot of **food/money/water.**
  (*singular verb*)

- There **are** a lot of **trees/stores/people.**
  (*plural verb*)
- A lot of **people like** soccer. (*not* likes)

B

We use **much** in *questions* and *negative sentences.*
- **Do** you **drink much** coffee?
- I **don't drink much** coffee.

But we do not often use **much** in *positive sentences.*
- I **drink a lot** of coffee. (*not* I drink much coffee)
- "Do you drink much coffee?" "Yes, **a lot.**" (*not* Yes, much)

We use **many** and **a lot of** in all kinds of sentences (question/positive/negative).
- **Do** you **have many** friends / **a lot of** friends?
- We **have many** friends / **a lot of** friends.
- We **don't have many** friends / **a lot of** friends.

C

much and **a lot** without a noun
- Diane spoke to me, but she didn't say **much.**
- "Do you watch TV **much?**" "No, **not much.**" (= not often)
- We like films, so we go to the movies **a lot.** (*not* much – see section B)
- I don't like him very **much.**

   Countable/Uncountable Units 68–69

Exercises

84.1 Write *much* or *many*.

1. Did you buy _much_ food?
2. There aren't _____ hotels in this town.
3. We don't have _____ gas.
4. Were there _____ people on the train?
5. Did _____ students fail the exam?
6. Paula doesn't have _____ money.
7. I wasn't hungry, so I didn't eat _____ .
8. I haven't seen Eric for _____ years.

Write *How much* or *How many*.

9. _____ people are coming to the party?
10. _____ milk should I get at the store?
11. _____ bread did you buy?
12. _____ players are there on a football team?

84.2 Complete the sentences. Use *much* or *many* with one of these words:

~~books~~   countries   luggage   people   time   times

1. I don't read very much. I don't have _many books_ .
2. Hurry up! We don't have _____ .
3. Do you travel a lot? Have you been to _____ ?
4. Tina hasn't lived here very long, so she doesn't know _____ .
5. "Do you have _____ ?" "No, only this suitcase."
6. I know Tokyo very well. I've been there _____ .

84.3 Complete the sentences with *a lot of* + one of these:

accidents   ~~books~~   fun   interesting things   traffic

1. I like to read. I have _a lot of books_ .
2. We enjoyed our visit to the museum. We saw _____ .
3. This road is very dangerous. There are _____ here.
4. We enjoyed our vacation. We had _____ .
5. It took me a long time to drive here. There was _____ .

84.4 In some of these sentences, *much* is not natural. Change the sentences or write *OK*.

1. Do you drink <u>much coffee</u>?   _OK_
2. I drink <u>much tea</u>.   _a lot of tea_
3. It was a cold winter. We had <u>much snow</u>.   _____
4. There wasn't <u>much snow</u> last winter.   _____
5. It costs <u>much money</u> to travel around the world. _____
6. This pen was cheap. It didn't cost <u>much</u>.   _____
7. Do you know <u>much</u> about computers?   _____
8. "Do you have any luggage?" "Yes, <u>much</u>."   _____

84.5 Write sentences about these people. Use *much* and *a lot*.

1. Jim loves movies. (go to the movies) _He goes to the movies a lot._
2. Nicole thinks TV is boring. (watch TV) _She doesn't watch TV much._
3. Tina is a good tennis player. (play tennis) She _____ .
4. Mark doesn't like to drive. (use his car) He _____ .
5. Paul spends most of his time at home. (go out) _____
6. Sue has been all over the world. (travel) _____

A little / a few and little / few

A

(a) little + *uncountable noun*

(a) little water
(a) little money
(a) little time
(a) little soup

a little water

(a) few + *plural noun*

(a) few books
(a) few questions
(a) few people
(a) few days

a few books

B

a **little** = some but not much

- She didn't eat anything, but she drank **a little water.**
- I speak **a little Spanish.** (= some Spanish but not much)
- *A:* Can you speak Spanish? *B:* **A little.**

a **few** = some but not many

- Last night I wrote **a few letters.**
- We're going away for **a few days.**
- I speak **a few words** of Spanish.

- *A:* Do you have any stamps? *B:* **A few.** Do you want one?

C

~~a~~ **little** (without **a**) = almost no *or* almost nothing

- There was **little food** in the fridge. It was almost empty.

You can say **very little.**

- Dan is very thin because he eats **very little.** (= almost nothing)

~~a~~ **few** (without **a**) = almost no

- There were **few people** in the theater. It was almost empty.

You can say **very few.**

- Your English is very good. You make **very few mistakes.**

D

little and **a little**

A little is a *positive* idea.

- They have **a little** money, but they're not rich. (= they have some money)

Little (or **very little**) is a *negative* idea.

- They are very poor. They have (**very**) **little** money. (= almost no money)

few and **a few**

A few is a *positive* idea.

- I have **a few** friends, so I'm not lonely. (= I have some friends)

Few (or **very few**) is a *negative* idea.s

- I'm sad and I'm lonely. I have (**very**) **few** friends. (= almost no friends)

I have a little money. I have little money. I have a few friends. I have few friends.

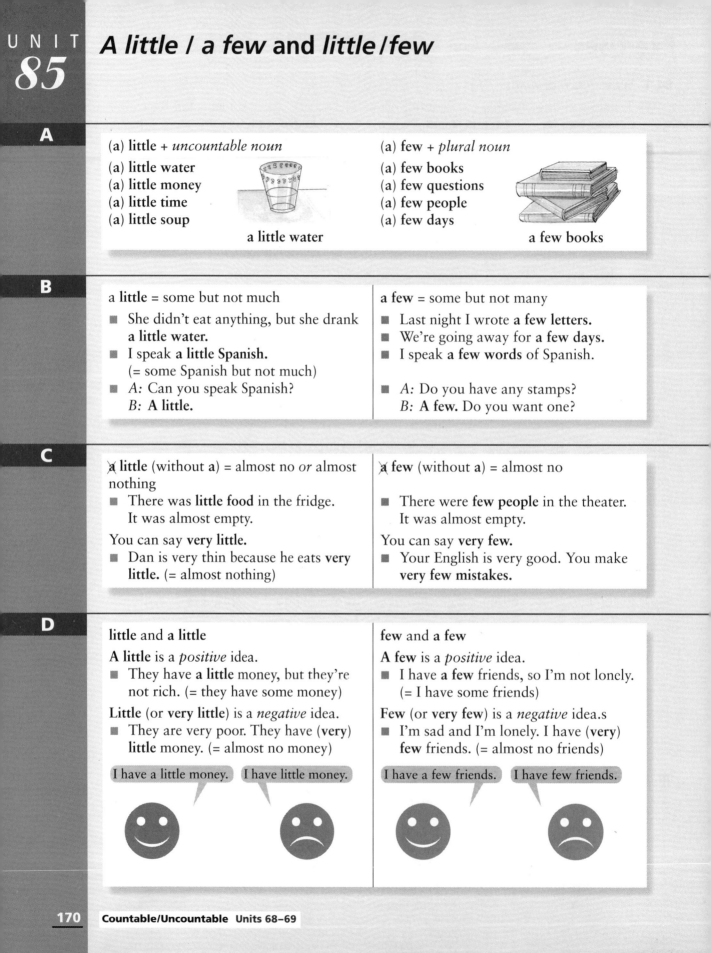

Exercises

85.1 Answer the questions with *a little* or *a few.*

1. "Do you have any money?" "Yes, *a little* _____."
2. "Do you have any envelopes?" "Yes, _____."
3. "Do you want sugar in your coffee?" "Yes, _____, please."
4. "Did you take any pictures when you were on vacation?" "Yes, _____."
5. "Does your friend speak English?" "Yes, _____."
6. "Are there any good restaurants in this town?" "Yes, _____."

85.2 Write *a little* or *a few* + one of these words:

chairs   days   fresh air   friends   ~~letters~~   milk   Russian   times

1. Last night I wrote *a few letters* _____ to my family and friends.
2. Can I have _____ in my coffee, please?
3. "When did Julia leave?" "_____ ago."
4. "Do you speak any foreign languages?" "I can speak _____."
5. "Are you going to the movies alone?" "No, I'm going with _____."
6. "Have you ever been to Mexico?" "Yes, _____."
7. There wasn't much furniture in the room – just a table and _____.
8. I'm going out for a walk. I need _____.

85.3 Complete the sentences. Use *very little* or *very few* + one of these words:

coffee   hotels   ~~mistakes~~   people   rain   time   work

1. Your English is very good. You make *very few mistakes* _____.
2. I drink _____. I don't like it much.
3. The weather here is very dry in the summer. There is _____.
4. It's difficult to find a place to stay in this town. There are _____.
5. Hurry up. There's _____ before the movie starts.
6. The town is very quiet at night. _____ go out.
7. Some people in my office are very lazy. They do _____.

85.4 Write *very little / a little / very few / a few.*

1. There was *very little* _____ food in the fridge. It was almost empty.
2. "When did Sarah go out?" "_____ minutes ago."
3. I can't decide now. I need _____ time to think about it.
4. There was _____ traffic, so we got there early.
5. Let's take a taxi. There are _____ buses after 9 o'clock at night.
6. "Would you like more soup?" "Yes, _____, please."
7. They sent us a map, so we had _____ trouble finding their house.

85.5 Right or wrong? Correct the sentences that are wrong. Write *OK* if the sentence is correct.

1. We're going away for few days next week.   *for a few days*
2. Everybody needs little luck.   _____
3. I can't talk to you now – I've got few things to do.   _____
4. I eat very little meat – I don't like it very much.   _____
5. Excuse me, can I ask you few questions?   *o k*
6. There were little people on the bus – it was almost empty.   _____

Old, nice, interesting, etc. (Adjectives)

A

Adjective + noun (**nice day / blue eyes**, etc.)

adjective + noun

It's a **nice**	**day** today.
Laura has **brown**	**eyes.**
There's a very **old**	**church** in this town.
Do you like **Italian**	**food?**
I don't speak any **foreign**	**languages.**
There are some **beautiful yellow**	**flowers** in the garden.

The adjective is *before* the noun.

- They live in a **modern house.** (*not* a house modern)
- Have you met any **famous people?** (*not* people famous)

The ending of an adjective is always the same.
   a **different** place   **different** places (*not* differents)

B

be (**am/is/was**, etc.) + adjective

- The weather **is nice** today.
- These flowers **are** very **beautiful.**
- **Are** you **cold?** Should I close the window?
- **I'm hungry.** Can I have something to eat?
- The movie **wasn't** very **good.** It **was boring.**
- Please **be quiet.** I'm studying.

I'm hungry.

C

look/feel/smell/taste/sound + adjective

You look tired.

I feel tired.

You sound happy.

It smells good.

It tastes good.

- "You **look tired.**" "Yes, I **feel tired.**"
- Eric told me about his new job. It **sounds** very **interesting.**
- I'm not going to eat this fish. It doesn't **smell good.**

Compare:

He	is feels looks	tired.		They	are look sound	happy.		It	is smells tastes	good.

*Get + Adjective (**get hungry/tired**, etc.)* **Unit 57**   *Something/anybody + Adjective* **Unit 80**

Exercises

86.1 Put the words in the right order.

1. (new / live in / house / they / a) _They live in a new house._
2. (like / jacket / I / that / green) I _____ .
3. (music / like / do / classical / you?) Do _____ ?
4. (had / wonderful / a / I / trip) _____
5. (went to / restaurant / a / Chinese / we) _____

86.2 The words in the box are adjectives (*dark*, *foreign*, etc.) or nouns (*air*, *job*, etc.). Use an adjective and a noun to complete each sentence.

air	dangerous	~~foreign~~	hot	knife	long	vacation
clouds	dark	fresh	job	~~languages~~	sharp	water

1. Do you speak any _foreign languages_ _____ ?
2. Look at those _____ . It's going to rain.
3. Sue works very hard, and she's very tired. She needs a _____ .
4. You need _____ to make tea.
5. Can you open the window? We need some _____ .
6. I need a _____ to cut these onions.
7. Fire fighting is a _____ .

86.3 Write sentences for the pictures. Choose from the boxes.

feel(s)	look(s)	~~sound(s)~~
look(s)	smell(s)	taste(s)

+

~~happy~~	nice	surprised
new	sick	terrible

1. You _sound happy_ .
2. It _____ .
3. I _____ .
4. You _____ .
5. They _____ .
6. It _____ .

86.4 A and B don't agree. Complete B's sentences. Use the word in parentheses ( ).

A

1. You look tired.
2. This is a new coat.
3. I'm American.
4. You look cold.
5. These bags are heavy.
6. The soup looks good.

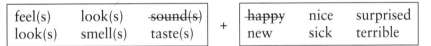

B

1. I do? I _don't feel tired_ . (feel)
2. Really? It _____ . (look)
3. You are? You _____ . (sound)
4. Really? I _____ . (feel)
5. They are? They _____ . (look)
6. Really? It _____ . (taste)

Quickly, badly, suddenly, etc. (Adverbs)

A

He ate his dinner very **quickly.**

Quickly and **suddenly** are adverbs.

Suddenly, the shelf fell down.

Adjective + -ly → adverb

adjective	quick	bad	sudden	careful	heavy	etc.
adverb	quickly	badly	suddenly	carefully	heavily	etc.

Spelling (see Appendix 5.2):   easy → easily   heavy → heavily

B

Adverbs tell you *how* something happens or *how* somebody does something.

- The train **stopped suddenly.**
- I **opened** the door **slowly.**
- Please **listen carefully.**
- I **understand** you **perfectly.**

It's **raining heavily.**

Compare:

adjective (see Unit 86)	*adverb*
■ Sue is very **quiet.**	■ Sue **speaks** very **quietly.** (*not* speaks very quiet)
■ **Be careful!**	■ **Listen carefully!** (*not* listen careful)
■ It was **a bad game.**	■ Our team **played badly.** (*not* played bad)
■ I **felt nervous.** (= I was nervous)	■ I **waited nervously.**

C

These words are adjectives *and* adverbs: **hard   fast   late   early**

■ Sue's job **is** very **hard.**	■ Sue **works** very **hard.** (*not* hardly)
■ Ben is **a fast runner.**	■ Ben can **run fast.**
■ The bus **was late/early.**	■ I **went** to bed **late/early.**

D

good *(adjective)* → **well** *(adverb)*

■ Your English **is** very **good.**	■ You **speak** English very **well.** (*not* very good)
■ It was **a good game.**	■ Our team **played well.**

But **well** is also an adjective (= not sick, in good health).

- "How are you?"   "I'm very **well,** thank you. And you?"

Exercises

87.1 Look at the pictures and complete the sentences with one of these adverbs:

angrily badly early fast ~~heavily~~ quietly

1. It's raining _heavily_ .
2. He sings very _____ .
3. They came in _____ .
4. She shouted at me _____ .
5. She can run very _____ .
6. He got to work _____ .

87.2 Complete the sentences. Choose from the boxes.

come	know	sleep	win		~~carefully~~	clearly	hard	well
explain	~~listen~~	think	work	+	carefully	easily	quickly	well

1. I'm going to tell you something very important, so please _listen carefully_ .
2. Amy! _____ ! Run!
3. They _____ . At the end of the day, they're always tired.
4. I'm tired this morning. I didn't _____ last night.
5. You play tennis much better than me. When we play, you always _____ .
6. _____ before you answer this question.
7. I've met Alice a few times, but I don't _____ her very _____ .
8. Our teacher doesn't _____ things very _____ . We never understand him.

87.3 Which is right?

1. Don't eat so ~~quick~~/quickly. It's not good for you. (*quickly* is right)
2. Why are you angry/angrily? I haven't done anything.
3. Can you speak slow/slowly, please?
4. Come on, Dave! Why are you always so slow/slowly?
5. Bill is a very careful/carefully driver.
6. Tracy is studying hard/hardly for her exams.
7. "Where's Diane?" "She was here, but she left sudden/suddenly."
8. Please be quiet/quietly. I'm studying.
9. Some companies pay their workers very bad/badly.
10. That jacket looks nice/nicely. Are you going to buy it?

87.4 Write *good* or *well*.

1. Your English is really _good_ . You speak it very _well_ .
2. Jackie did very _____ on her exams.
3. The food was very _____ . I enjoyed it a lot.
4. Mark has a difficult job, but he does it _____ .
5. How are your parents? Are they _____ ?
6. Did you have a _____ vacation? Was the weather _____ ?

Old/older and expensive / more expensive

A

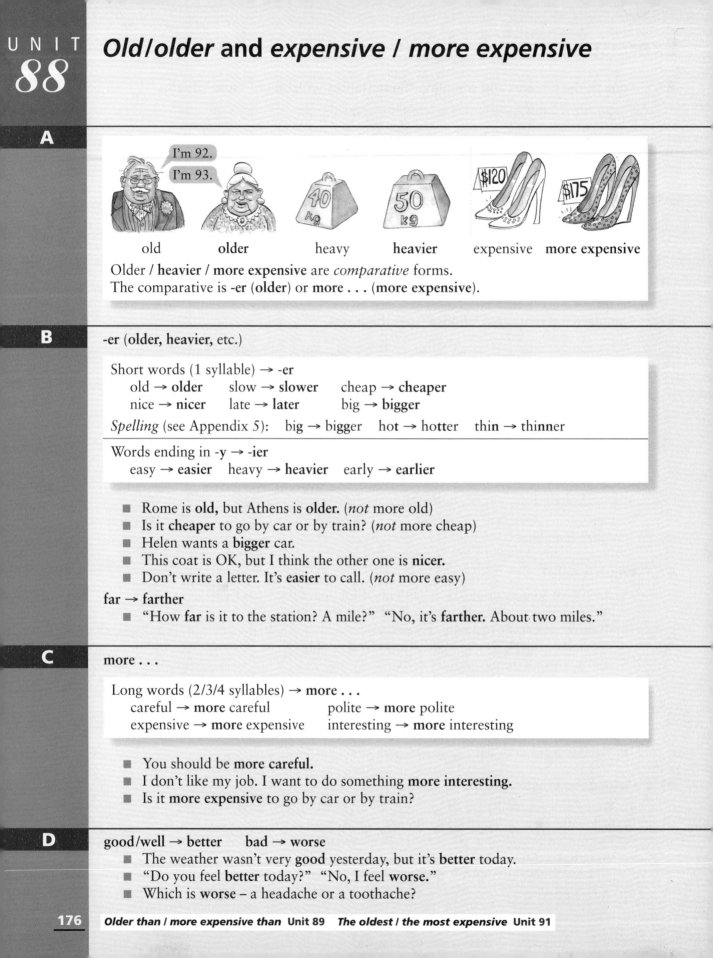

old   **older**   heavy   **heavier**   expensive   **more expensive**

Older / **heavier** / **more expensive** are *comparative* forms.
The comparative is -er (**older**) or **more . . .** (**more expensive**).

B

-er (**older, heavier,** etc.)

Short words (1 syllable) → -er
old → **older**   slow → **slower**   cheap → **cheaper**
nice → **nicer**   late → **later**   big → **bigger**

Spelling (see Appendix 5):   big → bigger   hot → hotter   thin → thinner

Words ending in -y → -ier
easy → **easier**   heavy → **heavier**   early → **earlier**

- Rome is **old,** but Athens is **older.** (*not* more old)
- Is it **cheaper** to go by car or by train? (*not* more cheap)
- Helen wants a **bigger** car.
- This coat is OK, but I think the other one is **nicer.**
- Don't write a letter. It's **easier** to call. (*not* more easy)

far → **farther**
- "How **far** is it to the station? A mile?" "No, it's **farther.** About two miles."

C

more . . .

Long words (2/3/4 syllables) → **more . . .**
careful → **more** careful   polite → **more** polite
expensive → **more** expensive   interesting → **more** interesting

- You should be **more careful.**
- I don't like my job. I want to do something **more interesting.**
- Is it **more expensive** to go by car or by train?

D

good/well → **better**   bad → **worse**
- The weather wasn't very **good** yesterday, but it's **better** today.
- "Do you feel **better** today?" "No, I feel **worse.**"
- Which is **worse** – a headache or a toothache?

    Older than / more expensive than Unit 89   *The oldest / the most expensive* Unit 91

Exercises

88.1 Look at the pictures and write the comparative (*older / more interesting*, etc.).

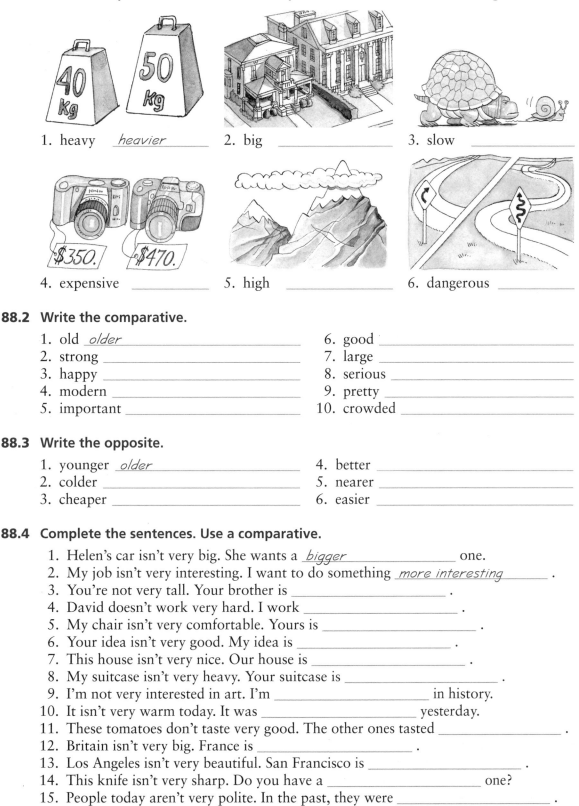

1. heavy _heavier_
2. big _____
3. slow _____

4. expensive _____
5. high _____
6. dangerous _____

88.2 Write the comparative.

1. old _older_
2. strong _____
3. happy _____
4. modern _____
5. important _____

6. good _____
7. large _____
8. serious _____
9. pretty _____
10. crowded _____

88.3 Write the opposite.

1. younger _older_
2. colder _____
3. cheaper _____

4. better _____
5. nearer _____
6. easier _____

88.4 Complete the sentences. Use a comparative.

1. Helen's car isn't very big. She wants a _bigger_ one.
2. My job isn't very interesting. I want to do something _more interesting_ .
3. You're not very tall. Your brother is _____ .
4. David doesn't work very hard. I work _____ .
5. My chair isn't very comfortable. Yours is _____ .
6. Your idea isn't very good. My idea is _____ .
7. This house isn't very nice. Our house is _____ .
8. My suitcase isn't very heavy. Your suitcase is _____ .
9. I'm not very interested in art. I'm _____ in history.
10. It isn't very warm today. It was _____ yesterday.
11. These tomatoes don't taste very good. The other ones tasted _____ .
12. Britain isn't very big. France is _____ .
13. Los Angeles isn't very beautiful. San Francisco is _____ .
14. This knife isn't very sharp. Do you have a _____ one?
15. People today aren't very polite. In the past, they were _____ .

Older than . . . and more expensive than . . .

A

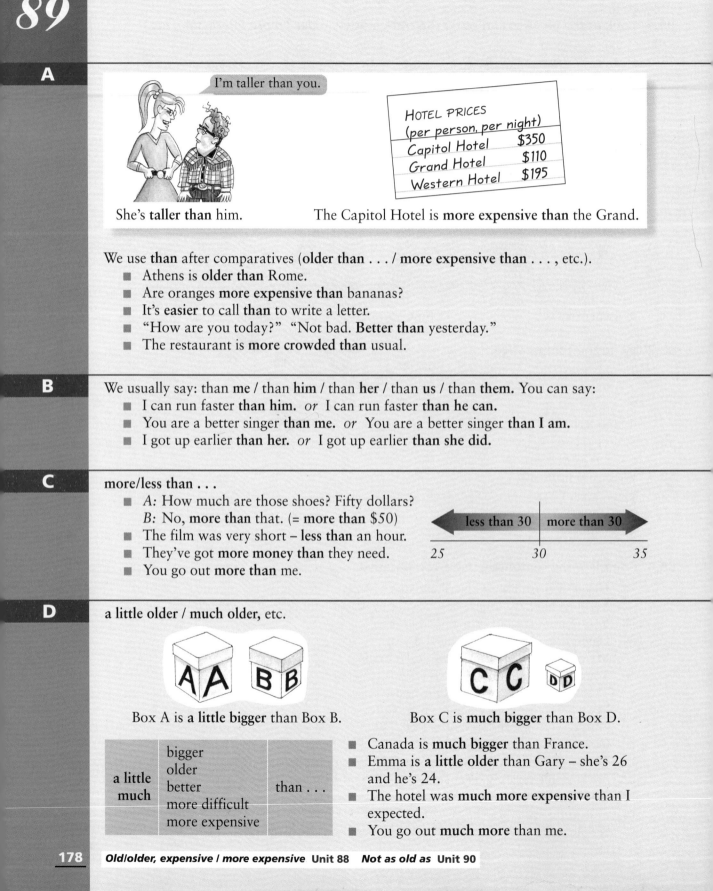

I'm taller than you.

HOTEL PRICES
(per person, per night)
Capitol Hotel $350
Grand Hotel $110
Western Hotel $195

She's **taller than** him.   The Capitol Hotel is **more expensive than** the Grand.

We use **than** after comparatives (**older than** . . . / **more expensive than** . . . , etc.).
- Athens is **older than** Rome.
- Are oranges **more expensive than** bananas?
- It's **easier** to call **than** to write a letter.
- "How are you today?" "Not bad. **Better than** yesterday."
- The restaurant is **more crowded than** usual.

B

We usually say: than **me** / than **him** / than **her** / than **us** / than **them**. You can say:
- I can run faster **than him**. *or* I can run faster **than he can**.
- You are a better singer **than me**. *or* You are a better singer **than I am**.
- I got up earlier **than her**. *or* I got up earlier **than she did**.

C

more/less than . . .
- A: How much are those shoes? Fifty dollars?
  B: No, **more than** that. (= **more than** $50)
- The film was very short – **less than** an hour.
- They've got **more money than** they need.
- You go out **more than** me.

less than 30 | more than 30

25   *30*   *35*

D

a little older / much older, etc.

Box A is **a little bigger** than Box B.   Box C is **much bigger** than Box D.

a little much	bigger older better more difficult more expensive	than . . .

- Canada is **much bigger** than France.
- Emma is **a little older** than Gary – she's 26 and he's 24.
- The hotel was **much more expensive** than I expected.
- You go out **much more** than me.

Exercises

89.1 Write sentences about Liz and Ben. Use *than.*

LIZ

1. I'm 26.
2. I'm not a good swimmer.
3. I'm 5 feet, 10 inches tall.
4. I start work at 8 o'clock.
5. I don't work very hard.
6. I don't have much money.
7. I'm a very good driver.
8. I'm not very patient.
9. I'm not a very good dancer.
10. I'm very intelligent.
11. I speak French very well.
12. I don't go to the movies much.

BEN

1. I'm 24.
2. I'm a very good swimmer.
3. I'm 5 feet, 8 inches tall.
4. I start work at 8:30.
5. I work very hard.
6. I have a lot of money.
7. I'm not a very good driver.
8. I'm very patient.
9. I'm a good dancer.
10. I'm not very intelligent.
11. I don't speak French well.
12. I go to the movies a lot.

1. Liz *is older than Ben*   .
2. Ben *is a better swimmer than Liz* .
3. Liz is *a*   .
4. Liz starts _____ Ben.
5. Ben _____ .
6. Ben has _____ .

7. Liz is a _____ .
8. Ben _____ .
9. Ben _____ .
10. Liz _____ .
11. Liz _____ .
12. Ben _____ .

89.2 Complete the sentences. Use *than.*

1. He isn't very tall. You *'re taller than him* OR *'re taller than he is* _____ .
2. She isn't very old. You're _____ .
3. I don't work very hard. You work _____ .
4. He doesn't watch TV very much. You _____ .
5. I'm not a very good cook. You _____ .
6. We don't know many people. You _____ .
7. They don't have much money. You _____ .
8. I can't run very fast. You can _____ .
9. She hasn't been here very long. You _____ .
10. They didn't get up very early. You _____ .
11. He wasn't very surprised. You _____ .

89.3 Complete the sentences with *a little* or *much* + a comparative (*older/better,* etc.).

1. Emma is 26. Gary is 24.
   Emma *is a little older than Gary* _____ .
2. Brian's mother is 52. His father is 69.
   Brian's mother _____ .
3. My camera cost $100. Yours cost $96.
   My camera _____ .
4. Yesterday I felt terrible. Today I feel great.
   I feel _____ .
5. Today the temperature is 12 degrees Celsius. Yesterday it was 10 degrees.
   It's _____ .
6. Amy is an excellent tennis player. I'm not very good.
   Amy _____ .

Not as . . . as

A

not as . . . as

She's old, but she's **not as old as** he is.

Box A **isn't as big as** Box B.

- Rome is **not as old as** Athens. (= Athens is **older**)
- The Grand Hotel **isn't as expensive as** the Western. (= the Western is **more expensive**)
- I **don't** play tennis **as often as** you. (= you play **more often**)
- The weather is better than it was yesterday. It **isn't as cold**. (= as cold **as it was yesterday**)

B

not as much as . . . / not as many as . . .
- I haven't got **as much money as** you. (= you've got **more money**)
- I don't know **as many people as** you. (= you know **more people**)
- I don't go out **as much as** you. (= you go out **more**)

C

Compare **not as . . . as** and **than:**
- Rome is **not as old as** Athens.
  Athens is **older than** Rome. (*not* older as Rome)
- Tennis **isn't as popular as** soccer.
  Soccer is **more popular than** tennis.
- I **don't** go out **as much as** you.
  You go out **more than** me.

D

We usually say: as **me** / as **him** / as **her**, etc. You can say:
- She's not as old **as him.** *or* She's not as old **as he is.**
- You don't work as hard **as me.** *or* You don't work as hard **as I do.**

E

We say **the same as** . . . .
- The weather today is **the same as** yesterday.
- Your son's hair is **the same color as** yours.
- I arrived at **the same time as** Tim.

Much/many Unit 84   ***Older than / more expensive than*** Unit 89

Exercises

90.1 Look at the pictures and write sentences about A, B, and C.

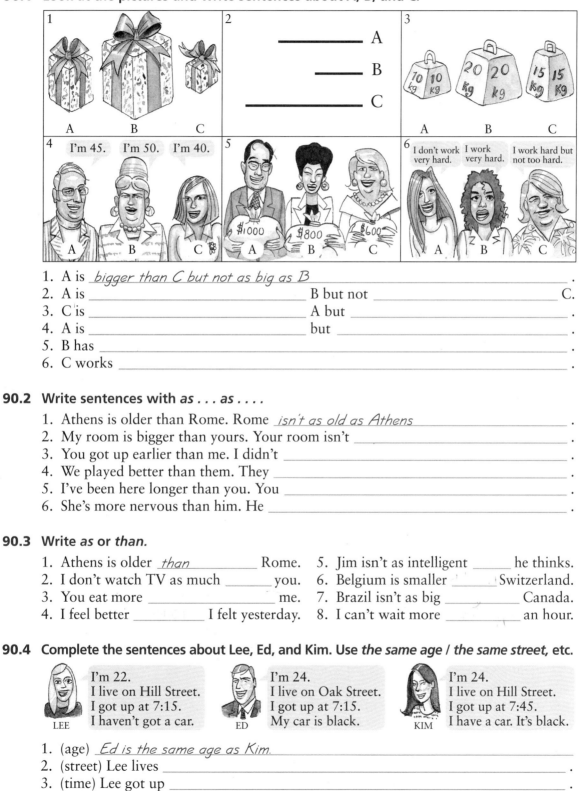

1. A is _bigger than C but not as big as B_ .
2. A is _____ B but not _____ C.
3. C is _____ A but _____ .
4. A is _____ but _____ .
5. B has _____ .
6. C works _____ .

90.2 Write sentences with *as . . . as . . . .*

1. Athens is older than Rome. Rome _isn't as old as Athens_ .
2. My room is bigger than yours. Your room isn't _____ .
3. You got up earlier than me. I didn't _____ .
4. We played better than them. They _____ .
5. I've been here longer than you. You _____ .
6. She's more nervous than him. He _____ .

90.3 Write *as* or *than*.

1. Athens is older _than_ Rome.
2. I don't watch TV as much _____ you.
3. You eat more _____ me.
4. I feel better _____ I felt yesterday.
5. Jim isn't as intelligent _____ he thinks.
6. Belgium is smaller _____ Switzerland.
7. Brazil isn't as big _____ Canada.
8. I can't wait more _____ an hour.

90.4 Complete the sentences about Lee, Ed, and Kim. Use *the same age / the same street*, etc.

LEE: I'm 22. I live on Hill Street. I got up at 7:15. I haven't got a car.

ED: I'm 24. I live on Oak Street. I got up at 7:15. My car is black.

KIM: I'm 24. I live on Hill Street. I got up at 7:45. I have a car. It's black.

1. (age) _Ed is the same age as Kim._
2. (street) Lee lives _____ .
3. (time) Lee got up _____ .
4. (color) Ed's _____ .

The oldest and the most expensive

Motel Prices in Jamestown

Best West Motel	$120	Oak Tree Motel	$85
Sleep Inn	$105	Cozy Cabins	$60
Rainbow Motel	$95		

Box A is **bigger than** Box B.

Box A is **bigger than** all the other boxes.

Box A is **the biggest** box.

The Best West Motel is **more expensive than** the Sleep Inn.

The Best West Motel is **more expensive than** all the other motels in town.

The Best West Motel is **the most expensive** motel in town.

Bigger / older / more expensive, etc., are *comparative* forms. (see Unit 88)
Biggest / oldest / most expensive, etc., are *superlative* forms.

The superlative form is **-est** (**oldest**) *or* **most . . .** (**most expensive**).

Short words (**old/cheap/nice**, etc.) → the **-est**
    old → **the oldest**   cheap → **the cheapest**   nice → **the nicest**
but good → **the best**   bad → **the worst**

Spelling (see Appendix 5): big → the biggest   hot → the hottest

Words ending in -y (**easy/heavy**, etc.) → the **-iest**
    easy → **the easiest**   heavy → **the heaviest**   pretty → **the prettiest**

Long words (**careful/expensive/interesting**, etc.) → the **most . . .**
    careful → **the most careful**   interesting → **the most interesting**

We say: **the** oldest . . . / **the** most expensive . . . , etc. (with **the**).
- The church is very old. It's **the oldest** building in the town.
  (= it is **older than** all the other buildings)
- What is **the longest** river in the world?
- Money is important, but it isn't **the most important** thing in life.
- Excuse me, where is **the nearest** bank?

You can use **the oldest / the best / the most expensive**, etc., without a noun.
- Ken is a good player, but he isn't **the best** on the team. (= the best player)

Superlative + **I've ever . . . / you've ever . . .** , etc.
- The movie was very bad. I think it's **the worst** movie **I've ever seen.**
- What is **the most unusual** thing **you've ever done?**

Present Perfect + *ever* Unit 16   *Older / more expensive* **Units 88–89**

Exercises

91.1 Write sentences with comparatives (*older*, etc.) and superlatives (*the oldest*, etc.).

1.

(big/small)
(A/D) _A is bigger than D._
(A)   _A is the biggest._
(B)   _B is the smallest._

2.

A ▬▬▬▬▬▬▬▬▬▬ A
B ▬▬▬▬▬▬▬ B
C ▬▬▬▬▬▬▬▬▬ C
D ▬▬▬▬▬▬▬▬ D

(long/short)
(C/A) C is _____ A.
(D)   D is _____ .
(B)   B _____ .

3. I'm 23.   I'm 19.   I'm 24.   I'm 21.

A   B   C   D

(young/old)
(D/C) D _____ .
(B)   _____
(C)   _____

4.

$25 $45 $50 $30

A   B   C   D

(expensive/cheap)
(D/A) _____
(C)   _____
(A)   _____

5.

Restaurant A   excellent
Restaurant B   good
Restaurant C   OK
Restaurant D   terrible

(good/bad)
(A/C) _____
(A)   _____
(D)   _____

91.2 Complete the sentences. Use a superlative + a noun (*the oldest building*, etc.).

1. This building is very old. It's _the oldest building_ in town.
2. It was a very happy day. It was _____ of my life.
3. It's a very good movie. It's _____ I've ever seen.
4. She's a very popular singer. She's _____ in the country.
5. It was a very bad mistake. It was _____ I've ever made.
6. It's a very pretty city. It's _____ I've ever seen.
7. It was a very cold day. It was _____ of the year.
8. He's a very boring person. He's _____ I've ever met.

91.3 Write sentences with a superlative (*the longest*, etc.). Choose from the boxes.

~~Alaska~~	Jupiter	high	city	planet	Africa	South America
Brazil	the Nile	large	country	river	Australia	~~the USA~~
Everest	Sydney	long	mountain	~~state~~	the solar system	the world

1. _Alaska is the largest state in the USA._
2. Brazil _____ .
3. _____
4. _____
5. _____
6. _____

A

I've only got $2.00.

SANDWICHES $4.00

She can't buy a sandwich.
She doesn't have **enough money**.

He can't reach the shelf.
He isn't **tall enough**.

B

enough + *noun* (**enough money / enough people**, etc.)

- ■ "Is there **enough salt** in the soup?" "Yes, it's fine."
- ■ We wanted to play football, but we didn't have **enough players**.
- ■ Why don't you buy a car? You have **enough money**. (*not* money enough)

enough without a noun

- ■ I've got some money, but not **enough** to buy a car. (= I need more money to buy a car)
- ■ "Would you like some more cake?" "No, thanks. I've had **enough**."
- ■ You're always at home. You don't go out **enough**.

C

Adjective + **enough** (**good enough / tall enough**, etc.)

- ■ "Do you want to go swimming?" "No, it isn't **warm enough**." (*not* enough warm)
- ■ Can you hear the radio? Is it **loud enough** for you?
- ■ Don't buy that coat. It's nice, but it isn't **long enough**. (= it's too short)

Remember:

enough + noun   *but*   adjective + **enough**

enough money	tall **enough**
enough time	good **enough**
enough people	old **enough**

D

We say:

enough for somebody/something	■ This sweater isn't **big enough for me**.
	■ I don't have **enough money for a car**.
enough to do something	■ I don't have **enough money to buy** a car. (*not* for buy a car)
	■ Is your English **good enough to have** a conversation? (*not* for have)
enough for somebody/something **to do** something	■ There aren't **enough chairs for everybody to sit down**.

Exercises

92.1 Look at the pictures and complete the sentences. Use *enough* + one of these words:

chairs   ~~money~~   paint   wind

1. She doesn't have *enough money*   .   3. She doesn't have _____.
2. There aren't _____.   4. There isn't _____.

92.2 Look at the pictures and complete the sentences. Use one of these adjectives + *enough*:

big   long   strong   ~~tall~~

1. She *isn't tall enough*   .   3. His legs _____.
2. The car _____.   4. He _____.

92.3 Complete the sentences. Use *enough* with one of these words:

big   eat   fruit   ~~loud~~   old   practice   ~~sugar~~   time   tired

1. "Is there *enough salt*_____ in the soup?" "Yes, it's fine."
2. Can you hear the radio? Is it *loud enough*_____ for you?
3. He can quit school if he wants – he's _____.
4. Did you have _____ to answer all the questions on the exam?
5. This house isn't _____ for a large family.
6. Tina is very thin. She doesn't _____.
7. Lisa isn't a very good tennis player because she doesn't _____.
8. You don't eat _____. You should eat a banana every day.
9. It's late, but I don't want to go to bed. I'm not _____ to sleep.

92.4 Complete the sentences. Use *enough* with the words in parentheses ( ).

1. We haven't got *enough money to buy*_____ a car. (money / buy)
2. This knife isn't _____ tomatoes. (sharp / cut)
3. The water wasn't _____ swimming. (warm / go)
4. Do we have _____ sandwiches? (bread / make)
5. We played well but not _____ the game. (well / win)
6. I don't have _____ the newspaper. (time / read)

Too

A

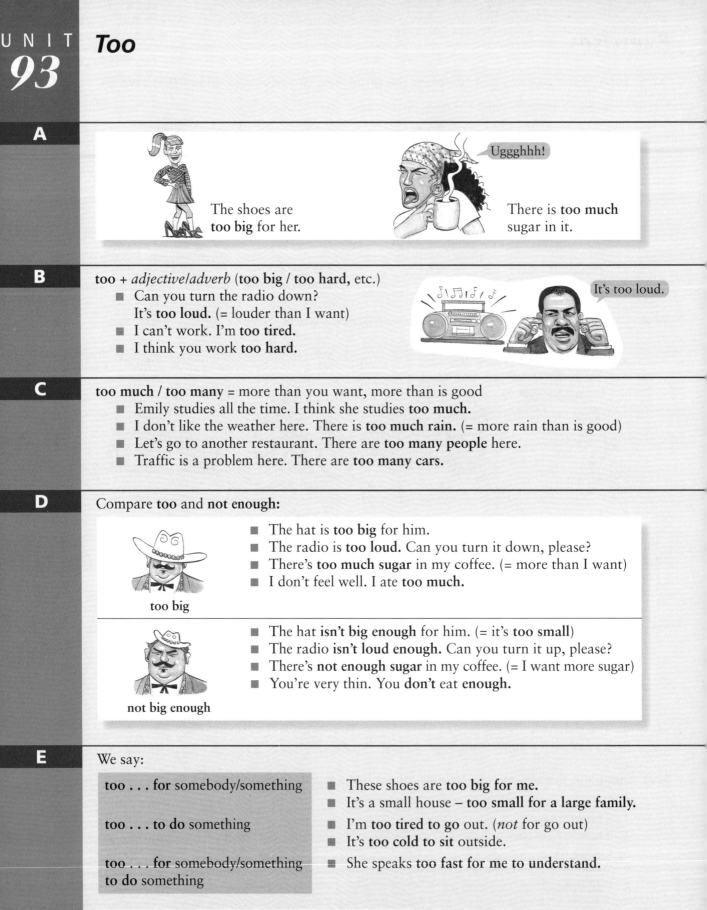

The shoes are **too big** for her.

Uggghhh!

There is **too much** sugar in it.

B

too + *adjective/adverb* (too big / too hard, etc.)

- Can you turn the radio down?
  It's **too loud.** (= louder than I want)
- I can't work. I'm **too tired.**
- I think you work **too hard.**

It's too loud.

C

too much / too many = more than you want, more than is good

- Emily studies all the time. I think she studies **too much.**
- I don't like the weather here. There is **too much rain.** (= more rain than is good)
- Let's go to another restaurant. There are **too many people** here.
- Traffic is a problem here. There are **too many cars.**

D

Compare **too** and **not enough:**

- The hat is **too big** for him.
- The radio is **too loud.** Can you turn it down, please?
- There's **too much sugar** in my coffee. (= more than I want)
- I don't feel well. I ate **too much.**

too big

- The hat **isn't big enough** for him. (= it's **too small**)
- The radio **isn't loud enough.** Can you turn it up, please?
- There's **not enough sugar** in my coffee. (= I want more sugar)
- You're very thin. You **don't** eat **enough.**

not big enough

E

We say:

too . . . for somebody/something	▪ These shoes are **too big for me.** ▪ It's a small house – **too small for a large family.**
too . . . to do something	▪ I'm **too tired to go** out. (*not* for go out) ▪ It's **too cold to sit** outside.
too . . . for somebody/something **to do** something	▪ She speaks **too fast for me to understand.**

To and for Unit 55   ***Much/many*** Unit 84   ***Enough*** Unit 92

Exercises

93.1 Look at the pictures and complete the sentences. Use *too* + one of these words:

big   crowded   fast   heavy   ~~loud~~   low

1. The radio is *too loud*   .   4. She's driving _____ .
2. The box is _____ .   5. The ball is _____ .
3. The net is _____ .   6. The restaurant is _____ .

93.2 Write *too / too much / too many / enough.*

1. You're always at home. You don't go out *enough*   .
2. I don't like the weather here. There's *too much*   rain.
3. I can't wait for them. I don't have _____ time.
4. There was nowhere to sit on the beach. There were _____ people.
5. You're always tired. I think you work _____ hard.
6. "Did you have _____ to eat?" "Yes, thank you."
7. You drink _____ coffee. It's not good for you.
8. You don't eat _____ vegetables. You should eat some every day.
9. I don't like the weather here. It's _____ cold.
10. Our team didn't play well. We made _____ mistakes.
11. "Would you like some ice in your tea?" "Yes, but not _____ ."

93.3 Complete the sentences. Use *too* or *enough* with the words in parentheses ( ).

1. I couldn't work. I *was too tired*   . (tired)
2. Can you turn the radio up, please? It *isn't loud enough*   . (loud)
3. I don't want to walk home. It's _____ . (far)
4. Don't buy anything at that store. It _____ . (expensive)
5. You can't put all your things in that bag. It _____ . (big)
6. I couldn't do the exercise. It _____ . (hard)
7. Your work needs to be better. It _____ . (good)
8. Sorry, I can't talk now. I _____ . (busy)
9. I thought the movie was boring. It _____ . (long)

93.4 Complete the sentences. Use *too* + adjective + *to* do something.

1. I'm not going out. *It's too cold to go out*   . (cold)
2. I'm not going to bed. It's _____ . (early)
3. They're not getting married. They're _____ . (young)
4. Nobody swims here. It's _____ . (dangerous)
5. Don't call her now. It's _____ . (late)
6. I didn't say anything. I was _____ . (surprised)

He speaks English very well. (Word Order 1)

A

Verb + object

Sue **reads** **the newspaper** every day.
| subject | verb | object |

The verb and the object are usually together.

We say:

Sue **reads the newspaper** every day.
(*not* Sue reads every day the newspaper)

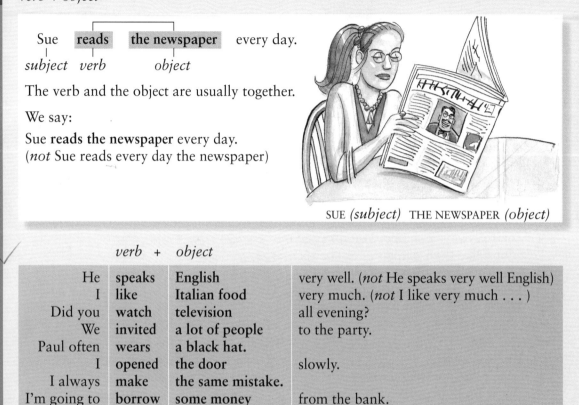

SUE (*subject*) THE NEWSPAPER (*object*)

	verb +	*object*	
He	speaks	English	very well. (*not* He speaks very well English)
I	like	Italian food	very much. (*not* I like very much . . .)
Did you	watch	television	all evening?
We	invited	a lot of people	to the party.
Paul often	wears	a black hat.	
I	opened	the door	slowly.
I always	make	the same mistake.	
I'm going to	borrow	some money	from the bank.

B

Place and time

We went **to a party** **last night** .
| place | time |

Place is usually before time. We say:

We went **to a party last night**. (*not* last night to a party)

	place (where?)	+	*time* (when? how long? how often?)
Liz walks	to work		every day. (*not* every day to work)
Will you be	at home		tonight? (*not* tonight at home?)
I usually go	to bed		early. (*not* early to bed)
We arrived	at the airport		at 7 o'clock.
They've lived	in the same house		for 20 years.
Jim's father has been	in the hospital		since June.

Exercises

94.1 Right or wrong? Correct the sentences that are wrong.

1. Did you watch all evening television?   _Did you watch television all evening?_
2. Sue reads a newspaper every day.   _OK_
3. I like very much this picture. _____
4. Tom started last week his new job. _____
5. I want to speak English fluently. _____
6. April bought for her friend a present. _____
7. I drink every day three cups of coffee. _____
8. Don't eat your dinner too quickly! _____
9. I borrowed from my brother fifty dollars. _____

94.2 Put the words in order.

1. (the door / opened / I / slowly) _I opened the door slowly._
2. (two letters / I / this morning / wrote) I _____ .
3. (entered / quietly / the house / the thief) _____
4. (Megan / very well / French / doesn't speak) _____
5. (a lot of work / did / I / yesterday) _____
6. (Mary / do you know / well?) _____
7. (we / enjoyed / very much / the party) _____
8. (the problem / carefully / I / explained) _____
9. (we / at the airport / some friends / met) _____
10. (did you buy / in Canada / that jacket?) _____
11. (every day / do / the same thing / we) _____
12. (football / don't like / very much / I) _____

94.3 Put the words in order.

1. (to work / every day / walks / Liz) Liz _walks to work every day_ .
2. (at the hotel / I / early / arrived) I _____ .
3. (goes / every year / to Puerto Rico / Julia) Julia _____ .
4. (we / since 1998 / here / have lived) We _____ .
5. (in Montreal / Sue / in 1980 / was born) Sue _____ .
6. (didn't go / yesterday / Paul / to work) Paul _____ .
7. (to the bank / yesterday afternoon / went / Megan)
   Megan _____ .
8. (I / in bed / this morning / had breakfast) I _____ .
9. (next September / Barbara / to college / is going)
   Barbara _____ .
10. (I / a beautiful bird / this morning / in the yard / saw)
    I _____ .
11. (many times / have been / my parents / to Tokyo)
    My _____ .
12. (my umbrella / I / last night / left / in the restaurant)
    I _____ .
13. (to the movies / tomorrow / are you going?)
    Are _____ ?
14. (the children / I / took / this morning / to school)
    I _____ .

Always/usually/often, etc. (Word Order 2)

A

We often use these words with the verb in the middle of a sentence.

always	often	ever	rarely	also	already	all
usually	sometimes	never	seldom	just	still	both

- My brother **never speaks** to me.
- She's **always** late.
- Do you **often go** to restaurants?
- I **sometimes eat** too much. (*or* **Sometimes** I eat too much.)
- I don't want to go to the movies. I've **already** seen that film.
- I've got three sisters. They're **all** married.

B

Always/never, etc., usually go *before* the verb.

	verb
always	go
often	play
never	feel
(etc.)	(etc.)

- I **always go** to work by car. (*not* I go always)
- Megan **often plays** tennis. (*not* Megan plays often tennis)
- You **sometimes look** unhappy.
- They **usually have** dinner at 7 o'clock.
- We **rarely** (*or* **seldom**) **watch** television.
- Richard is a good swimmer. He **also plays** tennis and volleyball. (*not* He plays also tennis)
- I've got three sisters. They **all live** in the same city.

Always/never, etc., go *after* am/is/are/was/were.

am is are was were	always often never (etc.)

- I **am never** sick. (*not* I never am sick)
- They **are usually** at home in the evening.
- It **is often** very cold here in the winter.
- When I was a child, I **was always** late for school.
- "Is Nicole **still** here?" "No, she went home."
- I've got two brothers. They're **both** doctors.

C

Always/never, etc., go *between* two verbs (**have . . . been / can . . . find**, etc.).

verb 1		*verb 2*
will can do (etc.)	always often never (etc.)	go find remember (etc.)
have has		gone been (etc.)

- I **will always remember** you.
- It **doesn't often rain** here.
- Do you **usually drive** to work?
- I **can never find** my keys.
- **Have** you **ever been** to Egypt?
- Nicole isn't here. She **just went** out.
- The children **have all finished** their homework.

***Always/never* + Simple Present** Unit 5 ***Just/already* + Present Perfect and Simple Past** Unit 20
All Units 81–82 ***Both*** Unit 83 ***Still*** Unit 96

Exercises

95.1 Look at Paul's answers. Write sentences with *often/never*, etc.

   PAUL

1.	Do you ever play tennis?	Yes, often.	*Paul often plays tennis.*
2.	Do you get up early?	Yes, always.	He _____.
3.	Are you ever late for work?	No, never.	He _____.
4.	Do you ever get angry?	Sometimes.	_____
5.	Do you go swimming much?	No, rarely.	_____
6.	Are you home in the evening much?	Yes, usually.	_____

95.2 Write these sentences with the words in parentheses ( ).

1. My brother calls me. (never) *My brother never calls me.*
2. Susan is polite. (always) Susan _____.
3. Kim started a new job. (just) Kim _____.
4. I go to bed before midnight. (rarely) _____
5. The bus isn't late. (usually) _____
6. I don't eat fish. (often) _____
7. I will forget what you said. (never) _____
8. Have you lost your passport? (ever) _____
9. Do you work in the same place? (still) _____
10. They stay at the same hotel. (always) _____
11. Diane doesn't work on Saturday. (usually) _____
12. Is Tina here? (already) _____
13. What do you have for breakfast? (usually) _____
14. I can remember his name. (never) _____

95.3 Write sentences with *also*. Use the words in parentheses ( ).

1. Do you play football? (tennis) *Yes, and I also play tennis.*
2. Do you speak Spanish? (Russian) Yes, and I _____.
3. Are you tired? (hungry) Yes, and _____
4. Have you been to England? (Ireland) Yes, _____.
5. Did you buy any clothes? (some books) _____

95.4 Write sentences with *both* and *all*.

I live in Buenos Aires. I play soccer. I'm a student. I have a car.	I live in Buenos Aires. I play soccer. I'm a student. I have a car.

I'm married. I was born in England. I live in Toronto.

1. *They both live in Buenos Aires.*
   They _____ soccer.
   They _____ students.
   _____ cars.

2. They _____ married.
   They _____ England.
   _____

Still, yet, and already

A

still

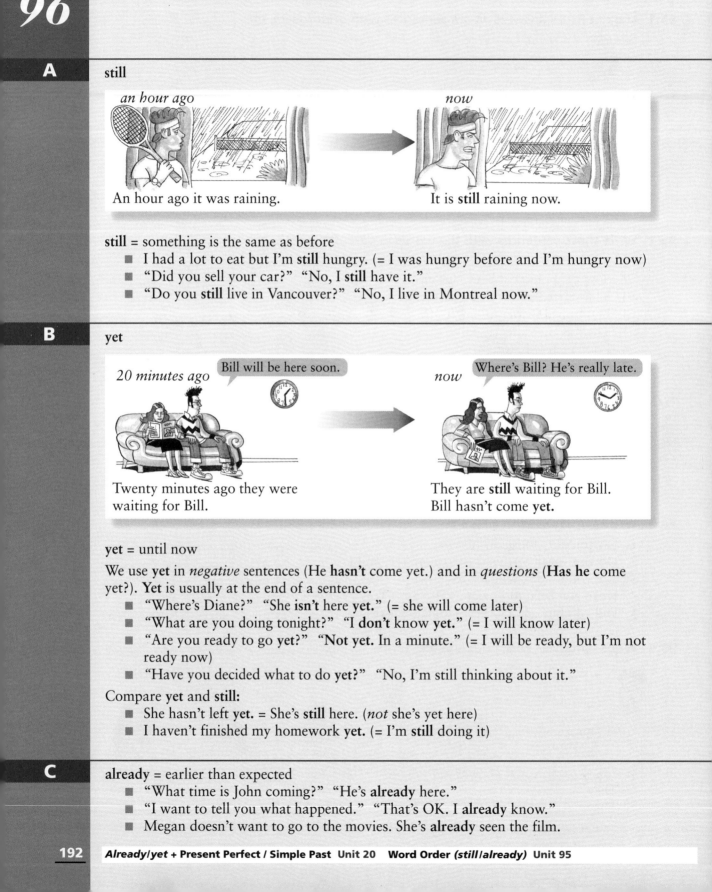

an hour ago

An hour ago it was raining.

now

It is **still** raining now.

still = something is the same as before

- I had a lot to eat but I'm **still** hungry. (= I was hungry before and I'm hungry now)
- "Did you sell your car?" "No, I **still** have it."
- "Do you **still** live in Vancouver?" "No, I live in Montreal now."

B

yet

20 minutes ago   Bill will be here soon.

Twenty minutes ago they were waiting for Bill.

now   Where's Bill? He's really late.

They are **still** waiting for Bill. Bill hasn't come **yet.**

yet = until now

We use **yet** in *negative* sentences (He **hasn't** come yet.) and in *questions* (**Has he** come yet?). **Yet** is usually at the end of a sentence.

- "Where's Diane?" "She **isn't** here **yet.**" (= she will come later)
- "What are you doing tonight?" "I **don't** know **yet.**" (= I will know later)
- "Are you ready to go **yet?**" "**Not yet.** In a minute." (= I will be ready, but I'm not ready now)
- "Have you decided what to do **yet?**" "No, I'm **still** thinking about it."

Compare **yet** and **still**:

- She hasn't left **yet.** = She's **still** here. (*not* she's yet here)
- I haven't finished my homework **yet.** (= I'm **still** doing it)

C

already = earlier than expected

- "What time is John coming?" "He's **already** here."
- "I want to tell you what happened." "That's OK. I **already** know."
- Megan doesn't want to go to the movies. She's **already** seen the film.

Exercises

96.1 You meet Lisa. The last time you saw her was two years ago. You ask her some questions with *still*.

LISA *two years ago*

I play the piano.
I have an old car.
I'm a student.
I'm studying Japanese.
I go to the movies a lot.
I want to be a teacher.

1. *Do you still play the piano?*
2. Do you _____ ?
3. Are _____ ?
4. _____
5. _____
6. _____

96.2 Write three sentences for each situation. Look at the example carefully.

before   *now*

1.
   (before) *They were waiting for the bus.*
   (still) *They are still waiting.*
   (yet) *The bus hasn't come yet.*

2. I'm looking for a job.
   (before) He was _____ .
   (still) He _____ .
   (yet) _____ yet.

3.
   (before) She _____ .
   (still) _____
   (yet) _____

4.
   dinner   *dinner*
   (before) They _____ .
   (still) _____
   (yet) _____

96.3 Write questions with *yet*.

1. You and Sue are going out together. You are waiting for her to get ready. Maybe she is ready now. You ask Sue: *Are you ready yet?*
2. You are waiting for Megan to arrive. She wasn't here ten minutes ago. Maybe she is here now. You ask somebody: _____ Megan _____ ?
3. Mary had a blood test and is waiting for the report. Maybe she has gotten the report now. You ask her: _____ you _____ ?
4. A few days ago you spoke to Tom. He couldn't decide where to go on vacation. Maybe he has decided now. You ask him: _____ ?

96.4 Complete the sentences. Use *already*.

1. What time is John coming?	He *'s already* _____ here.
2. Do you and Joe want to see the movie?	No, we *'ve already seen* _____ it.
3. I have to see Julie before she leaves.	It's too late. She _____ .
4. Do you need a pen?	No thanks. I _____ one.
5. Should I pay the bill?	No, it's OK. I _____ .
6. Should I tell Paul about the meeting?	No, he _____ . I told him.

Give me that book!   Give it to me!

A

give/lend/pass/send/show

After these verbs, there are two possible structures:

(give) **something to somebody**
- I gave **the keys to Liz.**

(give) **somebody something**
- I gave **Liz the keys.**

I   *the keys*   LIZ

B

(give) **something to somebody**

		something	to somebody
That's my book.	**Give**	it	**to** me.
These are Sue's keys. Can you	**give**	them	**to** her?
Can you	**give**	these flowers	**to** your mother?
I	**lent**	my car	**to** a friend of mine.
Did you	**send**	a postcard	**to** Kate?
We've seen these photos. You	**showed**	them	**to** us.

C

(give) **somebody something**

		somebody	something	
	Give	me	that book.	It's mine.
Tom	**gave**	his mother	some flowers.	
I	**lent**	John	some money.	
How much money did you	**lend**	him?		
I	**sent**	you	a postcard.	
Nicole	**showed**	us	her vacation photos.	
Can you	**pass**	me	the salt,	please?

You can also say: **buy/get** somebody something.
- I **bought** my mother some flowers. (= I bought some flowers **for** my mother)
- Can you **get** me a newspaper when you go out? (= get a newspaper **for** me)

D

Compare:
- I **gave** the keys **to Liz.**
  I **gave Liz** the keys. (*but not* I gave to Liz the keys)
- That's my book. Can you **give** it **to me**?
  Can you **give me** that book? (*but not* give to me that book)

We prefer the first structure (**give** something **to** somebody) when the *thing* is **it** or **them.**
- I gave **it to her.** (*not* I gave her it)
- Here are the keys. Give **them to your father.** (*not* Give your father them)

I/him/them, etc. Unit 60

Exercises

97.1 Mark had some things that he didn't want. He gave them to different people.

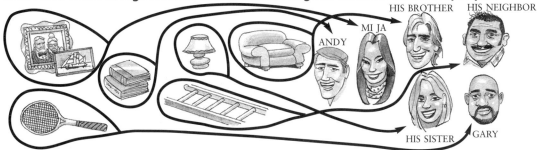

HIS BROTHER   HIS NEIGHBOR
ANDY   MI JA
HIS SISTER   GARY

Write sentences beginning *He gave* . . . .

1. What did Mark do with the armchair?   *He gave it to his brother.*
2. What did he do with the tennis rackct?   He gave _____ .
3. What happened to the books?   He _____ .
4. What about the lamp?   _____
5. What did he do with the pictures?   _____
6. And the ladder?   _____

97.2 You gave some gifts to these people. Write a sentence for each person.

1   PAUL   2   MIKA   3   ALAN   4   DIANE   5   LYNN   6   CARLOS

1. *I gave Paul a book.*   4. _____
2. I gave _____ .   5. _____
3. I _____ .   6. _____

97.3 Write questions beginning *Can you give me . . . ?* / *Can you pass me . . . ?*, etc.

1. (you want the salt – pass) *Can you pass me the salt?*
2. (you need an umbrella – lend) Can you _____ ?
3. (you want my address – give) Can _____ your _____ ?
4. (you need ten dollars – lend) _____
5. (you want some information – send) _____
6. (you want to see the letter – show) _____
7. (you want some stamps – get) _____

97.4 Which is right?

1. ~~I gave to Liz the keys.~~ / I gave Liz the keys.   (*I gave Liz the keys* is right.)
2. I'll <u>lend to you some money</u> if you want. / I'll <u>lend you some money</u> if you want.
3. Did you <u>send the letter me</u>? / Did you <u>send the letter to me</u>?
4. I want to <u>buy for you a present</u>. / I want to <u>buy you a present</u>.
5. Can you <u>pass to me the sugar</u>, please? / Can you <u>pass me the sugar</u>, please?
6. This is Megan's bag. Can you <u>give it to her</u>? / Can you <u>give her it</u>?
7. I showed <u>to the officer my driver's license</u>. / I showed <u>the officer my driver's license</u>.

At 8 o'clock, on Monday, in April, etc.

A at

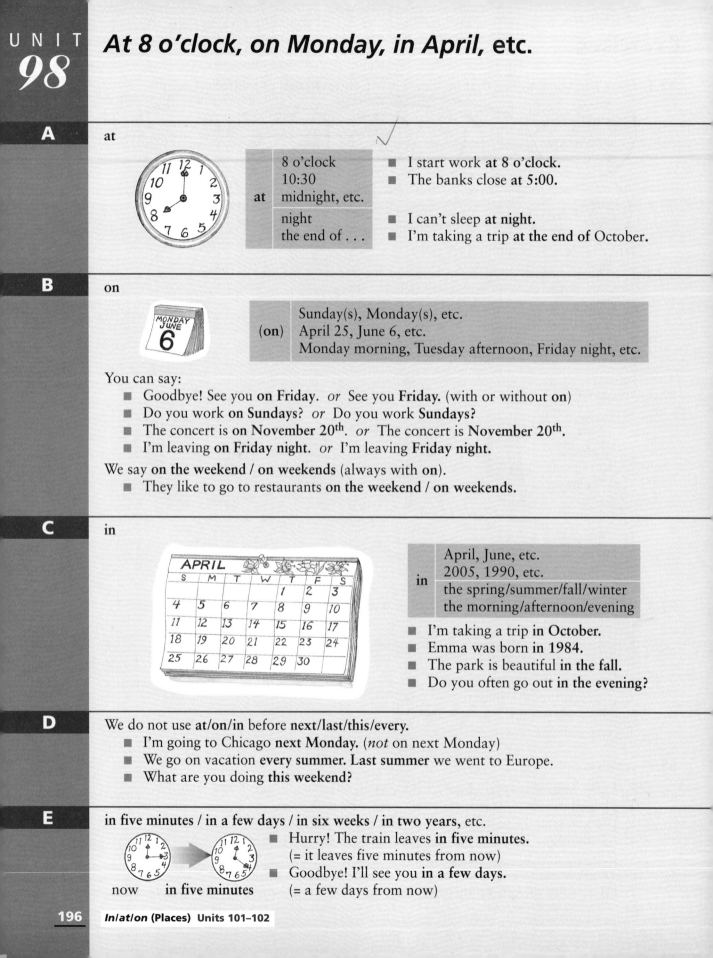

	8 o'clock 10:30 midnight, etc.
at	
	night the end of . . .

- I start work **at 8 o'clock.**
- The banks close **at 5:00.**

- I can't sleep **at night.**
- I'm taking a trip **at the end of** October.

B on

(on)	Sunday(s), Monday(s), etc. April 25, June 6, etc. Monday morning, Tuesday afternoon, Friday night, etc.

You can say:
- Goodbye! See you **on Friday.** *or* See you **Friday.** (with or without **on**)
- Do you work **on Sundays?** *or* Do you work **Sundays?**
- The concert is **on November 20th.** *or* The concert is **November 20th.**
- I'm leaving **on Friday night.** *or* I'm leaving **Friday night.**

We say **on the weekend / on weekends** (always with **on**).
- They like to go to restaurants **on the weekend / on weekends.**

C in

in	April, June, etc. 2005, 1990, etc. the spring/summer/fall/winter the morning/afternoon/evening

- I'm taking a trip **in October.**
- Emma was born **in 1984.**
- The park is beautiful **in the fall.**
- Do you often go out **in the evening?**

D We do not use **at/on/in** before **next/last/this/every.**
- I'm going to Chicago **next Monday.** (*not* on next Monday)
- We go on vacation **every summer. Last summer** we went to Europe.
- What are you doing **this weekend?**

E **in five minutes / in a few days / in six weeks / in two years,** etc.

now   **in five minutes**

- Hurry! The train leaves **in five minutes.**
  (= it leaves five minutes from now)
- Goodbye! I'll see you **in a few days.**
  (= a few days from now)

In/at/on (Places) **Units 101–102**

Exercises

98.1 Write *at* or *in*.

1. Emma was born _in___ 1984.
2. I got up _____ 8 o'clock this morning.
3. I like to get up early _____ the morning.
4. I like to look at the stars _____ night.
5. My brother got married _____ May.
6. We often go to the beach _____ the summer.
7. Let's meet _____ 7:30 tomorrow evening.
8. The company started _____ 1989.
9. I'll send you the money _____ the end of the month.
10. The café is open _____ the evening. It closes _____ midnight.

98.2 Write *at/in/on*.

1.	_in___ April	6.	_____ September	11.	_____ Friday morning
2.	_on___ June 6	7.	_____ September 24th	12.	_____ Saturday night
3.	_____ half past two	8.	_____ the weekend	13.	_____ night
4.	_____ 1987	9.	_____ 11:45	14.	_____ the end of the day
5.	_____ Wednesday	10.	_____ the morning	15.	_____ the winter

98.3 Which sentence is correct – A, B, or both of them?

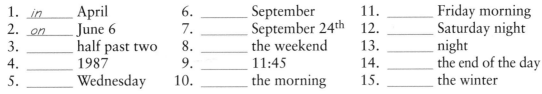

	A	**B**	
1.	I'm taking a trip in October.	I'm taking a trip on October.	_A__
2.	Do you work Sundays?	Do you work on Sundays?	_both_
3.	I always feel tired at the evening.	I always feel tired in the evening.	_____
4.	I'm leaving next Saturday.	I'm leaving on next Saturday.	_____
5.	Tim started his new job on May 18th.	Tim started his new job May 18th.	_____
6.	Laura finished high school in 1998.	Laura finished high school 1998.	_____
7.	We meet on every Tuesday.	We meet every Tuesday.	_____
8.	We don't often go out in night.	We don't often go out at night.	_____
9.	I can't meet you Thursday.	I can't meet you on Thursday.	_____
10.	Lisa saw Sam Monday night.	Lisa saw Sam at Monday night.	_____
11.	I'm leaving in the end of this month.	I'm leaving at the end of this month.	_____
12.	Tim goes to the gym on Fridays.	Tim goes to the gym Fridays.	_____

98.4 Write sentences with *in*.

1. It's 5:25 now. The train leaves at 5:30.
   The train leaves in five minutes.
2. It's Monday today. I'll call you on Thursday.
   I'll _____ .
3. Today is June 14th. My exam is June 28th.
   My _____ .
4. It's 3 o'clock now. Tom will be here at 3:30.
   Tom _____ .

From . . . to, until, since, and for

A

from . . . to . . .
- We lived in Canada **from** 1982 **to** 1990.
- I work **from** Monday **to** Friday.

You can also say **from . . . until . . . .**
- We lived in Canada **from** 1982 **until** 1990.

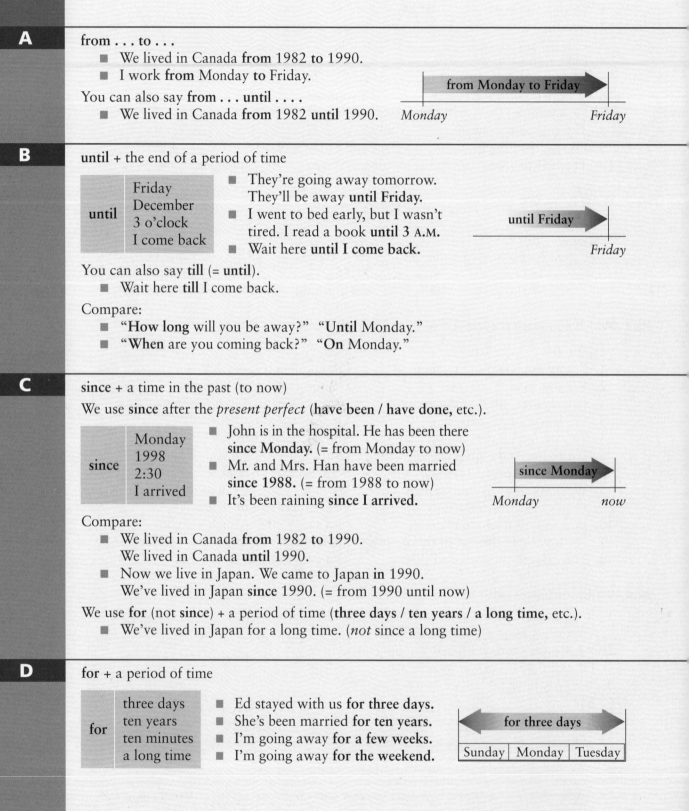

from Monday to Friday

Monday   *Friday*

B

until + the end of a period of time

until	Friday December 3 o'clock I come back

- They're going away tomorrow.
  They'll be away **until Friday.**
- I went to bed early, but I wasn't
  tired. I read a book **until 3 A.M.**
- Wait here **until I come back.**

until Friday

Friday

You can also say **till** (= until).
- Wait here **till** I come back.

Compare:
- "**How long** will you be away?" "**Until** Monday."
- "**When** are you coming back?" "**On** Monday."

C

since + a time in the past (to now)

We use **since** after the *present perfect* (**have been / have done,** etc.).

since	Monday 1998 2:30 I arrived

- John is in the hospital. He has been there
  since Monday. (= from Monday to now)
- Mr. and Mrs. Han have been married
  since 1988. (= from 1988 to now)
- It's been raining **since I arrived.**

since Monday

Monday   *now*

Compare:
- We lived in Canada **from** 1982 **to** 1990.
  We lived in Canada **until** 1990.
- Now we live in Japan. We came to Japan **in** 1990.
  We've lived in Japan **since** 1990. (= from 1990 until now)

We use **for** (not since) + a period of time (**three days / ten years / a long time,** etc.).
- We've lived in Japan **for** a long time. (*not* since a long time)

D

for + a period of time

for	three days ten years ten minutes a long time

- Ed stayed with us **for three days.**
- She's been married **for ten years.**
- I'm going away **for a few weeks.**
- I'm going away **for the weekend.**

for three days

Sunday	Monday	Tuesday

Present Perfect + *for/since* **Unit 18**   **Present Perfect (*I have done*) and Simple Past (*I did*) Unit 21**

Exercises

99.1 Read the information and complete the sentences. Use *from . . . to / until / since.*

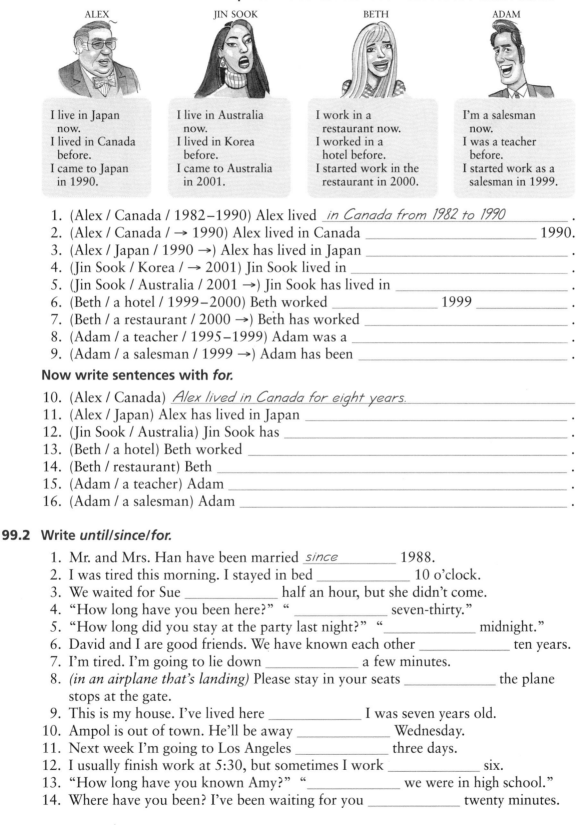

ALEX

I live in Japan now.
I lived in Canada before.
I came to Japan in 1990.

JIN SOOK

I live in Australia now.
I lived in Korea before.
I came to Australia in 2001.

BETH

I work in a restaurant now.
I worked in a hotel before.
I started work in the restaurant in 2000.

ADAM

I'm a salesman now.
I was a teacher before.
I started work as a salesman in 1999.

1. (Alex / Canada / 1982–1990) Alex lived _in Canada from 1982 to 1990_ .
2. (Alex / Canada / → 1990) Alex lived in Canada _____ 1990.
3. (Alex / Japan / 1990 →) Alex has lived in Japan _____ .
4. (Jin Sook / Korea / → 2001) Jin Sook lived in _____ .
5. (Jin Sook / Australia / 2001 →) Jin Sook has lived in _____ .
6. (Beth / a hotel / 1999–2000) Beth worked _____ 1999 _____ .
7. (Beth / a restaurant / 2000 →) Beth has worked _____ .
8. (Adam / a teacher / 1995–1999) Adam was a _____ .
9. (Adam / a salesman / 1999 →) Adam has been _____ .

Now write sentences with *for.*

10. (Alex / Canada) _Alex lived in Canada for eight years._
11. (Alex / Japan) Alex has lived in Japan _____ .
12. (Jin Sook / Australia) Jin Sook has _____ .
13. (Beth / a hotel) Beth worked _____ .
14. (Beth / restaurant) Beth _____ .
15. (Adam / a teacher) Adam _____ .
16. (Adam / a salesman) Adam _____ .

99.2 Write *until/since/for.*

1. Mr. and Mrs. Han have been married _since_ 1988.
2. I was tired this morning. I stayed in bed _____ 10 o'clock.
3. We waited for Sue _____ half an hour, but she didn't come.
4. "How long have you been here?" "_____ seven-thirty."
5. "How long did you stay at the party last night?" "_____ midnight."
6. David and I are good friends. We have known each other _____ ten years.
7. I'm tired. I'm going to lie down _____ a few minutes.
8. *(in an airplane that's landing)* Please stay in your seats _____ the plane stops at the gate.
9. This is my house. I've lived here _____ I was seven years old.
10. Ampol is out of town. He'll be away _____ Wednesday.
11. Next week I'm going to Los Angeles _____ three days.
12. I usually finish work at 5:30, but sometimes I work _____ six.
13. "How long have you known Amy?" "_____ we were in high school."
14. Where have you been? I've been waiting for you _____ twenty minutes.

Before, after, during, and while

A   before, during, and after

before the movie   **during** the movie   **after** the movie

- Everybody is nervous **before exams.**
- I fell asleep **during the movie.**
- We were tired **after our visit** to the museum.

B   before, while, and after

before we played   **while** we were playing   **after** we played

- Don't forget to close the window **before you go** out.
- I often fall asleep **while I'm reading.**
- They watched TV **after they did** the dishes.

C   during, while, and for

We use **during** + *noun* (during the movie). We use **while** + *verb* (while I'm watching).

- We didn't speak **during the meal.** *but*
- We didn't speak **while we were eating.** (*not* during we were eating)

Use **for** (*not* during) + *a period of time* (**three days / two hours / a year**, etc.).

- We played tennis **for two hours.** (*not* during two hours)
- I lived in London **for a year.** (*not* during a year)

D

You can use **before/after** + **-ing** (before going / after eating, etc.).

- I always have breakfast **before going** to work. (= before I go to work)
- **After doing** the dishes, they watched TV. (= after they did)

Do not say "before to go," "after to do," etc.

- **Before eating** the apple, I washed it carefully. (*not* before to eat)
- I started work **after reading** the newspaper. (*not* after to read)

I was -ing **(Past Continuous)** Units 13–14   *For* **Unit 99**   **Preposition + -ing** Unit 107
Before/after/while/when Unit 112

Exercises

100.1 Complete the sentences. Choose from the boxes.

after	during
before	while

+

lunch	the end	they went to Australia
the concert	the exam	you're waiting
the course	the night	

1. Everybody was nervous *before the exam* .
2. I usually work four hours in the morning and another three hours _____ .
3. The movie was really boring. We left _____ .
4. Anne went to night school to learn German. She learned a lot _____ .
5. My aunt and uncle lived in London _____ .
6. *A:* Somebody broke a window _____ . Did you hear anything?
   B: No, I was asleep.
7. Would you like to sit down _____ ?
8. "Are you going home _____ ?" "Yes, we have to get up early tomorrow."

100.2 Write *during/while/for.*

1. We didn't speak *while* _____ we were eating.
2. We didn't speak *during* _____ the meal.
3. Eric called _____ you were out.
4. I stayed in Rome _____ five days.
5. Karen wrote a lot of letters _____ she was on vacation.
6. The students looked very bored _____ the class.
7. I fell out of bed _____ I was asleep.
8. Last night I watched TV _____ six hours.
9. I don't usually watch TV _____ the day.
10. Do you ever watch TV _____ you're having dinner?

100.3 Complete the sentences. Use *-ing* (*doing,* etc.).

1. After *doing* _____ the dishes, they watched TV.
2. I felt sick after _____ too much chocolate.
3. I'm going to ask you a question. Think carefully before _____ it.
4. I felt terrible when I got up this morning. I felt better after _____ a shower.
5. After _____ my work, I left the office and went home.
6. Before _____ to a foreign country, you should learn a little of the language.

100.4 Write sentences with *before* + *-ing* and *after* + *-ing.*

1. They did the dishes. Then they watched TV.
   After *doing the dishes, they watched TV* .
2. John finished high school. Then he worked in a department store for two years.
   John worked _____ .
3. I read for a few minutes. Then I went to sleep.
   Before _____ .
4. We walked for three hours. We were very tired.
   After _____ .
5. Let's have a cup of coffee. Then we'll go out.
   Let's _____ .

In, at, and *on* (Places 1)

A

in

in a room
in a store
in a car
in the water

in a yard
in a town
in a park
in Brazil

- "Where's David?" "In the kitchen. / In the back yard. / In Tokyo."
- What's **in that box** / **in that bag** / **in that closet**?
- Angela works **in a store** / **in a bank** / **in a factory**.
- I went for a swim **in the river** / **in the pool** / **in the ocean**.
- Milan is **in northern Italy**.
- I live **in a city**, but I'd like to live **in the country**.

B

at

at the bus stop   at the door   at the traffic light   at her desk

- There's somebody **at the bus stop** / **at the door**.
- The car is waiting **at the traffic light**.
- Julia is working **at her desk**.

Also: **at the top** / **at the bottom** / **at the end** (of . . .)
- Write your name **at the top of the page**.
- My house is **at the end of the block**.

at the top (of the page)

at the bottom (of the page)

C

on

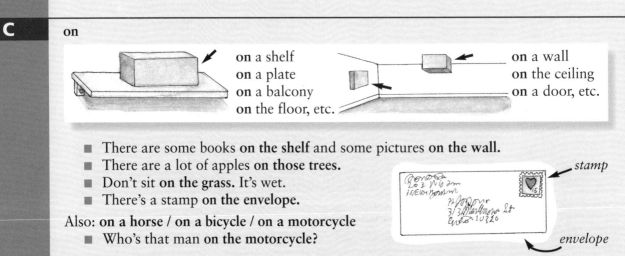

on a shelf
on a plate
on a balcony
on the floor, etc.

on a wall
on the ceiling
on a door, etc.

- There are some books **on the shelf** and some pictures **on the wall**.
- There are a lot of apples **on those trees**.
- Don't sit **on the grass**. It's wet.
- There's a stamp **on the envelope**.

Also: **on a horse** / **on a bicycle** / **on a motorcycle**
- Who's that man **on the motorcycle**?

stamp

envelope

In/at/on (Places 2) **Unit 102** *The top / the bottom, etc.* **Unit 71** *At/on/in* (Time) **Unit 98**

Exercises

101.1 Answer the questions. Use *in/at/on* + the words in parentheses ( ).

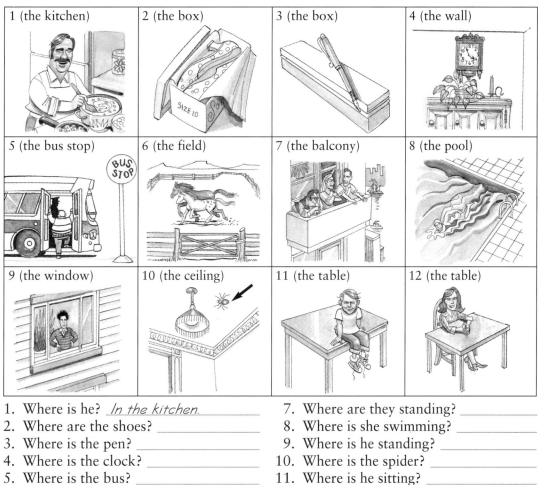

1 (the kitchen) 2 (the box) 3 (the box) 4 (the wall)

5 (the bus stop) 6 (the field) 7 (the balcony) 8 (the pool)

9 (the window) 10 (the ceiling) 11 (the table) 12 (the table)

1. Where is he? _In the kitchen._	7. Where are they standing? _____
2. Where are the shoes? _____	8. Where is she swimming? _____
3. Where is the pen? _____	9. Where is he standing? _____
4. Where is the clock? _____	10. Where is the spider? _____
5. Where is the bus? _____	11. Where is he sitting? _____
6. Where are the horses? _____	12. Where is she sitting? _____

101.2 Write *in/at/on*.

1. Don't sit _on____ the grass. It's wet.
2. What do you have _____ the bag?
3. Look! There's a man _____ the roof. What's he doing?
4. There are a lot of fish _____ this river.
5. Our house is number 45 – the number is _____ the door.
6. "Is the post office near here?" "Yes, turn left _____ the traffic light."
7. I have a small vegetable garden _____ the back yard.
8. My sister lives _____ Mexico City.
9. There's a small park _____ the top of the hill.
10. I think I heard the doorbell. There's somebody _____ the door.
11. Munich is a large city _____ southern Germany.
12. There's a gas station _____ the end of the block.
13. It's difficult to carry a lot of things _____ a bicycle.
14. I looked at the list of names. My name was _____ the bottom of the list.
15. There's a mirror _____ the wall _____ the living room.

In, at, and *on* (Places 2)

A

in

in bed	■ "Where's Kate?" "She's **in bed.**"
in prison / jail	■ Karen's husband is **in jail** for driving without a license.
in the hospital	■ David's father is sick. He's **in the hospital.**
in the sky	■ I like to look at the stars **in the sky** at night.
in the world	■ What's the largest city **in the world?**
in a newspaper / in a book	■ I read about the accident **in the newspaper.**
in a photograph / in a picture	■ You look sad **in this photograph.**
in a car / in a taxi	■ Did you come here **in your car?**
in the middle (of . . .)	■ There's a big tree **in the middle** of the yard.

B

at

at work	■ "Where's Kate?" "She's **at work.**"
at the station / at the airport	■ Do you want me to meet you **at the airport?**
at the post office / at the supermarket	■ I saw your brother **at the post office** today.
at Tracy's (house) / at the doctor's (office) / at the hairdresser's, etc.	■ "Where were you Friday?" "**At my sister's.**"
	■ I saw Tom **at the doctor's.**
at a concert / at a party / at a football game, etc.	■ There weren't many people **at the party.**

You can say **be/stay at home** or **be/stay home** (with or without **at**).
   ■ Is Tom **at home?** *or* Is Tom **home?**

You can often use **in** or **at** for hotels and restaurants.
   ■ We stayed **at** a nice hotel. *or* We stayed **in** a nice hotel.

C

You can say **in school** or **at school,** but there is a difference.

She's **at school** = she is there now
   ■ "Where's your sister? Is she home?" "No, she's **at school.**"

She's **in school** = she is a student (in high school / college / medical school, etc.)
   ■ "Does your sister have a job?" "No, she's still **in school.**"

D

on

on a bus / on a train / on a plane / on a boat	■ Did you come here **on the bus?**
on the first floor (*or* ground floor) / on the second floor, etc.	■ The office is **on the first floor.** (*not* in the first floor)
on a street	■ My brother lives **on a nice street.**
on the way (to . . .) / on the way home	■ I met Lee **on the way** to work / **on my way** home.

In/at/on (Places 1) Unit 101   *To/in/at* Unit 103   *On the left/right* Unit 104

Exercises

102.1 Answer the questions. Use *in/at/on* + the words in parentheses ( ).

1 (the hospital) 2 (the airport) CHECK IN 3 (bed) 4 (a boat)

5 (the sky) 6 (a party) 7 (the doctor's) BRIAN 8 (the second floor) RESTAURANT SECOND FLOOR MENU

9 (work) 10 (a plane) 11 (a taxi) TAXI 12 (a wedding)

1. Where is she? *In the hospital.* _____
2. Where are they? _____
3. Where is he? _____
4. Where are they? _____
5. Where are the stars? _____
6. Where are they? _____

7. Where is Brian? _____
8. Where is the restaurant? _____
9. Where is she? _____
10. Where are they? _____
11. Where are they? _____
12. Where are they? _____

102.2 Write *in/at/on*.

1. "Where's your sister? Is she home?" "No, she's _at_ school."
2. There was a big table _____ the middle of the room.
3. What is the longest river _____ the world?
4. Were there many people _____ the concert last night?
5. Will you be _____ home tomorrow afternoon?
6. Who is the man _____ this photograph? Do you know him?
7. "Is your son going to get married soon?" "No, he's still _____ college."
8. Eric is coming by train. I'm going to meet him _____ the station.
9. Charlie is _____ the hospital. He had an operation yesterday.
10. How many pages are there _____ that book?
11. "Are you hungry after your trip?" "No, I ate _____ the plane."
12. I'm sorry I'm late. My car broke down _____ the way.
13. "Is Tom here?" "No, he's _____ his brother's."
14. Don't believe everything you see _____ the newspaper!
15. I walked to work, but I came home _____ the bus.
16. *A (on the phone):* Can I speak to Anne, please?
    B: No, sorry. She'll be _____ the university until 5:00 today.

To, in, and at (Places 3)

A

to	in/at (see Units 101–102)

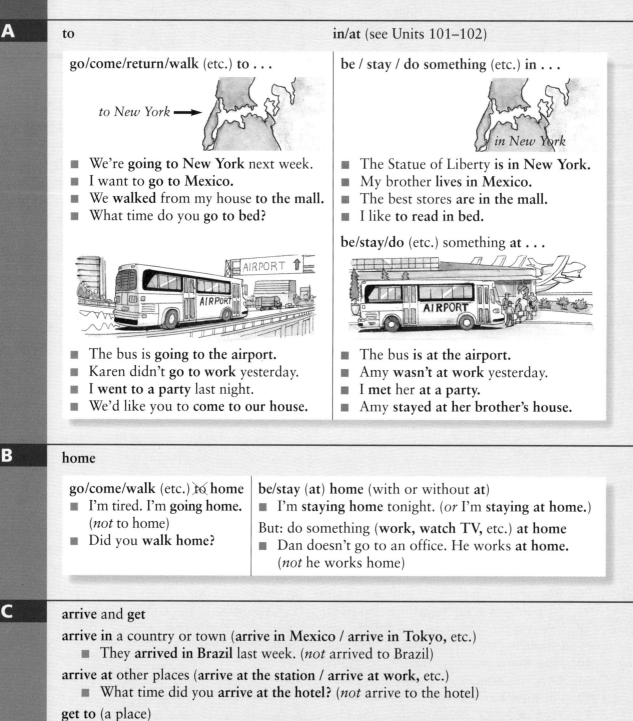

go/come/return/walk (etc.) to . . .

to New York ➡

- We're **going to New York** next week.
- I want to **go to Mexico**.
- We **walked** from my house **to the mall**.
- What time do you **go to bed**?

- The bus is **going to the airport**.
- Karen didn't **go to work** yesterday.
- I **went to a party** last night.
- We'd like you to **come to our house**.

be / stay / do something (etc.) in . . .

in New York

- The Statue of Liberty is **in New York**.
- My brother **lives in Mexico**.
- The best stores **are in the mall**.
- I like to **read in bed**.

be/stay/do (etc.) something at . . .

- The bus **is at the airport**.
- Amy **wasn't at work** yesterday.
- I met her **at a party**.
- Amy **stayed at her brother's house**.

B

home

go/come/walk (etc.) to home
- I'm tired. I'm **going home**.
  (*not* to home)
- Did you **walk home**?

be/stay (at) home (with or without at)
- I'm **staying home** tonight. (*or* I'm **staying at home**.)

But: do something (**work, watch TV,** etc.) **at home**
- Dan doesn't go to an office. He works **at home**.
  (*not* he works home)

C

arrive and get

arrive in a country or town (**arrive in Mexico** / **arrive in Tokyo**, etc.)
- They **arrived in Brazil** last week. (*not* arrived to Brazil)

arrive at other places (**arrive at the station** / **arrive at work**, etc.)
- What time did you **arrive at the hotel**? (*not* arrive to the hotel)

get to (a place)
- What time did you **get to the hotel**?
- When did you **get to Tokyo**?

get home / arrive home (no *preposition*)
- I was tired when I **got home**. (*or* I was tired when I **arrived home**.)

Exercises

103.1 Write *to* or *in*.

1. I like to read _in_ bed.
2. We're going _____ Italy next month.
3. Sue is on vacation _____ Chile right now.
4. I have to go _____ the bank today.
5. I was tired, so I stayed _____ bed.
6. What time do you go _____ bed?
7. Does this bus go _____ the airport?
8. Would you like to live _____ another country?

103.2 Write *to* or *at* if necessary. Sometimes no preposition is necessary.

1. Paula didn't go _to_ work yesterday.
2. I'm tired. I'm going ___—___ home. *(no preposition)*
3. Amy is sick. She went _____ the doctor.
4. Would you like to come _____ a party on Saturday?
5. "Is Liz _____ home?" "No, she went _____ work."
6. There were 20,000 people _____ the football game.
7. Why did you go _____ home early last night?
8. A boy jumped into the river and swam _____ the other side.
9. There were a lot of people waiting _____ the bus stop.
10. We had dinner _____ a restaurant, and then we went back _____ the hotel.

103.3 Write *to, at,* or *in* if necessary. Sometimes no preposition is necessary.

1. Joe is coming tomorrow. I'm meeting _at_ the airport.
2. We're going _____ a concert tomorrow night.
3. I went _____ Chile last year.
4. How long did you stay _____ Chile?
5. Next year we hope to go _____ Japan to visit some friends.
6. Do you want to go _____ the movies tonight?
7. Did you park your car _____ the airport?
8. After the accident three people were taken _____ the hospital.
9. How often do you go _____ the dentist?
10. "Is Diane here?" "No, she's _____ Amy's."
11. My house is _____ the end of the block on the left.
12. I went _____ Mary's house, but she wasn't _____ home.
13. There were no taxis, so we had to walk _____ home.
14. "Who did you see _____ the party?" "I didn't go _____ the party."

103.4 Write *to, at,* or *in* if necessary. Sometimes no preposition is necessary.

1. What time do you get _____ work?
2. What time do you get _____ home?
3. I arrived _____ the party after 9:00.
4. When did you arrive _____ Dallas?
5. The plane got _____ Paris on time.
6. We arrived _____ home very late.

103.5 Complete these sentences about yourself. Use *to/in/at*.

1. At three o'clock this morning I was _in bed_____ .
2. Yesterday I went _____ .
3. At 11 o'clock yesterday morning I was _____ .
4. Someday I'd like to go _____ .
5. At 9 o'clock last night I was _____ .

Next to, between, under, etc.

A

next to / between / in front of / in back of

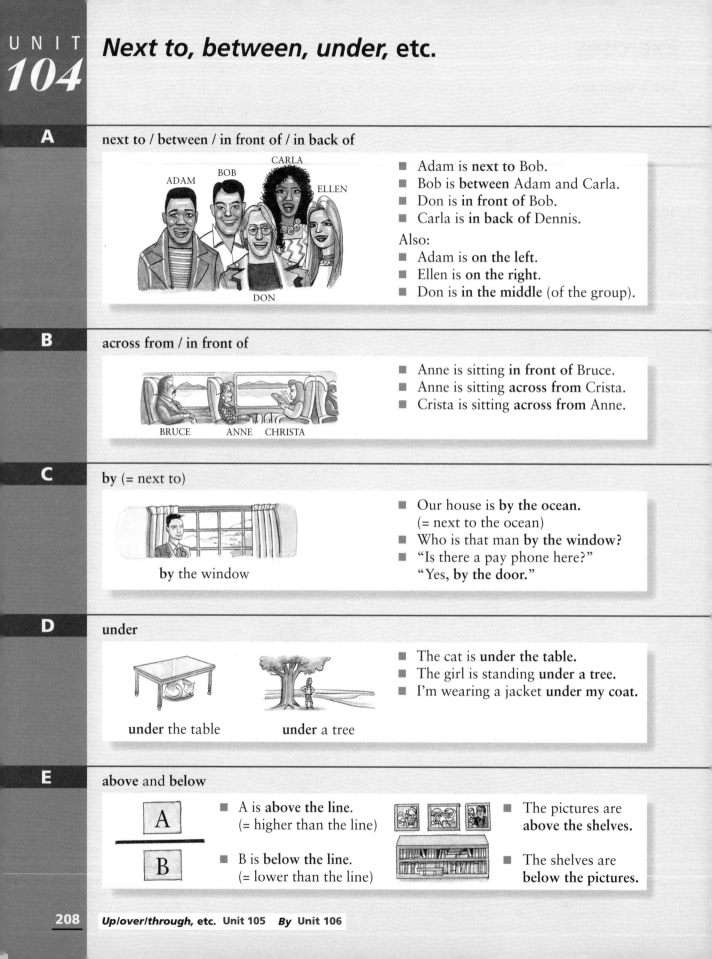

ADAM BOB CARLA ELLEN DON

- Adam is **next to** Bob.
- Bob is **between** Adam and Carla.
- Don is **in front of** Bob.
- Carla is **in back of** Dennis.

Also:
- Adam is **on the left**.
- Ellen is **on the right**.
- Don is **in the middle** (of the group).

B

across from / in front of

BRUCE ANNE CHRISTA

- Anne is sitting **in front of** Bruce.
- Anne is sitting **across from** Crista.
- Crista is sitting **across from** Anne.

C

by (= next to)

by the window

- Our house is **by the ocean**.
  (= next to the ocean)
- Who is that man **by the window**?
- "Is there a pay phone here?"
  "Yes, **by the door**."

D

under

under the table   **under** a tree

- The cat is **under the table**.
- The girl is standing **under a tree**.
- I'm wearing a jacket **under my coat**.

E

above and **below**

A

B

- A is **above the line**.
  (= higher than the line)

- B is **below the line**.
  (= lower than the line)

- The pictures are **above the shelves**.

- The shelves are **below the pictures**.

Up/over/through, etc. Unit 105   *By* Unit 106

Exercises

104.1 Where are the people in the picture? Complete the sentences.

left   *right*
DOT   CHRIS

ALAN   BETH   EMILY   FRED

1. Dot is standing ___*between*___ Alan and Chris.
2. Chris is standing _____ Fred.
3. Beth is sitting _____ Alan.
4. Emily is sitting _____ Beth and Fred.
5. Chris is standing _____ Dot.
6. Alan is standing _____ Beth.
7. Alan is standing _____ left.
8. Fred is sitting _____ right.
9. Emily is sitting _____ middle.

104.2 Look at the pictures and complete the sentences.

1. The cat is ___*under*___ the table.
2. There's a big tree _____ the house.
3. The plane is flying _____ the clouds.
4. She's standing _____ the piano.
5. The movie theater is _____ the right.
6. He's sitting _____ the phone.
7. The calendar is _____ the clock.
8. The cabinet is _____ the sink.
9. There are some shoes _____ the bed.
10. The plant is _____ the piano.
11. Paul is sitting _____ Anna.
12. In Japan people drive _____ the left.

104.3 Write sentences about the picture. Use the words in parentheses ( ).

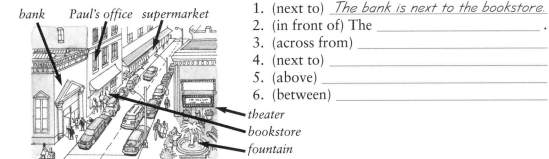

bank   *Paul's office*   *supermarket*

theater
bookstore
fountain

1. (next to) *The bank is next to the bookstore.*
2. (in front of) The _____.
3. (across from) _____
4. (next to) _____
5. (above) _____
6. (between) _____

Up, over, through, etc.

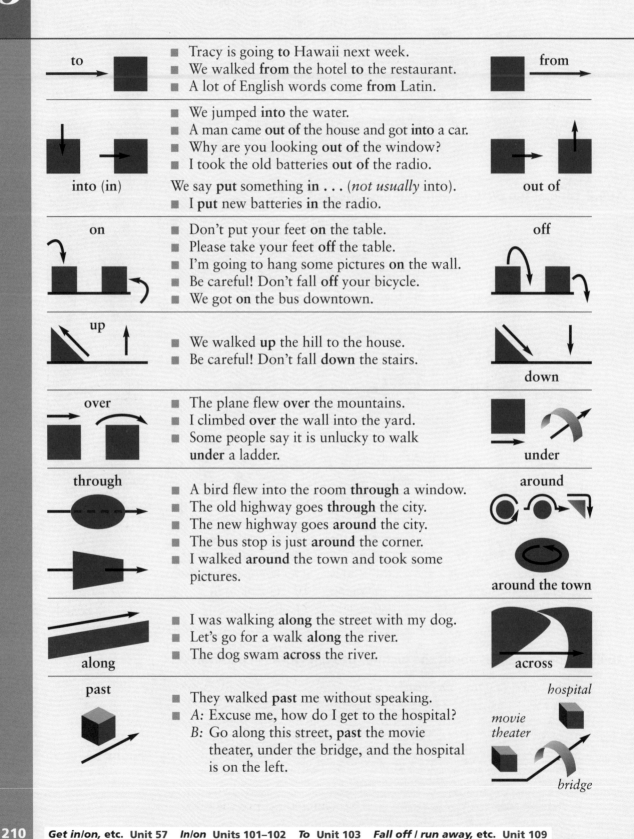

to
- Tracy is going **to** Hawaii next week.
- We walked **from** the hotel **to** the restaurant.
- A lot of English words come **from** Latin.

from

into (in)
- We jumped **into** the water.
- A man came **out of** the house and got **into** a car.
- Why are you looking **out of** the window?
- I took the old batteries **out of** the radio.

We say **put** something **in . . .** (*not usually* into).
- I **put** new batteries **in** the radio.

out of

on
- Don't put your feet **on** the table.
- Please take your feet **off** the table.
- I'm going to hang some pictures **on** the wall.
- Be careful! Don't fall **off** your bicycle.
- We got **on** the bus downtown.

off

up
- We walked **up** the hill to the house.
- Be careful! Don't fall **down** the stairs.

down

over
- The plane flew **over** the mountains.
- I climbed **over** the wall into the yard.
- Some people say it is unlucky to walk **under** a ladder.

under

through
- A bird flew into the room **through** a window.
- The old highway goes **through** the city.
- The new highway goes **around** the city.
- The bus stop is just **around** the corner.
- I walked **around** the town and took some pictures.

around

around the town

along
- I was walking **along** the street with my dog.
- Let's go for a walk **along** the river.
- The dog swam **across** the river.

across

past
- They walked **past** me without speaking.
- A: Excuse me, how do I get to the hospital?
  B: Go along this street, **past** the movie theater, under the bridge, and the hospital is on the left.

hospital

movie theater

bridge

Get in/on, etc. Unit 57   *In/on* Units 101–102   *To* Unit 103   *Fall off / run away, etc.* Unit 109

Exercises

105.1 Somebody asks you for directions.
Look at the pictures and write
sentences beginning *Go . . . .*

Excuse me, where is . . . ?

Go . . .

1. PUBLIC LIBRARY — *Go past the library.*
2. Go _____ the bridge.
3. _____ the hill.
4. _____ the steps.
5. _____ this street.
6. HOTEL
7. HOTEL
8. HOTEL
9.
10. PARK

105.2 Look at the pictures. Complete the sentences with a preposition.

1. The dog swam *across* the river.
2. A book fell _____ the shelf.
3. A plane flew _____ the town.
4. A woman got _____ the car.
5. A girl ran _____ the street.
6. Suddenly a car came _____ the corner.
7. They all drove _____ the town.
8. They got _____ the train.
9. The moon travels _____ the earth.
10. They got _____ the house _____ a window.

105.3 Write a preposition (*over / from / out of,* etc.).

1. I looked _____ the window and watched the people in the street.
2. My house is very near here. It's just _____ the corner.
3. Do you know how to put film _____ this camera?
4. How far is it _____ here _____ the airport?
5. We walked _____ the museum for an hour and saw a lot of beautiful pictures.
6. You can put your coat _____ the back of the chair.
7. In tennis, you have to hit the ball _____ the net.
8. Silvia took a key _____ her bag and opened the door.

On, at, by, with, and about

A

on

| on vacation |
| on television |
| on the radio |
| on the phone |
| on fire |
| on time (= not late) |

- Tracy isn't at work this week. She's **on vacation.**
- We watched the news **on television.**
- We listened to the news **on the radio.**
- I spoke to Carol **on the phone** last night.
- The house is **on fire!** Call the fire department.
- "Was the train late?" "No, it was **on time.**"

B

at (the age of) 21 / at 50 kilometers an hour / at 100 degrees, etc.

- Lisa got married **at 21.** (*or* . . . **at the age of 21**)
- A car uses more gas **at 70 miles an hour** than **at 55.**
- Water boils **at 100 degrees Celsius.**

C

by car / by bus / by plane (*or* **by air**) **/ by boat / by bicycle,** etc.

- Do you like traveling **by train?**
- Can you get there **by bike?**

But: **on foot**

- You can't get there by car.
  You have to go **on foot.**

by bus

on foot

a book **by . . . /** a painting **by . . . /**
a piece of music **by . . . ,** etc.

- Have you read any books
  by Charles Dickens?
- **Who** is that painting **by?** Picasso?

(the title)
by
(the writer)

by after the passive (see Unit 22)

- I was bitten **by a dog.**

D

with/without

- Did you stay at a hotel or **with friends?**
- Wait for me. Please don't go **without me.**
- Do you like your coffee **with** or **without milk?**
- I cut the paper **with a pair of scissors.**

a man **with** a beard / a woman **with** glasses, etc.

- Do you know that man **with the beard?**
- I'd like to have a house **with a big yard.**

a man **with**
a beard

a woman
with glasses

E

talk/speak/think/hear/know about . . .

- Some people **talk about their work** all the time.
- I don't **know** much **about cars.**

a book / a question / a program (etc.) **about . . .**

- Did you see **the program about computers** on TV last night?

Exercises

106.1 Complete the sentences. Use *on* + one of these:

> the phone   ~~the radio~~   TV   time   vacation

1. We listened to the news *on the radio* .
2. Please don't be late. Try to be here _____ .
3. I won't be here next week. I'm going _____ .
4. "Did you see Nicole?" "No, but I talked to her _____ ."
5. "What's _____ tonight?" "There's a movie at 9 o'clock."

106.2 Look at the pictures. Complete the sentences with a preposition (*at/by*, etc.).

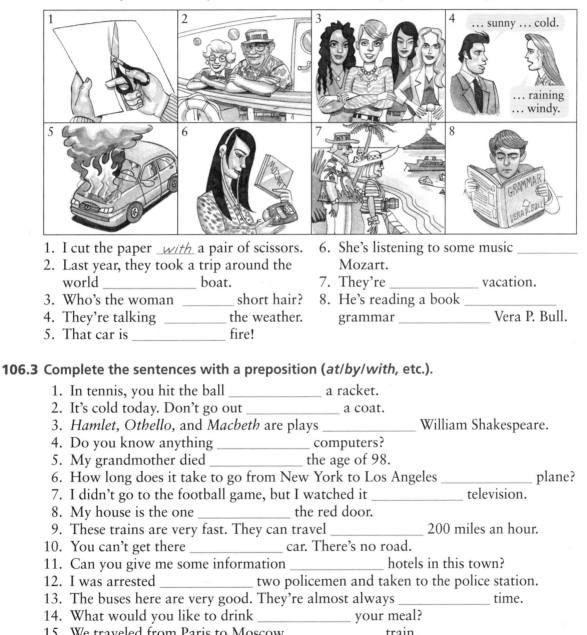

1. I cut the paper *with* a pair of scissors.
2. Last year, they took a trip around the world _____ boat.
3. Who's the woman _____ short hair?
4. They're talking _____ the weather.
5. That car is _____ fire!
6. She's listening to some music _____ Mozart.
7. They're _____ vacation.
8. He's reading a book _____ grammar _____ Vera P. Bull.

106.3 Complete the sentences with a preposition (*at/by/with*, etc.).

1. In tennis, you hit the ball _____ a racket.
2. It's cold today. Don't go out _____ a coat.
3. *Hamlet, Othello,* and *Macbeth* are plays _____ William Shakespeare.
4. Do you know anything _____ computers?
5. My grandmother died _____ the age of 98.
6. How long does it take to go from New York to Los Angeles _____ plane?
7. I didn't go to the football game, but I watched it _____ television.
8. My house is the one _____ the red door.
9. These trains are very fast. They can travel _____ 200 miles an hour.
10. You can't get there _____ car. There's no road.
11. Can you give me some information _____ hotels in this town?
12. I was arrested _____ two policemen and taken to the police station.
13. The buses here are very good. They're almost always _____ time.
14. What would you like to drink _____ your meal?
15. We traveled from Paris to Moscow _____ train.
16. The museum has some paintings _____ Rembrandt.

Afraid of, good at, etc. (Adjective + Preposition)
At -ing, with -ing, etc. (Preposition + -ing)

A

afraid of / good at, etc. (*adjective + preposition*)

afraid of . . .	■ Are you **afraid of** dogs?
angry/mad at somebody **angry/mad about** something	■ Why are you **mad at** me? What did I do? ■ Are you **angry about** last night? (= something that happened last night)
different from . . . / **different than . . .**	■ Lynn is very **different from** her sister. *or* Lynn is very **different than** her sister.
full of . . .	■ The room was **full of** people.
good at . . . **bad at . . .**	■ Are you **good at** math? ■ Tina is very **bad at** writing letters.
interested in . . .	■ I'm not **interested in** sports.
married to . . .	■ Sue is **married to** a dentist. (= her husband is a dentist)
nice/kind of somebody **to . . .** **nice/kind to** somebody	■ It was **kind of** you to help us. Thank you very much. ■ David is very friendly. He's always very **nice to** me.
sorry about something **sorry for** somebody	■ I'm **sorry about** your accident. Was anyone hurt? ■ I feel **sorry for** them. They work hard, but they never have enough money.
tired of . . .	■ I'm **tired of** my job. I need a change.

B

Preposition + -ing

After a preposition (**at/with/for**, etc.), a verb ends in **-ing**.

I'm not very good **at**	**telling**	stories.
Are you tired **of**	**doing**	the same thing every day?
Thank you **for**	**helping**	me.
Mark is thinking **of**	**buying**	a new car.
Tom left **without**	**saying**	goodbye. (= he didn't say goodbye)
After	**doing**	the housework, they went out.

Before/after -ing Unit 100   **Verb + Preposition** Unit 108

Exercises

107.1 Look at the pictures. Complete the sentences with a preposition (*of, in,* etc.).

1. He's afraid *of* _____ dogs.
2. She's interested _____ science.
3. She's married _____ a firefighter.
4. He's very good _____ languages.
5. "Can I help you?" "Thanks, that's very nice _____ you."

107.2 Write the correct preposition (*of/for/about,* etc.).

1. I'm not interested *in* _____ sports.
2. I'm not very good _____ sports.
3. I like Sarah. She's always very nice _____ me.
4. I'm sorry _____ your broken window. It was an accident.
5. He's very brave. He isn't afraid _____ anything.
6. It was very nice _____ Julia to let us stay in her apartment.
7. Life today is very different _____ life 50 years ago.
8. Are you interested _____ politics?
9. I feel sorry _____ her, but I can't help her.
10. Chris was angry _____ what happened.
11. These boxes are very heavy. They're full _____ books.
12. What's wrong? Are you mad _____ me?

107.3 Complete the sentences.

1. I'm not very *good at telling* _____ stories. (good / tell)
2. I wanted to go to the movies, but Paula wasn't _____ . (interested / go)
3. Sue isn't very _____ up in the morning. (good / get)
4. Let's go! I'm _____ . (tired / wait)
5. Sorry I'm late! _____ (thank you / wait)

107.4 Complete the sentences. Use *without -ing.*

1. (Tom left / he didn't say goodbye) *Tom left without saying goodbye.*
2. (Sue walked past me / she didn't speak) Sue walked _____ .
3. (don't do anything / ask me first) Don't _____ .
4. (I went out / I didn't lock the door) I _____ .

107.5 Write sentences about yourself. Use the words in parentheses ( ).

1. (interested) *I'm interested in sports.*
2. (afraid) I'm _____ .
3. (not very good) I'm not _____ .
4. (not interested) _____
5. (tired) _____

Listen to . . . , look at . . . , etc.
(Verb + Preposition)

ask somebody **for** . . .	■ A man stopped me and **asked me for** money.
belong **to** . . .	■ Does this book **belong to** you? (= Is this your book?)
happen **to** . . .	■ I can't find my pen. What **happened to** it?
listen **to** . . .	■ **Listen to** this music. It's great!
look **at** . . .	■ She's **looking at** her watch.
	■ **Look at** these flowers! They're beautiful.
	■ Why are you **looking at** me like that?
look **for** . . .	■ He lost his key. He's **looking for** it.
	■ I'm **looking for** Sarah. Have you seen her?
speak/talk **to** somebody **about** . . .	■ Did you **talk to** Paul **about** the problem?
	■ *(on the phone)* Can I **speak to** Chris, please?
take care **of** . . .	■ When Pat is at work, a friend of hers **takes care of** her children.
	■ Don't lose this book. **Take care of** it.
thank somebody **for** . . .	■ **Thank** you very much **for** your help.
think **about** . . . *or* think **of** . . .	■ He never **thinks about** (*or* **of**) other people.
	■ Mark is **thinking of** (*or* **about**) buying a new car.
wait **for** . . .	■ **Wait for** me! I'm almost ready.

write and call

write (to) somebody	**call** somebody *(no preposition)*
■ I never get letters. Nobody **writes to** me. (*or* Nobody **writes** me.)	■ I have to **call** my parents. (*not* call to . . .)

depend

We say **depend on** . . . :
- ■ *A:* Do you like to eat in restaurants?
  B: Sometimes. It **depends on** the restaurant. (*not* it depends of)

You can say **it depends what/where/how**, etc., with or without **on**.
- ■ *A:* Do you want to go out with us?
  B: It **depends where** you're going. (*or* It **depends on where** you're going.)

Exercises

108.1 Look at the pictures. Complete the sentences with a preposition (*to/for* etc.).

1. He's looking *at* his watch.
2. He's listening _____ the radio.
3. They're waiting _____ a taxi.
4. Paul is talking _____ Tracy.
5. They're looking _____ a picture.
6. Sue is looking _____ Tom.

108.2 Complete the sentences with a preposition (*to/for/about,* etc.) if necessary.

1. Thank you very much *for* your help.
2. This isn't my umbrella. It belongs _____ a friend of mine.
3. Who's going to take care _____ your dog while you're out of town?
4. *(on the phone)* Can I speak _____ Mr. Davis, please?
5. *(on the phone)* Thank you _____ calling. Goodbye.
6. Excuse me, I'm looking _____ Hill Street. Can you tell me where it is?
7. We're thinking _____ going to Australia next year.
8. We asked the waiter _____ tea, but he brought us coffee.
9. "Do you like to read books?" "It depends _____ the book."
10. John was talking, but nobody was listening _____ what he was saying.
11. I want to take your picture. Please look _____ the camera and smile.
12. We waited _____ Karen until 2 o'clock, but she didn't come.
13. What happened _____ Mary last night? Why didn't she come to the party?
14. Don't forget to call _____ your mother tonight.
15. He's alone all day. He never talks _____ anybody.
16. "How much does it cost to stay at this hotel?" "It depends _____ the room."
17. Kathy is thinking _____ changing jobs.
18. I looked _____ the newspaper, but I didn't read it carefully.
19. When you're sick, you need somebody to take care_____ you.
20. Barry is looking _____ a job. He wants to work in a hotel.

108.3 Answer these questions with *It depends . . . .*

1. Do you want to go out with us? *It depends where you're going.*
2. Do you like to eat in restaurants? *It depends on the restaurant.*
3. Do you enjoy watching TV? It depends _____ .
4. Can you do something for me? It _____ .
5. Are you leaving town this weekend? _____
6. Can you lend me some money? _____

UNIT
109

Go in, fall off, run away, etc. (Two-Word Verbs 1)

A *two-word verb* is a verb (**go/look/be**, etc.) + **in/out/up/down**, etc.

in

go in

- Erin opened the door of the car and **got in.** (= **into** the car)
- I waited outside the house. I didn't **go in.**

out

look out

- The car stopped and two women **got out.** (= **out of** the car)
- I went to the window and **looked out.**

on

get on

- The bus came, and I **got on.**

off

fall off

- Be careful! Don't **fall off.**

up

stand up

- He **stood up** and left the room.
- I usually **get up** early. (= get out of bed)
- We **looked up** at the stars.

down

fall down

- Would you like to **sit down?**
- The picture **fell down.**
- **Lie down** on the floor.

away or off

run away

- The thief **ran away.** (*or* . . . **ran off**)
- Erin got into the car and **drove away.** (*or* . . . **drove off**)

be/go away (= in/to another place)
- Erin has **gone away** for a few days.

back

go

come back

- We went out for dinner and then **went back** to our hotel.
- Go away and don't **come back!**

be back
- Erin is away. She'll **be back** on Monday.

around

look around

turn around

- I'm not sure what kind of car I want. I want to **look around** first.
- Somebody shouted my name, so I **turned around.**
- We went for a long walk. After six miles we **turned around** and went back.

Exercises

109.1 Look at the pictures and complete the sentences. Use the verbs + *in/out/up,* etc.

got   got   looked   ~~looked~~   rode   sat   turned   went

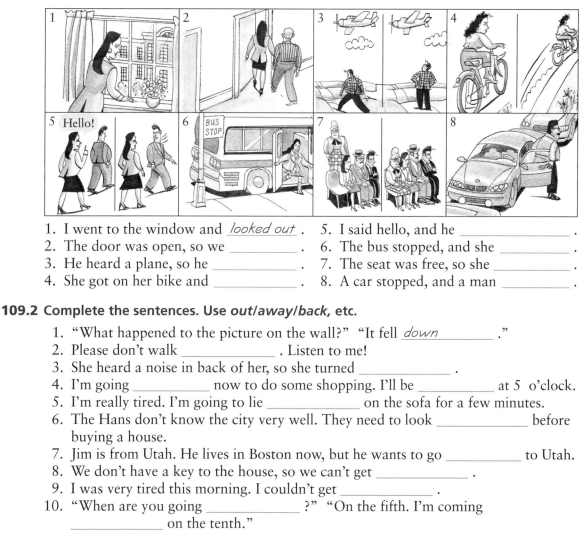

1. I went to the window and *looked out* .
2. The door was open, so we _____ .
3. He heard a plane, so he _____ .
4. She got on her bike and _____ .
5. I said hello, and he _____ .
6. The bus stopped, and she _____ .
7. The seat was free, so she _____ .
8. A car stopped, and a man _____ .

109.2 Complete the sentences. Use *out/away/back,* etc.

1. "What happened to the picture on the wall?" "It fell *down* ."
2. Please don't walk _____ . Listen to me!
3. She heard a noise in back of her, so she turned _____ .
4. I'm going _____ now to do some shopping. I'll be _____ at 5 o'clock.
5. I'm really tired. I'm going to lie _____ on the sofa for a few minutes.
6. The Hans don't know the city very well. They need to look _____ before buying a house.
7. Jim is from Utah. He lives in Boston now, but he wants to go _____ to Utah.
8. We don't have a key to the house, so we can't get _____ .
9. I was very tired this morning. I couldn't get _____ .
10. "When are you going _____ ?" "On the fifth. I'm coming _____ on the tenth."

109.3 Complete the sentences. Choose from the boxes. If necessary, put the verb in the correct form. All these verbs (*wake up,* etc.) are in Appendix 6.

break	give	slow	take	work		along	off	up
get	hurry	speak	~~wake~~		+	down	out	

1. I went to sleep at 10 o'clock and *woke up* at nine o'clock the next morning.
2. The train _____ and finally stopped.
3. I tried to find a job, but I _____ . It was impossible.
4. I like flying, but I'm always nervous when the plane _____ .
5. It's difficult to hear you. Can you _____ a little?
6. This car isn't very good. It has _____ many times.
7. Ben has gained weight because he doesn't _____ any more.
8. _____ , we have to leave. The movie starts in ten minutes.
9. Tony doesn't see his sister much. They don't _____ very well.

Put on your shoes and *put your shoes on* (Two-Word Verbs 2)

Sometimes a two-word verb (**put on / take off**, etc.) has an *object*. For example:

   verb   object

put on your coat

You can say:
   put on your coat
   put your coat **on**

   verb   object

take off your shoes

You can say:
   take off your shoes
   take your shoes **off**

But **it/them** *(pronouns)* always go before **on/off**, etc.
   put **it** on (*not* put on it)   take **them** off (*not* take off them)

- It was cold, so I **put on** my coat.
  or . . . I **put** my coat **on**.
- Here's your coat. **Put it on.**

- I'm going to **take off** my shoes.
  or . . . **take** my shoes **off**.
- Your shoes are dirty. **Take them off.**

More two-word verbs + object

turn on / turn off (lights, machines, faucets, etc.)
- It was dark, so I **turned on** the light.
  or . . . I **turned** the light **on**.
- I don't want to watch this program.
  You can **turn it off.**

on   *off*

pick up / put down
- Those are my keys on the floor.
  Can you **pick them up** for me?
- I stopped reading and **put** my book
  down. *or* . . . **put down** my book.

pick up   *put down*

bring back / take back / give back / put back
- You can take my umbrella but please
  bring it back.
- I **took** my new sweater **back** to the store.
  It was too small.
- I have Diane's keys. I have to **give them
  back** to her.
- I read the letter and then **put it back**
  in the envelope.

take

bring back

Go in / fall off, etc. **Unit 109** **Two-Word Verbs + Object Appendix 7**

Exercises

110.1 Look at the pictures. What did these people do?

1. He *turned on the light* .   4. He _____ .
2. She _____ .   5. He _____ .
3. She _____ .   6. She _____ .

110.2 You can write these sentences in three different ways. Complete the table.

1. I turned on the TV.	*I turned the TV on.*	*I turned it on.*
2. He put on his jacket.	He _____ .	He _____ .
3. I _____ .	I gave the keys back.	_____
4. She took off her hat.	_____	_____
5. Put down your pens.	_____	_____
6. _____	I turned the lights off.	_____

110.3 Complete the sentences. Use one of the verbs in the list + *it/them*.

bring   pick   take   ~~turn~~   turn   (+ on/off/up/back)

1. I wanted to watch something on television, so I *turned it on* .
2. My new lamp doesn't work. I'm going to _____ to the store.
3. Your gloves were on the floor, so I _____ and put them on the table.
4. When I finished working on the computer, I _____ .
5. Thank you for lending me these books. I won't forget to _____ .

110.4 Complete the sentences. Choose from the boxes. These verbs are in Appendix 7.

your cigarette ten houses		me them		around down out up
some shoes a glass	*or*	it	+	away on over

1. They tore *ten houses down* OR *down ten houses* to build the new road.
2. That music is very loud. Can you turn *it down* ?
3. I knocked _____ and broke it.
4. If you don't know a word, you can look _____ in a dictionary.
5. I want to keep these magazines. Please don't throw _____ .
6. Somebody gave me a form and told me to fill _____ .
7. I tried _____ at the store, but I didn't buy them.
8. I visited the school. One of the teachers showed _____ .
9. Mike loves skiing, but he had to give _____ when he hurt his leg.
10. You're not allowed to smoke here. Please put _____ .

UNIT 111

And, but, or, so, and because

A

and   but   or   so   because

We use these words *(conjunctions)* to join two sentences. They make one longer sentence from two shorter sentences:

sentence A The car stopped. ─── The driver got out. *sentence B*

The car stopped, **and** the driver got out.

B

and/but/or

sentence A		*sentence B*	
We stayed at home	**and**	(we)* watched television.	*We and she are
My sister is married	**and**	(she)* lives in London.	not necessary here.
He doesn't like her,	**and**	she doesn't like him.	
I bought a newspaper,	**but**	I didn't read it.	
It's a nice house,	**but**	it hasn't got a garage.	
Do you want to go out,	**or**	are you too tired?	

In lists, we use commas (,). We use **and** between the last two things.
- I got home, had something to eat, sat down to watch TV, **and** fell asleep.
- Amy is at work, Sue went shopping, **and** Chris is playing football.

C

so (the result of something)

sentence A		*sentence B*
It was very hot,	**so**	we opened the window.
They had some free time,	**so**	so they went for a drive.
I don't like to travel,	**so**	I haven't been to many places.

D

because (the reason for something)

sentence A		*sentence B*
We opened the window	**because**	it was very hot.
They didn't go for a drive	**because**	they didn't have time.
Lisa is hungry	**because**	she didn't have breakfast.

Because is also possible at the beginning. We use a comma.
- **Because they didn't have time,** they didn't go for a drive.

E

In these examples there is more than one conjunction.
- It was late **and** I was tired, **so** I went to bed.
- I love New York, **but** I wouldn't like to live there **because** it's too big.

When/while/before, etc. Unit 112

Exercises

111.1 Write sentences. Choose from the boxes and use *and/but/or*.

~~I stayed at home.~~
~~I bought a newspaper.~~
I went to the window.
I wanted to call you.
I jumped into the river.
I usually drive to work.
Do you want me to come with you?

I didn't have your number.
Should I wait here?
~~I didn't read it.~~
I took the bus this morning.
~~I watched television.~~
I swam to the other side.
I looked out.

1. *I stayed at home and watched television.*
2. *I bought a newspaper, but I didn't read it.*
3. I _____ .
4. _____
5. _____
6. _____
7. _____

111.2 Look at the pictures and complete the sentences. Use *and/but/so/because*.

1. It was very hot, *so he opened the window* _____ .
2. They didn't play tennis _____ .
3. They went to the museum, _____ .
4. Bill wasn't hungry, _____ .
5. Amy was late _____ .
6. Sue said _____ .

111.3 Write sentences about what you did yesterday. Use the words in parentheses ( ).

1. (and) *Last night I stayed home and studied.*
2. (because) *I went to bed very early because I was tired.*
3. (but) _____
4. (and) _____
5. (so) _____
6. (because) _____

When . . .

A

When I went out, it was raining.

This sentence has two parts:

| when I went out | + | it was raining |

The **when** part can be first or second.

- { **When I went out**, it was raining.
  { It was raining **when I went out**.

We use a comma (,) if the **when** part is first.

- { **When** you're tired, don't drive.
  { Don't drive **when** you're tired.

- { Joy was very happy **when** she passed the exam.
  { **When** Joy passed the exam, she was very happy.

We do the same in sentences with **before/while/after**.

- { Always look both ways **before** you cross the street.
  { **Before** you cross the street, always look both ways.

- { **While** I was waiting for the bus, it began to rain.
  { It began to rain **while** I was waiting for the bus.

- { He never played football again **after** he broke his leg.
  { **After** he broke his leg, he never played football again.

B

When I am . . . / When I go . . . , etc.

Next week Kim is going to New York. She has a friend, Lily, who lives in New York, but Lily is also going away – to Mexico. So they won't see each other in New York.

Lily **will be** in Mexico **when** Kim **is** in New York.

The time is *future* (next week), but we say: . . . when Kim **is** in New York. (*not* when Kim will be)

I'll be in Mexico when you're here.

LILY   KIM

We use the *present* (I **am** / I **go**, etc.) with a *future meaning* after **when**.

- **When I get** home tonight, I'm going to take a shower. (*not* When I will get home)
- I can't talk now. I'll talk to you later **when I have** more time.

We do the same after **before/while/after/until**.

- Please close the windows **before** you **go** out. (*not* before you will go)
- Julia is going to stay in our apartment **while** we **are** away. (*not* while we will be)
- I'll wait here **until** you **come** back. (*not* until you will come back)

Exercises

112.1 Write sentences beginning with *when*. Choose from the boxes.

When +

I went out
I'm tired
I called her
I go on vacation
the program was over
I got to the hotel

+

I turned off the TV
I always go to the same place
there were no rooms
it was raining
there was no answer
I like to watch TV

1. *When I went out, it was raining.*
2. _____
3. _____
4. _____
5. _____
6. _____

112.2 Complete the sentences. Choose from the box.

somebody broke into the house	before they came here	when they heard the news
before they crossed the street	while they were away	they didn't believe me
they went to live in New Zealand		

1. They looked both ways *before they crossed the street* .
2. They were very surprised _____ .
3. After they got married, _____ .
4. The letter arrived _____ .
5. Where did they live _____ ?
6. While they were asleep, _____ .
7. When I told them the news, _____ .

112.3 Which is right? Choose the correct form.

1. ~~I stay~~ / I'll stay here until <u>you come</u> / ~~you'll come~~ back. (*I'll stay* and *you come* are right.)
2. I'm going to bed when <u>I finish</u> / <u>I'll finish</u> my work.
3. We should do something before <u>it's</u> / <u>it will be</u> too late.
4. Julia is moving soon. <u>I'm</u> / <u>I'll be</u> very sad when <u>she leaves</u> / <u>she'll leave</u>.
5. Don't go out yet. Wait until the rain <u>stops</u> / <u>will stop</u>.
6. <u>We come</u> / <u>We'll come</u> and visit you when <u>we're</u> / <u>we'll be</u> in Toronto again.
7. When <u>I come</u> / <u>I'll come</u> to see you tomorrow, <u>I bring</u> / <u>I'll bring</u> your CDs.
8. I'm going to Quebec next week. I hope to see Sam while <u>I'm</u> / <u>I'll be</u> there.
9. "I need your address." "OK, <u>I give</u> / <u>I'll give</u> it to you before <u>I go</u> / <u>I'll go</u>."

112.4 Use your own ideas to complete these sentences.

1. Can you close the window before *you go out* ?
2. What are you going to do when _____ ?
3. When I have more time, _____ .
4. I'll wait for you while _____ .
5. When I start my new job, _____ .
6. Will you be here when _____ ?

If we go . . . , If you see . . . , etc.

A

If can be at the beginning of a sentence or in the middle.

If at the beginning

If we take the bus,	it will be cheaper.
If you don't hurry,	you'll miss the train.
If you're hungry,	have something to eat.
If the phone rings,	can you answer it, please?

if in the middle

It will be cheaper	if we take the bus.
You'll miss the train	if you don't hurry.
I'm going to the concert	if I can get a ticket.
Is it OK	if I use your phone?

In conversation, we often use the if part of the sentence alone.
■ "Are you going to the concert?" "Yes, if I can get a ticket."

B

if you see Amy tomorrow, etc.

After if, we use the present (*not* will). We say if you see . . . (*not* if you will see).
■ If you **see** Amy tomorrow, can you ask her to call me?
■ If I'm late tonight, don't wait for me. (*not* if I will be)
■ What should we do if it **rains**? (*not* if it will rain)
■ If I **don't feel** well tomorrow, I'll stay home.

C

if and when

if I go out = it is possible that I will go out, but I'm not sure
■ A: Are you going out later?
   B: Maybe. **If I go out,** I'll close the windows.

Are you going out later?

when I go out = I'm going out (for sure)
■ A: Are you going out later?
   B: Yes, I am. **When I go out,** I'll close the windows.

■ **When** I get home tonight, I'm going to take a shower.
■ If I'm late tomorrow, don't wait for me. (*not* When I'm late)
■ We're going to play tennis if it doesn't rain. (*not* when it doesn't rain)

Exercises

113.1 Write sentences beginning with *If.* Choose from the boxes.

If +

~~you don't hurry~~
you pass the driving test
you fail the driving test
you don't want this magazine
you want those pictures
you're busy now
you're hungry
you need money

+

we can have lunch now
you can have them
I can lend you some
you'll get your license
~~you'll be late~~
I'll throw it away
we can talk later
you can take it again

1. *If you don't hurry, you'll be late.* _____
2. If you pass _____ .
3. If _____ .
4. _____
5. _____
6. _____
7. _____
8. _____

113.2 Which is right?

1. If <u>I'm</u> / ~~I'll be~~ late tonight, don't wait for me. (*I'm* is right.)
2. Will you write to me if <u>I give / I'll give</u> you my address?
3. If there <u>is /will be</u> a fire, the alarm will ring.
4. If I don't see you tomorrow morning, <u>I call / I'll call</u> you in the afternoon.
5. <u>I'm / I'll be</u> surprised if Mark and Julia <u>get / will get</u> married.
6. <u>Do you go / Will you go</u> to the party if <u>they invite / they'll invite</u> you?

113.3 Use your own ideas to complete these sentences.

1. I'm going to the concert if *I can get a ticket* _____ .
2. If you don't hurry *you'll miss the train* _____ .
3. I don't want to go swimming if _____ .
4. If you go to bed early tonight, _____ .
5. Turn the television off if _____ .
6. Lisa won't pass her driving test if _____ .
7. If I have time tomorrow, _____ .
8. We can go to the beach tomorrow if _____ .

113.4 Write *if* or *when.*

1. *If* _____ I'm late tomorrow, don't wait for me.
2. I'm going shopping now. _____ I come back, we can have lunch.
3. I'm thinking of going to see Tim. _____ I go, will you come with me?
4. _____ you don't want to go out tonight, we can stay home.
5. Do you mind _____ I close the window?
6. John is still in high school. _____ he finishes, he wants to go to college.
7. Do you want to go on a picnic tomorrow _____ the weather is good?
8. We're going to Oslo tomorrow. We're going to look for a hotel _____ we get there. I don't know what we'll do _____ we don't find a room.

If I had . . . , if we went . . . , etc.

A

Dan likes fast cars, but he doesn't have one.
He doesn't have enough money.

If I had the money . . .

If he **had** the money, he **would buy** a fast car.

Usually **had** is *past*, but in this sentence **had**
is *not* past. If he **had** the money = if he had
the money *now* (but he doesn't have it).

| If | I
you
it
they, etc. | had/knew/went (etc.) . . . ,
didn't have/know/go (etc.) . . . ,
could have/know/go (etc.) . . . ,
was/were . . . , | I
you
it
they, etc. | would(n't)
could(n't) | buy . . .
be . . .
have . . .
go . . . |

I'd / she'd / they'd, etc. = I **would** / she **would** / they **would**, etc.
- I don't know the answer. If I **knew** the answer, **I'd tell** you.
- It's raining, so we're not going out. **We'd get** wet **if** we **went** out.
- Ellie lives in a city. She **wouldn't be** happy **if** she **lived** in the country.
- **If** you **didn't have** a job, what **would** you **do**? (but you have a job)
- I'm sorry I can't help you. **I'd help** you **if** I **could.** (but I can't)
- **If** we **had** a car, we **could travel** more. (but we don't have a car)

B

if I were/was . . .
You can say **if** (I/he/she/it) **were** *or* **was** . . . .
- It's cold. **If** I **were** you, **I'd put** a coat on.
  (*or* If I **was** you . . .)
- It's not a good restaurant. I **wouldn't eat** there
  if I **were** you. (*or* . . . if I **was** you)
- **I'd be** happier **if** the weather **were** (*or* **was**) nicer.

I wouldn't go out if I were you.

C

Compare:

if I **have** / if it **is**, etc.	if I **had** / if it **was**, etc.
■ I want to go and see Judy. **If** I **have** time, I **will go** today. (= maybe I'll have time, so maybe I'll go)	■ I want to go and see Judy. **If** I **had** time, I **would go** today. (= I don't have time today, so I won't go)
■ I like that jacket. **I'll buy** it **if** it **isn't** too expensive. (= maybe it is not too expensive)	■ I like that jacket, but it's very expensive. **I'd buy** it **if** it **weren't** so expensive. (= it is expensive, so I'm not going to buy it)
■ **I'll help** you **if** I **can.** (= maybe I can help)	■ **I'd help** you **if** I **could,** but I can't.

Exercises

114.1 Complete the sentences.

1. I don't know the answer. If I _knew_ the answer, I'd tell you.
2. I have a car. I couldn't travel much if I _didn't have_ a car.
3. I don't want to go out. If I _____ to go out, I'd go.
4. We don't have a key. If we _____ a key, we could get into the house.
5. I'm not hungry. I would have something to eat if I _____ hungry.
6. Sue enjoys her work. She wouldn't do it if she _____ it.
7. You can't drive. If you _____ drive, I would lend you my car.
8. He speaks too fast. I could understand him better if he _____ more slowly.
9. I have a lot to do today. If I _____ so much to do, we could go out.

114.2 Write the verb in the correct form.

1. If _he had_ the money, he would buy a fast car. (he / have)
2. If I wanted to learn Chinese, _____ to China. (I / go)
3. I haven't told Joy what happened. She'd be angry if _____ . (she / know)
4. If _____ a map, I could show you where I live. (we / have)
5. What would you do if _____ a lot of money? (you / win)
6. It's not a very good hotel. _____ there if I were you. (I / not / stay)
7. If _____ closer to Miami, we would go there more often. (we / live)
8. I'm sorry you have to go. _____ nice if you had more time. (it / be)
9. I'm not going to take the job. I'd take it if _____ better. (the salary / be)
10. I don't understand cars. If my car broke down, _____ what to do. (I / not / know)
11. If you could change one thing in the world, what _____ ? (you / change)

114.3 Complete the sentences. Choose from the box and put the verb in the correct form.

we (have) a bigger house	~~it (be) a little cheaper~~	I (watch) it
we (buy) a bigger house	every day (be) the same	I (be) bored
we (have) some pictures on the wall	the air (be) cleaner	

1. I'd buy that jacket if _it were a little cheaper_ .
2. If there was a good film on TV tonight, _____ .
3. This room would be nicer if _____ .
4. If there weren't so much traffic, _____ .
5. Life would be boring if _____ .
6. If I had nothing to do, _____ .
7. We could invite all our friends to stay if _____ .
8. If we had more money, _____ .

114.4 Complete the sentences. Use your own ideas.

1. I'd go to the dentist if _I had a toothache_ .
2. If I could go anywhere in the world, _____ .
3. I wouldn't be very happy if _____ .
4. I'd buy a house if _____ .
5. If I saw an accident in the street, _____ .
6. The world would be a better place if _____ .

A person who . . . and *a thing that/which . . .* (Relative Clauses 1)

A

I can speak six languages.

I met a woman. **She** can speak six languages.	*2 sentences*
I met a woman **who** can speak six languages.	*1 sentence*

JIM

Jim was wearing a hat. **It** was too big for him.	*2 sentences*
Jim was wearing a hat **that** was too big for him.	
or	*1 sentence*
Jim was wearing a hat **which** was too big for him.	

B

Who is for people (not things).

A thief is **a person**	who steals things.	
Do you know **anybody**	who can play the piano?	
The man	who called	didn't give his name.
The people	who work in the office	are very friendly.

C

That is for things or people.

An airplane is **a machine**	that flies.	
Amy lives in **a house**	that is 100 years old.	
The people	that work in the office	are very friendly.

You can use **that** for people, but **who** is more usual.

D

Which is for things (not people).

An airplane is **a machine**	which flies. (*not* a machine who . . .)
Amy lives in **a house**	which is 100 years old.

Do not use **which** for people.
- Do you know **the woman who** sang at the party? (*not* the woman which . . .)

Exercises

115.1 Choose from the boxes and write sentences: *A . . . is a person who . . . .* Use a dictionary if necessary.

~~a thief~~	a dentist
a butcher	a fool
a musician	a genius
a patient	a liar

doesn't tell the truth	is seeing a doctor
takes care of your teeth	~~steals things~~
is very intelligent	does stupid things
plays music	sells meat

1. *A thief is a person who steals things.* _____
2. A butcher is a person _____ .
3. A musician _____ .
4. _____
5. _____
6. _____
7. _____
8. _____

115.2 Make one sentence from two.

1. (A man phoned. He didn't give his name.)
   The man who phoned didn't give his name. _____
2. (A woman opened the door. She was wearing a yellow dress.)
   The woman _____ a yellow dress.
3. (Some students took the exam. Most of them passed.)
   Most of the students _____ .
4. (A police officer stopped our car. He wasn't very friendly.)
   The _____ .

115.3 Write *who* or *which*.

1. I met a woman *who* _____ can speak six languages.
2. What's the name of the woman _____ lives next door?
3. What's the name of the river _____ flows through the town?
4. Where is the picture _____ was hanging on the wall?
5. Do you know anybody _____ wants to buy a car?
6. You always ask questions _____ are difficult to answer.
7. I have a friend _____ is very good at repairing cars.
8. I think everybody _____ went to the party enjoyed it a lot.
9. Why does he always wear clothes _____ are too small for him?

115.4 Right or wrong? Correct the mistakes.

1. A thief is a person which steals things.   *a person who steals* _____
2. An airplane is a machine that flies.   *OK* _____
3. A coffee maker is a machine who makes coffee.   _____
4. Have you seen the money that was on the table?   _____
5. I don't like people which never stop talking.   _____
6. I know somebody that can help you.   _____
7. I know somebody who works in that store.   _____
8. Correct the sentences who are wrong.   _____

The people we met and the hotel you stayed at (Relative Clauses 2)

A

The man is carrying a bag. ⎫
It's very heavy. ⎭ *2 sentences*

The bag (that) he is carrying is very heavy.   *1 sentence*

Kim took some pictures. ⎫
Did you see them? ⎭ *2 sentences*

Did you see **the pictures (that) Kim took?**   *1 sentence*

You can say:
- The bag **that** he is carrying ... *or* The bag he is carrying ... (with or without **that**)
- ... the pictures **that** Kim took? *or* ... the pictures Kim took?

You do not need **that/who/which** when it is the *object*.

subject	verb	object	
the man	was carrying	a bag	→ **the bag (that) the man was carrying**
Kim	took	some pictures	→ **the pictures (that) Kim took**
you	wanted	the book	→ **the book (that) you wanted**
we	met	some people	→ **the people (who) we met**

- Did you find **the book you wanted?** *or* ... the book **that** you wanted?
- **The people we met** were very nice. *or* The people **who** we met ...
- **Everything I said** was true. *or* Everything **that** I said ...

Note that we say:
- The movie **we saw** was very good. (*not* The movie we saw it was ...)

B

Sometimes there is a *preposition* (**to/in/at,** etc.) after the verb.

Erica **is talking to** a man.	→	Do you know **the man Erica is talking to?**
We **stayed at** a hotel.	→	**The hotel we stayed at** was near the station.
I told you **about** some books.	→	These are **the books I told you about.**
		(*not* the books I told you about them)

You can say (a place) **where** ....
- **The hotel where** we stayed was near the station. (= The hotel we stayed **at** ...)

C

You must use **that/who/which** when it is the *subject* (see Unit 115).
- I met a woman **who can speak** six languages. (**who** is the subject)
- Jim was wearing a hat **that was** too big for him. (**that** is the subject)

A person who ..., a thing that/which ... (Relative Clauses 1) **Unit 115**

Exercises

116.1 Make one sentence from two.

1. (Kim took some picturess. Did you see them?)
   Did you see the pictures Kim took?
2. (You gave me a pen. I lost it.)
   I lost the _____ .
3. (Sue is wearing a jacket. I like it.)
   I like the _____ .
4. (I gave you some flowers. Where are they?)
   Where are the _____ ?
5. (He told us a story. I didn't believe it.)
   I _____ .
6. (You bought some oranges. How much were they?)
   How _____ ?

116.2 Make one sentence from two.

1. (I was carrying a bag. It was very heavy.)
   The bag I was carrying was very heavy.
2. (You cooked a meal. It was excellent.)
   The _____ .
3. (I'm wearing shoes. They aren't very comfortable.)
   The shoes _____ .
4. (We invited some people to dinner. They didn't come.)
   The _____ .

116.3 Complete the sentences. Use the information in the box.

I looked at a map	I was sitting on a chair	you were looking for some keys
they live in a house	we were waiting for a bus	Nicole is dancing with a man
~~you stayed at a hotel~~	you spoke to some people	

1. What's the name of _the hotel you stayed at_ ?
2. Who are the people _____ ?
3. Did you find the _____ ?
4. The _____ is too small for them.
5. The _____ wasn't very clear.
6. I fell off _____ .
7. _____ was very late.
8. Who is _____ ?

116.4 Read the situations and complete the questions. Use _where_.

1. John stayed at a hotel. You ask him: Did you like _the hotel where you stayed_ ?
2. Sue had dinner at a restaurant. You ask her:
   What's the name of the restaurant _____ ?
3. Sarah lives in a town. You ask her:
   Do you like _____ ?
4. Richard works in a factory. You ask him:
   How big is _____ ?

APPENDIX 1: Active and Passive

1.1 *Present* and *past*

	active	passive
simple present	■ We **make** butter from cream. ■ Somebody **cleans** these rooms every day. ■ People never **invite** me to parties. ■ How **do** they **make** butter?	■ Butter **is made** from cream. ■ These rooms **are cleaned** every day. ■ I **am** never **invited** to parties. ■ How **is** butter **made**?
simple past	■ Somebody **stole** my car last week. ■ Somebody **stole** my keys yesterday. ■ They **didn't invite** me to the party. ■ When **did** they **build** these houses?	■ My car **was stolen** last week. ■ My keys **were stolen** yesterday. ■ I **wasn't invited** to the party. ■ When **were** these houses **built**?
present continuous	■ They **are building** a new airport. (= it isn't finished) ■ They **are building** some new houses near the river.	■ A new airport **is being built**. ■ Some new houses **are being built** near the river.
past continuous	■ When I was here a few years ago, they **were building** a new airport. (= it wasn't finished at that time)	■ When I was here a few years ago, a new airport **was being built**.
present perfect	■ Look! They **have painted** the door. ■ These shirts are clean. Somebody **has washed** them. ■ Somebody **has stolen** my car.	■ Look! The door **has been painted**. ■ These shirts are clean. They **have been washed**. ■ My car **has been stolen**.
past perfect	■ Ann said that somebody **had stolen** her car.	■ Ann said that her car **had been stolen**.

1.2 will / can / must / have to, etc.

active	passive
■ Somebody **will clean** the office tomorrow. ■ Somebody **must clean** the office at night. ■ I think they**'ll invite** you to the party. ■ They **can't repair** my watch. ■ You **should wash** this sweater by hand.	■ The office **will be cleaned** tomorrow. ■ The office **must be cleaned** at night. ■ I think you**'ll be invited** to the party. ■ My watch **can't be repaired**. ■ This sweater **should be washed** by hand.
■ They **are going to build** a new airport. ■ Somebody **has to wash** these clothes. ■ They **had to take** the injured man to the hospital.	■ A new airport **is going to be built**. ■ These clothes **have to be washed**. ■ The injured man **had to be taken** to the hospital.

APPENDIX 2: List of Irregular Verbs

See Unit 25.

base form	simple past	past participle
be	was/were	been
beat	beat	beaten
become	became	become
begin	began	begun
bite	bit	bitten
blow	blew	blown
break	broke	broken
bring	brought	brought
build	built	built
buy	bought	bought
catch	caught	caught
choose	chose	chosen
come	came	come
cost	cost	cost
cut	cut	cut
do	did	done
draw	drew	drawn
drink	drank	drunk
drive	drove	driven
eat	ate	eaten
fall	fell	fallen
feel	felt	felt
fight	fought	fought
find	found	found
fly	flew	flown
forget	forgot	forgotten
get	got	gotten
give	gave	given
go	went	gone
grow	grew	grown
hang	hung	hung
have	had	had
hear	heard	heard
hide	hid	hidden
hit	hit	hit
hold	held	held
hurt	hurt	hurt
keep	kept	kept
know	knew	known
leave	left	left
lend	lent	lent
let	let	let

base form	simple past	past participle
lie	lay	lain
light	lit	lit
lose	lost	lost
make	made	made
mean	meant	meant
meet	met	met
pay	paid	paid
put	put	put
quit	quit	quit
read	read*	read*
ride	rode	ridden
ring	rang	rung
rise	rose	risen
run	ran	run
say	said	said
see	saw	seen
sell	sold	sold
send	sent	sent
shine	shone	shone
shoot	shot	shot
show	showed	shown/showed
shut	shut	shut
sing	sang	sung
sit	sat	sat
sleep	slept	slept
speak	spoke	spoken
spend	spent	spent
stand	stood	stood
steal	stole	stolen
swim	swam	swum
take	took	taken
teach	taught	taught
tear	tore	torn
tell	told	told
think	thought	thought
throw	threw	thrown
understand	understood	understood
wake	woke	woken
wear	wore	worn
win	won	won
write	wrote	written

*pronounced [rɛd]

APPENDIX 3: Irregular Verbs in Groups

Simple past and *past participle* are the same.

Simple past and *past participle* are different.

1.
cost	→ cost	let	→ let
cut	→ cut	put	→ put
hit	→ hit	quit	→ quit
hurt	→ hurt	shut	→ shut

2.
lend	→ lent	lose	→ lost
send	→ sent	shoot	→ shot
spend	→ spent		
		light	→ lit
build	→ built	sit	→ sat

keep	→ kept	feel	→ felt
sleep	→ slept	leave	→ left
		meet	→ met
		dream	→ dreamed
			or dreamt
		mean	→ meant

3.
bring	→ brought
buy	→ bought
fight	→ fought
think	→ thought

catch	→ caught
teach	→ taught

4.
sell	→ sold
tell	→ told

find	→ found
have	→ had
hear	→ heard
hold	→ held
read	→ read*
say	→ said

pronounced [rɛd]

pay	→ paid
make	→ made

stand	→ stood
understand	→ understood

1.
break	→ broke	broken
choose	→ chose	chosen
speak	→ spoke	spoken
steal	→ stole	stolen
wake	→ woke	woken

2.
drive	→ drove	driven
ride	→ rode	ridden
rise	→ rose	risen
write	→ wrote	written

beat	→ beat	beaten
bite	→ bit	bitten
hide	→ hid	hidden

3.
eat	→ ate	eaten
fall	→ fell	fallen
forget	→ forgot	forgotten
get	→ got	gotten
give	→ gave	given
see	→ saw	seen
take	→ took	taken

4.
blow	→ blew	blown
grow	→ grew	grown
know	→ knew	known
throw	→ threw	thrown
fly	→ flew	flown

draw	→ drew	drawn

show	→ showed	shown

5.
begin	→ began	begun
drink	→ drank	drunk
swim	→ swam	swum

ring	→ rang	rung
sing	→ sang	sung

run	→ ran	run

6.
come	→ came	come
become	→ became	become

APPENDIX 4: Short Forms (*he's/I'd/don't*, etc.)

4.1 In spoken English, we usually pronounce **I am** as one word. The short form (**I'm**) is a way of writing this.

I am → **I'm**	
it is → **it's**	
they have → **they've**	

- **I'm** feeling tired this morning.
- "Do you like this jacket?" "Yes, **it's** very nice."
- "Where are your friends?" "**They've** gone home."

When we write short forms, we use an *apostrophe* (').

I ~~a~~m → **I'm**   he ~~i~~s → **he's**   you ~~ha~~ve → **you've**   she ~~wi~~ll → **she'll**

4.2 We use 'm / 's / 're / 've / 'd / 'll with I/he/she, etc.

		I	he	she	it		we	you	they
am →	**'m**	I'm							
is →	**'s**		he's	she's	it's				
are →	**'re**						we're	you're	they're
have →	**'ve**	I've					we've	you've	they've
has →	**'s**		he's	she's	it's				
had →	**'d**	I'd	he'd	she'd			we'd	you'd	they'd
will →	**'ll**	I'll	he'll	she'll			we'll	you'll	they'll
would →	**'d**	I'd	he'd	she'd			we'd	you'd	they'd

- **I've** lost your address.
- **We'll** probably go out tonight.
- **It's** 10 o'clock. **You're** late again.

's = is or **has**
- **She's** going out tonight. (she's going = she **is** going)
- **She's** gone out. (she's gone = she **has** gone)

'd = would or **had**
- *A:* What would you like to eat?
  B: **I'd** like a salad, please. (I'd like = I **would** like)
- I told the police that **I'd** lost my passport. (I'd lost = I **had** lost)

Do not use 'm / 's / 're / 've / 'd / 'll at the end of a sentence (see Unit 41).
- "Are you tired?" "Yes, I **am**." (*not* Yes, I'm)
- She isn't tired, but he **is**. (*not* he's)

4.3 We use short forms with **I/you/he/she**, etc., but you can use short forms (especially 's) with other words too.
- **Who's** your favorite singer? (= who **is**)
- **What's** the time? (= what **is**)
- **There's** a big tree in the yard. (= there **is**)
- **My sister's** working in London. (= my sister **is** working)
- **Paul's** gone out. (= Paul **has** gone out)
- **What color's** your car? (= What color **is** your car?)

4.4 Negative short forms (see Unit 44)

isn't	(= is not)	**don't**	(= do not)	**hasn't**	(= has not)
aren't	(= are not)	**doesn't**	(= does not)	**haven't**	(= have not)
wasn't	(= was not)	**didn't**	(= did not)	**hadn't**	(= had not)
weren't	(= were not)				
can't	(= cannot)	**won't**	(= will not)	**mustn't**	(= must not)
couldn't	(= could not)	**wouldn't**	(= would not)	**shouldn't**	(= should not)

- We went to her house but she **wasn't** at home.
- "Where's David?" "I **don't** know. I **haven't** seen him."
- You work all the time. You **shouldn't** work so hard.
- I **won't** be here tomorrow. (= I will not)

4.5 **'s** (apostrophe + s) can mean different things.

1. **'s** = **is** or **has** (see section 4.2 of this appendix)

2. **let's** = let **us** (see Unit 37)
   - The weather is nice. **Let's** go out. (= Let **us** go out.)

3. Kate's camera (= her camera) / my brother's car (= his car) / the manager's office (= his/her office), etc. (see Unit 65)

Compare:
- **Kate's** camera was very expensive. (**Kate's** camera = **her** camera)
- **Kate's** a very good photographer. (**Kate's** = Kate **is**)
- **Kate's** got a new camera. (**Kate's** got = Kate **has** got)

APPENDIX 5: Spelling

5.1 Words + -s and -es (birds/watches, *etc.*)

noun + **s** (plural) (see Unit 67)		
bird → birds	mistake → mistakes	hotel → hotels

verb + **s** (he/she/it **-s**) (see Unit 5)		
think → thinks	live → lives	remember → remembers

But:

+ **es** after -s / -sh / -ch / -x		
bus → buses	pass → passes	address → addresses
dish → dishes	wash → washes	finish → finishes
watch → watches	teach → teaches	sandwich → sandwiches
box → boxes		

also	
potato → potatoes	tomato → tomatoes
do → does	go → goes

-f / **-fe** → **-ves**		
shelf → shelves	knife → knives	*but* roof → roofs

5.2 Words ending in -y (baby → babies / study → studied, *etc.*)

-y → **-ies**		
study → studies (*not* studys)	family → families (*not* familys)	
story → stories	city → cities	baby → babies
try → tries	marry → marries	fly → flies

-y → **-ied** (see Unit 11)		
study → studied (*not* studyed)		
try → tried	marry → married	copy → copied

-y → **-ier** / **-iest** (see Units 88 and 91)	
easy → easier/easiest (*not* easyer/easyest)	
happy → happier/happiest	lucky → luckier/luckiest
heavy → heavier/heaviest	funny → funnier/funniest

-y → **-ily** (see Unit 87)		
easy → easily (*not* easyly)		
happy → happily	lucky → luckily	heavy → heavily

Y does not change to **i** if the ending is **-ay** / **-ey** / **-oy** / **-uy**.			
holiday → holidays (*not* holidaies)			
enjoy → enjoys/enjoyed	stay → stays/stayed	buy → buys	key → keys

but		
say → said	pay → paid	(*irregular verbs*)

5.3 -ing

> Verbs that end in -e (make/write/drive, etc.) → -~~e~~ing
>   make → making   write → writing   come → coming   dance → dancing

> Verbs that end in -ie → -ying
>   lie → lying   die → dying   tie → tying

5.4 stop → stopped, big → bigger, etc.

Vowels and consonants

Vowel letters: a e i o u
Consonant letters: b c d f g k l m n p r s t w y

Sometimes a word ends in a *vowel* + a *consonant,* for example, **stop, big, get.** Before -ing / -ed / -er / -est, the consonant at the end (-**p** / -**g** / -**t**, etc.) is "doubled" (-**pp**- / -**gg**- / -**tt**-, etc.). For example:

V+C

stop	ST **O** P	p → **pp**	stopping	stopped
run	R **U** N	n → **nn**	running	
get	G **E** T	t → **tt**	getting	
swim	SW **I** M	m → **mm**	swimming	
big	B **I** G	g → **gg**	bigger	biggest
hot	H **O** T	t → **tt**	hotter	hottest
thin	TH **I** N	n → **nn**	thinner	thinnest

V = *vowel*
C = *consonant*

The letters are not doubled:

(1) if the word ends in *two* consonant letters (C + C)

C+C

help	HE **L** **P**	helping	helped
work	WO **R** **K**	working	worked
fast	FA **S** **T**	faster	fastest

(2) if the word ends in two vowel letters + a consonant letter (V + V + C)

V+V+C

need	N **E** **E** D	needing	needed
wait	W **A** **I** T	waiting	waited
cheap	CH **E** **A** P	cheaper	cheapest

(3) in longer words (two syllables or more) if the last part of the word is *not* stressed

stress

happen	**HAP**-pen	→	happening/happened (*not* happenned)
visit	**VIS**-it	→	visiting/visited
remember	re-**MEM**-ber	→	remembering/remembered

but	prefer	pre-**FER** (*stress at the end*)	→	preferring/preferred
	begin	be-**GIN** (*stress at the end*)	→	beginning

(4) if the word ends in -**y** or -**w** (At the end of words, **y** and **w** are not consonants.)
    enjoy/enjoying/enjoyed   snow/snowing/snowed   few/fewer/fewest

APPENDIX 6: Two-Word Verbs
(*look out / take off*, etc.)

This is a list of some important two-word verbs (see Unit 109).

out	**look out** / **watch out** = be careful ■ **Look out!** There's a car coming! **work out** = exercise (to become stronger or more fit) ■ Sarah **works out** at the gym two or three times a week.

work out

on	**come on** = be quick / hurry ■ **Come on!** Everybody is waiting for you. **go on** = continue ■ I'm sorry I interrupted you. **Go on.** (= continue what you were saying) ■ How long will my cold **go on,** Doctor? **keep on** = continue (talking, etc.) ■ I asked them to be quiet, but they **kept on** talking.

off	**take off** = leave the ground (for airplanes) ■ The plane **took off** 20 minutes late but landed on time.

take off

up	**wake up** = stop sleeping ■ I often **wake up** in the middle of the night. **speak up** = speak more loudly ■ I can't hear you. Can you **speak up,** please? **hurry up** = do something more quickly ■ **Hurry up!** We haven't got much time. **clean up** = make neat or clean ■ After the party, it took two hours to **clean up.** **grow up** = become an adult ■ What does your son want to do when he **grows up?** **give up** = stop trying ■ I know it's difficult, but don't **give up.**

wake up

1980   2002
grow up

down	**slow down** = go more slowly ■ You're driving too fast. **Slow down!** **break down** = stop working (for cars/machines, etc.) ■ Sue was very late because her car **broke down.**

break down

along	**get along** = be together without problems ■ Do you like living with Mike? Do you two **get along?** ■ Sam doesn't visit his parents often. He doesn't **get along** with his father.

APPENDIX 7: Two-Word Verbs + Object (*put out* a fire / *try on* clothes, etc.)

This is a list of some important two-word verbs + object (see Unit 110).

out	**put out** (a fire / a cigarette) ■ The fire department arrived and **put the fire out.** **cross out** (a mistake / a word, etc.) ■ If you make a mistake, **cross it out.** **fill out** (a form) = complete ■ Can you **fill out this form,** please?
on	**try on** (clothes) = put on clothes to see if they fit you ■ *(in a store)* Where can I **try** these pants **on?**
up	**give up** (something) = stop doing/having something ■ Tom's doctor told him he had to **give up smoking.** (= stop smoking) ■ Sheila **gave up her job** when her baby was born. **call up** = call on the telephone ■ Sue **called me up** last night. *or* Sue **called me** last night. (*without* up) **look up** (a word in a dictionary, etc.) ■ I didn't know the meaning of the word, so I **looked it up.** **turn up** = make louder (TV, radio, music, etc.) ■ Can you **turn the radio up?** I can't hear it. **wake up** = make someone stop sleeping ■ The baby just fell asleep. Try to be quiet so you don't **wake her up.**
down	**tear down** (a building) = demolish ■ They are going to **tear down** the school and build a new one. **knock down** = make (somebody) fall ■ A man was **knocked down** by the car. **turn down** = make quieter (TV, radio, music, etc.) ■ The music is too loud. Can you **turn it down?**
back	**pay** somebody **back** (money that you borrowed) ■ Thank you for lending me the money. I'll **pay you back** next week.
away	**throw away** (things you don't want) ■ These apples are bad. Shall I **throw them away?** ■ Don't **throw away that picture.** I want it. **put away** = put something in the place where you usually keep it ■ After they finished playing, the children **put their toys away.**
over	**knock over** (a cup / a glass, etc.) ■ Be careful! Don't **knock your cup over.**
around	**show** (somebody) **around** = take somebody on a tour of a place ■ We visited a factory last week. The manager **showed us around.**

Additional Exercises

Am/is/are   **Units 1–2**

1   **Write sentences for the pictures. Use the words in the boxes + *is/isn't/are/aren't*.**

The windows ~~The windows~~	a doctor
~~Amy~~	asleep
Kate	crowded
The children	~~happy~~
Bill	hungry
The books	near the station
The hotel	on the table
The bus	~~open~~

1. *The windows are open.*
2. *Amy isn't happy.*
3. Kate _____ .
4. _____
5. _____
6. _____
7. _____
8. _____

2 **Complete the sentences.**

1. "Are you hungry?" "No, but *I'm* _____ thirsty."
2. "*How are* _____ your parents?" "They're fine."
3. "Is Lisa at home?" "No, _____ at work."
4. "_____ my keys?" "In the kitchen."
5. Where is John from? _____ American or Canadian?
6. _____ very hot today. The temperature is 38 degrees Celsius.
7. "Are you a teacher?" "No, _____ a student."
8. "_____ your umbrella?" "Green."
9. Where's your car? _____ in the parking lot?
10. "_____ tired?" "No, I'm fine."
11. "_____ these oranges?" "Seventy-five cents each."

Present Continuous (*I'm working / are you working?*, etc.)   Units 3–4

3 **Write sentences. Use the words in parentheses ( ).**

1. *A:* Where are your parents?
   B: *They're watching TV.* _____ (they / watch / TV)
2. *A:* Paula is going out.
   B: *Where's she going?* _____ (where / she / go?)
3. *A:* Where's David?
   B: _____ (he / take / a bath)
4. *A:* _____ (the children / play?)
   B: No, they're asleep.
5. *A:* _____ (it / rain?)
   B: No, not any more.
6. *A:* Where are Sue and Steve?
   B: _____ (they / come / now)
7. *A:* _____ (why / you / stand / here?)
   B: _____ (I / wait / for somebody)

Simple Present (*I work / she doesn't work / do you work?*, etc.)   Units 5–7

4 **Complete the sentences. Use the simple present.**

1. *Sue always gets* _____ to work early. (Sue / always / get)
2. *We don't watch* _____ TV very often. (we / not / watch)
3. How often *do you wash* _____ your hair? (you / wash)
4. I want to go to the movies, but _____ to go. (Chris / not / want)
5. _____ to go out tonight? (you / want)
6. _____ near here? (Amy / live)
7. _____ a lot of people. (Sarah / know)
8. I enjoy traveling, but _____ very much. (I / not / travel)
9. What time _____ in the morning? (you / usually / get up)
10. My parents are usually home in the evening.
    _____ very often. (they / not / go out)
11. _____ work at five o'clock. (Adam / always / leave)
12. *A:* What _____ ? (Kim / do)
    B: _____ in a hotel. (she / work)

5 **Read the questions and Claire's answers. Write sentences about Claire.**

CLAIRE

Are you married?	No.
Do you live in Toronto?	Yes.
Are you a student?	Yes.
Do you have a car?	No.
Do you go out a lot?	Yes.
Do you have a lot of friends?	Yes.
Do you like Toronto?	No.
Do you like to dance?	Yes.
Are you interested in sports?	No.

1. *She isn't married.*
2. *She lives in Toronto.*
3. _____
4. _____
5. _____
6. _____
7. _____
8. _____
9. _____

6 **Complete the questions.**

1.
What's your name ?	Brian.
_____ married?	Yes, I am.
Where _____ ?	On State Street.
_____ any children?	Yes, a daughter.
How _____ ?	She's three.

2.
_____ ?	I'm 29.
_____ ?	I work in a supermarket.
_____ your job?	No, I hate it.
_____ a car?	Yes, I do.
_____ to work?	No, I usually take the bus.

3.
Who is this man?	That's my brother.
_____ ?	Alex.
_____ ?	He's a travel agent.
_____ in New York?	No, Los Angeles.

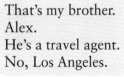

7 **Write sentences with these words. All of the sentences are present.**

1. (Sarah often / tennis) *Sarah often plays tennis.*
2. (they / a new car) *They have a new car.* OR *They've got a new car.*
3. (my shoes / dirty) *My shoes are dirty.*
4. (Sonia / 32 years old) Sonia _____ .
5. (he / six sisters) _____
6. (we often / TV at night) _____
7. (Amy never / a hat) _____
8. (my car / a flat tire) _____
9. (these flowers / beautiful) _____
10. (Mary / German very well) _____

8   Complete the sentences.

1 (I / work)
Please be quiet.
I'm working.

2 (you / often go)
Do you often go
to the movies?

3 (you / cook)
What _____ ?

4 (play)
Roy _____
the piano very well.

5 (I / leave)
_____
now. Good night.

6 (it / rain)
_____
Can I take this umbrella?

7 (I / not / watch)
_____
TV very much.

8 (we / look)
Excuse me, _____
_____ for the museum.

9 (you / pronounce)
What's this word? How
_____ it?

9   Which is right?

1. "~~Are you speaking~~ / Do you speak English?" "Yes, a little." (*Do you speak* is right.)
2. Sometimes <u>we're going / we go</u> away on weekends.
3. It's a nice day today. The sun <u>is shining / shines</u>.
4. *(You meet Amy in the street.)* Hello, Amy. Where <u>are you going / do you go</u>?
5. How often <u>are you taking / do you take</u> a vacation?
6. Emily is a writer. <u>She's writing / She writes</u> books for children.
7. <u>I'm never reading / I never read</u> newspapers.
8. "Where are Ed and Lee?" "<u>They're watching / They watch</u> TV in the living room."
9. Beth is in her office. <u>She's talking / She talks</u> to somebody.
10. What time <u>are you usually having / do you usually have</u> dinner?
11. John isn't home right now. <u>He's visiting / He visits</u> some friends.
12. "Would you like some tea?" "No, thank you. <u>I'm not drinking / I don't drink</u> tea."

10   **Complete the sentences. Use only one word.**

1. I got up early and *took*_____ a shower.
2. Tom was tired last night, so he _____ to bed early.
3. I _____ this pen on the floor. Is it yours?
4. Kate got married when she _____ 23.
5. Beth is learning to drive. She _____ her first lesson yesterday.
6. "I've got a new job." "Yes, I know. David _____ me."
7. "Where did you buy that book?" "It was a present. Andy _____ it to me."
8. We _____ hungry, so we had something to eat.
9. "Did you enjoy the movie?" "Yes, I did. I _____ it was very good."
10. "Did Ed come to your party?" "No, I _____ him, but he didn't come."

11   **Look at the questions and Joe's answers. Write about Joe when he was a child.**

When you were a child . . .

Were you tall?	No.	1. *He wasn't tall.*
Did you like school?	Yes.	2. *He liked school.*
Were you good at sports?	Yes.	3. He _____.
Did you play basketball?	Yes.	4. _____
Did you work hard in school?	No.	5. _____
Did you have a lot of friends?	Yes.	6. _____
Did you have a bicycle?	No.	7. _____
Were you a quiet child?	No.	8. _____

JOE

12   **Complete the questions.**

1. | *Did you have* _____ a nice vacation? | Yes, it was great, thanks.
2. | *Where did you go* _____ ? | To Vancouver.
3. | _____ there? | Five days.
4. | _____ Vancouver? | Yes, very much.
5. | _____ ? | I have friends there. I stayed with them.
6. | _____ good? | Yes, it was warm and sunny.
7. | _____ back? | Yesterday.

13   **Put the verb in the right form (positive, negative, or question).**

1. It was a good party. *I enjoyed*_____ it. (I / enjoy)
2. "*Did you do*___ the dishes?" (you / do) "No, *I didn't have*___ time." (I / have)
3. "Did you call Alan?" "No, I'm sorry. _____" (I / forget)
4. I like your watch. Where _____ it? (you / get)
5. I saw Lucy at the party, but _____ to her. (I / speak)
6. "_____ a nice weekend?" (you / have) "Yes, I saw a friend of mine."
7. Paul was sick yesterday, so _____ to work. (he / go)
8. "Is Mary here?" "Yes, _____ here five minutes ago." (she / get)
9. Where _____ before he moved here? (Bob / live)
10. The restaurant wasn't expensive. _____ very much. (the meal / cost)

14   Complete the sentences. Use the simple past or past continuous.

1. It _was raining_____ (rain) when
   we _went_____ (go) out.

AL   JAN

2. When I got to the office, Al and Jan
   _____ (work).

3. I _____ (open) the
   window because it was hot.

SUE

4. The phone _____ (ring)
   while Sue _____ (cook) dinner.

5. I _____ (hear) a
   noise, so I _____ (look)
   out the window.

TOM

6. Tom _____ (look)
   out the window when the accident
   _____ (happen).

BRUCE

7. Bruce had a book in his hand, but he
   _____ (not / read) it.
   He _____ (watch) TV.

ERIN

8. Erin bought a magazine, but she
   _____ (not / read) it.
   She didn't have time.

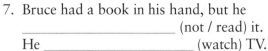

9. I _____ (finish) lunch,
   _____ (pay), and
   _____ (leave) the
   restaurant.

KATE

10. I _____ (see) Kate this
    morning. I _____
    (walk) along the street, and she
    _____ (wait) for the bus.

15   Complete the sentences. Use one of these forms.

> the simple present (*I work*, etc.)   the present continuous (*I am working*, etc.)
> the simple past (*I worked*, etc.)   the past continuous (*I was working*, etc.)

1. You can turn off the TV. I *'m not watching* _____ (not / watch) it.
2. Last night Amy *fell* _____ (fall) asleep while she *was reading* ____ (read).
3. Listen! Somebody _____ (play) the piano.
4. "Do you have my key?" "No, I _____ (give) it back to you."
5. David is very lazy. He _____ (not / like) to work hard.
6. Where _____ (your family / go) for vacation last year?
7. I _____ (see) Diane yesterday. She _____ (drive) her new car.
8. "_____ (you / watch) TV very much?" "No, I don't have a TV."
9. *A:* What _____ (you / do) at six o'clock last Sunday morning?
   B: I was in bed asleep.
10. Andy isn't at home very much. He _____ (go) out a lot.
11. I _____ (try) to find a job right now. It's very hard.
12. I'm tired this morning. I _____ (not / sleep) very well last night.

Present Perfect (*I have done / she has been*, etc.)   **Units 16–20**

16   Look at the pictures and complete the sentences. Use the present perfect.

1. Who's that man?
   I don't know. I *'ve never seen* _____ him before.

2. Is this a good book?
   I don't know. I _____ it.

3. I'm looking for Julia. _____ her?
   Yes, she was here a few minutes ago.

4. More coffee?
   No, thanks. I _____ enough.

5. _____ to Chile?

Yes, I was there a few years ago.

6. How long _____ here?

Since 1994.

7. Do you know Al?

Yes, we _____ each other for years.

8. The weather is terrible today. It _____ all day.

AL

17 Complete the sentences (1, 2 or 3 words).

1. Mark and Liz are married. They _have been_ married for five years.
2. David has been watching TV _since_ five o'clock.
3. Mark is at work. He _____ at work since 8:30.
4. "Did you just arrive in Ottawa?" "No, I've been here _____ five days."
5. I've known Amy _____ we were in high school.
6. "My brother lives in Los Angeles." "Really? How long _____ there?"
7. Eric has had the same job _____ twenty years.
8. Some friends are staying with us. They _____ here since Monday.

18 Complete the sentences. Write about yourself.

1. I've never _ridden a horse_ .
2. I've _been to Los Angeles_ many times.
3. I've _____ .
   (once / twice / a few times / many times)
4. I haven't _____ yet.
5. I've never _____ .
6. I've _____ since _____ .
7. I've _____ for _____ .

19 Present perfect or simple past? Complete the sentences (positive or negative).

1. *A:* Do you like London?
   B: I don't know. I *haven't been* _____ there.
2. *A:* Have you seen Amy?
   B: Yes, I *saw* _____ her five minutes ago.
3. *A:* That's a nice sweater. Is it new?
   B: Yes, I _____ it last week.
4. *A:* Are you tired this morning?
   B: Yes, I _____ to bed late last night.
5. *A:* Is that new French movie good?
   B: Yes, really good. _____ it three times.
6. *A:* The weather isn't very nice today, is it?
   B: No, but it _____ nice yesterday.
7. *A:* Was Lisa at the party on Saturday?
   B: I don't think so. I _____ her there.
8. *A:* How long does it take to make pizza?
   B: I have no idea. I _____ pizza.
9. *A:* Is your son still in school?
   B: No, he _____ college two years ago.
10. *A:* Is Sylvia married?
    B: Yes, she _____ married for five years.
11. *A:* Have you heard of George Washington?
    B: Of course. He _____ the first President of the United States.

20 Write sentences with the words in parentheses ( ). Use the present perfect or the simple past.

1. *A:* Have you been to Thailand?
   B: Yes, *I went there last year* _____ . (I / go / there / last year)
2. *A:* Do you like London?
   B: I don't know. *I've never been there* _____ . (I / never / there)
3. *A:* Where is Paul these days?
   B: He's living in Chicago. _____ (live / there / since last May)
4. *A:* Has Erin gone home?
   B: Yes, _____ . (she / leave / at four o'clock)
5. *A:* New York is my favorite city.
   B: Is it? _____ (how many times / you / there?)
6. *A:* You look tired.
   B: Yes, _____ (I / tired / all day)
7. *A:* I can't find my address book. Have you seen it?
   B: _____ (it / on the table / last night)
8. *A:* Is that restaurant good?
   B: Yes, it is. _____ (eat / there / many times)
9. *A:* Paula and Sue are here.
   B: They are? _____ (what time / they / arrive?)

21 Present perfect or simple past? Complete the sentences.

1. *A:* *Have you been* _____ to France?
   B: Yes, many times.
   A: When _____
      the last time?
   B: Two years ago.

2. *A:* Is this your car?
   B: Yes, it is.
   A: How long _____ it?
   B: It's new. I _____ it yesterday.

3. *A:* Where do you live?
   B: On Maple Street.
   A: How long _____ there?
   B: Five years. Before that _____
      _____ on Mill Road.
   A: Really? How long _____
      _____ on Mill Road?
   B: About three years.

4. *A:* What do you do?
   B: I work in a store.
   A: How long _____ there?
   B: Almost two years.
   A: What _____
      before that?
   B: I _____taxi driver.

22 Write sentences about yourself.

1. (yesterday morning) *I was late for work yesterday morning.*
2. (last night) _____
3. (yesterday afternoon) _____
4. (. . . days ago) _____
5. (last week) _____
6. (last year) _____

Present, Past, and Present Perfect   **Units 3–21**

23 Which is right?

1. "_____?" "No, she's on vacation."
   A. Does Sue work   B. Is working Sue   (C.)Is Sue working   D. Does work Sue
2. "Where _____?" "In Dallas."
   A. lives your uncle   B. does your uncle live   C. your uncle lives
   D. does live your uncle
3. I speak Italian, but _____ French.
   A. I no speak   B. I'm not speaking   C. I doesn't speak   D. I don't speak
4. "Where's Tom?" "_____ a shower right now."
   A. He's taking   B. He take   C. He takes   D. He has taken

5. Why _____ angry with me yesterday?
   A. were you   B. was you   C. you were   D. have you been
6. My favorite film is *Cleo's Dream*. _____ it four times.
   A. I'm seeing   B. I see   C. I seen   D. I've seen
7. I _____ out last night. I was too tired.
   A. don't go   B. didn't went   C. didn't go   D. haven't gone
8. Liz is from Chicago. She _____ there all her life.
   A. is living   B. has lived   C. lives   D. lived
9. My friend _____ for me when I arrived.
   A. waited   B. has waited   C. was waiting   D. has been waiting
10. "How long _____ English?" "Six months."
    A. do you learn   B. are you learning   C. you are learning
    D. have you been learning
11. Joel is Canadian, but he lives in Chile. He has been there _____ .
    A. for three years   B. since three years   C. three years ago   D. during three years
12. "What time _____ ?" "About an hour ago."
    A. has Amy called   B. Amy called   C. did Amy call   D. is Amy calling
13. What _____ when you saw her?
    A. did Sue wear   B. was Sue wearing   C. has Sue worn   D. was wearing Sue
14. "Can you drive?" "No, _____ a car, but I want to learn."
    A. I never drive   B. I'm never driving   C. I've never driven   D. I was never driving
15. I saw Ruth at the train station this morning, but she _____ me.
    A. didn't see   B. don't see   C. hasn't seen   D. didn't saw

---

Passive   **Units 22–23, Appendix 1**

24 **Complete the sentences.**

1. These houses *were built*
   20 years ago. Before that there was a
   church here, but the church _____
   _____ (damage) in a fire and had
   to _____ (tear down).

2. This bridge _____ (build)
   in 1925. It _____ (use)
   by hundreds of people every day. At
   present the bridge _____
   (paint).

3. This street _____ (call)
   Kennedy Street. It used to _____
   _____ (call) Hill Street, but the name
   _____ (change) in 1964.

4. This is a bicycle factory. Bicycles _____
   _____ (make) here since 1931.
   It is the oldest bicycle factory in the
   country. Thousands of bicycles _____
   _____ (produce) here every year.

25 Complete the sentences.

1. We _were invited_ _____ to the party, but we didn't go. (invite)
2. The museum is very popular. Every year it _____ by thousands of people. (visit)
3. Many buildings _____ in the storm last week. (damage)
4. A new road is going to _____ next year. (build)
5. "Where's your jacket?" "It _____ . It will be ready tomorrow." (clean)
6. She's famous now, but in a few years her name will _____ . (forget)
7. "Are you happy with your washing machine?" "Not really. It _____ three times since we bought it." (repair)
8. Milk should _____ in the refrigerator. (keep)
9. _____ by a snake? (you / ever / bite)
10. My bag _____ from my car yesterday afternoon. (steal)

26 Write a new sentence with the same meaning.

1. Somebody has stolen my keys.   _My keys have been stolen._ _____
2. Somebody stole my car last week.   My car _____ .
3. Somebody wants you on the phone.   You _____ .
4. Somebody has eaten the ice cream.   The _____ .
5. Somebody will repair the machine.   The _____ .
6. Somebody is watching us.   We _____ .
7. Somebody has to buy the food.   The _____ .

27 Active or passive? Complete the sentences.

1. They _are building_ _____ a new airport now. (build)
2. These shirts are clean now. They _have been washed_ OR _were washed_ . (wash)
3. "How did you fall?" "Somebody _____ me." (push)
4. "How did you fall?" "I _____ ." (push)
5. I can't find my bag. Somebody _____ it! (take)
6. My watch is broken. It _____ at the moment. (repair)
7. Who _____ the camera? (invent)
8. When _____ ? (the camera / invent)
9. The letter was for me, so why _____ it to you? (they / send)
10. The information will _____ to you as soon as possible. (send)

Future   **Units 26–29**

28 Which is right?

1. _____ a party next Sunday. I hope you can come.
   (A.) We're having   B. We'll have
2. Did you hear about Karen? _____ her job. She told me last week.
   A. She's going to quit   B. She'll quit
3. There's a program on TV that I want to watch. _____ in five minutes.
   A. It starts   B. It's starting
4. The weather is nice now, but I think _____ later.
   A. it's raining   B. it will rain

5. "What _____ next weekend?" "Nothing special. Why?"
   A. are you doing   B. do you do

6. "When you see Amy, can you ask her to call me?" "OK, _____ her."
   A. I ask   B. I'll ask

7. "What would you like to drink, tea or coffee?" "_____ tea, please."
   A. I have   B. I'll have

8. Don't take that newspaper away. _____ it.
   A. I'm going to read   B. I'll read

9. Rachel is sick, so _____ to the party tomorrow night.
   A. she doesn't come   B. she isn't coming

10. I want to meet Sarah at the station. What time _____ ?
    A. does her train arrive   B. is her train arriving

11. "Will you be at home tomorrow night?" "No, _____ ."
    A. I'm going out   B. I go out

12. "_____ you at six tomorrow?" "Yes, fine."
    A. Do I call   B. Shall I call

Past, Present, and Future   Units 3–21, 26–29

29   **Complete the sentences.**

1. *A:* _Did you go_ _____ (you / go) out last night?
   B: No, _____ (I / stay) home.
   A: What _____ (you / do) ?
   B: _____ (I / watch) TV.
   A: _____ (you / go) out tomorrow night?
   B: Yes, _____ (I / go) to the movies.
   A: What movie _____ (you / see) ?
   B: _____ (I / not / know) .
      _____ (I / not / decide) yet.

2. *A:* Are you visiting here?
   B: Yes, we are.
   A: How long _____
      _____ (you / be) here?
   B: _____
      (we / arrive) yesterday.
   A: And how long _____ (you / stay) ?
   B: Until the end of next week.
   A: And _____ (you / like) it here?
   B: Yes, _____ (we / have) a wonderful time.

3. *A:* Oh, _____ (I / just / remember) –
      _____ (Kim / call) while you were out.
   B: _____ (she / always / call) when I'm not here.
      _____ (she / leave) a message?
   A: No, but _____ (she / want) you to call her back as
      soon as possible.
   B: OK, _____ (I / call) her now.
      _____ (you / know) her number?
   A: It's in my address book. _____ (I / get) it for you.

4. *A:* _____ (I / go) out with Chris and Steve tonight.
   _____ (you / want) to come with us?
   B: Yes, where _____ (you / go)?
   A: To the Italian restaurant on North Street.
   _____ (you / ever / eat) there?
   B: Yes, _____ (I / be) there two or three times. In fact I
   _____ (go) there last night, but I'd love to go again!

5. *A:* _____ (I / lose) my glasses again.
   _____ (you / see) them?
   B: _____ (you / wear) them when
   _____ (I / come) in.
   A: Well, _____ (I / not / wear) them
   now, so where are they?
   B: _____ (you / look) in the kitchen?
   A: No. _____ (I / go) and look now.

***-ing* and *to* . . .**   Units 52–56, 100, 107

30 **Which is right?**

1. Don't forget _____ off the light when you leave.
   A. turn   (B.) to turn   C. turning
2. It's late. I should _____ now.
   A. go   B. to go   C. going
3. I'm sorry but I haven't got time _____ to you now.
   A. for talking   B. to talk   C. talking
4. Bill is always in the kitchen. He enjoys _____ .
   A. cook   B. to cook   C. cooking
5. We've decided _____ away for a few days.
   A. go   B. to go   C. going
6. You're making too much noise. Can you please stop _____ ?
   A. shout   B. to shout   C. shouting
7. Would you like _____ to dinner on Sunday?
   A. come   B. to come   C. coming
8. That bag is too heavy for you. Let me _____ you.
   A. help   B. to help   C. helping
9. There's a swimming pool near my house. I go _____ every day.
   A. swim   B. to swimming   C. swimming
10. Did you use a dictionary _____ the letter?
    A. to translate   B. for translating   C. for translate
11. I'd love _____ a car like yours.
    A. have   B. to have   C. to having
12. Could you _____ me with this bag, please?
    A. help   B. to help   C. helping
13. I don't mind _____ here, but I'd prefer to sit by the window.
    A. sit   B. to sit   C. sitting
14. Do you want _____ you?
    A. that I help   B. me to help   C. me helping

15. I always read the newspaper before _____ work.
    A. start   B. to start   C. starting
16. I wasn't feeling very well, but the medicine made me _____ better.
    A. feel   B. to feel   C. feeling
17. Shall I call the restaurant _____ a table?
    A. for reserve   B. for reserving   C. to reserve
18. Tom looked at me without _____ anything.
    A. say   B. saying   C. to say

A and **the**   Units 66, 70–74

31 **Complete the sentences.**

1. Can you pass ___the sugar___, please?
2. Do you have _____? No, I can't drive.
3. Have you got any milk? Yes, there's some in _____.
4. What do you do? I'm _____.
5. I don't feel very well. I don't want to go to _____.
6. What did you do last night? We went to _____.
7. Shall we walk home? No, let's take _____.
8. Can you play _____? Yes, but not very well.
9. I'm interested in _____.
10. What's the difference between those cars? Nothing. They're _____.

32 Write *a/an* or *the* if necessary.

1. Who is *the* _____ best player on your team?
2. I don't watch — _____ television very often.
3. "Is there *a* _____ bank near here?" "Yes, at *the* _____ end of this block."
4. I can't ride _____ horse.
5. _____ sky is very clear tonight.
6. Do you live here, or are you _____ tourist?
7. What did you have for _____ lunch?
8. Who was _____ first President of _____ United States?
9. "What time is it?" "I don't know. I don't have _____ watch."
10. I'm sorry but I've forgotten your name. I can never remember _____ names.
11. What time is _____ next train to Boston?
12. Kate never writes _____ letters. She prefers to call people.
13. "Where's Sue?" "She's in _____ yard."
14. Excuse me, I'm looking for _____ Majestic Hotel. Is it near here?
15. Gary was sick _____ last week, so he didn't go to _____ work.
16. Everest is _____ highest mountain in _____ world.
17. I usually listen to _____ radio while I'm having _____ breakfast.
18. I like _____ sports. My favorite sport is _____ basketball.
19. Julia is _____ doctor. Her husband is _____ art teacher.
20. My apartment is on _____ second floor. Turn left at _____ top of _____ stairs, and it's on _____ right.
21. After _____ dinner, we watched _____ television.
22. I've been to _____ northern Mexico, but not to _____ south.

Prepositions   Units 98–103, 106

33 Write a preposition (*in/for/by*, etc.).

1. Beth is studying math *in* _____ college.
2. What is the longest river _____ Europe?
3. Is there anything _____ television tonight?
4. We arrived _____ the hotel after midnight.
5. "Where's Mike?" "He's _____ vacation."
6. Tom hasn't gotten up yet. He's still _____ bed.
7. Lisa is away. She's been away _____ Monday.
8. The next meeting is _____ April 15.
9. We traveled across Canada _____ train.
10. There's too much sugar _____ my coffee.
11. Kevin lived in Chicago _____ six months. He didn't like it very much.
12. Were there a lot of people _____ the party?
13. I don't know any of the people _____ this photograph.
14. The train was very slow. It stopped _____ every station.
15. I like this room. I like the pictures _____ the walls.
16. "Did you buy that picture?" "No, it was given to me _____ a friend of mine."
17. I'm going away _____ a few days. I'll be back _____ Thursday.
18. Lynn has gone _____ Italy. She's _____ Milan right now.
19. Amy quit school _____ sixteen and got a job _____ a bookstore.

Study Guide

If you are not sure which units you need to study, use this study guide.

You have to decide which alternative is right (A, B, C, etc.). **Sometimes more than one alternative is correct.**

If you don't know (or if you are not sure) which alternatives are correct, study the unit (or units) on the right. You will find the correct sentence in the unit.

The Answer Key to this study guide is on page 296.

IF YOU ARE NOT SURE WHICH IS RIGHT	STUDY UNIT

Present

1.1 _____ . Can you close the window, please?   **1**
A. I cold   B. I'm cold   C. I have cold   D. It has cold

1.2 Tom _____ in politics.   **1**
A. isn't interested   B. not interested   C. doesn't interested   D. don't interest

1.3 "_____ ?" "No, she's out."   **2**
A. Is at home your mother   B. Does your mother at home
C. Is your mother at home   D. Are your mother at home

1.4 "How much _____ ?" "Fifty cents."   **2**
A. are these postcards   B. is these postcards   C. these postcards
D. do these postcards

1.5 Look at Michiko! _____ her new hat.   **3, 24**
A. She wearing   B. She has wearing   C. She is wearing   D. She's wearing

1.6 You can turn off the television. _____ it.   **3, 24**
A. I'm not watch   B. I'm not watching   C. I not watching   D. I don't watching

1.7 "_____ today?" "No, he's at home."   **4, 24**
A. Is working Luis   B. Is work Luis   C. Is Luis work   D. Is Luis working

1.8 Look, there's Hannah! _____ ?   **4, 24**
A. Where she is going   B. Where she go   C. Where's she going
D. Where she going

1.9 The earth _____ around the sun.   **5, 24**
A. going   B. go   C. goes   D. does go   E. is go

1.10 We _____ late on weekends.   **5, 24, 95**
A. often sleep   B. sleep often   C. often sleeping   D. are often sleep

1.11 We _____ television very often.   **6, 24**
A. not watch   B. doesn't watch   C. don't watch   D. don't watching

1.12 "_____ on Saturdays?" "No, not usually."   **7, 24**
A. Do you work   B. Are you work   C. Does you work   D. Do you working

1.13 I don't understand this sentence. What _____ ?   **7, 24**
A. mean this word   B. means this word   C. does mean this word
D. does this word mean   E. this word means

1.14 Please be quiet. _____ .
A. I working   B. I work   C. I'm working   D. I'm work

8, 24

1.15 Tom _____ a shower every morning.
A. takes   B. taking   C. is taking   D. take

8

1.16 What _____ on weekends?
A. do you usually   B. are you usually doing   C. are you usually do
D. do you usually do   E. you do usually

7, 8, 24

1.17 Li Jing isn't feeling well. _____ a headache.
A. She have   B. She have got   C. She has   D. She's got

9, 59

1.18 Mr. and Mrs. Harris _____ any children.
A. don't have   B. doesn't have   C. no have   D. haven't got

9, 59

Past

2.1 The weather _____ last week.
A. is nice   B. was nice   C. were nice   D. nice   E. had nice

10

2.2 Why _____ late this morning?
A. you was   B. did you   C. was you   D. you were   E. were you

10

2.3 Terry _____ in a bank from 1987 to 1998.
A. work   B. working   C. works   D. worked   E. was work

11, 24

2.4 Caroline _____ to the movies three times last week.
A. go   B. went   C. goes   D. got   E. was

11

2.5 I _____ television yesterday.
A. didn't watch   B. didn't watched   C. wasn't watch   D. don't watch
E. didn't watching

12, 24

2.6 "How _____ ?" "I don't know. I didn't see it"
A. happened the accident   B. did happen the accident   C. does the accident happen
D. did the accident happen   E. the accident happened

12

2.7 What _____ at 11:30 yesterday?
A. were you doing   B. was you doing   C. you were doing   D. were you do
E. you was doing

13

2.8 Eric was reading a book when the phone _____ .
A. ringing   B. rang   C. was ringing   D. was ring

14

2.9 I saw Lucy and Steve this morning. They _____ at the bus stop.
A. waiting   B. waited   C. were waiting   D. was waiting   E. were waited

14

2.10 Dave _____ in a factory. Now he works in a supermarket.
A. working   B. works   C. worked   D. use to work   E. used to work

15

Present Perfect

3.1 My mother _____ by plane.
A. has never travel   B. has never traveled   C. is never traveled
D. has never been traveled   E. have never traveled

16, 24

3.2 _____ that woman before, but I can't remember where.   **16, 24**
    A. I see   B. I seen   C. I've saw   D. I've seen   E. I've seeing

3.3 "How long _____ married?" "Since 1992."   **17**
    A. you are   B. you have been   C. has you been   D. are you
    E. have you been

3.4 "Do you know Lynn?" "Yes, _____ her for a long time."   **17**
    A. I knew   B. I've known   C. I know   D. I am knowing

3.5 Richard has been in Canada _____ .   **18, 99**
    A. for six months   B. since six months   C. six months ago   D. in six months

3.6 "When did Tom go out?" " _____ ."   **18**
    A. For ten minutes   B. Since ten minutes   C. Ten minutes ago
    D. In ten minutes

3.7 "Is Peter here?" "No, _____ home."   **19, 21**
    A. he went   B. he have gone   C. he's went   D. hc's gone   E. he go

3.8 "Are you hungry?" "No, _____ dinner."   **20**
    A. I just had   B. I just have   C. I just having   D. I've just had

3.9 We _____ a vacation last year.   **21**
    A. don't take   B. haven't taken   C. hasn't taken   D. didn't take
    E. didn't took

3.10 Where _____ on Sunday afternoon? I couldn't find you.   **21**
    A. you were   B. you have been   C. was you   D. have you been   E. were you

Passive

4.1 This house _____ 100 years ago.   **22, 24**
    A. is built   B. is building   C. was building   D. was built   E. built

4.2 We _____ to the party last week.   **22, 23**
    A. didn't invite   B. didn't invited   C. weren't invited   D. wasn't invited
    E. haven't been invited

4.3 "Where _____ born?" "In Los Angeles."   **22**
    A. you are   B. you were   C. was you   D. are you   E. were you

4.4 I took the bus this morning because my car _____ .   **23**
    A. is being repaired   B. is repairing   C. has been repaired   D. repaired

4.5 I can't find my keys. I think _____ .   **23**
    A. they've been stolen   B. they are stolen   C. they've stolen
    D. they're being stolen

Verb Forms

5.1 It _____ , so we went out.   **24**
    A. wasn't rained   B. wasn't rain   C. didn't raining   D. wasn't raining

5.2 Somebody _____ this window.   **25**
    A. has broke   B. has broken   C. has breaked   D. has break

Future

6.1 Andrew _____ tennis tomorrow.　26
　　 A. is playing　　B. play　　C. plays　　D. is play

6.2 _____ out tonight?　26
　　 A. Are you going　　B. Are you go　　C. Do you go　　D. Go you　　E. Do you going

6.3 What time _____ tonight?　26
　　 A. is the concert start　　B. does the concert start　　C. starts the concert
　　 D. does the concert starting

6.4 What _____ to the party tonight?　27
　　 A. are you wearing　　B. are you going to wear　　C. do you wear
　　 D. you are going to wear

6.5 I think Diana _____ her driver's test.　28
　　 A. passes　　B. will pass　　C. will be pass　　D. will passing

6.6 _____ to the movies on Saturday. Do you want to come with us?　26, 28
　　 A. We go　　B. We'll go　　C. We're going　　D. We will going

6.7 "_____ you tomorrow, OK?" "OK. Goodbye."　29
　　 A. I call　　B. I'll call　　C. I'm calling　　D. I calling

6.8 There's a good program on TV tonight. _____ it.　27, 29
　　 A. I watch　　B. I'll watch　　C. I'm going to watch　　D. I'll watching

6.9 It's a nice day. _____ for a walk?　29
　　 A. Do we go　　B. Shall we go　　C. Should we go

Modals, Imperatives, etc.

7.1 _____ to the movies tonight, but I'm not sure.　30
　　 A. I'll go　　B. I'm going　　C. I may go　　D. I might go

7.2 "_____ here?" "Sure."　30, 31
　　 A. Can I sit　　B. Do I sit　　C. May I sit　　D. Can I to sit

7.3 I'm having a party next week, but Scott and Angela _____ .　31
　　 A. can't come　　B. can't to come　　C. can't coming　　D. couldn't come

7.4 Before Shu Ling came to Canada, she _____ understand much English.　31
　　 A. can　　B. can't　　C. not　　D. couldn't　　E. doesn't

7.5 You worked ten hours today. You _____ tired.　32
　　 A. must　　B. can　　C. must be　　D. can be　　E. must to be

7.6 Carlos takes the bus everywhere. He _____ a car.　32
　　 A. must have　　B. must not have　　C. must not to have　　D. no have

7.7 They were in a dangerous situation. They _____ careful.　32, 34
　　 A. must to be　　B. must be　　C. have to be　　D. had to be　　E. had be

7.8 I _____ study tonight, but I think I'll go to the movies.　33
　　 A. must　　B. have to　　C. should　　D. ought to　　E. will

7.9 What time _____ go to the dentist tomorrow?　34
　　 A. you must　　B. you have to　　C. have you to　　D. do you have to

7.10 " _____ some coffee?" "No, thank you."   35
A. Are you liking   B. You like   C. Would you like   D. Do you like

7.11 I don't really want to go out. _____ home.   36
A. I rather stay   B. I'd rather stay   C. I'd rather to stay   D. I'd prefer to stay

7.12 Stay here. Please _____ .   37
A. don't go   B. you no go   C. you not to go   D. go not

7.13 It's a nice day. _____ out.   37
A. Let's to go   B. Let's go   C. Let's to go   D. We go

There and *it*

8.1 Excuse me, _____ a hotel near here?   38
A. has there   B. is there   C. there is   D. is it

8.2 _____ a lot of accidents on this road.   38
A. Have   B. It has   C. There have   D. They are   E. There are

8.3 When I got home, I was hungry, but _____ anything to eat.   39
A. there wasn't   B. there weren't   C. it wasn't   D. there hasn't been

8.4 _____ three miles from our house to the mall.   40
A. It's   B. It has   C. There is   D. There are

8.5 _____ true that you're moving to Australia?   40
A. Is there   B. Is it   C. Is   D. Are you

Auxiliary Verbs

9.1 I haven't seen the movie but my sister _____ .   41
A. does   B. is   C. has seen   D. has   E. hasn't

9.2 I don't like hot weather, but Megan _____ .   41
A. does   B. doesn't   C. do   D. does like   E. likes

9.3 "Nicole got married last week." "_____ ? Really?"   42
A. Got she   B. She got   C. She did   D. She has

9.4 You haven't met my mother, _____ ?   42
A. haven't you   B. have you   C. did you   D. you have   E. you haven't

9.5 Bill doesn't watch TV. He doesn't read newspapers _____ .   43
A. too   B. either   C. neither   D. never

9.6 "I'd like to go to Australia." "_____ ."   43
A. So do I   B. So am I   C. So would I   D. Neither do I   E. So I would

9.7 Sue _____ much on weekends.   44
A. don't   B. doesn't   C. don't do   D. doesn't do

Questions

10.1 "When _____ ?" "I'm not sure. More than 100 years ago."   45
A. did the telephone invent   B. was invented the telephone
C. was the telephone invented   D. the telephone was invented

10.2 "I broke my finger last week." " How _____ that?"   `45`
A. did you   B. you did   C. you did do   D. did you do

10.3 Why _____ me last night? I was waiting for you to call.   `45`
A. didn't you call   B. you no call   C. you don't call   D. you didn't call

10.4 "Who _____ in this house?" "I don't know."   `46`
A. lives   B. does live   C. does lives   D. living

10.5 What _____ when you told him the story?   `46`
A. said Paul   B. did Paul say   C. Paul said   D. did Paul said

10.6 "Tom's father is in the hospital." "_____ ?"   `47`
A. In which hospital he is   B. In which hospital he is in
C. Which hospital he is in   D. Which hospital is he in

10.7 Did you have a good vacation? _____ ?   `47`
A. How was the weather like   B. What was the weather like
C. What the weather was like   D. Was the weather like

10.8 _____ taller – Bill or Sam?   `48`
A. Who is   B. What is   C. Which is   D. Who has

10.9 There are four umbrellas here. _____ is yours?   `48, 76`
A. What   B. Who   C. Which   D. How   E. Which one

10.10 How long _____ to get from Washington to New York by plane?   `49`
A. is it   B. does it need   C. does it take   D. it wants

10.11 I don't remember what _____ at the party.   `50`
A. Dawn was wearing   B. was wearing Dawn   C. was Dawn wearing

10.12 "Do you know _____ ?" "Yes, I think so."   `50`
A. if Jack is at home   B. is Jack at home   C. whether Jack is at home
D. that Jack is at home

Reported Speech

11.1 I saw Steve a week ago. He said _____ me but he didn't.   `51`
A. he call   B. he call   C. he'll call   D. he's going to call   E. he would call

11.2 "Why did Tim go to bed so early?" "He _____ ."   `51`
A. said he was tired   B. said that he was tired   C. said me he was tired
D. told me he was tired

-ing and to . . .

12.1 You shouldn't _____ so hard.   `52`
A. working   B. work   C. to work   D. worked

12.2 I _____ now. See you tomorrow.   `52`
A. must to go   B. have go   C. have to going   D. have to go

12.3 Tina has decided _____ her house.   `53`
A. sell   B. to sell   C. selling   D. to selling

12.4 I don't mind _____ early.   `53`
A. get up   B. to get up   C. getting up   D. to getting up

12.5	Do you like _____ early? A. get up B. to get up C. getting up D. to getting up	53
12.6	Do you want _____ you some money? A. me lend B. me lending C. me to lend D. that I lend	54
12.7	He's very funny. He makes _____ . A. me laugh B. me laughing C. me to laugh D. that I laugh	54
12.8	Kelly went to the store _____ a newspaper. A. for buy B. for to buy C. for buying D. to buy E. buy	55

Go, get, do, make, and have

13.1	It's a nice day. Let's go _____ . A. for a swim B. on a swim C. to swimming D. swimming	56
13.2	I'm sorry your mother is sick. I hope she _____ better soon. A. has B. makes C. gets D. goes	57
13.3	Kate _____ the car and drove away. A. went into B. went in C. got in D. got into	57
13.4	"Shall I open the window?" "No, it's OK. I'll _____ it. A. do B. make C. have	58
13.5	I'm sorry, I _____ a mistake. A. did B. made C. got D. had	58
13.6	" _____ a nice weekend?" "Yes, thanks. It was very nice!" A. Have you B. Had you C. Do you have D. Did you have	59

Pronouns and Possessives

14.1	I don't want this book. You can have _____ . A. it B. them C. her D. him	60, 63
14.2	Sue and Kevin are going to the movies. Do you want to go with _____ ? A. her B. they C. them D. him	60, 63
14.3	I saw Mr. and Mrs. Lee with _____ daughter. A. her B. his C. they D. their	61, 63
14.4	Hawaii is famous for _____ beaches. A. his B. its C. it's D. their	61
14.5	I didn't have an umbrella, so Mary gave me _____ . A. her B. hers C. her umbrella D. she's	62, 63
14.6	I went to the movies with a friend of _____ . A. mine B. my C. me D. I	62,63
14.7	We had a good vacation. We enjoyed _____ . A. us B. our C. ours D. ourselves	64
14.8	Kim and Amy are good friends. They know _____ well. A. each other B. them C. themselves D. theirselves	64

14.9 Have you met _____ ?
  A. the wife of Mr. Suzuki   B. Mr. Suzuki wife   C. the wife Mr. Suzuki
  D. Mr. Suzuki's wife   E. the Mr. Suzuki's wife

65

14.10 Have you seen _____ ?
  A. the car of my parents   B. my parent's car   C. my parents' car
  D. my parents car

65

A and the

15.1 I'm going to buy _____ .
  A. hat and umbrella   B. a hat and a umbrella   C. a hat and an umbrella
  D. an hat and an umbrella

66, 68

15.2 "What do you do?" "_____ ."
  A. I dentist   B. I'm a dentist   C. I'm dentist   D. I do dentist

66

15.3 I'm going shopping. I need _____ .
  A. some new jeans   B. a new jeans   C. a new pair of jeans   D. a new pair jeans

67

15.4 I like the people here. _____ very friendly.
  A. She is   B. They are   C. They is   D. It is

67

15.5 I'm very thirsty. I need _____ .
  A. some water   B. a water   C. a glass of water

68, 69

15.6 I need _____ about hotels in Mexico City.
  A. some information   B. some informations   C. an information

69

15.7 We enjoyed our vacation. _____ was very nice.
  A. Hotel   B. A hotel   C. An hotel   D. The hotel

70, 71

15.8 The table is in _____ .
  A. middle of room   B. middle of the room   C. the middle of the room
  D. the middle of room

71

15.9 What did you have for _____ ?
  A. the breakfast   B. breakfast   C. a breakfast

71

15.10 I finish _____ at five o'clock every day.
  A. the work   B. work   C. a work

71

15.11 I never go to _____ , but I go to the movies a lot.
  A. the theater   B. theater   C. a theater

72

15.12 We don't eat _____ very often.
  A. the meat   B. meat   C. a meat   D. some meat

73

15.13 _____ is in New York.
  A. The Times Square   B. Times Square

74

15.14 My friends are staying at _____ .
  A. the Milton Hotel   B. Milton Hotel

74

Determiners and Pronouns

16.1 "I'm going on vacation next week." "Oh, _____ nice."
  A. it's   B. this is   C. that's

75

16.2 "Is there a bank near here?" "Yes, there's _____ on the corner."   76
A. some   B. it   C. one   D. a one

16.3 This cup is dirty. Can I have _____ ?   76
A. clean one   B. a clean one   C. clean   D. a clean

16.4 There's _____ in the fridge.   77
A. a milk   B. some milk   C. any milk

16.5 "Where's your luggage?" "I don't have _____ ."   77
A. one   B. some   C. any

16.6 Karen and Steve _____ .   78, 79
A. have no children   B. don't have no children   C. don't have any children
D. have any children

16.7 "How much money do you have?" "_____ ."   78
A. No   B. No one   C. Any   D. None

16.8 There's _____ in the room. It's empty.   79, 80
A. anybody   B. nobody   C. anyone   D. no one

16.9 "What did you say?" "_____ ."   79, 80
A. Nothing   B. Nobody   C. Anything   D. Not anything

16.10 I'm hungry. I want _____ .   80
A. something for eat   B. something to eat   C. something for eating

16.11 "How often do you read a newspaper?" "_____ ."   81
A. All day   B. All days   C. Every days   D. Every day

16.12 _____ friends.   81
A. Everybody need   B. Everybody needs   C. Everyone need   D. Everyone needs

16.13 _____ children like to play.   81
A. Most   B. The most   C. Most of   D. The most of

16.14 I like _____ those pictures.   83
A. both   B. both of   C. either   D. either of

16.15 I haven't read _____ these books.   83
A. neither   B. neither of   C. either   D. either of

16.16 Do you have _____ friends?   84
A. a lot of   B. much   C. many   D. much of   E. many of

16.17 We like films, so we go to the movies _____ .   84
A. a lot of   B. much   C. many   D. a lot

16.18 There were _____ people in the theatre. It was almost empty.   85
A. a little   B. few   C. little   D. a few of

16.19 They have _____ money, but they're not rich.   85
A. a little   B. a few   C. few   D. little   E. little of

Adjectives and Adverbs

17.1 Do you speak any _____ ?   86
A. foreign languages   B. languages foreign   C. languages foreigns

17.2   He ate his dinner very _____ .   **87**
        A. quick   B. quicker   C. quickly

17.3   You speak English very _____ .   **87**
        A. good   B. fluent   C. well   D. slow

17.4   Helen wants a _____ .   **88**
        A. more big car   B. car more big   C. car bigger   D. bigger car

17.5   "Do you feel better today?" "No, I feel _____ ."   **88**
        A. good   B. worse   C. more bad   D. more worse

17.6   Athens is older _____ Rome.   **89**
        A. as   B. than   C. that   D. of

17.7   I can run faster _____ .   **89**
        A. than him   B. that he can   C. than he can   D. as he can   E. as he

17.8   Tennis isn't _____ soccer.   **90**
        A. popular as   B. popular than   C. so popular that   D. as popular as

17.9   The weather today is the same _____ yesterday.   **90**
        A. as   B. that   C. than   D. like

17.10   The Best West is _____ in town.   **91**
        A. the more expensive motel   B. the most expensive motel
        C. the motel most expensive   D. the motel the more expensive

17.11   The movie is very bad. I think it's the _____ movie I've ever seen. **91**
        A. worse   B. baddest   C. most bad   D. worst   E. more worse

17.12   Why don't you buy a car? You have _____ .   **92**
        A. enough money   B. money enough   C. enough of money

17.13   Is your English _____ a conversation?   **92**
        A. enough good to have   B. good enough for have   C. enough good for
        D. good enough to have

17.14   I'm _____ out.   **93**
        A. too tired for go   B. too much tired for going   C. too tired to go
        D. too much tired to go

Word Order

18.1   Sue is interested in the news. She _____ .   **94**
        A. reads every day the newspaper   B. reads the newspaper every day
        C. every day reads the newspaper

18.2   "Do you ever take the bus to work?" "No, _____ ."   **95**
        A. I go to work always by car   B. I go always to work by car
        C. I always go to work by car   D. always I go to work by car

18.3   I'm very healthy. _____ .   **95**
        A. I am sick never   B. I am never sick   C. I never am sick   D. Never I am
        sick

18.4   "Where's Diane?" "She _____ ."   **96**
        A. isn't here yet   B. isn't here already   C. isn't here still

18.5 I locked the door and I gave _____ .
A. Liz the keys   B. to Liz the keys   C. the keys to Liz   D. the keys Liz

97

Prepositions

19.1 Goodbye! See you _____ .
A. Friday   B. at Friday   C. in Friday   D. on Friday

98

19.2 Hurry! The train leaves _____ five minutes.
A. at   B. on   C. from   D. after   E. in

98

19.3 "How long will you be away?" "_____ Monday."
A. On   B. To   C. Until   D. Till   E. Since

99

19.4 We played tennis yesterday. We played _____ two hours.
A. in   B. for   C. since   D. during

100

19.5 I always have breakfast before _____ to work.
A. I go   B. go   C. to go   D. going

100

19.6 Write your name _____ the top of the page.
A. at   B. on   C. in   D. to

101

19.7 There are a lot of apples _____ those trees.
A. at   B. on   C. in   D. to

101

19.8 What's the largest city _____ the world?
A. at   B. on   C. in   D. of

102

19.9 The office is _____ the first floor.
A. at   B. on   C. in   D. to

102

19.10 I want to go _____ Mexico next year.
A. at   B. on   C. in   D. to

103

19.11 I'm staying _____ tonight.
A. home   B. at home   C. to home   D. in home

103

19.12 What time did you arrive _____ the hotel?
A. at   B. on   C. in   D. to

103

19.13 "Where is Dennis in this picture?" "He's _____ Bob."
A. at front of   B. in the front of   C. in front of   D. in front from

104

19.14 I climbed _____ the wall and into the yard.
A. on   B. through   C. across   D. over   E. above

105

19.15 Tracy isn't at work this week. She's _____ vacation.
A. on   B. in   C. for   D. to   E. at

105

19.16 Do you like traveling _____ ?
A. with train   B. with the train   C. in train   D. on train   E. by train

106

19.17 Tina is very bad _____ writing letters.
A. on   B. with   C. at   D. in   E. for

107

19.18 Tom left without _____ goodbye.
A. say   B. saying   C. to say   D. that he said

107

19.19 I never get letters. Nobody writes _____ .
A. for me   B. to me   C. at me   D. me

108

19.20 "Do you like to eat in restaurants?" "It depends _____ the restaurant."
A. in   B. at   C. of   D. on   E. over

108

Two-Word Verbs

20.1 The car stopped and two women got _____ .
A. off   B. down   C. out   D. out of

109

20.2 It was cold, so I _____ .
A. put on my coat   B. put my coat on   C. put me my coat   D. put my coat

110

20.3 I have Diane's keys. I have to _____ to her.
A. give back they   B. give them back   C. give back them   D. give it back

110

Conjunctions and Clauses

21.1 I can't talk to you now. I'll talk to you later when _____ more time.
A. I have   B. I had   C. I'll have   D. I'm going to have

112

21.2 _____ late tomorrow, don't wait for me.
A. If I'm   B. If I'll be   C. When I'm   D. When I'll be

113

21.3 I don't know the answer. If I _____ the answer, I'd tell you.
A. know   B. would know   C. have known   D. knew

114

21.4 I like this jacket. _____ it if it weren't so expensive.
A. I buy   B. I'll buy   C. I bought   D. I'd bought   E. I'd buy

114

21.5 Amy lives in a house _____ is 100 years old.
A. who   B. that   C. which   D. what

115

21.6 The people _____ work in the office are very friendly.
A. who   B. that   C. which   D. what

115

21.7 Did you find the book _____ ?
A. who you wanted   B. that you wanted   C. what you wanted   D. you wanted

116

21.8 I met _____ can speak six languages.
A. a woman who   B. a woman which   C. a woman   D. a woman she

116

Answer Key to Exercises

In some of the exercises, you have to use your own ideas to write sentences, and sample answers are given in the key. If possible, check your answers with someone who speaks English well.

UNIT 1

1.1
2. they're
3. it's not / it isn't
4. that's
5. I'm not
6. you're not / you aren't

1.2
3. is
4. are
5. is ('s)
6. are
7. is; are
8. am ('m); is

1.3
2. brother is a teacher
3. This house isn't (is not) very big.
4. The stores aren't (are not) open today.
5. My keys are in my bag.
6. Jenny is 18 years old.

1.4
Sample answers:
1. name's (name is) Roberto
2. 'm (am) from Colombia
3. 'm (am) 26 years old
4. 'm (am) a computer programmer
5. 'm (am) not married
6. favorite colors are black and white
7. 'm (am) interested in computers

1.5
2. 're (are) cold
3. 's (is) hot
4. She's (She is) afraid.
5. They're (They are) hungry.
6. She's (She is) angry.

1.6
2. 'm (am) hungry *or* 'm not (am not) hungry
3. 's (is) warm today *or* isn't / 's not (is not) warm today
4. I'm (I am) afraid of dogs. *or* I'm not (I am not) afraid of dogs.
5. My hands are cold. *or* My hands aren't (are not) cold.
6. Canada is a very big country.

7. I'm (I am) interested in soccer. *or* I'm not (I am not) interested in soccer.
8. Tokyo isn't (is not) in China.

UNIT 2

2.1
2. f
3. h
4. c
5. a
6. e
7. b
8. d

2.2
2. Is your job interesting?
3. Are the stores open today?
4. Are you interested in sports?
5. Is the post office near here?
6. Are your children at school?
7. Why are you late?

2.3
2. Where's (Where is)
3. How old are
4. How much are
5. What's (What is)
6. Who's (Who is)
7. What color are

2.4
2. Are you married or single?
3. Are you Australian?
4. How old are you?
5. Are you a lawyer?
6. Is your wife a teacher?
7. Where is she from?
8. What's (What is) her name?
9. How old is she?

2.5
2. Yes, I am. *or* No, I'm not (I am not).
3. Yes, it is. *or* No, it isn't (is not). *or* No, it's not (it is not).
4. Yes, they are. *or* No, they aren't (are not). *or* No, they're not (they are not).
5. Yes, it is. *or* No, it isn't (is not). *or* No, it's not (it is not).
6. Yes, I am. *or* No, I'm not (I am not).

UNIT 3

3.1
2. 's waiting (is waiting)

3. 're playing (are playing)
4. He's lying (He is lying)
5. They're having (They are having)
6. She's sitting (She is sitting)

3.2
2. 's cooking (is cooking)
3. 're standing (are standing)
4. is swimming
5. 're staying (are staying)
6. 's taking (is taking)
7. 're building (are building)
8. 'm leaving (am leaving)

3.3
3. 's sitting (is sitting) on the floor
4. She isn't reading / 's not reading (is not reading) a book.
5. She isn't playing / 's not playing (is not playing) the piano.
6. She's laughing. (She is laughing.)
7. She's wearing (She is wearing) a hat.
8. She isn't writing / 's not writing (is not writing) a letter.

3.4
3. I'm sitting (I am sitting) on a chair. *or* I'm not sitting (I am not sitting) on a chair.
4. I'm eating. (I am eating.) *or* I'm not eating (I am not eating.)
5. It's raining. (It is raining.) *or* It isn't raining / 's not raining (is not raining).
6. I'm studying (I am studying) English.
7. I'm listening (I am listening) to music. *or* I'm not listening (I am not listening) to music.
8. The sun is shining. *or* The sun isn't shining (is not shining).
9. I'm wearing (I am wearing) shoes. *or* I'm not wearing (I am not wearing) shoes.
10. I'm not reading (I am not reading) a newspaper.

UNIT 4

4.1
2. Are you leaving now?
3. Is it raining?
4. Are you enjoying the movie?
5. Is that clock working?
6. Are you writing a letter?

4.2

2. is; going
3. are you eating
4. are you crying
5. are they looking at
6. is he laughing

4.3

3. Are you listening to me?
4. Where are your friends going?
5. Are your parents watching television?
6. What is Jessica cooking?
7. Why are you looking at me?
8. Is the bus coming?

4.4

2. Yes, I am. *or* No, I'm not (I am not).
3. Yes, I am. *or* No, I'm not (I am not).
4. Yes, it is. *or* No, it's not (it is not). *or* No, it isn't (is not).
5. Yes, I am. *or* No, I'm not (I am not).
6. Yes, I am. *or* No, I'm not (I am not).

UNIT 5

5.1

2. thinks
3. flies
4. dances
5. has
6. finishes

5.2

2. live
3. She eats
4. They play
5. They go
6. He sleeps

5.3

2. open
3. closes
4. teaches
5. meet
6. washes
7. costs
8. cost
9. boils
10. like; likes

5.4

2. always enjoys parties
3. Megan usually works hard.
4. Jenny always wears nice clothes.
5. We always have dinner at 6:30.
6. Mario never watches television.
7. Children usually like chocolate.
8. I often play basketball after work.

5.5

Sample answers:
2. usually read in bed
3. I often get up before 7 o'clock.
4. I never go to work by bus.

5. I always drink coffee in the morning.

UNIT 6

6.1

2. doesn't play (does not play) the piano very well
3. They don't know (do not know) my phone number.
4. We don't work (do not work) very hard.
5. He doesn't have (does not have) a car.
6. You don't do (do not do) the same thing every day.

6.2

1. doesn't like (does not like) jazz; like *or* don't like (do not like)
2. don't like (do not like) boxing; likes boxing; like boxing *or* don't like (do not like) boxing
3. Bill and Rose like horror movies.; Carol doesn't like (does not like) horror movies.; I like horror movies. *or* I don't like (do not like) horror movies.

6.3

Sample answers:
2. I don't go (do not go) to the theater very often.
3. I ride a bicycle a lot.
4. I don't eat (do not eat) in restaurants very often.
5. I never travel by train.

6.4

2. doesn't use (does not use)
3. don't go (do not go)
4. doesn't wear (does not wear)
5. don't know (do not know)
6. doesn't cost (does not cost)
7. don't see (do not see)

6.5

3. don't know (do not know)
4. doesn't talk (does not talk)
5. drinks
6. don't believe (do not believe)
7. like
8. doesn't eat (does not eat)

UNIT 7

7.1

2. Do; play tennis
3. Does; play tennis

4. Do your friends live near here?
5. Does your brother speak English?
6. Do you do yoga every morning?
7. Does Paul often travel on business?
8. Do you want to be famous?
9. Does Nicole work hard?

7.2

3. How often do you watch TV?
4. What do you want for dinner?
5. Do you like football?
6. Does your brother like football?
7. What do you do in your free time?
8. Where does your sister work?
9. Do you ever go to the movies?
10. What does this word mean?
11. Does it ever snow here?
12. What time do you usually go to bed?
13. How much does it cost to call Mexico?
14. What do you usually have for breakfast?

7.3

2. Do you like/enjoy
3. do you start
4. Do you work
5. do you get
6. does he do
7. does he teach
8. Does he enjoy/like

7.4

2. Yes, it does. *or* No, it doesn't (does not).
3. Yes, they do. *or* No, they don't (do not).
4. Yes, I do. *or* No, I don't (do not).
5. Yes, I do. *or* No, I don't (do not).

UNIT 8

8.1

2. No, she isn't / 's not (is not).; Yes, she does.; She's playing (She is playing) the piano.
3. Yes, he does.; Yes, he is.; He's washing (He is washing) a window.
4. No, they aren't / 're not (are not).; Yes, they do.; They're (They are) teachers.

8.2

2. don't (do not)
3. are
4. does
5. 's (is); don't (do not)
6. do
7. does
8. doesn't (does not)

8.3

4. is singing
5. She wants
6. do you read
7. you're sitting (you are sitting)
8. I don't understand (do not understand)
9. I'm going (I am going); Are you coming
10. does you father finish
11. I'm not listening (I am not listening)
12. He's cooking (He is cooking)
13. doesn't usually drive (does not usually drive); usually walks
14. doesn't like (does not like); she prefers

UNIT 9

9.1

2. Bill has got a headache.
3. I haven't got (have not got) any free time.
4. Have you got a watch?
5. We've got (We have got) a lot of work at the office now.
6. My brother hasn't got (has not got) a college degree.
8. You have a phone call from Japan.
9. Do you have any aspirin?
10. Sara doesn't have (does not have) much money.
11. Do your parents have any friends in Hawaii?

9.2

2. hasn't got (has not got) a bicycle; 've got (have got) a bicycle *or* haven't got (have not got) a bicycle
3. Tina has got long hair. I've got (I have got) long hair. *or* I haven't got (have not got) long hair.
4. Tina has got two brothers and two sisters.
   Sample answers:
   I've got (I have got) one brother and two sisters.
   I've got (I have got) one brother. I haven't got (have not got) any brothers or sisters.

9.3

3. have four wheels
4. has a lot of friends
5. have a toothache

6. doesn't have (does not have) a key
7. don't have (do not have) much time

9.4

3. 's (has)
4. Do
5. don't (do not)
6. got
7. have
8. doesn't (does not)
9. Have

UNIT 10

10.1

2. were; school
3. was; the airport
4. Mr. and Mrs. Hall were; the/a bus
5. Gary was; the beach
6. Sample answer: was at work

10.2

2. is; was
3. 'm (am)
4. was
5. were
6. 're (are)
7. Was
8. are; were

10.3

2. wasn't (was not); was
3. was; were
4. Were; was; wasn't (was not) *or* wasn't (was not); was
5. were
6. weren't (were not); were

10.4

2. Was your exam hard?
3. Where were Beth and Bill last week?
4. Why were you angry yesterday?
5. Was the weather nice last week?

UNIT 11

11.1

2. started; ended
3. wanted
4. happened
5. rained
6. enjoyed; stayed
7. died

11.2

2. saw
3. played
4. paid
5. visited
6. bought
7. went
8. thought
9. copied
10. knew
11. put
12. spoke

11.3

2. got
3. had
4. left
5. drove
6. arrived
7. parked
8. went
9. checked
10. had
11. waited
12. departed
13. arrived
14. took

11.4

2. lost her keys
3. met her friends
4. bought two newspapers
5. went to the movies
6. ate an apple
7. took a shower

11.5

Sample answers:
2. I met some friends for lunch.
3. I bought some shoes.
4. I visited my grandmother.

UNIT 12

12.1

2. didn't work (did not work)
3. didn't go (did not go)
4. didn't have (did not have)
5. didn't do (did not do)

12.2

2. Did you enjoy the party?
3. Did you have a nice vacation?
4. Did you finish work early?
5. Did you sleep well last night?

12.3

2. got up before 7 o'clock *or* didn't get up (did not get up) before 7 o'clock
3. I took a shower. *or* I didn't take (did not take) a shower.
4. I bought a magazine. *or* I didn't buy (did not buy) a magazine.
5. I ate meat. *or* I didn't eat (did not eat) meat.
6. I went to bed before 10:30. *or* I didn't go (did not go) to bed before 10:30.

12.4

2. did you get to work
3. Did you win?
4. did you go
5. did it cost
6. Did you go to bed late?
7. Did you have a nice time?
8. did it happen

12.5

2. bought
3. Did it rain
4. didn't stay (did not stay)
5. opened
6. didn't have (did not have)
7. did you do

UNIT 13

13.1

2. were at the supermarket; were buying food
3. was in his car; He was driving.
4. Tracy was at the station.; She was waiting for a train.
5. Mr. and Mrs. Cody were in the park.; They were walking.
6. Sample answers: was at home; I was listening to music.

13.2

2. was swimming
3. she was reading the newspaper / drinking coffee
4. she was making lunch
5. she was having breakfast
6. she was listening to music

13.3

2. What were you doing
3. Was it raining
4. Why was Ann driving
5. Was Lee wearing

13.4

2. He was carrying a bag.
3. He wasn't going (was not going) to the dentist.
4. He was eating an ice cream cone.
5. He wasn't carrying (was not carrying) an umbrella.
6. He wasn't going (was not going) home.
7. He was wearing a hat.
8. He wasn't riding (was not riding) a bicycle.

UNIT 14

14.1

1. happened; was painting; fell
2. arrived; got; were waiting
3. was walking; met; was going; was carrying; stopped

14.2

2. was studying
3. did the mail come; came; was having
4. didn't go (did not go)
5. were you driving; stopped; wasn't driving (was not driving)
6. Did your team win; didn't play (did not play)
7. did you break; were playing; hit; broke

8. Did you see; was wearing
9. were you doing
10. lost; did you get; climbed

UNIT 15

15.1

2. used to play
3. She used to be
4. They used to live
5. He used to wear glasses.
6. used to be a hotel

15.2

2. used to play volleyball
3. She used to go out a lot / three or four nights a week.
4. She used to play the guitar.
5. She used to read a lot.
6. She used to travel a lot. *or* She used to take two or three trips a year.

15.3

3. used to have
4. used to be
5. go
6. used to eat
7. watches
8. used to live
9. get *or* wake
10. did; use to play

UNIT 16

16.1

3. you ever been to Australia
4. Have you ever lost your passport?
5. Have you ever flown in a helicopter?
6. Have you ever eaten Chinese food?
7. Have you ever been to London?
8. Have you ever driven a bus?

16.2

2. has never been to Australia
3. She/Angela has eaten Chinese food a few times.
4. She/Angela has never driven a bus.
Sample answers:
5. I've never been (I have never been) to London.
6. I've played (I have played) tennis many times.
7. I've never flown (I have never flown) in a helicopter.

16.3

(Answers can be in any order.)
2. has traveled / has been all over the world
3. She has met a lot of interesting people.

4. She has done a lot of interesting things.
5. She has been married three times.
6. She has written ten books.

16.4

3. Have you ever written
4. she's never met (she has never met)
5. they've read (they have read)
6. I've never been (I have never been); my brother has been
7. She's seen (She has seen); I've never seen (I have never seen)
8. I've traveled (I have traveled)

UNIT 17

17.1

3. 've been (have been)
4. 's been (has been)
5. 've lived (have lived)
6. 's worked (has worked)
7. 's had (has had)
8. 've been studying (have been studying)

17.2

2. have they been there / in Canada
3. have; known her/Amy?
4. How long has she been studying it / studying Italian?
5. How long has he lived there / in Seattle?
6. How long have you been one / a teacher?
7. How long has it been raining?

17.3

2. 's lived (has lived) in Korea all her life
3. 've been (have been) on vacation since Sunday
4. has been shining all day / for ten minutes
5. 's been waiting (has been waiting) for ten minutes
6. 's had (has had) a beard since he was 20

17.4

2. know
3. have known
4. have you been
5. works
6. has been
7. have you lived
8. I've had
9. is; has been

UNIT 18

18.1

3. for
5. since
7. for
4. since
6. for
8. for; since

18.2

Sample answers:
2. A year ago.
3. A few days ago.
4. Two hours ago.
5. Six months ago.

18.3

3. for 20 years
4. 20 years ago
5. ten minutes ago
6. an hour ago
7. for six months
8. a few days ago

18.4

2. been here since Tuesday
3. raining for an hour
4. known her for two years
5. had it since 1999
6. been studying medicine for three years
7. been playing the piano since he was seven [years old].

18.5

Sample answers:
1. I've lived (I have lived) in . . . all my life.
2. I've never been (I have never been) to New York.
3. I've been studying (I have been studying) English for two years.
4. I've known (I have known) my friend Rick since 1998.
5. I've had (I have had) my car for seven years.

UNIT 19

19.1

2. 's closed (has closed) the door
3. 've gone (have gone) to bed
4. 's stopped (has stopped) raining
5. 's taken (has taken) a shower
6. picture has fallen down

19.2

2. I've written (I have written) them a letter.
3. She's broken (She has broken) her arm.

4. They've moved (They have moved) to Seattle.
5. I've made (I have made) a big mistake.
6. I've lost (I have lost) my wallet. Have you seen it anywhere?
7. Have you heard? Mark has gotten married!
9. Brian took my bike again without asking.
10. Did you tell your friends the good news?
11. We didn't pay (did not pay) the electric bill.

UNIT 20

20.1

2. 's just gotten/woken (has just gotten/woken) up
3. 've just bought (have just bought) a [new] car
4. has just started

20.2

2. 've already seen (have already seen)
3. 've already called (have already called) him
4. 's already gone (has already gone)
5. 've already read (have already read) it
6. 's already started (has already started) it

20.3

2. Have you told your father about the accident yet?
3. I've just eaten (I have just eaten) a big dinner, so I'm not (I am not) hungry.
4. Jenny can watch TV because she's already done (she has already done) her homework.
5. You can't go (cannot go) to bed – you haven't brushed (have not brushed) your teeth yet.
6. You can't talk (cannot talk) to Pete because he's just gone (he has just gone) home.
7. Sarah has just gotten out of the hospital, so she can't go (cannot go) to work.
9. The mailman didn't come (did not come) yet.
10. I just spoke to your sister.
11. Did Mario buy a new computer yet?

12. Ted and Alice didn't tell (did not tell) anyone they're getting married (they are getting married) yet.
13. We already did our packing for our trip.
14. I was just at the gym. *or* I just went to the gym.

20.4

2. Have; met your new neighbors yet
3. Have you written the letter yet
4. Has Jiro sold his car yet

UNIT 21

21.1

2. started it
3. arrived on Friday
4. she went out at 5 o'clock
5. I wore it yesterday

21.2

3. WRONG; I finished
4. RIGHT
5. WRONG; did you finish
6. RIGHT
7. WRONG; Jim's grandmother died
8. WRONG; were you

21.3

3. played
4. did you go
5. 's visited (has visited)
6. lived
7. wasn't (was not)
8. 's been (has been)
9. washed

21.4

1. Did you have; was
2. 's won (has won); Have you seen; I saw
3. 's had (has had); was; worked; didn't enjoy (did not enjoy)
4. 've seen (have seen); 've never spoken (have never spoken); Have you ever spoken; met

UNIT 22

22.1

3. is made from sand
4. Stamps are sold in a post office.
5. This word isn't used (is not used) very often.
6. Are we allowed to park here?
7. How is this word pronounced?
9. The house was painted last month.

10. Three people were injured in the accident.
11. My bicycle was stolen a few days ago.
12. When was this bridge built?
13. Were you invited to the party last week?
14. I wasn't woken up (was not woken up) by the noise.

22.2

2. Soccer is played in most countries of the world.
3. Why was the letter sent to the wrong address?
4. A garage is a place where cars are repaired.
5. Where were you born?
6. How many languages are spoken in Canada?
7. Somebody broke into our house, but nothing was stolen.
8. When was the bicycle invented?

22.3

3. is made
4. were damaged
5. was given
6. are shown
7. were invited
8. was made
9. was stolen; was found

22.4

2. was born in São Paulo
3. parents were born in Rio de Janeiro
Sample answers:
4. was born in Seoul
5. My mother was born in Seoul too.

UNIT 23

23.1

2. is being built
3. are being washed/cleaned
4. is being cut

23.2

3. has been broken
4. is being repaired
5. The car has been damaged.
6. The buildings are being knocked down.
7. The trees have been cut down.
8. They have been invited to a party.

23.3

3. has been / was repaired
4. was repaired
5. are made
6. were they built
7. Is the computer being used

8. are they called
9. were stolen
10. was damaged; hasn't been repaired (has not been repaired) *or* wasn't repaired (was not repaired)

UNIT 24

24.1

3. are
4. Does
5. Do
6. Is
7. do
8. Is
9. does
10. Are

24.2

2. don't (do not)
3. 'm not (am not)
4. isn't (is not)
5. don't (do not)
6. doesn't (does not)
7. 'm not (am not)
8. aren't (are not)

24.3

2. Did
3. were
4. was
5. Has
6. did
7. were
8. Has
9. did
10. have

24.4

2. was
3. Have
4. are
5. were
6. 've (have)
7. is
8. was
9. has

24.5

3. eaten
4. enjoying
5. damaged
6. use
7. gone away
8. understand
9. listening
10. pronounced
11. open

UNIT 25

25.1

3. said
4. brought
5. paid
6. enjoyed
7. bought
8. sat
9. left
10. happened
11. heard
12. put
13. caught
14. watched
15. understood

25.2

2. began; begun
3. ate; eaten
4. drank; drunk
5. drove; driven
6. ran; run
7. spoke; spoken
8. wrote; written
9. came; come
10. knew; known
11. took; taken
12. went; gone
13. gave; given
14. threw; thrown
15. got; gotten

25.3

3. slept
4. saw
5. rained
6. lost; seen
7. stolen
8. went
9. finished
10. built
11. learned
12. ridden
13. known
14. fell; hurt

25.4

2. told
3. met
4. woken up (waked up)
5. swam
6. thought
7. spoken
8. cost
9. driven
10. sold
11. flew

UNIT 26

26.1

2. is going
3. is meeting Dave [. . . at 9:30]
4. Denise is having
5. Sue and Tom are going to a party.

26.2

2. Are you working next week?
3. What are you doing tomorrow night?
4. What time are your friends coming?
5. When is Liz going on vacation?

26.3

Sample answers (answers can be in any order):
3. I'm going (I am going) away next weekend.
4. I'm playing (I am playing) basketball tomorrow.
5. I'm meeting (I am meeting) a friend this evening.
6. I'm going (I am going) to the movies on Thursday.

26.4

3. Karen is getting
4. are going; are they going
5. ends
6. I'm not going (I am not going)
7. I'm going (I am going); We're meeting (We are meeting)
8. are you getting; leaves
9. does the movie begin
10. are you doing; I'm working. (I am working.)

UNIT 27

27.1

2. I'm going (I am going) to take a bath.

3. We're going (We are going) to buy a car.
4. I'm going (I am going) to play the piano.

27.2
3. 'm going (am going) to walk
4. 's going (is going) to visit
5. 'm going (am going) to eat
6. 're going (are going) to give
7. 's going (is going) to lie down
8. Are you going to watch
9. is; going to do

27.3
2. is going to fall [down]
3. is going to turn
4. 's going (is going) to kick

27.4
Sample answers (answers can be in any order.):
1. I'm going (I am going) to call my brother this evening.
2. I'm going (I am going) to get up early tomorrow.
3. I'm going (I am going) to go to the gym after work.

UNIT 28

28.1
2. she'll be (she will be)
3. she was
4. she'll be (she will be)
5. she's (she is)
6. she was
7. she'll be (she will be)

28.2
Sample answers:
2. I'll be (I will be) at home.
3. I'll probably be (I will probably be) in bed.
4. I'll be (I will be) at work.
5. I don't know (do not know) where I'll be (I will be).

28.3
2. 'll (will)   5. 'll (will)
3. won't (will not)   6. 'll (will)
4. won't (will not)   7. won't (will not)

28.4
3. I think we'll win (we will win) the game.
4. I don't think (do not think) I'll be (I will be) here tomorrow.
5. I think Rika will like her present.

6. I don't think (do not think) they'll get married (they will get married).
7. I don't think (do not think) you'll like (you will like) the movie.

28.5
2. are you doing
3. They're leaving
4. she'll lend
5. I'm going
6. will call
7. He's working

UNIT 29

29.1
2. I'll send (I will send)
3. I'll eat (I will eat)
4. I'll sit (I will sit)
5. I'll do (I will do)
6. I'll stay (I will stay)
7. I'll show (I will show)

29.2
2. think I'll have (I will have)
3. I don't think (do not think) I'll play (I will play)
4. I don't think (do not think) I'll buy (I will buy)

29.3
2. I'll do
3. I watch
4. I'll go
5. is going to buy
6. I'll give
7. Are you doing; I'm going (I am going)
8. I'll tell
9. I'm going to do
10. I'm working
11. I'll buy

29.4
2. g	4. e	6. a	8. c
3. b	5. i	7. h	9. f

UNIT 30

30.1
2. I might see you tomorrow.
3. Sarah might forget to call.
4. It might snow today.
5. I might be late tonight.
6. Mark might not be here.
7. I might not have time to go out tonight.

30.2
2. might take a trip *or* might buy a new car *or* might shop for a new car
3. I might see her [on] Monday
4. I might have fish.
5. I might take a taxi.
6. I might buy a new car. *or* . . . take a trip.

30.3
3. might get up early
4. He's not working / He isn't working (He is not working) tomorrow.
5. He might be at home tomorrow night.
6. He might watch television.
7. He's going out (He is going out) this afternoon.
8. He might go shopping.

30.4
Sample answers (answers can be in any order):
1. I might read the newspaper.
2. I might go out with some friends.
3. I might have pancakes for breakfast.

UNIT 31

31.1
2. Can you ski?
3. Can you play chess?
4. Can you run 10 kilometers?
5. Can you drive?
6. Can you ride a horse?
7. can/can't swim (cannot swim)
8. I can/can't ski (cannot ski).
9. I can/can't play (cannot play) chess.
10. I can/can't run (cannot run) 10 kilometers.
11. I can/can't drive (cannot drive).
12. I can/can't ride (cannot ride) a horse.

31.2
2. can see
3. can't hear (cannot hear)
4. can't find (cannot find)
5. can speak

31.3
2. couldn't eat (could not eat)
3. can't decide (cannot decide)
4. couldn't find (could not find)

5. can't go (cannot go)
6. couldn't go (could not go)

31.4

2. Can/Could you pass the salt [, please]?
3. Can/Could I look at your paper [, please]?
4. Can/Could you turn off the radio [, please]?
5. Can/Could I have your phone number [, please]?
6. Can/Could I use your pen [, please]?

UNIT 32

32.1

2. must be hungry
3. must be good
4. must be very happy
5. must be for you
6. must be in the kitchen

32.2

2. must like   4. must drink
3. must have   5. must work

32.3

3. must not   5. must not   7. must
4. must   6. must not

32.4

2. must know   5. must take
3. must wear   6. must be
4. must get

32.5

3. had to   6. must
4. had to   7. mustn't (must
5. mustn't (must   not)
   not)   8. had to

UNIT 33

33.1

2. You should go
3. You should brush
4. you should visit
5. you should wear
6. You should read

33.2

2. shouldn't eat (should not eat) so much.
3. She shouldn't work (should not work) so hard.
4. He shouldn't drive (should not drive) so fast.

33.3

2. I should learn [how] to drive
3. Do you think I should get another job?
4. Do you think I should invite Scott [to my party]?

33.4

3. I think you should sell it.
4. I think she should take a trip.
5. I don't think (do not think) they should get married.
6. I don't think (do not think) you should go to work.
7. I think he should go to the doctor.
8. I don't think (do not think) we should stay here.

33.5

Sample answers:
2. should have enough food
3. people should drive carefully
4. the police should carry guns
5. exercise more

UNIT 34

34.1

2. have to take   5. has to travel
3. has to read   6. have to hit
4. have to speak

34.2

2. have to go   5. had to answer
3. had to buy   6. have to wake
4. have to change   7. have to take

34.3

2. did he have to wait
3. does she have to go
4. did you have to pay
5. do you have to do
6. did they have to leave early

34.4

2. doesn't have to wait (does not have to wait)
3. didn't have to get up (did not have to get up) early
4. doesn't have to work (does not have to work) so hard
5. don't have to leave (do not have to leave) now

34.5

Sample answers:
2. I have to cook dinner every day.
3. I have to pay my bills tomorrow.

4. I had to go to the dentist yesterday.
5. I had to take the bus to work last week.
6. I had to go to bed at 9 o'clock when I was younger.

UNIT 35

35.1

2. Would you like an apple / some fruit / a piece of fruit?
3. Would you like some / a cup of coffee?
4. Would you like some / a piece of cheese?
5. Would you like a sandwich?
6. Would you like some / a piece of cake?

35.2

2. Would you like to play tennis with me tomorrow?
3. Would you like to see my vacation pictures?
4. Would you like to go to a/the concert with me next week?
5. Would you like to borrow my umbrella?

35.3

2. Do you like
3. Would you like
4. would you like
5. Would you like
6. I like
7. would you like
8. Would you like
9. Do you like
10. I'd like

UNIT 36

36.1.

2. 'd rather read (would rather read)
3. I'd rather have (I would rather have)
4. I'd rather wait (I would rather wait)

36.2

2. would you rather have/eat it/dinner
3. would you rather have
4. would you rather watch

36.3

2. take   6. see / call / talk
3. to go   to / speak to; to
4. get/have/find   send / to write
5. carry/do

36.4

2. I'd rather be (I would rather be) a journalist / a school teacher.
3. I'd rather live (I would rather live) in a big city / in a small town.
4. I'd rather have (I would rather have) a cat / a dog.
5. I'd rather study (I would rather study) electronics / philosophy.

UNIT 37

37.1

2. Don't buy (Do not buy)
3. smile
4. Don't drink (Do not drink)
5. Turn
6. Don't sit (Do not sit)
7. don't talk (do not talk)
8. Sleep

37.2

2. let's take the bus
3. No, let's watch TV.
4. No, let's go to a restaurant.
5. No, let's wait.

37.3

3. No, let's not go out.
4. No, don't close (do not close) it / the door.
5. No, don't call (do not call) me [tonight].
6. No, let's not wait for him/Dave.
7. No, don't turn (do not turn) it on. *or* . . . the light on *or* . . . on the light
8. No, let's not take one/a taxi.

UNIT 38

38.1

3. There's (There is) a hospital.
4. There isn't / (is not) a swimming pool.
5. There are two movie theaters.
6. There isn't / (is not) a university.
7. There aren't (are not) any big hotels.

38.2

Sample answers (answers can be in any order):
3. There isn't (is not) an airport in . . . .
4. There aren't (aren't) any hotels.
5. There are four schools.
6. There's (There is) a post office.

38.3

2. There's (There is)
3. is there
4. There are
5. are there
6. there isn't (is not)
7. Is there
8. Are there
9. There's (There is); There aren't (are not)

38.4

(Answers can be in any order.)
2. There are nine planets in the solar system.
3. There are eleven players on a hockey team.
4. There are twenty-six letters in the English alphabet.
5. There are thirty days in September.
6. There are fifty states in the USA.

38.5

2. It's (It is)
3. There's (There is)
4. There's (There is); Is it
5. Is there; there's (there is)
6. It's (It is)
7. Is there

UNIT 39

39.1

2. There was a rug
3. There were three pictures
4. There was a coffee table
5. There were some flowers
6. There were some books
7. There was an armchair
8. There was a sofa

39.2

3. There was
4. Was there
5. there weren't (were not)
6. Were there
7. There wasn't (was not)
8. There was
9. there weren't (were not)

39.3

2. There are
3. There was
4. There's (There is)
5. There was *or* There has been
6. there was
7. there will be
8. there were; there are
9. There have been *or* There were *or* There are
10. there will be

UNIT 40

40.1

2. It's (It is) cold.
3. It's (It is) windy.
4. It's (It is) sunny.
5. It's (It is) snowing.
6. It's (It is) cloudy.

40.2

2. It's (It is)   6. It's (It is)
3. Is it   7. is it
4. is it; it's (it is) 8. It's (It is)
5. Is it   9. It's (It is)

40.3

2. far is it from the hotel to the beach
3. How far is it from New York to Washington?
4. How far is it from your house to the airport?

40.4

3. It   5. It   7. There
4. There   6. it   8. It

40.5

2. It's (It is) nice to see you again.
3. It's (It is) impossible to work in this office
4. It's (It is) easy to make friends.
5. It's (It is) interesting to visit different places.
6. It's (It is) dangerous to go out alone

UNIT 41

41.1

2. is   4. has   6. was
3. can   5. will

41.2

2. 'm not (am not)
3. weren't (were not)
4. haven't (have not)
5. isn't / 's not (is not)
6. hasn't (has not)

41.3

3. doesn't   6. does
   (does not)   7. don't (do not)
4. do   8. didn't (did not)
5. did

41.4

Sample answers:
2. I like sports, but my brothers don't (do not).

3. I don't eat (do not eat) meat, but my parents do.
4. I'm (I am) Mexican, but my daughter isn't (is not).
5. I haven't been (have not been) to Japan, but my son has.

41.5

2. wasn't (was not)
3. is
4. does
5. can't (can not / cannot)
6. did
7. has
8. do
9. will
10. might

41.6

Sample answers:
2. Yes, I do. *or* No, I don't (do not).
3. Yes, it is. *or* No, it isn't / it's not (it is not).
4. Yes, I do. *or* No, I don't (do not).
5. Yes, I am. *or* No, I'm not (I am not).
6. Yes, I do. *or* No, I don't (do not).
7. Yes, I will. *or* No, I won't (will not).
8. Yes, I have. *or* No, I haven't (have not).
9. Yes, I did. *or* No, I didn't (did not).
10. Yes, I was. *or* No, I wasn't (was not).

UNIT 42

42.1

2. You do?
3. You didn't (did not)?
4. She doesn't (does not)?
5. I do?
6. She did?

42.2

3. You have?
4. She can't (cannot)?
5. You were?
6. You didn't (did not)?
7. There is?
8. You're not / You aren't (you are not)?
9. You did?
10. She does?
11. You won't (will not)?
12. It isn't / 's not (is not)?

42.3

2. aren't they
3. wasn't she
4. haven't you
5. don't you
6. doesn't he
7. won't you

42.4

2. are you
3. isn't she
4. can't you
5. do you
6. didn't he
7. was it
8. doesn't she
9. will you

UNIT 43

43.1

2. either
3. too
4. too
5. either
6. either
7. too

43.2

2. So am I.
3. So have I.
4. So do I.
5. So will I.
6. So was I.
7. Neither can I.
8. Neither did I.
9. Neither have I.
10. Neither am I.
11. Neither do I.

43.3

1. So am I. *or* I'm not (I am not).
2. So can I. *or* I can't (cannot).
3. I am. *or* Neither am I.
4. So do I. *or* I don't (do not).
5. I do. *or* Neither do I.
6. So did I. *or* I didn't (did not).
7. I have. *or* Neither have I.
8. I do. *or* Neither do I.
9. So am I. *or* I'm not (I am not).
10. I was. *or* Neither was I.
11. I did. *or* Neither did I.
12. So do I. *or* I don't (do not).

UNIT 44

44.1

2. They aren't / 're not (are not) married.
3. I haven't had (have not had) dinner.
4. It isn't / 's not (is not) cold today.
5. We won't be (will not be) late.
6. You shouldn't go (should not go).

44.2

2. I don't like (do not like) cheese.
3. They don't/didn't understand (do not / did not understand).
4. He doesn't live (does not live) here.
5. Don't go (Do not go) away!
6. I didn't do (did not do) the dishes.

44.3

2. They haven't arrived (have not arrived).
3. I didn't go (did not go) to the bank.
4. He doesn't speak (does not speak) Japanese.
5. We weren't (were not) angry.

6. He won't be (will not be) pleased.
7. Don't call (Do not call) me tonight.
8. It didn't rain (did not rain) yesterday.
9. I couldn't hear (could not hear) them.
10. I don't have (do not have) a camera.

44.4

2. 'm not (am not)
3. can't (cannot)
4. doesn't (does not)
5. isn't / 's not (is not)
6. don't (do not); haven't (have not)
7. Don't (Do not)
8. didn't (did not)
9. haven't (have not)
10. won't (will not)
11. didn't (did not)
12. weren't (were not)

44.5

3. He wasn't born (was not born) in Los Angeles.
4. He doesn't like (does not like) Los Angeles.
5. He'd like (He would like) to live someplace else.
6. He can drive.
7. He hasn't traveled (has not traveled) abroad.
8. He doesn't read (does not read) newspapers.
9. He isn't / 's not (is not) interested in politics.
10. He watches TV at night.
11. He didn't watch (did not watch) TV last night.
12. He went out last night.

UNIT 45

45.1

3. Were you late [this morning]?
4. Has Anne had lunch? *or* Did Anne have lunch?
5. Will you be here [tomorrow]?
6. Is Paul going out [tonight]?
7. Do you like your job?
8. Does Nicole live near here?
9. Did you enjoy the movie/it?
10. Did you have a nice vacation/one?

45.2

2. Do you use it a lot?
3. Did you use it yesterday?
4. Do you enjoy driving?

5. Are you a good driver?
6. Have you ever had an accident? *or* Did you ever have . . . ?

45.3

3. are the children doing
4. How is cheese made?
5. Is your sister coming to the party?
6. Why don't you tell the truth?
7. Have your guests arrived yet?
8. What time does your plane leave?
9. Was you car damaged in the accident?
10. Why didn't Anne go to work?

45.4

3. What are you reading?
4. What time did she go to bed?
5. When are they going [on vacation]?
6. Where did you see him?
7. Why can't you come [to the party]?
8. How much [money] do you need?
9. Why doesn't she like you?
10. How often does it rain?
11. When did you do it / the shopping?

UNIT 46

46.1

2. fell off the shelf
3. Who wants to see
4. Who took your umbrella?
5. What made you sick?
6. Who's (Who is) coming?

46.2

3. Who did you call?
4. What happened [last night]?
5. Who knows it / the answer?
6. Who did them / the dishes?
7. What did she/Jane do?
8. What woke you [up]? *or* What was it?
9. Who saw it / the accident?
10. Who did you see?
11. Who has it / your pen?
12. What does it / the word mean?

46.3

2. Who called you?; What did she want?
3. Who did you ask?; What did he say?
4. Who got married?; Who told you?
5. Who did you meet?; What did she tell you?

6. Who won?; What did you do [after the game]?
7. Who gave you a book?; What did Catherine give you?

UNIT 47

47.1

2. are; looking for
3. Who did you go [to the movies] with?
4. What was it / the movie about?
5. Who did you give it / the money to?
6. Who was it / the book written by?

47.2

2. are they looking at
3. is he writing to
4. are they talking about
5. is she listening to
6. are they waiting for

47.3

2. Which one/hotel did you stay at?
3. Which one/club does he belong to?
4. Which one / high school did you go to?

47.4

2. What's (What is) the food like?
3. What are the people like?
4. What's (What is) the weather like?

47.5

2. What was the movie like?
3. What were the classes like?
4. What was the hotel like?

UNIT 48

48.1

3. color is it
4. What time did you
5. What type [of music] do you like?
6. What kind [of car] do you want [to buy]?

48.2

2. Which coat   4. Which bus
3. Which movie

48.3

3. Which   6. What   9. What
4. What   7. Which   10. Which
5. Which   8. Who

48.4

2. How far   4. How often/
3. How old   frequently

5. How deep   6. How long

48.5

2. How heavy is this box? *or* How much does this box weigh?
3. How old are you?
4. How much did you spend?
5. How often do you watch TV?
6. How far is it from New York to Los Angeles?

UNIT 49

49.1

2. How long does it take to get from Houston to Mexico City by car?
3. How long does it take to get from Tokyo to Kyoto by train?
4. How long does it take to get from Kennedy Airport to Manhattan by bus?

49.2

Sample answers:
2. It takes . . . hours to fly from . . . to Australia.
3. It takes . . . years to become a doctor in . . . .
4. It takes . . . minutes/hours to walk from my house to the nearest school.
5. It takes . . . minutes/hours to get from my house to the nearest airport.

49.3

2. How long did it take you to walk there / to the station?
3. How long did it take him to wash them / the windows?
4. How long did it take you to learn [to ski]?
5. How long did it take them to repair it / the car?

49.4

2. It took us 20 minutes to walk/get home.
3. It took me nine months to learn to fly / to get my pilot's license.
4. It took him two hours to get to Houston / drive there.
5. It took her a long time to find it / a job.
Sample answer:
6. It took me an hour to write a letter yesterday.

UNIT 50

50.1

2. where she/Kate is
3. I don't know (do not know) how old it / the building is.
4. I don't know (do not know) when he'll (he will) / Paul will be here.
5. I don't know (do not know) why he was angry.
6. I don't know (do not know) how long she's (she has) / Mary has lived here.

50.2

2. where Susan works
3. what Peter said
4. why he went home early
5. what time the meeting begins
6. how the accident happened

50.3

2. are you
3. they are
4. the museum is
5. do you want
6. elephants eat

50.4

2. if they're (they are) married
3. Do you know if Sue knows Bill?
4. Do you know if Justin will be here tomorrow?
5. Do you know if he passed his exam?

50.5

2. you know where Lynn is
3. Do you know if/whether she's working (she is working) today?
4. Do you know what time she starts work?
5. Do you know if/whether the banks are open tomorrow?
6. Do you know where Sarah and Tim live?
7. Do you know if/whether they went to Ji Yoo's party?

50.6

Sample answers:
2. the movie starts
3. the bus station is
4. I'm going (I am going) to do tonight
5. Tom is working today

UNIT 51

51.1

2. She said [that] she was very busy.
3. She said [that] she couldn't go (could not go) to the party.
4. He said [that] he had to go out.
5. He said [that] he was learning Russian.
6. She said [that] she didn't feel (did not feel) very well.
7. They said [that] they'd be (they would be) home late.
8. He said [that] he'd (he had) just gotten back from vacation.
9. She said [that] she was going to buy a new computer.
10. They said [that] they didn't have (did not have) a key.

51.2

2. [that] she wasn't (was not) hungry
3. [that] he needed it
4. [that] she didn't want (did not want) to go
5. [that] I could have it
6. [that] he'd send (he would send) me a postcard
7. [that] he'd gone (he had gone) home
8. [that] he wanted to watch TV
9. [that] she was going to the movies

51.3

3. said
4. told
5. tell
6. say
7. said
8. told
9. tell
10. say

UNIT 52

52.1

3. call Paul
4. call Paul
5. to call Paul
6. to call Paul
7. call Paul
8. to call Paul
9. call Paul
10. call Paul

52.2

3. get
4. going
5. watch
6. flying
7. listening
8. eat
9. waiting
10. wear
11. doing; staying

52.3

4. to go
5. rain
6. to leave
7. help
8. studying
9. to go
10. wearing
11. to stay
12. be
13. taking
14. to have
15. hear
16. go
17. listening
18. to make
19. take
20. use

UNIT 53

53.1

3. to see
4. to swim
5. cleaning
6. to go
7. visiting
8. going
9. to be
10. waiting
11. to do
12. to speak
13. to ask
14. to cry / crying
15. to work; talking

53.2

2. reading
3. to see
4. to send
5. walking
6. to lose
7. to help
8. to go
9. to watch / watching
10. to wait
11. raining
12. to cook / cooking

53.3

2. to go / going to museums
3. to write / writing letters
4. to go [there / to Rome]
5. traveling by train
6. going to / eating at; to eat at

53.4

Sample answers:
1. cooking
2. to drive
3. to have a picnic by the lake
4. to relax
5. traveling alone; I prefer to travel with somebody
6. to live in a big city

UNIT 54

54.1

2. you to listen carefully
3. want you to be angry
4. want me to wait for you
5. I don't want (do not want) you to call me tonight.
6. I want you to meet Sarah.

54.2

2. me to turn left after the bridge
3. me to help her
4. her not to call after eleven o'clock
5. me use his phone
6. her to play the piano

54.3

2. to repeat
3. wait
4. to arrive
5. to get
6. go
7. borrow
8. to tell
9. to make
10. think

UNIT 55

55.1

(Answers can be in any order.)
2. to a coffee shop to meet a friend
3. I went to the post office to get some stamps.
4. I went to the supermarket to buy some food.

55.2

2. to read the newspaper
3. to open this door
4. to get some fresh air
5. to wake him up
6. to see who it was

55.3

Sample answers:
2. to talk to you now
3. to tell her about the party
4. to do some shopping
5. to buy a car

55.4

2. to	5. to	8. to
3. to	6. for	9. for
4. for	7. to	10. to; for

55.5

2. for the film to begin
3. for it to arrive
4. for you to tell me

UNIT 56

56.1

3. to	8. on; to	12. —
4. to	9. for	13. on
5. —	10. on	14. for/to
6. for	11. to	15. on
7. to		

56.2

2. fishing
3. goes swimming
4. going skiing
5. go shopping
6. went running/jogging

56.3

2. to the bank
3. shopping
4. to bed
5. home
6. skiing
7. riding
8. for a walk
9. on vacation; to Hawaii
or to Hawaii; on vacation

UNIT 57

57.1

2. get your jacket
3. get a room
4. get the job
5. get a lot of snow
6. get a ticket
7. get a new computer
8. get the manager

57.2

2. getting dark	4. getting ready
3. getting married	5. getting late

57.3

2. get wet	6. get old
3. got married	7. got better
4. got angry	8. get nervous
5. got lost	

57.4

2. got to New York at 11:45
3. I left the party at 11:15 and got home at midnight.
Sample answer:
4. home at 7:30 and got to work at nine o'clock

57.5

2. got off   3. got out of   4. got on

UNIT 58

58.1

2. do	6. do	9. making
3. make	7. done	10. do
4. made	8. make	11. doing
5. did		

58.2

2. 're doing (are doing) [their] homework
3. 's making (is making) a dress.
4. They're doing (They are doing) [their] laundry.
5. She's making (She is making) a phone call.
6. He's making (He is making) the bed.
7. He's doing (He is doing) the dishes.
8. She's making (She is making) a list.
9. They're making (They are making) a movie.
10. He's taking (He is taking) a picture.

58.3

2. make	6. did	9. making
3. do	7. do	10. made
4. done	8. do	11. make; do
5. made		

UNIT 59

59.1

3. He doesn't (does not) have / hasn't got (has not got)
4. Eric had
5. Do you have / Have you got
6. didn't have (did not have)
7. She doesn't have (does not have) / hasn't got (has not got)
8. Did you have

59.2

2. 's having (is having) a cup of tea
3. 's having (is having) breakfast
4. 're having (are having) fun
5. He's having (He is having) a terrible flight.
6. They're having (They are having) an argument.

59.3

3. Have a good/great trip!
4. Did you have a good/nice weekend?
5. Did you have a nice/good vacation?
6. Have fun! or Have a good/great time!

59.4

2. have something to eat
3. had a glass of water
4. had a strange dream
5. had an accident
6. have a baby

UNIT 60

60.1

2. him	4. her	6. them
3. them	5. him	7. her

60.2

2. I; them	6. she; them
3. he; her	7. they; me
4. they; us	8. she; you
5. we; him	

60.3

2. him	5. don't like her
3. like it	6. Do you like them
4. you like it	

60.4

2. him   5. us   8. me
3. them   6. She   9. her
4. they   7. them   10. He; it

60.5

2. it to him   5. give it to them
3. give them to her   6. give them to us
4. give it to me

UNIT 61

61.1

2. her hands   5. their hands
3. our hands   6. your hands
4. his hands

61.2

2. their
3. live with our
4. with her parents
5. live with my
6. lives with his
7. with your parents
8. live with their parents

61.3

2. their   5. her   7. her
3. his   6. their   8. their
4. his

61.4

2. his   6. my   10. my
3. Their   7. your   11. Its
4. our   8. her   12. His; his
5. her   9. their

61.5

2. my key   5. their homework
3. Her husband   6. his name
4. your coat   7. Our house

UNIT 62

62.1

2. mine   5. theirs   7. mine
3. ours   6. yours   8. his
4. hers

62.2

2. yours   6. My; hers
3. my; Mine   7. their
4. Yours; mine   8. Ours
5. her

62.3

3. friend of hers   6. friend of his
4. friends of ours   7. friends of
5. friend of mine   yours

62.4

2. Whose camera; hers
3. Whose gloves are; 're (are) mine
4. Whose hat is this?; It's (It is) his.
5. Whose money is this?; It's (It is) yours.
6. Whose books are these?; They're (They are) ours.

UNIT 63

63.1

2. her; her name
3. know them; can't remember (cannot remember) their
4. know you; I can't remember (cannot remember) your name

63.2

2. him at his
3. them at their
4. to stay with me at my house
5. to stay with her at her house
6. to stay with you at your house

63.3

2. my; hers
3. his; him mine
4. our; us theirs
5. her; he gave her his
6. your; we gave you ours
7. their; you gave them yours

63.4

2. them   5. yours   8. their
3. him   6. us   9. mine
4. our   7. her

UNIT 64

64.1

2. myself   5. himself
3. herself   6. yourself
4. themselves   7. yourselves

64.2

2. was by himself
3. go out by yourself
4. went to the movies by myself
5. lives by herself
6. live by themselves

64.3

2. see each other
3. often write to each other
4. They don't know (do not know) each other.
5. They're sitting (They are sitting) next to each other.

6. They just gave each other a present / presents.

64.4

3. each other   7. each other
4. yourselves   8. them
5. us   9. themselves
6. ourselves

UNIT 65

65.1

3. Pedro's
4. is Julia's brother
5. Alberto is Daniel's
6. is Paul's wife
7. Blanca is Daniel's grandmother.
8. Julia is Alberto's sister.
9. Paul is Julia's husband.
10. Paul is Daniel's father.
11. Daniel is Alberto's nephew.

65.2

2. Andy's   4. Jane's   6. Alice's
3. Dave's   5. Diane's

65.3

3. OK
4. Bill's phone number
5. My brother's job
6. OK
7. OK
8. Paula's favorite color
9. your mother's birthday
10. My parents' house
11. OK
12. OK
13. Silvia's party
14. OK

UNIT 66

66.1

2. a   4. an   6. an   8. an
3. a   5. a   7. a   9. an

66.2

2. a vegetable   7. a fruit
3. a sport   8. a river
4. an airplane   9. a flower
5. a mountain   10. an insect
6. a planet

66.3

2. a sales clerk
3. an auto mechanic
4. He's an electrician.
5. She's a taxi driver.
6. She's a photographer.

7. He's an architect.
Sample answer:
8. a teacher

66.4

(Answers can be in any order.)
2. Lucia works in an office.
3. Tom never wears a hat.
4. Amy wants to learn a foreign language.
5. I can't ride (cannot ride) a bicycle.
6. Jim lives in an old house.
7. My brother is an artist.
8. Tonight I'm going (I am going) to a party.

UNIT 67

67.1

2. boats	8. sandwiches
3. women	9. families
4. cities	10. feet
5. umbrellas	11. holidays
6. addresses	12. potatoes
7. knives	

67.2

2. teeth	4. children	6. leaves
3. people	5. fish	

67.3

3. . . . a lot of beautiful trees
4. . . . with two men
5. OK
6. . . . has three children
7. . . . my friends are students
8. . . . his pajamas . . .
9. OK
10. . . . many people . . .
11. . . . your pants; . . . get them
12. . . . full of tourists
13. OK
14. These scissors aren't (are not) . . .

67.4

2. are	7. Do
3. don't (do not)	8. are
4. watch	9. them
5. were	10. some
6. live	

UNIT 68

68.1

3. tea	8. money
4. a teapot	9. a wallet
5. toothpaste	10. sand
6. a toothbrush	11. a bucket
7. an egg	12. an envelope

68.2

3. . . . a hat
4. . . . a job
5. OK
6. . . . eats an apple . . .
7. . . . to a concert . . .
8. . . . a beautiful day
9. . . . is an island
10. . . . need a key
11. OK
12. . . . a good idea
13. . . . drive a car
14. . . . a cup of tea
15. OK
16. . . . without a coat

68.3

2. a piece of wood
3. a glass of water
4. a bottle of juice
5. a cup of coffee
6. a piece of paper
7. a bowl of soup
8. a can of beans
9. a jar of honey

UNIT 69

69.1

2. a newspaper, some flowers, and a pen
3. I bought some / a loaf of bread, some post cards, and some stamps.
4. I bought some / a tube of toothpaste, some / a bar of soap, and a comb.

69.2

2. some coffee
3. you like a cookie / some cookies
4. Would you like some bread?
5. Would you like a sandwich?
6. Would you like some candy / a piece of candy?

69.3

2. some; some	6. a; a; some
3. some	7. some
4. a; some	8. some
5. an; some	9. some; a

69.4

2. eyes	6. furniture
3. hair	7. job
4. information	8. wonderful weather
5. chairs	

UNIT 70

70.1

3. a	7. a; a
4. the	8. a; a
5. an	9. a; a; an; the; The
6. the	10. a; a; The; the; a; a

70.2

2. the airport	5. the radio
3. a cup	6. the floor
4. a; picture	

70.3

2. . . . send me a postcard
3. . . . the name of this town
4. . . . a very big country
5. . . . the largest city . . .
6. . . . the color of the ceiling
7. . . . a headache
8. . . . an old house near the station
9. . . . the name of the director of the movie . . .

UNIT 71

71.1

3. . . . the second floor
4. . . . to the moon
5. . . . the best hotel . . .
6. OK
7. . . . the football stadium
8. . . . at the end of May
9. OK
10. . . . the first time . . .
11. OK
12. . . . the biggest city . . .
13. OK
14. . . . on the top shelf on the right
15. . . . in the country . . . from the nearest town

71.2

2. the same time
3. the same age
4. the same color
5. the same problem

71.3

2. the guitar	5. TV/television
3. breakfast	6. the ocean
4. the radio/music	

71.4

2. the name	6. the capital
3. The sky	7. lunch
4. television	8. the middle
5. The police	

UNIT 72

72.1

2. the movies   5. home
3. the hospital   6. jail/prison
4. the airport

72.2

3. school   6. bed
4. the station   7. the post office
5. home

72.3

2. the theater / movie theater
3. go to bed
4. go to jail/prison
5. go to the dentist
6. go to college
7. go to the hospital

72.4

3. to the doctor   9. OK
4. OK   10. At the station
5. OK   11. in the hospital
6. OK   12. OK
7. in the bank   13. OK
8. OK   14. to the theater

UNIT 73

73.1

Sample answers (answers can be in any order):
2. I don't like (do not like) dogs.
3. I don't mind (do not mind) loud music.
4. I love big cities.
5. I like basketball.
6. I love TV quiz shows.
7. I don't like (do not like) computer games.
8. I don't mind (do not mind) hard work.

73.2

Sample answers:
2. 'm not (am not) interested in politics
3. I'm (I am) interested in sports.
4. I don't know (do not know) much about art.
5. I don't know (do not know) anything about astronomy.
6. I know a little about economics.

73.3

3. friends   6. the milk
4. parties   7. milk
5. The stores   8. football

9. computers   16. pictures
10. The water   17. the pictures
11. cold water   18. English;
12. the salt   international
13. the people   business
14. Vegetables 19. Money;
15. the words   happiness

UNIT 74

74.1

3. Sweden
4. The Amazon
5. Asia
6. The Pacific
7. The Rhine
8. Kenya
9. The United States
10. The Andes
11. Bangkok
12. The Himalayas
13. The Mediterranean
14. Jamaica
15. The Bahamas

74.2

3. OK
4. the Philippines
5. the Westside Cineplex
6. OK
7. the Museum of Modern Art
8. the Washington Monument
9. the east; the west
10. OK
11. the Mississippi; the Nile
12. the Park Hotel
13. OK
14. The Rocky Mountains
15. OK
16. The Panama Canal; the Atlantic Ocean; the Pacific Ocean
17. the United States
18. the University of Michigan

UNIT 75

75.1

2. that house   5. this chair
3. these postcards 6. These dishes
4. those birds

75.2

2. Is that your umbrella?
3. Is this your book?
4. Are those your books?
5. Is that your bike?
6. Are these your keys?
7. Are those your keys?
8. Is this your watch?

9. Are those your glasses?
10. Are these your gloves?

75.3

2. that's (that is)   6. this is
3. This is   7. That's (That is)
4. That's (That is) 8. that's (that is)
5. that

UNIT 76

76.1

2. need one
3. I'm going (I am going) to buy one
4. I don't have (do not have) one
5. I just had one.
6. there's (there is) one on First Avenue

76.2

2. a new/better one
3. a better one
4. an old / a different one
5. a big one
6. a different/new one

76.3

2. ones; brown
3. Which one?; The one . . . a/the red door
4. Which one?; The black one.
5. Which one?; The one on the wall.
6. Which ones?; The ones on the top shelf.
7. Which one?; The tall one with long hair.
8. Which ones?; The yellow ones.
9. Which one?; The one with a/the moustache and glasses.
10. Which ones?; The ones I took at the beach last week.

UNIT 77

77.1

2. some 6. some 10. any; any
3. any   7. any   11. some; any
4. any   8. some 12. some
5. any   9. some

77.2

2. some letters 6. some milk
3. any pictures 7. any batteries
4. any . . .   8. some . . . air
   languages 9. some fruit
5. some friends 10. any help

77.3

3. I have some
4. I don't have (do not have) any

5. I didn't buy (did not buy) any
6. I bought some

77.4

2. something
3. anything
4. anything
5. Somebody
6. anything
7. anybody
8. something
9. anything
10. anybody

UNIT 78

78.1

2. no stores near here
3. Carol has no free time.
4. There's (There is) no light in this room.
6. There isn't (is not) any gas in the car.
7. There aren't (are not) any buses today.
8. Marcos doesn't have (does not have) any brothers or sisters.

78.2

2. any
3. any
4. no
5. any
6. no
7. any
8. no
9. any
10. no
11. None
12. any

78.3

2. no money
3. any questions
4. no friends
5. no difference
6. any furniture
7. no answer
8. any air conditioning
9. any photographs; no film

78.4

Sample answers:
2. One.
3. Three cups.
4. None.
5. None.

UNIT 79

79.1

2. nobody / no one in the office
3. have nothing to do
4. There's (There is) nothing on TV.
5. There was nobody / no one at home.
6. We found nothing.

79.2

2. anybody/anyone on the bus
3. I don't have (do not have) anything to read.
4. I don't have (do not have) anybody/anyone to help me.
5. Sarai didn't hear (did not hear) anything.
6. We don't have (do not have) anything for dinner.

79.3

3a. Nothing.
4a. Nobody / No one.
5a. Nobody / No one.
6a. Nothing.
7a. Nothing.
8a. Nobody / No one.
3b. want anything
4b. didn't meet (did not meet) anybody/anyone
5b. Nobody / No one knows
6b. I didn't buy (did not buy) anything.
7b. Nothing happened.
8b. Nobody / No one was late.

79.4

3. anything
4. Nobody / No one
5. Nothing
6. anything
7. anybody/anyone
8. nothing
9. anything
10. anything
11. nobody / no one
12. anything
13. Nothing
14. Nobody / No one; anybody/anyone

UNIT 80

80.1

2. something
3. somewhere
4. somebody/someone

80.2

2a. Nowhere.
3a. Nothing.
4a. Nobody / No one.
2b. going anywhere
3b. I don't want (do not want) anything.
4b. I'm not looking (I am not looking) for anybody/anyone.

80.3

3. anything
4. anything
5. somebody/someone
6. something
7. anybody/anyone; nobody / no one

8. anything
9. Nobody / No one
10. anybody/anyone
11. Nothing
12. anywhere
13. somewhere
14. anything
15. anybody/anyone

80.4

2. anything to eat
3. nothing to do
4. anywhere to sit
5. something to drink
6. nowhere to stay
7. something to read
8. somewhere to play

UNIT 81

81.1

2. Every day
3. every time
4. Every room
5. every word

81.2

2. every day
3. all day
4. every day
5. all day
6. every day
7. all day / every day

81.3

2. every
3. all
4. all
5. Every
6. all
7. every
8. all
9. every

81.4

2. everything
3. Everybody
4. everything
5. everywhere
6. Everybody
7. everywhere
8. Everything

81.5

2. is
3. likes
4. has
5. was
6. makes

UNIT 82

82.1

3. Some
4. Most of
5. some
6. any of
7. all / all of
8. None of
9. any of
10. Most
11. most of
12. Some
13. All / All of
14. some of
15. most of

82.2

2. All of them.
3. Some of them.
4. None of them.
5. Most of them.
6. None of it.

82.3

3. Some people
4. Some questions / Some of the questions
5. OK
6. All insects
7. OK
8. Most students / Most of the students
9. OK
10. most of the night

UNIT 83

83.1

3. Both
4. Neither
5. Neither
6. both
7. Either
8. neither of

9. Neither
10. either of
11. Both
12. neither of
13. Both
14. either of

83.2

2. Both windows
3. Neither man is
4. Both people have

5. Both buses go
6. Neither answer is

83.3

3. Both of them are
4. Neither of them has
5. Both of them live in Boston.
6. Both of them like to cook.
7. Neither of them can play the piano.
8. Both of them read the newspaper.
9. Neither of them is interested in sports.

UNIT 84

84.1

2. many
3. much
4. many
5. many

6. much
7. much
8. many

9. How many
10. How much
11. How much
12. How many

84.2

2. much time
3. many countries
4. many people

5. much luggage
6. many times

84.3

2. a lot of interesting things
3. a lot of accidents

4. a lot of fun
5. a lot of traffic

84.4

3. a lot of snow
4. OK
5. a lot of money

6. OK
7. OK
8. a lot

84.5

3. plays tennis a lot
4. doesn't use (does not use) his car much
5. He doesn't go (does not go) out much.
6. She travels a lot.

UNIT 85

85.1

2. a few
3. a little

4. a few
5. a little

6. a few

85.2

2. a little milk
3. A few days
4. a little Russian
5. a few friends

6. a few times
7. a few chairs
8. a little fresh air

85.3

2. very little coffee
3. very little rain
4. very few hotels
5. very little time
6. Very few people
7. very little work

85.4

2. A few
3. a little

4. very little
5. very few

6. a little
7. very little

85.5

2. a little luck
3. a few things
4. OK

5. a few questions
6. few people

UNIT 86

86.1

2. I like that green jacket.
3. Do you like classical music?
4. I had a wonderful trip.
5. We went to a Chinese restaurant.

86.2

2. dark clouds
3. long vacation
4. hot water

5. fresh air
6. sharp knife
7. dangerous job

86.3

2. looks new
3. feel sick/terrible
4. look surprised

5. smell nice
6. tastes terrible

86.4

2. doesn't look (does not look) new
3. don't sound (do not sound) American
4. don't feel (do not feel) cold
5. don't look (do not look) heavy
6. doesn't taste (does not taste) good

UNIT 87

87.1

2. badly
3. quietly

4. angrily
5. fast

6. early

87.2

2. Come quickly
3. work hard
4. sleep well
5. win easily

6. Think carefully
7. know; well
8. explain; clearly/well

87.3

2. angry
3. slowly
4. slow

5. careful
6. hard
7. suddenly

8. quiet
9. badly
10. nice

87.4

2. well
3. good

4. well
5. well

6. good; good

UNIT 88

88.1

2. bigger
3. slower
4. more expensive

5. higher
6. more dangerous

88.2

2. stronger
3. happier
4. more modern
5. more important
6. better

7. larger
8. more serious
9. prettier
10. more crowded

88.3

2. hotter
3. more expensive
4. worse

5. farther
6. harder / more difficult

88.4

3. taller
4. harder
5. more comfortable
6. better
7. nicer
8. heavier

9. more interested
10. warmer
11. better
12. bigger
13. more beautiful
14. sharper
15. more polite

UNIT 89

89.1

3. taller than Ben
4. work earlier than
5. works harder than Liz

6. more money than Liz
7. better driver than Ben
8. is more patient than Liz
9. is a better dancer than Liz
10. is more intelligent than Ben
11. speaks French better than Ben
12. goes to the movies more than Liz

89.2

2. older than her / she is
3. harder than me / I do
4. watch TV more than him / he does
5. 're a better cook than me / I am
6. know more people than us / we do
7. have more money than them / they do
8. run faster than me / I can
9. 've been (have been) here longer than her / she has
10. got up earlier than them / they did
11. were more surprised than him / he was

89.3

2. is much younger than his father
3. cost a little more than yours
4. much better than yesterday
5. a little warmer than yesterday
6. is a much better tennis player than me / I am

UNIT 90

90.1

2. longer than; as long as
3. heavier than; not as heavy as B
4. older than C; not as old as B *or* younger than B; not as young as C
5. more money than C but not as much [money] as A
6. harder than A but not as hard as B

90.2

2. as big as mine
3. get up as early as you / you did
4. didn't play (did not play) as well as us / we did
5. haven't been (have not been) here as long as me / I have
6. isn't (is not) as nervous as her / she is

90.3

2. as   5. as   7. as
3. than   6. than   8. than
4. than

90.4

2. on the same street as Kim
3. at the same time as Ed
4. car is the same color as Kim's

UNIT 91

91.1

2. longer than; the longest; is the shortest
3. is younger than C; B is the youngest.; C is the oldest.
4. D is more expensive than A.; C is the most expensive.; A is the cheapest.
5. A is better than C.; A is the best.; D is the worst.

91.2

2. the happiest day
3. the best movie
4. the most popular singer
5. the worst mistake
6. the prettiest city
7. the coldest day
8. the most boring person

91.3

2. is the largest country in South America
(Answers 3–6 can be in any order.)
3. Everest is the highest mountain in the world.
4. Jupiter is the largest planet in the solar system.
5. The Nile is the longest river in Africa / the world.
6. Sydney is the largest city in Australia.

UNIT 92

92.1

2. enough chairs   4. enough wind
3. enough paint

92.2

2. isn't (is not) big enough
3. aren't (are not) long enough
4. isn't (is not) strong enough

92.3

3. old enough   7. practice
4. enough time   enough
5. big enough   8. enough fruit
6. eat enough   9. tired enough

92.4

2. sharp enough to cut
3. warm enough to go
4. enough bread to make
5. well enough to win
6. enough time to read

UNIT 93

93.1

2. too heavy   5. too big
3. too low   6. too crowded
4. too fast

93.2

3. enough   8. enough
4. too many   9. too
5. too   10. too many
6. enough   11. too much
7. too much

93.3

3. too far
4. 's (is) too expensive
5. isn't (is not) big enough
6. was too hard
7. isn't (is not) good enough
8. 'm (am) too busy
9. was too long

93.4

2. too early to go to bed
3. too young to get married
4. too dangerous to swim here
5. too late to call [her]
6. too surprised to say anything

UNIT 94

94.1

3. I like this picture very much.
4. Tom started his new job last week.
5. OK
6. April bought a present for her friend *or* her friend a present
7. I drink three cups of coffee every day.
8. OK
9. I borrowed fifty dollars from my brother.

94.2

2. wrote two letters this morning
3. The thief entered the house quietly.
4. Megan doesn't speak (does not speak) French very well.
5. I did a lot of work yesterday.
6. Do you know Mary well?
7. We enjoyed the party very much.
8. I explained the problem carefully.
9. We met some friends at the airport.
10. Did you buy that jacket in Canada?

11. We do the same thing every day.
12. I don't like (do not like) football very much.

94.3

2. arrived at the hotel early
3. goes to Puerto Rico every year
4. have lived here since 1998
5. was born in Montreal in 1980
6. didn't go (did not go) to work yesterday
7. went to the bank yesterday afternoon
8. had breakfast in bed this morning
9. is going to college next September
10. saw a beautiful bird in the yard this morning
11. parents have been to Tokyo many times
12. left my umbrella in the restaurant last night
13. you going to the movies tomorrow
14. took the children to school this morning

UNIT 95

95.1

2. always gets up early
3. is never late for work
4. He sometimes gets angry.
5. He rarely goes swimming.
6. He's (He is) usually home in the evening.

95.2

2. is always polite
3. just started a new job
4. I rarely go to bed before midnight.
5. The bus isn't (is not) usually late.
6. I don't often eat (do not often eat) fish.
7. I will never forget what you said.
8. Have you ever lost your passport?
9. Do you still work in the same place?
10. They always stay at the same hotel.
11. Diane doesn't usually work (does not usually work) on Saturday.
12. Is Tina already here?
13. What do you usually have for breakfast?
14. I can never remember his name.

95.3

2. also speak Russian
3. I'm (I am) also hungry

4. and I've also been (I have also been) to Ireland
5. Yes, and I also bought some books.

95.4

1. both play; both; They both have
2. 're (are) all; were all born in; They all live in Toronto.

UNIT 96

96.1

2. still have an old car
3. you still a student
4. Are you still studying Japanese?
5. Do you still go to the movies a lot?
6. Do you still want to be a teacher?

96.2

2. looking for a job; is still looking for a job; He hasn't found (has not found) a job
3. was sleeping; She's still sleeping (She is still sleeping).; She hasn't woken up / gotten up (has not woken up / gotten up) yet.
4. were having/eating dinner; They are still having/eating dinner.; They haven't finished (have not finished) dinner/eating yet.

96.3

2. Is; here yet *or* Has; arrived yet
3. Have; gotten the report yet *or* Did; get the report yet
4. Have you decided where to go yet? *or* Do you know where you're going (you are going) yet?

96.4

3. ['s (has)] already left
4. already have *or* 've (have) already got
5. ['ve (have)] already paid it
6. already knows [about it]

UNIT 97

97.1

2. it to Gary
3. gave them to Andy
4. He gave it to his sister.
5. He gave them to Mi Ja.
6. He gave it to his neighbor.

97.2

2. Mika a plant
3. gave Alan a tie
4. I gave Diane [some] candy.

5. I gave Lynn [some] flowers.
6. I gave Carlos a pen.

97.3

2. lend me an/your umbrella
3. you give me; address
4. Can you lend me ten dollars?
5. Can you send me some information?
6. Can you show me the letter?
7. Can you get me some stamps?

97.4

2. lend you some money
3. send the letter to me
4. buy you a present
5. pass me the sugar
6. give it to her
7. the officer my driver's license

UNIT 98

98.1

2. at	5. in	8. in
3. in	6. in	9. at
4. at	7. at	10. in; at

98.2

3. at	8. on	12. on
4. in	9. at	13. at
5. on	10. in	14. at
6. in	11. on	15. in
7. on		

98.3

3. B	7. B	10. A
4. A	8. B	11. B
5. both	9. both	12. both
6. A		

98.4

2. call you in three days
3. exam is in two weeks / fourteen days
4. will be here in half an hour / thirty minutes

UNIT 99

99.1

2. until
3. since 1990
4. Korea until 2001
5. Australia since 2001
6. in a hotel from; to 2000
7. in a restaurant since 2000
8. teacher from 1995 to 1999
9. a salesman since 1999
11. for ___ years

12. lived in Australia for ___ years
13. in a hotel for one year
14. has worked in a restaurant for ___ years
15. was a teacher for four years
16. has been a salesman for ___ years

99.2

2. until	7. for	11. for
3. for	8. until	12. until
4. Since	9. since	13. Since
5. Until	10. until	14. for
6. for		

UNIT 100

100.1

2. after lunch
3. before the end
4. during the course
5. before they went to Australia
6. during the night
7. while you're waiting (you are waiting)
8. after the concert

100.2

3. while	6. during	9. during
4. for	7. while	10. while
5. while	8. for	

100.3

2. eating   5. finishing/doing
3. answering   6. going/traveling
4. taking

100.4

2. in a department store for two years after finishing high school
3. going to sleep, I read for a few minutes
4. walking for three hours, we were very tired
5. have a cup of coffee before going out

UNIT 101

101.1

2. In the box.	7. On the balcony.
3. On the box.	8. In the pool.
4. On the wall.	9. At the window.
5. At the bus stop.	10. On the ceiling.
	11. On the table.
6. In the field.	12. At the table.

101.2

2. in	4. in	6. at	8. in
3. on	5. on	7. in	9. at

10. at	12. at	14. at	
11. in	13. on	15. on; in	

UNIT 102

102.1

2. At the airport.	8. On the second floor.
3. In bed.	
4. On a boat.	9. At work.
5. In the sky.	10. On a plane.
6. At a party.	11. In a taxi.
7. At the doctor's.	12. At a wedding.

102.2

2. in	6. in	10. in	14. in
3. in	7. in	11. on	15. on
4. at	8. at	12. on	16. at
5. at/—	9. in	13. at	

UNIT 103

103.1

2. to	4. to	6. to	8. in
3. in	5. in	7. to	

103.2

3. to	6. at	9. at
4. to	7. —	10. in/at; to
5. —; to	8. to	

103.3

2. to	6. to	9. to	12. to; —
3. to	7. at	10. at	13. —
4. in	8. to	11. at	14. at; to
5. to			

103.4

1. to 2. — 3. at 4. in 5. to 6. —

103.5

Sample answers:
2. to work   4. to Europe
3. at work   5. at a friend's house

UNIT 104

104.1

2. next to / by	6. in back of
3. in front of	7. on the
4. between	8. on the
5. next to / by	9. in the

104.2

2. in back of	8. above
3. above	9. under
4. in front of	10. next to / by
5. on	11. across from
6. next to / by	12. on
7. below/under	

104.3

2. fountain is in front of the theater
3. The bank is across from the theater. *or* The theater/fountain is across from the bank.
4. The bank/supermarket is next to the bookstore. *or* The bookstore is next to the bank/supermarket.
5. Paul's office is above the bookstore.
6. The bookstore / Paul's office is between the bank and the supermarket.

UNIT 105

105.1

2. under	7. Go past the hotel.
3. Go up	8. Go out of the hotel.
4. Go down	9. Go over the
5. Go along	bridge.
6. Go into	10. Go through the
the hotel.	park.

105.2

2. off	6. around	9. around
3. over	7. through	10. into;
4. out of	8. on	through
5. across		

105.3

1. out of	5. around
2. around	6. on
3. in	7. over/across
4. from; to	8. out of

UNIT 106

106.1

2. on time	4. on the phone
3. on vacation	5. on TV

106.2

2. by	5. on	7. on
3. with	6. by	8. about; by
4. about		

106.3

1. with	7. on	12. by
2. without	8. with	13. on
3. by	9. at	14. with
4. about	10. by	15. by
5. at	11. about	16. by
6. by		

UNIT 107

107.1

2. in   3. to   4. at   5. of

107.2

2. at   6. of   10. about
3. to   7. from/than   11. of
4. about   8. in   12. at
5. of   9. for

107.3

2. interested in going
3. good at getting
4. tired of waiting
5. Thank you for waiting.

107.4

2. past me without speaking
3. do anything without asking me first
4. went out without locking the door

107.5

Sample answers:
2. afraid of the dark
3. very good at drawing
4. I'm not interested (I am not interested) in cars.
5. I'm tired (I am tired) of cooking every day.

UNIT 108

108.1

2. to   3. for   4. to   5. at   6. for

108.2

2. to   9. on   15. to
3. of   10. to   16. on
4. to   11. at   17. about/of
5. for   12. for   18. at
6. for   13. to   19. of
7. about/of   14. —   20. for
8. for

108.3

3. on the program *or* [on] what's (what is) on
4. depends [on] what it is
5. It depends on the weather.
6. It depends [on] how much [you need].

UNIT 109

109.1

2. went in   6. got off
3. looked up   7. sat down
4. rode away   8. got out
5. turned around

109.2

2. away   4. out; back   6. around
3. around   5. down   7. back

8. in   9. up   10. away; back

109.3

2. slowed down   6. broken down
3. gave up   7. work out
4. takes off   8. Hurry up
5. speak up   9. get along

UNIT 110

110.1

2. took off her hat *or* took her hat off
3. put down her bag *or* put her bag down
4. picked up the magazine *or* picked the magazine up
5. put on his sunglasses *or* put his sunglasses on
6. turned off the faucet *or* turned the faucet off

110.2

2. put his jacket on; put it on
3. gave back the keys; I gave them back.
4. She took her hat off.; She took it off.
5. Put your pens down.; Put them down.
6. I turned off the lights.; I turned them off.

110.3

2. take/bring it back
3. picked them up
4. turned it off
5. bring them back

110.4

3. a glass over *or* over a glass
4. it up
5. them away
6. it out
7. on some shoes *or* some shoes on
8. me around
9. it up
10. your cigarette out *or* out your cigarette

UNIT 111

111.1

(Answers can be in any order.)
3. went to the window and looked out
4. I wanted to call you, but I didn't have (did not have) your number.
5. I jumped into the river and swam to the other side.

6. I usually drive to work, but I took the bus this morning.
7. Do you want me to come with you, or should I wait here?

111.2

2. because it rained / was raining *or* because the weather was bad
3. but it was closed
4. so he didn't eat (did not eat) [anything] *or* so he didn't have (did not have) anything to eat
5. because there was a lot of traffic *or* because the traffic was bad *or* so she apologized *or* so she said she was sorry
6. goodbye, got in/into her car, and drove away

111.3

Sample answers:
3. I went to the movies, but the tickets were sold out.
4. I called my friend in France and talked for an hour.
5. There was nothing good on TV, so I went to bed early.
6. I got up in the middle of the night because I couldn't sleep (could not sleep).

UNIT 112

112.1

(Answers can be in any order.)
2. When I'm (I am) tired, I like to watch TV.
3. When I called her, there was no answer.
4. When I go on vacation, I always go to the same place.
5. When the program was over, I turned off the TV.
6. When I got to the hotel, there were no rooms.

112.2

2. when they heard the news
3. they went to live in New Zealand
4. while they were away
5. before they came here
6. somebody broke into the house
7. they didn't believe (did not believe) me

112.3

2. I finish
3. it's
4. I'll be; she leaves

5. stops
6. We'll come; we're (we are)
7. I come; I'll bring
8. I'm
9. I'll give; I go

112.4

Sample answers:
2. you finish school
3. I'll go (I will go) to the dentist
4. you get ready
5. I won't have (will not have) much free time
6. I get back

UNIT 113

113.1

2. the driving test, you'll get (you will get) your license
(Answers 3–8 can be in any order.)
3. you fail the driving test, you can take it again
4. If you don't want (do not want) this magazine, I'll throw (I will throw) it away.
5. If you want those pictures, you can have them.
6. If you're (you are) busy now, we can talk later.
7. If you're (you are) hungry, we can have lunch now.
8. If you need money, I can lend you some.

113.2

2. I give
3. is
4. I'll call
5. I'll be; get
6. Will you go; they invite

113.3

Sample answers:
3. the water is cold
4. you'll feel (you will feel) better in the morning
5. you're not watching (you are not watching) it
6. she doesn't practice (does not practice)
7. I'll call (I will call) Chris
8. it doesn't rain (does not rain)

113.4

2. When   5. if   7. if
3. If   6. When   8. when; if
4. If

UNIT 114

114.1

3. wanted   7. could
4. had   8. spoke
5. were/was   9. didn't have
6. didn't enjoy   (did not have)
   (did not enjoy)

114.2

2. I'd go (I would go)
3. she knew
4. we had
5. you won
6. I wouldn't stay (would not stay)
7. we lived
8. It would be
9. the salary were/was
10. I wouldn't know (would not know)
11. would you change

114.3

2. I'd watch (I would watch) it
3. we had some pictures on the wall
4. the air would be cleaner
5. every day were / was the same
6. I'd be (I would be) bored
7. we had/bought a bigger house
8. we could buy a bigger house

114.4

Sample answers:
2. I'd go (I would go) to Antarctica
3. I didn't have (did not have) my friends
4. I had enough money
5. I'd call (I would call) the police
6. there were no guns

UNIT 115

115.1

2. who sells meat
3. is a person who plays music
(Answers 4–8 can be in any order.)
4. A patient is a person who is seeing a doctor.
5. A dentist is a person who takes care of your teeth.

6. A fool is a person who does stupid things.
7. A genius is a person who is very intelligent.
8. A liar is a person who doesn't tell (does not tell) the truth.

115.2

2. who opened the door was wearing
3. who took the exam passed [it]
4. police officer who stopped our car wasn't (was not) very friendly

115.3

2. who   5. who   8. who
3. which   6. which   9. which
4. which   7. who

115.4

3. a machine that/which makes
4. OK (*which* is also correct)
5. people who/that never stop
6. OK (*who* is also correct)
7. OK (*that* is also correct)
8. the sentences that/which are

UNIT 116

116.1

2. pen you gave me
3. jacket Sue is wearing
4. flowers I gave you
5. didn't believe (did not believe) the story he told us
6. much were the oranges you bought

116.2

2. meal you cooked was excellent
3. I'm wearing (I am wearing) aren't (are not) very comfortable
4. people we invited to dinner didn't come (did not come)

116.3

2. you spoke to
3. keys you were looking for
4. house they live in
5. map I looked at
6. the chair I was sitting on
7. The bus we were waiting for
8. the man Nicole is dancing with

116.4

2. where you had dinner
3. the town where you live
4. the factory where you work

Answer Key to Additional Exercises

1

3. Kate is a doctor.
4. The children are asleep.
5. Bill isn't hungry.
6. The books aren't (are not) on the table.
7. The hotel is near the station.
8. The bus isn't crowded.

2

3. she's (she is)
4. Where are
5. Is he
6. It's (It is)
7. I'm (I am) *or* I'm not (I am not). I'm (I am)
8. What color is
9. Is it
10. Are you
11. How much are

3

3. He's taking (He is taking) a bath
4. Are the children playing?
5. Is it raining?
6. They're coming (They are coming) now.
7. Why are you standing here? I'm waiting (I am waiting) for somebody.

4

4. Chris doesn't want (does not want)
5. Do you want
6. Does Amy live
7. Sarah knows
8. I don't travel (do not travel)
9. do you usually get up
10. They don't go out (do not go out)
11. Adam always leaves
12. does Kim do; She works

5

3. She's (She is) a student.
4. She doesn't have (does not have) a car.
5. She goes out a lot.
6. She has a lot of friends.
7. She doesn't like (does not like) Toronto.
8. She likes to dance.
9. She isn't / 's not (She is not) interested in sports.

6

1. Are you; do you live; Do you have; old is she
2. How old are you; What do you do; Do you like; Do you have; Do you drive
3. What's (What is) his name; What does he do; Does he live

7

4. is 32 years old
5. He has six sisters.
6. We often watch TV at night.
7. Amy never wears a hat.
8. My car has a flat tire. *or* My car's got (car has got) a flat tire.
9. These flowers are beautiful.
10. Mary speaks German very well.

8

3. are you cooking
4. plays
5. I'm leaving (I am leaving)
6. It's raining (It is raining).
7. I don't watch (do not watch)
8. we're looking (we are looking)
9. do you pronounce

9

2. we go
3. is shining
4. are you going
5. do you take
6. She writes
7. I never read
8. They're watching
9. She's talking
10. do you usually have
11. He's visiting
12. I don't drink

10

2. went
3. found
4. was
5. had/took
6. told
7. gave
8. were
9. thought
10. invited/asked

11

3. was good at sports
4. He played basketball.
5. He didn't work (did not work) hard in school.
6. He had a lot of friends.

7. He didn't have (did not have) a bicycle.
8. He wasn't (was not) a quiet child.

12

3. How long were you
4. Did you like
5. Where did you stay
6. Was the weather
7. When did you get

13

3. I forgot.
4. did you get
5. I didn't speak (did not speak)
6. Did you have
7. he didn't go (did not go)
8. she got
9. did Bob live
10. The meal didn't cost (did not cost)

14

2. were working
3. opened
4. rang; was cooking
5. heard; looked
6. was looking; happened
7. wasn't reading (was not reading); was watching
8. didn't read (did not read)
9. finished; paid; left
10. saw; was walking; was waiting

15

3. is playing
4. gave
5. doesn't like (does not like)
6. did your family go
7. saw; was driving
8. Do you watch
9. were you doing
10. goes
11. 'm trying (am trying)
12. didn't sleep (did not sleep)

16

2. haven't read (have not read) *or* didn't read (did not read) *or* 've never read (have never read)
3. Have you seen *or* Did you see
4. 've had (have had)
5. Have you [ever] been *or* Did you [ever] go

6. have you lived
7. 've known (have known)
8. 's been raining (has been raining) *or* 's rained (has rained)

17

3. has been   6. has he lived
4. for   7. for
5. since   8. 've been (have been)

18

Sample sentences:
3. played golf a few times
4. had dinner
5. been to Australia
6. lived here; I was born
7. worked here; three years

19

3. bought/got
4. went
5. I've seen (I have seen)
6. was
7. didn't see (did not see)
8. 've never made (have never made)
9. finished / graduated from
10. 's been (has been)
11. was

20

3. He's lived (He has lived) there since last May.
4. she left at four o'clock
5. How many times have you been there?
6. I've been/felt (I have been/felt) tired all day
7. It was on the table last night.
8. I've eaten (I have eaten) there many times. *or* We've (We have) . . .
9. What time did they arrive?

21

1. was
2. have you had/owned; bought/got
3. have you lived; I lived/was *or* we lived/were; did you live *or* were you
4. have you worked/been; did you do; was

22

Sample sentences:
2. I didn't go out (did not go out) last night.
3. I was at work yesterday afternoon.
4. I went to a party a few days ago.
5. It was my birthday last week.
6. I went to Europe last year.

23

2. B	7. C	12. C
3. D	8. B	13. B
4. A	9. C	14. C
5. A	10. D	15. A
6. D	11. A	

24

1. was damaged; be torn down
2. was built; is used; is being painted
3. is called; be called; was changed
4. have been made; are produced

25

2. is visited
3. were damaged
4. be built
5. 's being cleaned (is being cleaned)
6. be forgotten
7. 's been repaired (has been repaired) *or* 's had to be repaired (has had to be repaired)
8. be kept
9. Have you ever been bitten
10. was stolen

26

2. was stolen last week
3. 're wanted (are wanted) on the phone
4. ice cream has been eaten
5. machine will be repaired
6. 're being watched (are being watched)
7. food has to be bought

27

3. pushed
4. was pushed
5. took *or* 's taken (has taken)
6. 's being repaired (is being repaired)
7. invented
8. was the camera invented
9. did they send
10. be sent

28

2. A	6. B	10. A*
3. A*	7. B	11. A
4. B	8. A	12. B
5. A	9. B	

* The present continuous (B) is also possible, but it is less common.

29

1. I stayed; did you do; I watched; Are you going out; I'm going (I am going); are you seeing *or* are you going to see; I don't know (do not know); I haven't decided (have not decided)
2. have you been; We arrived; are you staying *or* are you going to stay; do you like; we're having (we are having)
3. I just remembered; Kim called; She always calls *or* She's always calling (She is always calling); Did she leave; she wants *or* she wanted; I'll call (I will call), Do you know; I'll get (I will get)
4. I'm going (I am going); Do you want; are you going; Have you ever eaten; 've been (have been); went
5. I lost *or* I've lost (I have lost); Have you seen; You were wearing, I came in; I'm not wearing (I am not wearing); Have you looked; I'll go (I will go)

30

2. A	8. A	14. B
3. B	9. C	15. C
4. C	10. A	16. A
5. B	11. B	17. C
6. C	12. A	18. B
7. B	13. C	

31

2. a car   6. the movies
3. the refrigerator/   7. a taxi
   fridge   8. the piano
4. a teacher   9. computers
5. school   10. the same

32

4. a	14. the
5. The	15. —; —
6. a	16. the; the
7. —	17. the; —
8. the; the	18. —; —
9. a	19. a; an
10. —	20. the; the;
11. the	the; the
12. —	21. —; —
13. the	22. —; the

33

2. in	11. for
3. on	12. at
4. at	13. in
5. on	14. at
6. in	15. on
7. since	16. by
8. on	17. for; on
9. by	18. to; in
10. in	19. at; in

Answer Key to Study Guide

Present

1.1 B	1.10 A
1.2 A	1.11 C
1.3 C	1.12 A
1.4 A	1.13 D
1.5 C/D	1.14 C
1.6 B	1.15 A
1.7 D	1.16 D
1.8 C	1.17 C/D
1.9 C	1.18 A/D

Past

2.1 B	2.6 D
2.2 E	2.7 A
2.3 D	2.8 B
2.4 B	2.9 C
2.5 A	2.10 C/E

Present Perfect

3.1 B	3.6 C
3.2 D	3.7 A/D
3.3 E	3.8 A/D
3.4 B	3.9 D
3.5 A	3.10 E

Passive

4.1 D	4.4 A
4.2 C	4.5 A
4.3 E	

Verb Forms

5.1 D	5.2 B

Future

6.1 A	6.6 C
6.2 A	6.7 B
6.3 B	6.8 C
6.4 A/B	6.9 B/C
6.5 B	

Modals, Imperatives, etc.

7.1 C/D	7.8 C/D
7.2 A/C	7.9 D
7.3 A	7.10 C
7.4 D	7.11 B/D
7.5 C	7.12 A
7.6 B	7.13 B
7.7 D	

There and *it*

8.1 B	8.4 A
8.2 E	8.5 B
8.3 A	

Auxiliary Verbs

9.1 D	9.5 B
9.2 A	9.6 C
9.3 C	9.7 D
9.4 B	

Questions

10.1 C	10.7 B
10.2 D	10.8 A
10.3 A	10.9 C/E
10.4 A	10.10 C
10.5 B	10.11 A
10.6 D	10.12 A/C

Reported Speech

11.1 E	11.2 A/B/D

-ing and *to . . .*

12.1 B	12.5 B/C
12.2 D	12.6 C
12.3 B	12.7 A
12.4 C	12.8 D

Go, get, do, make, and *have*

13.1 A/D	13.4 A
13.2 C	13.5 B
13.3 C/D	13.6 D

Pronouns and Possessives

14.1 A	14.6 A
14.2 C	14.7 D
14.3 D	14.8 A
14.4 B	14.9 D
14.5 B/C	14.10 C

A and *the*

15.1 C	15.8 C
15.2 B	15.9 B
15.3 A/C	15.10 B
15.4 B	15.11 A
15.5 A/C	15.12 B
15.6 A	15.13 B
15.7 D	15.14 A

Determiners and Pronouns

16.1 C	16.11 D
16.2 C	16.12 B/D
16.3 B	16.13 A
16.4 B	16.14 A/B
16.5 C	16.15 D
16.6 A/C	16.16 A/C
16.7 D	16.17 D
16.8 B/D	16.18 B
16.9 A	16.19 A
16.10 B	

Adjectives and Adverbs

17.1 A	17.8 D
17.2 C	17.9 A
17.3 C	17.10 B
17.4 D	17.11 D
17.5 B	17.12 A
17.6 B	17.13 D
17.7 A/C	17.14 C

Word Order

18.1 B	18.4 A
18.2 C	18.5 A/C
18.3 B	

Prepositions

19.1 A/D	19.11 A/B
19.2 E	19.12 A
19.3 C/D	19.13 C
19.4 B	19.14 D
19.5 A/D	19.15 A
19.6 A	19.16 E
19.7 B	19.17 C
19.8 C	19.18 B
19.9 B	19.19 B/D
19.10 D	19.20 D

Two-Word Verbs

20.1 C	20.3 B
20.2 A/B	

Conjunctions and Clauses

21.1 A	21.5 B/C
21.2 A	21.6 A/B
21.3 D	21.7 B/D
21.4 E	21.8 A

Index

The numbers in the index are *unit* numbers, not page numbers.